Four Great Histories

DOVER · **GIANT THRIFT** · EDITIONS

Four Great Histories

Henry IV, Part 1
Henry IV, Part 2
Henry V
and
Richard III

WILLIAM SHAKESPEARE

DOVER PUBLICATIONS, INC.
Mineola, New York

DOVER GIANT THRIFT EDITIONS

GENERAL EDITOR: MARY CAROLYN WALDREP
EDITOR OF THIS VOLUME: JANET BAINE KOPITO

Theatrical Rights

This Dover Thrift Edition may be used in its entirety, in adaptation, or in any other way for theatrical productions, professional and amateur, in the United States, without fee, permission, or acknowledgment. (This may not apply outside of the United States, as copyright conditions may vary.)

Bibliographical Note

This Dover edition, first published in 2006, contains the unabridged texts of four plays: *Henry IV, Part 1*, published as *The First Part of King Henry IV* in Volume XII of *The Caxton Edition of the Complete Works of William Shakespeare*, Caxton Publishing Company, London, n.d., and republished as a Dover Thrift Edition in 1997; *Henry IV, Part 2*, published as *The Second Part of King Henry IV* in Volume XII of *The Caxton Edition of the Complete Works of William Shakespeare*, n.d., 1910; *Henry V*, published as *The Life of King Henry V* in Volume XIII of *The Caxton Edition of the Complete Works of William Shakespeare*, n.d., and republished as a Dover Thrift Edition in 2003; and *Richard III*, as published in Volume X of *The Caxton Edition of the Complete Works of William Shakespeare*, n.d., and republished as a Dover Thrift Edition in 1995. Introductory Notes were written, and explanatory footnotes revised or written anew, specially for the Dover editions of *Henry IV, Part 1*; *Henry IV, Part 2*; *Henry V*; and *Richard III*.

Library of Congress Cataloging-in-Publication Data

Shakespeare, William, 1564–1616.
    [Plays. Selections]
    Four great histories / William Shakespeare.
        p. cm. — (Dover giant thrift editions)
    ISBN 0-486-44629-8 (pbk.)
        1. Henry IV, King of England, 1367–1413—Drama. 2. Henry V, King of England, 1387–1422—Drama. 3. Richard III, King of England, 1452–1485—Drama. 4. Great Britain—Kings and rulers—Drama. 5. Historical drama, English. I. Title. II. Series.

PR2762 2006
822.3'3—dc22

                                                                    2005049692

Manufactured in the United States of America
Dover Publications, Inc., 31 East 2nd Street, Mineola, N.Y. 11501

Contents

Henry IV, Part 1

Henry IV, Part 1

Henry IV, Part 1 (c. 1596–1597) follows closely upon the action of Shakespeare's *Richard II*, which ended with Henry Bolingbroke newly crowned as the King of England. Echoing the conclusion of that play, *1 Henry IV* opens with the king planning to undertake a crusade to the Holy Land, in part to assuage his guilt over the death of his predecessor and in part to unify his countrymen now that civil strife within England has seemingly come to an end. His plans are soon shattered, however, by the news of rebellion in Wales and in Scotland, and of the disobedience of his former ally Henry Spencer (called Hotspur). The play thus begins with conflict, and conflict marks it throughout, from Hotspur's early defiance of the king's orders, to the split between the king and his old supporters, to the battle of Shrewsbury with which the action closes.

Besides being a portrait of a nation's unrest, *1 Henry IV* is a study in contrasts. Sir John Falstaff, for instance, comic and vice-ridden, acts as a foil to the careworn King Henry: the men compete as father-figures to Harry, Prince of Wales, the one leading him toward vice and folly, the other demanding the prince uphold the responsibilities of his position. The dissolute prince himself has his opposite in the other Harry, the impetuous Hotspur. It is King Henry's regret that the one is his son and not the other, for in Hotspur he finds conduct becoming of a prince, while "riot and dishonour stain the brow / Of my young Harry." The prince is not blind to his father's preference, and all along he plans to redeem his father's favor by reforming, even while reveling in the company of Falstaff; by mending his ways, he thinks, he will stand in marked contrast to his former self and win more acclaim than would have been his had he played the dutiful prince from the start. That his reformation will require him to cast off Falstaff is an unfortunate necessity; that it leads to the killing of his rival Hotspur is inevitable.

As he had for many of his history plays, Shakespeare used Raphael Holinshed's *Chronicles of England, Scotland and Ireland* (1587) as the principal source of the historical material in *1 Henry IV*, and some of Holinshed's factual errors have been carried over into this play. The anonymous play *The Famous Victories of Henry V* may have provided Shakespeare with the details of the young prince's dissipated behavior, although the theme had long been a part of popular tradition. Probably composed soon after *The Merchant of Venice*, *1 Henry IV* was first entered in the Stationers' Register on February 25th, 1598, and was printed later that year. It has since proved to be one of Shakespeare's most popular plays, and Sir John Falstaff has become one of his best-loved creations.

ADAM FROST

Dramatis Personae

KING HENRY the Fourth.
HENRY, Prince of Wales, } sons to the King.
JOHN of Lancaster,
EARL OF WESTMORELAND.
SIR WALTER BLUNT.
THOMAS PERCY, Earl of Worcester.
HENRY PERCY, Earl of Northumberland.
HENRY PERCY, surnamed HOTSPUR, his son.
EDMUND MORTIMER, Earl of March.
RICHARD SCROOP, Archbishop of York.
ARCHIBALD, Earl of DOUGLAS.
OWEN GLENDOWER.
SIR RICHARD VERNON.
SIR JOHN FALSTAFF.
SIR MICHAEL, a friend to the Archbishop of York.
POINS.
GADSHILL.
PETO.
BARDOLPH.

LADY PERCY, wife to Hotspur, and sister to Mortimer.
LADY MORTIMER, daughter to Glendower, and wife to Mortimer.
MISTRESS QUICKLY, hostess of a tavern in Eastcheap.

Lords, Officers, Sheriff, Vintner, Chamberlain, Drawers, two
Carriers, Travellers, and Attendants

SCENE: *England and Wales*

ACT I.

SCENE I. *London. The Palace.*

Enter KING HENRY, LORD JOHN of LANCASTER, the EARL of
WESTMORELAND, SIR WALTER BLUNT, *and others*

KING. So shaken as we are, so wan with care,
Find we a time for frighted peace to pant,
And breathe short-winded accents of new broils
To be commenced in stronds afar remote.[1]
No more the thirsty entrance of this soil
Shall daub her lips with her own children's blood;
No more shall trenching war channel her fields,
Nor bruise her flowerets with the armed hoofs
Of hostile paces: those opposed[2] eyes,
Which, like the meteors of a troubled heaven,
All of one nature, of one substance bred,
Did lately meet in the intestine[3] shock
And furious close[4] of civil butchery,
Shall now, in mutual well-beseeming[5] ranks,
March all one way, and be no more opposed
Against acquaintance, kindred and allies:
The edge of war, like an ill-sheathed knife,
No more shall cut his master. Therefore, friends,
As far as to the sepulchre of Christ,
Whose soldier now, under whose blessed cross
We are impressed and engaged to fight,
Forthwith a power of English shall we levy;
Whose arms were moulded in their mothers' womb
To chase these pagans in those holy fields
Over whose acres walk'd those blessed feet,

---

1. *Find we . . . remote*] Let us allow domestic peace time to recover breath, and speak briefly
of new campaigns to be waged on foreign shores.
2. *opposed*] hostile.
3. *intestine*] domestic, coming to pass between people of the same nation.
4. *close*] hand-to-hand grapple.
5. *mutual well-beseeming*] united (by common sentiment) and fitly equipped.

Which fourteen hundred years ago were nail'd
For our advantage on the bitter cross.
But this our purpose now is twelve month old,
And bootless 'tis to tell you we will go:
Therefore we meet not now.[6] Then let me hear
Of you, my gentle cousin Westmoreland,
What yesternight our council did decree
In forwarding this dear expedience.[7]

WEST. My liege, this haste was hot in question,
And many limits of the charge[8] set down
But yesternight: when all athwart there came
A post from Wales loaden with heavy news;
Whose worst was, that the noble Mortimer,
Leading the men of Herefordshire to fight
Against the irregular and wild Glendower,
Was by the rude hands of that Welshman taken,
A thousand of his people butchered;
Upon whose dead corpse[9] there was such misuse,
Such beastly shameless transformation,
By those Welshwomen done, as may not be
Without much shame retold or spoken of.

KING. It seems then that the tidings of this broil
Brake off our business for the Holy Land.

WEST. This match'd with other did, my gracious lord;
For more uneven[10] and unwelcome news
Came from the north and thus it did import:
On Holy-rood day,[11] the gallant Hotspur there,
Young Harry Percy, and brave Archibald,[12]
That ever-valiant and approved Scot,
At Holmedon met,
Where they did spend a sad and bloody hour;
As by discharge of their artillery,
And shape of likelihood, the news was told;
For he that brought them, in the very heat
And pride of their contention did take horse,
Uncertain of the issue any way.

KING. Here is a dear, a true industrious friend,

---

6. *Therefore we meet not now*] This is not the object of our present meeting.
7. *this dear expedience*] this important expedition.
8. *limits of the charge*] definite arrangements of the undertaking.
9. *corpse*] used for the plural "corpses."
10. *more uneven*] more troublesome.
11. *Holy-rood day*] September 14.
12. *brave Archibald*] Archibald Douglas, the fourth Earl of Douglas.

Sir Walter Blunt, new lighted from his horse,
Stain'd with the variation of each soil
Betwixt that Holmedon and this seat of ours;
And he hath brought us smooth and welcome news.
The Earl of Douglas is discomfited:
Ten thousand bold Scots, two and twenty knights,
Balk'd[13] in their own blood did Sir Walter see
On Holmedon's plains. Of prisoners, Hotspur took
Mordake the Earl of Fife, and eldest son
To beaten Douglas;[14] and the Earl of Athol,
Of Murray, Angus, and Menteith:
And is not this an honourable spoil?
A gallant prize? ha, cousin, is it not?

WEST.   In faith,
It is a conquest for a prince to boast of.

KING.   Yea, there thou makest me sad and makest me sin
In envy that my Lord Northumberland
Should be the father to so blest a son,
A son who is the theme of honour's tongue;
Amongst a grove, the very straightest plant;
Who is sweet Fortune's minion[15] and her pride:
Whilst I, by looking on the praise of him,
See riot and dishonour stain the brow
Of my young Harry. O that it could be proved
That some night-tripping fairy had exchanged
In cradle-clothes our children where they lay,
And call'd mine Percy, his Plantagenet!
Then would I have his Harry, and he mine.
But let him from my thoughts. What think you, coz,[16]
Of this young Percy's pride? the prisoners,
Which he in this adventure hath surprised,
To his own use he keeps; and sends me word,
I shall have none but Mordake Earl of Fife.

WEST.   This is his uncle's teaching; this is Worcester,
Malevolent to you in all aspects;
Which makes him prune[17] himself, and bristle up
The crest of youth against your dignity.

KING.   But I have sent for him to answer this;

---

13. *Balk'd*] Heaped up.
14. *Mordake . . . Douglas*] Murdoch, Earl of Fife, was not in fact related to Douglas. He was
  . also the Earl of Menteith mentioned in the following line.
15. *minion*] favorite.
16. *coz*] cousin, kinsman.
17. *prune*] preen.

And for this cause awhile we must neglect
Our holy purpose to Jerusalem.
Cousin, on Wednesday next our council we
Will hold at Windsor; so inform the lords:
But come yourself with speed to us again;
For more is to be said and to be done
Than out of anger can be uttered.

WEST. I will, my liege. [*Exeunt.*

SCENE II. *London. An Apartment of the Prince's.*

Enter the PRINCE OF WALES *and* FALSTAFF

FAL. Now, Hal, what time of day is it, lad?

PRINCE. Thou art so fat-witted,[1] with drinking of old sack[2] and unbuttoning thee after supper and sleeping upon benches after noon, that thou hast forgotten to demand that truly which thou wouldst truly know. What a devil hast thou to do with the time of the day? Unless hours were cups of sack, and minutes capons, and clocks the tongues of bawds, and dials the signs of leaping-houses,[3] and the blessed sun himself a fair hot wench in flame-coloured taffeta, I see no reason why thou shouldst be so superfluous to demand the time of the day.

FAL. Indeed, you come near me now, Hal; for we that take purses go by the moon and the seven stars,[4] and not by Phœbus,[5] he, "that wandering knight so fair." And, I prithee, sweet wag, when thou art king, as, God save thy grace, — majesty I should say, for grace thou wilt have none, —

PRINCE. What, none?

FAL. No, by my troth, not so much as will serve to be prologue to an egg and butter.

PRINCE. Well, how then? come, roundly, roundly.[6]

---

1. *fat-witted*] dull-witted.
2. *sack*] a dry Spanish wine.
3. *leaping-houses*] brothels.
4. *the seven stars*] the Pleiades.
5. *Phœbus*] the sun.
6. *roundly*] directly, without evasion.

FAL. Marry, then, sweet wag, when thou art king, let not us that are
squires of the night's body be called thieves of the day's beauty:[7]
let us be Diana's foresters,[8] gentlemen of the shade, minions of the
moon; and let men say we be men of good government,[9] being
governed, as the sea is, by our noble and chaste mistress the moon,
under whose countenance we steal.

PRINCE. Thou sayest well, and it holds well too; for the fortune of us that
are the moon's men doth ebb and flow like the sea, being governed,
as the sea is, by the moon. As, for proof, now: a purse of gold most
resolutely snatched on Monday night and most dissolutely spent
on Tuesday morning; got with swearing "Lay by"[10] and spent with
crying "Bring in;"[11] now in as low an ebb as the foot of the ladder,
and by and by in as high a flow as the ridge of the gallows.

FAL. By the Lord, thou sayest true, lad. And is not my hostess of the
tavern a most sweet wench?

PRINCE. As the honey of Hybla,[12] my old lad of the castle.[13] And is not
a buff jerkin a most sweet robe of durance?[14]

FAL. How now, how now, mad wag! what, in thy quips and thy
quiddities?[15] what a plague have I to do with a buff jerkin?

PRINCE. Why, what a pox have I to do with my hostess of the tavern?

FAL. Well, thou hast called her to a reckoning many a time and oft.

PRINCE. Did I ever call for thee to pay thy part?

FAL. No; I'll give thee thy due, thou hast paid all there.

PRINCE. Yea, and elsewhere, so far as my coin would stretch; and where
it would not, I have used my credit.

FAL. Yea, and so used it that, were it not here apparent that thou art heir
apparent — But, I prithee, sweet wag, shall there be gallows standing in England when thou art king? and resolution thus fobbed[16]
as it is with the rusty curb of old father antic[17] the law? Do not thou,
when thou art king, hang a thief.

---

7. *let not us . . . day's beauty*] The general sense is that we who ply a (dishonest) trade by
    night have no wish to be called thieves in daytime.
8. *Diana's foresters*] Diana was goddess both of the moon and of the chase.
9. *good government*] good conduct.
10. *"Lay by"*] The meaning is here "Stand close," the highwaymen's word to prepare for
    attack on a passer-by.
11. *"Bring in"*] sc. drink.
12. *Hybla*] A town in Sicily celebrated for the sweetness of its honey.
13. *my old lad of the castle*] a punning allusion to the name of Sir John Oldcastle, which
    Shakespeare bestowed on Falstaff in the first draft of the piece.
14. *a buff jerkin . . . durance*] Sheriff's officers were dressed in buff, and "durance" means
    both "imprisonment" and a coarse cloth well known for its durability.
15. *quiddities*] quibbles.
16. *resolution thus fobbed*] boldness or courage thus foiled or deluded.
17. *antic*] buffoon.

PRINCE. No; thou shalt.

FAL. Shall I? O rare! By the Lord, I'll be a brave judge.

PRINCE. Thou judgest false already: I mean, thou shalt have the hanging of the thieves and so become a rare hangman.

FAL. Well, Hal, well; and in some sort it jumps with my humour as well as waiting in the court, I can tell you.

PRINCE. For obtaining of suits?

FAL. Yea, for obtaining of suits, whereof the hangman hath no lean wardrobe.[18] 'Sblood, I am as melancholy as a gib cat or a lugged bear.[19]

PRINCE. Or an old lion, or a lover's lute.

FAL. Yea, or the drone of a Lincolnshire bagpipe.

PRINCE. What sayest thou to a hare,[20] or the melancholy of Moorditch?[21]

FAL. Thou hast the most unsavoury similes, and art indeed the most comparative,[22] rascalliest, sweet young prince. But, Hal, I prithee, trouble me no more with vanity. I would to God thou and I knew where a commodity of good names were to be bought. An old lord of the council rated me the other day in the street about you, sir, but I marked him not; and yet he talked very wisely, but I regarded him not; and yet he talked wisely, and in the street too.

PRINCE. Thou didst well; for wisdom cries out in the streets, and no man regards it.[23]

FAL. O, thou hast damnable iteration,[24] and art indeed able to corrupt a saint. Thou hast done much harm upon me, Hal; God forgive thee for it! Before I knew thee, Hal, I knew nothing; and now am I, if a man should speak truly, little better than one of the wicked. I must give over this life, and I will give it over: by the Lord, an I do not, I am a villain: I'll be damned for never a king's son in Christendom.

PRINCE. Where shall we take a purse to-morrow, Jack?

FAL. 'Zounds, where thou wilt, lad; I'll make one; an I do not, call me villain and baffle[25] me.

PRINCE. I see a good amendment of life in thee; from praying to purse-taking.

---

18. *wardrobe*] The apparel of executed persons was the hangman's perquisite.

19. *gib cat . . . lugged bear*] a tomcat or a showman's chained bear.

20. *a hare*] The hare was credited by Elizabethans with a melancholy temperament.

21. *Moor-ditch*] A section of Finsbury which had a reputation for generating a very depressing climate. For Finsbury in general, see note 29 to Scene I of Act III.

22. *comparative*] fond of comparisons.

23. *wisdom . . . regards it*] Cf. *Proverbs*, 1:20, 24.

24. *damnable iteration*] an exasperating habit of repeating my words.

25. *baffle*] disgrace, degrade.

FAL. Why, Hal, 'tis my vocation. Hal; 'tis no sin for a man to labour in
his vocation.

Enter POINS

Poins! Now shall we know if Gadshill have set a match.[26] O, if men
were to be saved by merit, what hole in hell were hot enough for
him? This is the most omnipotent villain that ever cried "Stand" to
a true man.

PRINCE. Good morrow, Ned.

POINS. Good morrow, sweet Hal. What says Monsieur Remorse? what
says Sir John Sack and Sugar?[27] Jack! how agrees the devil and thee
about thy soul, that thou soldest him on Good Friday last for a cup
of Madeira and a cold capon's leg?

PRINCE. Sir John stands to his word, the devil shall have his bargain; for
he was never yet a breaker of proverbs: he will give the devil his due.

POINS. Then art thou damned for keeping thy word with the devil.

PRINCE. Else he had been damned for cozening the devil.

POINS. But, my lads, my lads, to-morrow morning, by four o'clock, early
at Gadshill! there are pilgrims going to Canterbury with rich offer-
ings, and traders riding to London with fat purses: I have vizards[28]
for you all; you have horses for yourselves: Gadshill lies to-night in
Rochester: I have bespoke supper to-morrow night in Eastcheap:
we may do it as secure as sleep. If you will go, I will stuff your purses
full of crowns; if you will not, tarry at home and be hanged.

FAL. Hear ye, Yedward;[29] if I tarry at home and go not, I'll hang you for
going.

POINS. You will, chops?[30]

FAL. Hal, wilt thou make one?

PRINCE. Who, I rob? I a thief? not I, by my faith.

FAL. There's neither honesty, manhood, nor good fellowship in thee,
nor thou camest not of the blood royal, if thou darest not stand for
ten shillings.

PRINCE. Well then, once in my days I'll be a madcap.

FAL. Why, that's well said.

PRINCE. Well, come what will, I'll tarry at home.

FAL. By the Lord, I'll be a traitor then, when thou art king.

PRINCE. I care not.

POINS. Sir John, I prithee, leave the prince and me alone: I will lay him
down such reasons for this adventure that he shall go.

---

26. *set a match*] made an appointment for nefarious purposes.
27. *Sack and Sugar*] It was the habit of Elizabethan topers to mix sugar with their wine.
28. *vizards*] masks.
29. *Yedward*] A colloquial form of Edward.
30. *chops*] flesh meat, "fat chops."

FAL. Well, God give thee the spirit of persuasion and him the ears of profiting, that what thou speakest may move and what he hears may be believed, that the true prince may, for recreation sake, prove a false thief; for the poor abuses of the time want countenance. Farewell: you shall find me in Eastcheap.

PRINCE. Farewell, thou latter spring! farewell, All-hallown summer![31]

                                                 [Exit Falstaff.

POINS. Now, my good sweet honey lord, ride with us to-morrow: I have a jest to execute that I cannot manage alone. Falstaff, Bardolph, Peto and Gadshill shall rob those men that we have already waylaid; yourself and I will not be there; and when they have the booty, if you and I do not rob them, cut this head off from my shoulders.

PRINCE. How shall we part with them in setting forth?

POINS. Why, we will set forth before or after them, and appoint them a place of meeting, wherein it is at our pleasure to fail, and then will they adventure upon the exploit themselves; which they shall have no sooner achieved, but we'll set upon them.

PRINCE. Yea, but 'tis like that they will know us by our horses, by our habits, and by every other appointment,[32] to be ourselves.

POINS. Tut! our horses they shall not see; I'll tie them in the wood; our vizards we will change after we leave them: and, sirrah, I have cases[33] of buckram for the nonce, to immask our noted outward garments.

PRINCE. Yea, but I doubt they will be too hard for us.

POINS. Well, for two of them, I know them to be as true-bred cowards as ever turned back; and for the third, if he fight longer than he sees reason, I'll forswear arms. The virtue of this jest will be, the incomprehensible lies that this same fat rogue will tell us when we meet at supper: how thirty, at least, he fought with; what wards,[34] what blows, what extremities he endured; and in the reproof[35] of this lies the jest.

PRINCE. Well, I'll go with thee: provide us all things necessary and meet me to-morrow night in Eastcheap; there I'll sup. Farewell.

POINS. Farewell, my lord.   *[Exit.*

PRINCE. I know you all, and will a while uphold
The unyoked[36] humour of your idleness:
Yet herein will I imitate the sun,

---

31. *All-hallown summer*] Falstaff's summer (youth) has lasted to All-hallows Day, November 1.
32. *appointment*] equipment.
33. *cases*] overcoats.
34. *wards*] guards.
35. *reproof*] refutation.
36. *unyoked*] untamed, undisciplined, licentious.

Who doth permit the base contagious clouds
To smother up his beauty from the world,
That, when he please again to be himself,
Being wanted, he may be more wonder'd at,
By breaking through the foul and ugly mists
Of vapours that did seem to strangle him.
If all the year were playing holidays,
To sport would be as tedious as to work;
But when they seldom come they wish'd for come,
And nothing pleaseth but rare accidents.
So, when this loose behavior I throw off
And pay the debt I never promised,
By how much better than my word I am,
By so much shall I falsify men's hopes;
And like bright metal on a sullen ground,
My reformation, glittering o'er my fault,
Shall show more goodly and attract more eyes
Than that which hath no foil to set it off.
I'll so offend, to make offence a skill;[37]
Redeeming time when men think least I will.   [*Exit.*

SCENE III. *London. The Palace.*

Enter the KING, NORTHUMBERLAND, WORCESTER, HOTSPUR,
SIR WALTER BLUNT, *with others*

KING.   My blood hath been too cold and temperate,
Unapt to stir at these indignities,
And you have found me;[1] for accordingly
You tread upon my patience: but be sure
I will from henceforth rather be myself,
Mighty and to be fear'd, than my condition;[2]
Which hath been smooth as oil, soft as young down,
And therefore lost that title of respect
Which the proud soul ne'er pays but to the proud.

---

37. *to make offence a skill*] so as to derive advantage from obnoxious conduct.

---

1. *found me*] found me out, *i.e.*, discovered my easy-going tendency.
2. *I will . . . my condition*] I will choose from now on to act the king, mighty and to be feared, than follow my natural temper.

WOR.   Our house, my sovereign liege, little deserves
        The scourge of greatness to be used on it;
        And that same greatness to which our own hands
        Have holp to make so portly.
NORTH.   My lord, —
KING.   Worcester, get thee gone; for I do see
        Danger and disobedience in thine eye:
        O, sir, your presence is too bold and peremptory,
        And majesty might never yet endure
        The moody frontier[3] of a servant brow.
        You have good leave[4] to leave us: when we need
        Your use and counsel, we shall send for you.   [*Exit Wor.*
        You were about to speak.   [*To North.*
NORTH.   Yea, my good lord.
        Those prisoners in your highness' name demanded,
        Which Harry Percy here at Holmedon took,
        Were, as he says, not with such strength denied
        As is deliver'd[5] to your majesty:
        Either envy, therefore, or misprision[6]
        Is guilty of this fault and not my son.
HOT.   My liege, I did deny no prisoners.
        But I remember, when the fight was done,
        When I was dry with rage and extreme toil,
        Breathless and faint, leaning upon my sword,
        Came there a certain lord, neat, and trimly dress'd,
        Fresh as a bridegroom; and his chin new reap'd[7]
        Show'd like a stubble-land at harvest-home;
        He was perfumed like a milliner;[8]
        And 'twixt his finger and his thumb he held
        A pouncet-box,[9] which ever and anon
        He gave his nose and took 't away again;
        Who therewith angry, when it next came there,
        Took it in snuff;[10] and still he smiled and talk'd,
        And as the soldiers bore dead bodies by,
        He call'd them untaught knaves, unmannerly,

---

    3. *frontier*] front or forehead.
    4. *good leave*] our full assent.
    5. *deliver'd*] portrayed.
    6. *envy . . . misprision*] malice . . . misunderstanding.
    7. *chin new reap'd*] freshly trimmed, cropped close in accord with the fashionable vogue.
    8. *milliner*] dealer in fancy articles of attire.
    9. *A pouncet-box*] A box containing aromatic herbs, with a perforated cover.
    10. *Took it in snuff*] Snuffed it up. The phrase, which also meant "took offence," has a double
        meaning here.

To bring a slovenly unhandsome corse
Betwixt the wind and his nobility.
With many holiday and lady terms
He question'd me; amongst the rest, demanded
My prisoners in your majesty's behalf.
I then, all smarting with my wounds being cold,
To be so pester'd with a popinjay,
Out of my grief[11] and my impatience,
Answer'd neglectingly I know not what,
He should, or he should not; for he made me mad
To see him shine so brisk, and smell so sweet,
And talk so like a waiting-gentlewoman
Of guns and drums and wounds, — God save the mark! —
And telling me the sovereign'st thing on earth
Was parmaceti[12] for an inward bruise;
And that it was great pity, so it was,
This villanous salt-petre should be digg'd
Out of the bowels of the harmless earth,
Which many a good tall fellow had destroy'd
So cowardly; and but for these vile guns,
He would himself have been a soldier.
This bald unjointed[13] chat of his, my lord,
I answer'd indirectly, as I said;
And I beseech you, let not his report
Come current for an accusation
Betwixt my love and your high majesty.
BLUNT.   The circumstance consider'd, good my lord,
Whate'er Lord Harry Percy then had said
To such a person and in such a place,
At such a time, with all the rest re-told,
May reasonably die and never rise
To do him wrong, or any way impeach
What then he said,[14] so he unsay it now.
KING.   Why, yet he doth deny his prisoners,
But with[15] proviso and exception,
That we at our own charge shall ransom straight
His brother-in-law, the foolish Mortimer;
Who, on my soul, hath wilfully betray'd

---

11. *grief*] pain.
12. *parmaceti*] a popular form of spermaceti.
13. *unjointed*] incoherent.
14. *impeach What . . . said*] make what he then said matter for accusation.
15. *But with*] save with.

The lives of those that he did lead to fight
Against that great magician, damn'd Glendower,
Whose daughter, as we hear, the Earl of March
Hath lately married. Shall our coffers, then,
Be emptied to redeem a traitor home?
Shall we buy treason? and indent[16] with fears,
When they have lost and forfeited themselves?
No, on the barren mountains let him starve;
For I shall never hold that man my friend
Whose tongue shall ask me for one penny cost
To ransom home revolted Mortimer.

HOT.   Revolted Mortimer!
He never did fall off,[17] my sovereign liege,
But by the chance of war: to prove that true
Needs no more but one tongue for all those wounds,
Those mouthed[18] wounds, which valiantly he took,
When on the gentle Severn's sedgy bank,
In single opposition, hand to hand,
He did confound the best part of an hour
In changing hardiment[19] with great Glendower:
Three times they breathed and three times did they drink,
Upon agreement, of swift Severn's flood;
Who then, affrighted with their bloody looks,
Ran fearfully among the trembling reeds,
And hid his crisp head in the hollow bank
Bloodstained with these valiant combatants.
Never did base and rotten policy
Colour her working with such deadly wounds;
Nor never could the noble Mortimer
Receive so many, and all willingly:
Then let not him be slander'd with revolt.

KING.   Thou dost belie[20] him, Percy, thou dost belie him;
He never did encounter with Glendower:
I tell thee,
He durst as well have met the devil alone
As Owen Glendower for an enemy.
Art thou not ashamed? But, sirrah, henceforth
Let me not hear you speak of Mortimer:

---

16. *indent*] bargain.
17. *fall off*] abandon his allegiance.
18. *mouthed*] gaping.
19. *In changing hardiment*] Exchanging blows.
20. *belie*] praise falsely.

Send me your prisoners with the speediest means,
Or you shall hear in such a kind from me
As will displease you. My Lord Northumberland,
We license your departure with your son.
Send us your prisoners, or you will hear of it.

                              [*Exeunt King Henry, Blunt, and train.*

HOT.   An if the devil come and roar for them,
        I will not send them: I will after straight
        And tell him so; for I will ease my heart,
        Albeit I make a hazard of my head.
NORTH.   What, drunk with choler? stay and pause a while:
        Here comes your uncle.

                    Re-enter WORCESTER

HOT.   Speak of Mortimer!
        'Zounds, I will speak of him; and let my soul
        Want mercy, if I do not join with him:
        Yea, on his part[21] I'll empty all these veins,
        And shed my dear blood drop by drop in the dust,
        But I will lift the down-trod Mortimer
        As high in the air as this unthankful king,
        As this ingrate and canker'd[22] Bolingbroke.
NORTH.   Brother, the king hath made your nephew mad.
WOR.   Who struck this heat up after I was gone?
HOT.   He will, forsooth, have all my prisoners;
        And when I urged the ransom once again
        Of my wife's brother, then his cheek look'd pale,
        And on my face he turn'd an eye of death,[23]
        Trembling even at the name of Mortimer.
WOR.   I cannot blame him: was not he proclaim'd
        By Richard that dead is the next of blood?[24]
NORTH.   He was; I heard the proclamation:
        And then it was when the unhappy king, —
        Whose wrongs in us[25] God pardon! — did set forth
        Upon his Irish expedition;

---

21. *on his part*] on his behalf.
22. *canker'd*] corroded, malignant.
23. *an eye of death*] a ghastly look of death.
24. *was not he . . . blood?*] Shakespeare here confuses the captured Mortimer with both his brother Roger Mortimer, fourth Earl of March, and his nephew Edmund Mortimer, the fifth Earl. Roger Mortimer was proclaimed heir to the crown by Richard II; when he predeceased the king, the claim was left to his son.
25. *Whose wrongs in us*] Whose wrongs as far as our responsibility for them goes.

       From whence he intercepted did return
       To be deposed and shortly murdered.
WOR.   And for whose death we in the world's wide mouth
       Live scandalized[26] and foully spoken of.
HOT.   But, softly, I pray you; did King Richard then
       Proclaim my brother Edmund Mortimer
       Heir to the crown?
NORTH.   He did; myself did hear it.
HOT.   Nay, then I cannot blame his cousin king,
       That wish'd him on the barren mountains starve.
       But shall it be, that you, that set the crown
       Upon the head of this forgetful man,
       And for his sake wear the detested blot
       Of murderous subornation,[27] shall it be,
       That you a world of curses undergo,
       Being the agents, or base second means,
       The cords, the ladder, or the hangman rather?
       O, pardon me that I descend so low,
       To show the line and the predicament
       Wherein you range under this subtle king;
       Shall it for shame be spoken in these days,
       Or fill up chronicles in time to come,
       That men of your nobility and power
       Did gage them both in an unjust behalf,
       As both of you — God pardon it! — have done,
       To put down Richard, that sweet lovely rose,
       And plant this thorn, this canker,[28] Bolingbroke?
       And shall it in more shame be further spoken,
       That you are fool'd, discarded and shook off
       By him for whom these shames ye underwent?
       No; yet time serves wherein you may redeem
       Your banish'd honours, and restore yourselves
       Into the good thoughts of the world again,
       Revenge the jeering and disdain'd[29] contempt
       Of this proud king, who studies day and night
       To answer all the debt he owes to you
       Even with the bloody payment of your deaths:
       Therefore, I say, —
WOR.   Peace, cousin, say no more:

---

26. *scandalized*] defamed.
27. *the detested blot . . . subornation*] the hateful stigma of having instigated murder.
28. *canker*] the dog-rose of the hedge.
29. *disdain'd*] disdainful.

And now I will unclasp a secret book,
And to your quick-conceiving discontents
I'll read you matter deep and dangerous,
As full of peril and adventurous spirit
As to o'er-walk a current roaring loud
On the unsteadfast footing of a spear.
HOT.   If he fall in, good night! or sink or swim:[30]
Send danger from the east unto the west,
So honour cross it from the north to south,
And let them grapple: O, the blood more stirs
To rouse a lion than to start a hare!
NORTH.   Imagination of some great exploit
Drives him beyond the bounds of patience.
HOT.   By heaven, methinks it were an easy leap,
To pluck bright honour from the pale-faced moon,
Or dive into the bottom of the deep,
Where fathom-line could never touch the ground,
And pluck up drowned honour by the locks;
So he that doth redeem her thence might wear
Without corrival[31] all her dignities:
But out upon this half-faced fellowship![32]
WOR.   He apprehends a world of figures here
But not the form of what he should attend.
Good cousin, give me audience for a while.
HOT.   I cry you mercy.
WOR.   Those same noble Scots
That are your prisoners, —
HOT.   I'll keep them all;
By God, he shall not have a Scot of them;
No, if a Scot would save his soul, he shall not:
I'll keep them, by this hand.
WOR.   You start away
And lend no ear unto my purposes.
Those prisoners you shall keep.
HOT.   Nay, I will; that's flat:
He said he would not ransom Mortimer;
Forbad my tongue to speak of Mortimer;
But I will find him when he lies asleep,
And in his ear I'll holla "Mortimer!"

---

30. *or sink or swim*] that is, such a man is doomed if he fall in, whether he sink or swim.
31. *corrival*] rival, competitor.
32. *out upon this half-faced fellowship*] shame on this half-hearted, insincere sort of friendship.

Nay,
I'll have a starling shall be taught to speak
Nothing but "Mortimer," and give it him,
To keep his anger still in motion.

WOR.   Hear you, cousin; a word.

HOT.   All studies here I solemnly defy,[33]
Save how to gall and pinch this Bolingbroke:
And that same sword-and-buckler[34] Prince of Wales,
But that I think his father loves him not
And would be glad he met with some mischance,
I would have him poison'd with a pot of ale.

WOR.   Farewell, kinsman: I'll talk to you
When you are better temper'd to attend.

NORTH.   Why, what a wasp-stung[35] and impatient fool
Art thou to break into this woman's mood,
Tying thine ear to no tongue but thine own!

HOT.   Why, look you, I am whipp'd and scourged with rods,
Nettled, and stung with pismires,[36] when I hear
Of this vile politician, Bolingbroke.
In Richard's time, — what do you call the place? —
A plague upon it, it is in Gloucestershire;
'Twas where the madcap duke his uncle kept,[37]
His uncle York; where I first bow'd my knee
Unto this king of smiles, this Bolingbroke, —
'Sblood! —
When you and he came back from Ravenspurgh.

NORTH.   At Berkley-castle.

HOT.   You say true:
Why, what a candy[38] deal of courtesy
This fawning greyhound then did proffer me!
Look, "when his infant fortune came to age,"
And "gentle Harry Percy," and "kind cousin;"
O, the devil take such cozeners! God forgive me!
Good uncle, tell your tale; I have done.

WOR.   Nay, if you have not, to it again;
We will stay your leisure.

HOT.   I have done, i' faith.

WOR.   Then once more to your Scottish prisoners.

---

33. *defy*] renounce.
34. *sword-and-buckler*] improper arms for a prince, who should carry a rapier and dagger.
35. *wasp-stung*] irritated.
36. *pismires*] ants.
37. *kept*] resided.
38. *candy*] sweet, flattering.

Deliver them up without their ransom straight,
And make the Douglas' son your only mean
For powers[39] in Scotland; which, for divers reasons
Which I shall send you written, be assured,
Will easily be granted. You, my lord,   [*To Northumberland.*
Your son in Scotland being thus employ'd,
Shall secretly into the bosom creep
Of that same noble prelate, well beloved,
The archbishop.

HOT.   Of York, is it not?

WOR.   True; who bears hard
His brother's death at Bristol, the Lord Scroop.
I speak not this in estimation,[40]
As what I think might be, but what I know
Is ruminated, plotted and set down,
And only stays but to behold the face
Of that occasion that shall bring it on.

HOT.   I smell it: upon my life, it will do well.

NORTH.   Before the game is a-foot, thou still let'st slip.[41]

HOT.   Why, it cannot choose but be a noble plot:
And then the power of Scotland and of York,
To join with Mortimer, ha?

WOR.   And so they shall.

HOT.   In faith, it is exceedingly well aim'd.

WOR.   And 'tis no little reason bids us speed,
To save our heads by raising of a head;
For, bear ourselves as even as we can,
The king will always think him in our debt,
And think we think ourselves unsatisfied,
Till he hath found a time to pay us home:
And see already how he doth begin
To make us strangers to his looks of love.

HOT.   He does, he does: we'll be revenged on him.

WOR.   Cousin, farewell: no further go in this
Than I by letters shall direct your course.
When time is ripe, which will be suddenly,
I'll steal to Glendower and Lord Mortimer;
Where you and Douglas and our powers at once,
As I will fashion it, shall happily meet,

---

39. *mean For powers*] means or agent for raising forces.
40. *in estimation*] on conjecture, mere inference.
41. *let'st slip*] i.e., let loose the hounds from their leashes.

> To bear our fortunes in our own strong arms,
> Which now we hold at much uncertainty.
> NORTH. Farewell, good brother: we shall thrive, I trust.
> HOT. Uncle, adieu: O, let the hours be short
> Till fields and blows and groans applaud our sport!   [*Exeunt.*

ACT II.

SCENE I. *Rochester. An Inn Yard.*

Enter a CARRIER *with a lantern in his hand*

FIRST CARRIER.   Heigh-ho! An it be not four by the day,[1] I'll be hanged:
  Charles' wain[2] is over the new chimney, and yet our horse not
  packed. What, ostler!

OST.   [*Within*] Anon, anon.

FIRST CAR.   I prithee, Tom, beat Cut's saddle,[3] put a few flocks in the
  point;[4] poor jade, is wrung in the withers out of all cess.[5]

Enter another CARRIER

SEC. CAR.   Peas and beans are as dank here as a dog, and that is the next[6]
  way to give poor jades the bots:[7] this house is turned upside down
  since Robin Ostler died.

FIRST CAR.   Poor fellow, never joyed since the price of oats rose; it was
  the death of him.

SEC. CAR.   I think this be the most villanous house in all London road
  for fleas: I am stung like a tench.[8]

FIRST CAR.   Like a tench! by the mass, there is ne'er a king christen[9]
  could be better bit than I have been since the first cock.

SEC. CAR.   Why, they will allow us ne'er a jordan, and then we leak in
  your chimney;[10] and your chamber-lie[11] breeds fleas like a loach.[12]

FIRST CAR.   What, ostler! come away and be hanged! come away.

---

1. *by the day*] by the morning light.
2. *Charles' wain*] The constellation called "Ursa Major" or Great Bear.
3. *beat Cut's saddle*] soften the horse's saddle. "Cut" is used as a general name for a horse because of its docked tail.
4. *flocks in the point*] i.e., wool in the pommel of the saddle, so that it won't chafe.
5. *cess*] measure.
6. *next*] surest.
7. *bots*] worms.
8. *stung like a tench*] it was thought that the spots on some fish were due to flea bites.
9. *christen*] in Christendom.
10. *jordan . . . leak . . . chimney*] chamber-pot . . . make water . . . fireplace.
11. *chamber-lie*] urine.
12. *loach*] a highly reproductive fish.

SEC. CAR. I have a gammon of bacon and two razes[13] of ginger, to be delivered as far as Charing-cross.

FIRST CAR. God's body! the turkeys in my pannier are quite starved. What, ostler! A plague on thee! hast thou never an eye in thy head? canst not hear? An 'twere not as good deed as drink, to break the pate on thee, I am a very villain. Come, and be hanged! hast no faith in thee?

Enter GADSHILL

GADS. Good morrow, carriers. What's o'clock?

FIRST CAR. I think it be two o'clock.

GADS. I prithee, lend me thy lantern, to see my gelding in the stable.

FIRST CAR. Nay, by God, soft; I know a trick worth two of that, i' faith.

GADS. I pray thee, lend me thine.

SEC. CAR. Ay, when? canst tell?[14] Lend me thy lantern, quoth he? marry, I'll see thee hanged first.

GADS. Sirrah carrier, what time do you mean to come to London?

SEC. CAR. Time enough to go to bed with a candle, I warrant thee. Come, neighbour Mugs, we'll call up the gentlemen: they will along with company, for they have great charge.[15]

[*Exeunt Carriers.*

GADS. What, ho! chamberlain!

CHAM. [*Within*] At hand, quoth pick-purse.[16]

GADS. That's even as fair as — at hand, quoth the chamberlain; for thou variest no more from picking of purses than giving direction doth from labouring; thou layest the plot how.[17]

Enter CHAMBERLAIN

CHAM. Good morrow, Master Gadshill. It holds current that I told you yesternight: there's a franklin[18] in the wild of Kent hath brought three hundred marks with him in gold: I heard him tell it to one of his company last night at supper; a kind of auditor; one that hath abundance of charge too, God knows what. They are up already, and call for eggs and butter: they will away presently.

GADS. Sirrah, if they meet not with Saint Nicholas' clerks,[19] I'll give thee this neck.

CHAM. No, I'll none of it: I pray thee, keep that for the hangman;

---

13. *razes*] packages.
14. *Ay, when? canst tell?*] Don't you wish I would?
15. *charge*] baggage, goods.
16. *At hand, quoth pick-purse*] a slang phrase for "coming at once."
17. *layest the plot how*] arrange the plot how (robbery is to be effected).
18. *franklin*] yeoman.
19. *Saint Nicholas' clerks*] thieves, highwaymen.

for I know thou worshippest Saint Nicholas as truly as a man of falsehood may.

GADS. What talkest thou to me of the hangman? if I hang, I'll make a fat pair of gallows; for if I hang, old Sir John hangs with me, and thou knowest he is no starveling. Tut! there are other Trojans that thou dreamest not of, the which for sport sake are content to do the profession some grace; that would, if matters should be looked into, for their own credit sake, make all whole. I am joined with no foot land-rakers,[20] no long-staff sixpenny strikers,[21] none of these mad mustachio purple-hued malt-worms;[22] but with nobility and tranquillity, burgomasters and great oneyers;[23] such as can hold in,[24] such as will strike sooner than speak, and speak sooner than drink, and drink sooner than pray: and yet, 'zounds, I lie; for they pray continually to their saint, the commonwealth; or rather, not pray to her, but prey on her, for they ride up and down on her and make her their boots.[25]

CHAM. What, the commonwealth their boots? will she hold out water in foul way?

GADS. She will, she will; justice hath liquored[26] her. We steal as in a castle, cock-sure; we have the receipt of fern-seed,[27] we walk invisible.

CHAM. Nay, by my faith, I think you are more beholding to the night than to fern-seed for your walking invisible.

GADS. Give me thy hand: thou shalt have a share in our purchase, as I am a true man.

CHAM. Nay, rather let me have it, as you are a false thief.

GADS. Go to; "homo" is a common name to all men.[28] Bid the ostler bring my gelding out of the stable. Farewell, you muddy knave.

                                                    [*Exeunt.*

---

20. *foot land-rakers*] common thieves, footpads.
21. *long-staff sixpenny strikers*] thieves who would knock passers-by down with a long stick to rob them of sixpences.
22. *mustachio purple-hued malt-worms*] drunkards with their mustachios dyed with purple wine.
23. *great oneyers*] possibly an amplification of "great ones."
24. *hold in*] keep their counsel.
25. *make her their boots*] booty, with a pun on "boots."
26. *liquored*] waterproofed, as well as made drunk.
27. *receipt of fern-seed*] Those who carried fern-seed about with them were, it was believed, thereby rendered invisible.
28. "*homo*" . . . *all men*] a thief being a man is entitled to that designation.

SCENE II. *The Highway, near Gadshill*

Enter PRINCE HENRY *and* POINS

POINS. Come, shelter, shelter: I have removed Falstaff's horse, and he
frets like a gummed velvet.[1]
PRINCE. Stand close.

Enter FALSTAFF

FAL. Poins! Poins, and be hanged! Poins!
PRINCE. Peace, ye fat-kidneyed rascal! what a brawling dost thou keep!
FAL. Where's Poins, Hal?
PRINCE. He is walked up to the top of the hill: I'll go seek him.
FAL. I am accursed to rob in that thief's company: the rascal hath removed my horse, and tied him I know not where. If I travel but
four foot by the squier[2] further afoot, I shall break my wind. Well,
I doubt not but to die a fair death for all this, if I 'scape hanging for
killing that rogue. I have forsworn his company hourly any time this
two and twenty years, and yet I am bewitched with the rogue's company. If the rascal have not given me medicines[3] to make me love
him, I'll be hanged; it could not be else; I have drunk medicines.
Poins! Hal! a plague upon you both! Bardolph! Peto! I'll starve ere
I'll rob a foot further. An 'twere not as good a deed as drink, to turn
true man and to leave these rogues, I am the veriest varlet that ever
chewed with a tooth. Eight yards of uneven ground is threescore
and ten miles afoot with me; and the stony-hearted villains know
it well enough: a plague upon it when thieves cannot be true one
to another! [*They whistle.*] Whew! A plague upon you all! Give me
my horse, you rogues; give me my horse, and be hanged!
PRINCE. Peace, ye fat-guts! lie down; lay thine ear close to the ground
and list if thou canst hear the tread of travellers.
FAL. Have you any levers to lift me up again, being down? 'Sblood, I'll
not bear mine own flesh so far afoot again for all the coin in thy
father's exchequer. What a plague mean ye to colt[4] me thus?
PRINCE. Thou liest; thou art not colted, thou art uncolted.
FAL. I prithee, good Prince Hal, help me to my horse, good king's son.

---

1. *frets . . . velvet*] inferior velvets would easily fret or fray.
2. *squier*] square, measure.
3. *medicines*] love philtres or powders.
4. *colt*] trick.

PRINCE. Out, ye rogue! shall I be your ostler?

FAL. Go hang thyself in thine own heir-apparent garters! If I be ta'en,
I'll peach[5] for this. An I have not ballads made on you all and sung
to filthy tunes, let a cup of sack be my poison: when a jest is so
forward, and afoot too! I hate it.

Enter GADSHILL, BARDOLPH *and* PETO *with him*

GADS. Stand.

FAL. So I do, against my will.

POINS. O, 'tis our setter:[6] I know his voice. Bardolph, what news?

BARD. Case ye,[7] case ye; on with your vizards: there's money of the
king's coming down the hill; 'tis going to the king's exchequer.

FAL. You lie, ye rogue; 'tis going to the king's tavern.

GADS. There's enough to make us all.

FAL. To be hanged.

PRINCE. Sirs, you four shall front them in the narrow lane; Ned Poins
and I will walk lower: if they 'scape from your encounter, then they
light on us.

PETO. How many be there of them?

GADS. Some eight or ten.

FAL. 'Zounds, will they not rob us?

PRINCE. What, a coward, Sir John Paunch?

FAL. Indeed, I am not John of Gaunt,[8] your grandfather; but yet no
coward, Hal.

PRINCE. Well, we leave that to the proof.

POINS. Sirrah Jack, thy horse stands behind the hedge: when thou
needest him, there thou shalt find him. Farewell, and stand fast.

FAL. Now cannot I strike him, if I should be hanged.

PRINCE. Ned, where are our disguises?

POINS. Here, hard by: stand close.   [*Exeunt Prince and Poins.*

FAL. Now, my masters, happy man be his dole,[9] say I: every man to his
business.

Enter the Travellers

FIRST TRAV. Come, neighbour: the boy shall lead our horses down the
hill; we'll walk afoot awhile, and ease our legs.

THIEVES. Stand!

TRAVELLERS. Jesus bless us!

---

5. *peach*] give information.
6. *setter*] organizer of a robbery.
7. *Case ye*] Cover yourselves.
8. *Gaunt*] a pun on *gaunt*, thin.
9. *happy man be his dole*] good fortune be his lot.

FAL.   Strike; down with them; cut the villains' throats: ah! whoreson cat-
       erpillars![10] bacon-fed knaves! they hate us youth: down with them;
       fleece them.
TRAVELLERS. O, we are undone, both we and ours for ever!
FAL.   Hang ye, gorbellied[11] knaves, are ye undone? No, ye fat chuffs;[12]
       I would your store were here! On, bacons,[13] on! What, ye knaves!
       young men must live. You are grandjurors, are ye? we'll jure[14] ye,
       'faith.   [*Here they rob them and bind them. Exeunt.*

                Re-enter PRINCE HENRY *and* POINS, *disguised*

PRINCE.   The thieves have bound the true men. Now could thou and I
       rob the thieves and go merrily to London, it would be argument[15]
       for a week, laughter for a month and a good jest for ever.
POINS.   Stand close; I hear them coming.

                        Enter the Thieves *again*

FAL.   Come, my masters, let us share, and then to horse before day. An
       the Prince and Poins be not two arrant cowards, there's no equity
       stirring: there's no more valour in that Poins than in a wild-duck.
PRINCE.   Your money!
POINS.   Villains!
                [*As they are sharing, the Prince and Poins set upon them;
                    they all run away; and Falstaff, after a blow or two,
                        runs away too, leaving the booty behind them.*]
PRINCE.   Got with much ease. Now merrily to horse:
       The thieves are all scatter'd and possess'd with fear
       So strongly that they dare not meet each other;
       Each takes his fellow for an officer.
       Away, good Ned. Falstaff sweats to death,
       And lards the lean earth as he walks along:
       Were 't not for laughing, I should pity him.
POINS.   How the rogue roar'd!   [*Exeunt.*

----

  10. *caterpillars*] idlers, parasites.
  11. *gorbellied*] potbellied, paunchy.
  12. *chuffs*] rich but miserly boors.
  13. *bacons*] swine.
  14. *jure*] Falstaff coins the verb out of "grandjurors."
  15. *argument*] theme of talk.

SCENE III. *Warkworth Castle.*

Enter HOTSPUR *solus, reading a letter*

HOT. "But, for mine own part, my lord, I could be well contented to be there, in respect of the love I bear your house." He could be contented: why is he not, then? In respect of the love he bears our house: he shows in this, he loves his own barn better than he loves our house. Let me see some more. "The purpose you undertake is dangerous;" — why, that's certain: 'tis dangerous to take a cold, to sleep, to drink; but I tell you, my lord fool, out of this nettle, danger, we pluck this flower, safety. "The purpose you undertake is dangerous; the friends you have named uncertain; the time itself unsorted;[1] and your whole plot too light for the counterpoise of so great an opposition." Say you so, say you so? I say unto you again, you are a shallow cowardly hind, and you lie. What a lack-brain is this! By the Lord, our plot is a good plot as ever was laid; our friends true and constant: a good plot, good friends, and full of expectation; an excellent plot, very good friends. What a frosty-spirited rogue is this! Why, my lord of York commends the plot and the general course of the action. 'Zounds, an I were now by this rascal, I could brain him with his lady's fan. Is there not my father, my uncle, and myself? lord Edmund Mortimer, my lord of York, and Owen Glendower? is there not besides the Douglas? have I not all their letters to meet me in arms by the ninth of the next month? and are they not some of them set forward already? What a pagan rascal is this! an infidel! Ha! you shall see now in very sincerity of fear and cold heart, will he to the king, and lay open all our proceedings. O, I could divide myself, and go to buffets,[2] for moving such a dish of skim milk with so honourable an action! Hang him! let him tell the king: we are prepared. I will set forward to-night.

Enter LADY PERCY

How now, Kate! I must leave you within these two hours.

LADY. O, my good Lord, why are you thus alone?
For what offence have I this fortnight been
A banish'd woman from my Harry's bed?
Tell me, sweet Lord, what is 't that takes from thee

---

1. *unsorted*] ill-chosen, unsuitable.
2. *I could . . . go to buffets*] I could fight against myself.

Thy stomach, pleasure, and thy golden sleep?
Why dost thou bend thine eyes upon the earth,
And start so often when thou sit'st alone?
Why hast thou lost the fresh blood in thy cheeks,
And given my treasures and my rights of thee[3]
To thick-eyed musing and cursed melancholy?
In thy faint slumbers I by thee have watch'd,
And heard thee murmur tales of iron wars;
Speak terms of manage to thy bounding steed;
Cry "Courage! to the field!" And thou hast talk'd
Of sallies and retires,[4] of trenches, tents,
Of palisadoes, frontiers, parapets,
Of basilisks, of cannon, culverin,[5]
Of prisoners' ransom, and of soldiers slain,
And all the currents of a heady fight.
Thy spirit within thee hath been so at war
And thus hath so bestirr'd thee in thy sleep,
That beads of sweat have stood upon thy brow,
Like bubbles in a late-disturbed stream;
And in thy face strange motions have appear'd,
Such as we see when men restrain their breath
On some great sudden hest.[6] O, what portents are these?
Some heavy business hath my lord in hand,
And I must know it, else he loves me not.

HOT.   What, ho!

Enter SERVANT

          Is Gilliams with the packet gone?
SERV.   He is, my lord, an hour ago.
HOT.   Hath Butler brought those horses from the sheriff?
SERV.   One horse, my lord, he brought even now.
HOT.   What horse? a roan, a crop-ear, is it not?
SERV.   It is, my lord.
HOT.   That roan shall be my throne.
    Well, I will back him[7] straight: O esperance![8]
    Bid Butler lead him forth into the park.   [*Exit Servant.*
LADY.   But hear you, my lord.

---

3. *my treasures . . . thee*] my treasured wifely rights.
4. *sallies and retires*] sorties and retreats.
5. *basilisks . . . culverin*] large pieces of ordnance . . . small cannon.
6. *hest*] command.
7. *back him*] mount him.
8. *O esperance*] O hope; the motto of the Percy family.

HOT.   What say'st thou, my lady?
LADY.   What is it carries you away?[9]
HOT.   Why, my horse, my love, my horse.
LADY.   Out, you mad-headed ape!
    A weasel hath not such a deal of spleen
    As you are toss'd with. In faith,
    I'll know your business, Harry, that I will.
    I fear my brother Mortimer doth stir
    About his title, and hath sent for you
    To line[10] his enterprise: but if you go —
HOT.   So far afoot, I shall be weary, love.
LADY.   Come, come, you paraquito,[11] answer me
    Directly unto this question that I ask:
    In faith, I'll break thy little finger, Harry,
    An if thou wilt not tell me all things true.
HOT.   Away,
    Away, you trifler! Love! I love thee not,
    I care not for thee, Kate: this is no world
    To play with mammets[12] and to tilt with lips:
    We must have bloody noses and crack'd crowns,
    And pass them current too.[13] God's me, my horse!
    What say'st thou, Kate! what wouldst thou have with me?
LADY.   Do you not love me? do you not, indeed?
    Well, do not then; for since you love me not,
    I will not love myself. Do you not love me?
    Nay, tell me if you speak in jest or no.
HOT.   Come, wilt thou see me ride?
    And when I am o' horseback, I will swear
    I love thee infinitely. But hark you, Kate;
    I must not have you henceforth question me
    Whither I go, nor reason whereabout:
    Whither I must, I must; and, to conclude,
    This evening must I leave you, gentle Kate.
    I know you wise, but yet no farther wise
    Than Harry Percy's wife: constant you are,
    But yet a woman: and for secrecy,
    No lady closer; for I well believe
    Thou wilt not utter what thou dost not know;

---

9. *carries you away*] distracts, transports you.
10. *line*] strengthen, support.
11. *paraquito*] little parrot.
12. *mammets*] puppets, dolls.
13. *crowns . . . current*] a quibble on the double meaning of the word "crowns" as "heads" and "coins."

　　And so far will I trust thee, gentle Kate.
LADY.　　How! so far?
HOT.　　Not an inch further. But hark you, Kate:
　　Whither I go, thither shall you go too;
　　To-day will I set forth, to-morrow you.
　　Will this content you, Kate?
LADY.　　　　　　　　　　It must of force.　　　　　　[*Exeunt.*

SCENE IV. *The Boar's-Head Tavern in Eastcheap.*

Enter the PRINCE, *and* POINS

PRINCE.　Ned, prithee, come out of that fat[1] room, and lend me thy hand
　　to laugh a little.
POINS.　Where hast been, Hal?
PRINCE.　With three or four loggerheads amongst three or fourscore
　　hogsheads. I have sounded the very base-string of humility. Sirrah,
　　I am sworn brother to a leash of drawers;[2] and can call them all
　　by their christen names, as Tom, Dick, and Francis. They take it
　　already upon their salvation, that though I be but Prince of Wales,
　　yet I am the king of courtesy; and tell me flatly I am no proud
　　Jack, like Falstaff, but a Corinthian,[3] a lad of mettle, a good boy,
　　by the Lord, so they call me, and when I am king of England, I
　　shall command all the good lads in Eastcheap. They call drink-
　　ing deep, dyeing scarlet; and when you breathe in your water-
　　ing, they cry "hem!" and bid you play it off. To conclude, I am
　　so good a proficient in one quarter of an hour, that I can drink
　　with any tinker in his own language during my life. I tell thee,
　　Ned, thou hast lost much honour, that thou wert not with me
　　in this action. But, sweet Ned, — to sweeten which name of Ned,
　　I give thee this pennyworth of sugar, clapped even now into my
　　hand by an under-skinker,[4] one that never spake other English
　　in his life than "Eight shillings and sixpence," and "You are wel-

---

1. *fat*] stuffy; also, vat room.
2. *leash of drawers*] three tapsters.
3. *a Corinthian*] a buck, a blood, a young man of spirit.
4. *under-skinker*] inferior tapster or pot-boy.

come," with this shrill addition, "Anon, anon, sir! Score a pint of bastard[5] in the Half-moon,"[6] or so. But, Ned, to drive away the time till Falstaff come, I prithee, do thou stand in some by-room, while I question my puny drawer to what end he gave me the sugar; and do thou never leave calling "Francis," that his tale to me may be nothing but "Anon." Step aside, and I'll show thee a precedent.

POINS. Francis!

PRINCE. Thou art perfect.

POINS. Francis!   [*Exit Poins.*

Enter FRANCIS

FRAN. Anon, anon, sir. Look down into the Pomgarnet,[7] Ralph.

PRINCE. Come hither, Francis.

FRAN. My lord?

PRINCE. How long hast thou to serve, Francis?

FRAN. Forsooth, five years, and as much as to —

POINS. [*Within*] Francis!

FRAN. Anon, anon, sir.

PRINCE. Five year! by 'r lady, a long lease for the clinking of pewter. But, Francis, darest thou be so valiant as to play the coward with thy indenture and show it a fair pair of heels and run from it?

FRAN. O Lord, sir, I'll be sworn upon all the books in England, I could find in my heart.

POINS. [*Within*] Francis!

FRAN. Anon, sir.

PRINCE. How old art thou, Francis?

FRAN. Let me see — about Michaelmas next I shall be —

POINS. [*Within*] Francis!

FRAN. Anon, sir. Pray stay a little, my lord.

PRINCE. Nay, but hark you, Francis: for the sugar thou gavest me, 'twas a pennyworth, was 't not?

FRAN. O Lord, I would it had been two!

PRINCE. I will give thee for it a thousand pound: ask me when thou wilt, and thou shalt have it.

POINS. [*Within*] Francis!

FRAN. Anon, anon.

PRINCE. Anon, Francis? No, Francis; but to-morrow, Francis; or Francis, o' Thursday; or indeed, Francis, when thou wilt. But, Francis!

FRAN. My lord?

---

5. *bastard*] a sweet Spanish wine.
6. *Half-moon*] the name of a room in the inn.
7. *Pomgarnet*] another room in the inn.

PRINCE. Wilt thou rob this leathern jerkin, crystal-button, not-pated,[8] agate-ring, puke-stocking, caddis-garter, smooth-tongue, Spanish-pouch,[9] —

FRAN. O lord, sir, who do you mean?

PRINCE. Why, then, your brown bastard is your only drink; for look you, Francis, your white canvas doublet will sully: in Barbary, sir, it cannot come to so much.[10]

FRAN. What, sir?

POINS. [*Within*] Francis!

PRINCE. Away, you rogue! dost thou not hear them call?

[*Here they both call him; the drawer stands amazed, not knowing which way to go.*

Enter VINTNER

VINT. What, standest thou still, and hearest such a calling? Look to the guests within. [*Exit Francis.*] My lord, old Sir John, with half-a-dozen more, are at the door: shall I let them in?

PRINCE. Let them alone awhile, and then open the door. [*Exit Vintner.*] Poins!

Re-enter POINS

POINS. Anon, anon, sir.

PRINCE. Sirrah, Falstaff and the rest of the thieves are at the door: shall we be merry?

POINS. As merry as crickets, my lad. But hark ye; what cunning match have you made with this jest of the drawer? come, what's the issue?

PRINCE. I am now of all humours that have showed themselves humours since the old days of goodman Adam to the pupil age of this present twelve o'clock at midnight.

Re-enter FRANCIS

What's o'clock, Francis?

FRAN. Anon, anon, sir.　　　　　　　　　　　　　　　　[*Exit.*

PRINCE. That ever this fellow should have fewer words than a parrot, and yet the son of a woman! His industry is up-stairs and down-stairs; his eloquence the parcel[11] of a reckoning. I am not yet of Percy's mind, the Hotspur of the north; he that kills me some six or seven dozen of Scots at a breakfast, washes his hands, and says to his wife "Fie upon this quiet life! I want work." "O my sweet Harry,"

---

8. *not-pated*] crop-haired. The prince is describing the vintner, the boy's master.

9. *Spanish-pouch*] with a paunch filled with Spanish wine.

10. *Why . . . much*] The Prince is here mystifying Francis by the irrelevance and incoherence of his remarks.

11. *parcel*] items.

says she, "how many hast thou killed to-day?" "Give my roan horse a drench," says he; and answers "Some fourteen," an hour after; "a trifle, a trifle." I prithee, call in Falstaff: I'll play Percy, and that damned brawn shall play Dame Mortimer his wife. "Rivo!"[12] says the drunkard. Call in ribs, call in tallow.

Enter FALSTAFF, GADSHILL, BARDOLPH, *and* PETO; FRANCIS *following with wine*

POINS. Welcome, Jack: where hast thou been?

FAL. A plague of all cowards, I say, and a vengeance too! marry, and amen! Give me a cup of sack, boy. Ere I lead this life long, I'll sew nether stocks[13] and mend them and foot them too. A plague of all cowards! Give me a cup of sack, rogue. Is there no virtue extant?

[*He drinks.*

PRINCE. Didst thou never see Titan[14] kiss a dish of butter? pitiful-hearted Titan,[15] that melted at the sweet tale of the sun's! if thou didst, then behold that compound.

FAL. You rogue, here's lime in this sack[16] too: there is nothing but roguery to be found in villanous man: yet a coward is worse than a cup of sack with lime in it. A villanous coward! Go thy ways, old Jack; die when thou wilt, if manhood, good manhood, be not forgot upon the face of the earth, then am I a shotten herring.[17] There lives not three good men unhanged in England; and one of them is fat, and grows old: God help the while! a bad world, I say. I would I were a weaver;[18] I could sing psalms or any thing. A plague of all cowards, I say still.

PRINCE. How now, wool-sack! what mutter you?

FAL. A king's son! If I do not beat thee out of thy kingdom with a dagger of lath,[19] and drive all thy subjects afore thee like a flock of wild-geese, I'll never wear hair on my face more. You Prince of Wales!

PRINCE. Why, you whoreson round man, what's the matter?

FAL. Are not you a coward? answer me to that: and Poins there?

POINS. 'Zounds, ye fat paunch, an ye call me coward, by the Lord, I'll stab thee.

FAL. I call thee coward! I'll see thee damned ere I call thee coward: but

---

12. *Rivo!*] An exclamation, probably of Spanish origin, common among Elizabethan topers.
13. *nether stocks*] stockings.
14. *Titan*] the sun.
15. *pitiful-hearted Titan*] it has been suggested that substituting "butter" for this second "Titan" will make sense of this barely intelligible passage.
16. *lime in this sack*] i.e., added to make the drink sparkle.
17. *a shotten herring*] a herring that has shed its roe.
18. *weaver*] many weavers were psalm-singing Calvinists from the Netherlands.
19. *dagger of lath*] the weapon of Vice in the old morality plays.

I would give a thousand pound I could run as fast as thou canst. You are straight enough in the shoulders, you care not who sees your back: call you that backing of your friends? A plague upon such backing! give me them that will face me. Give me a cup of sack: I am a rogue, if I drunk to-day.

PRINCE.   O villain! thy lips are scarce wiped since thou drunkest last.

FAL.   All's one for that. [*He drinks.*] A plague of all cowards, still say I.

PRINCE.   What's the matter?

FAL.   What's the matter! there be four of us here have ta'en a thousand pounds this day morning.

PRINCE.   Where is it, Jack? where is it?

FAL.   Where is it! taken from us it is: a hundred upon poor four of us.

PRINCE.   What, a hundred, man?

FAL.   I am a rogue, if I were not at half-sword[20] with a dozen of them two hours together. I have 'scaped by miracle. I am eight times thrust through the doublet, four through the hose; my buckler cut through and through; my sword hacked like a hand-saw — ecce signum! I never dealt better since I was a man: all would not do. A plague of all cowards! Let them speak: if they speak more or less than truth, they are villains and the sons of darkness.

PRINCE.   Speak, sirs; how was it?

GADS.   We four set upon some dozen —

FAL.   Sixteen at least, my lord.

GADS.   And bound them.

PETO.   No, no, they were not bound.

FAL.   You rogue, they were bound, every man of them; or I am a Jew else, an Ebrew Jew.

GADS.   As we were sharing, some six or seven fresh men set upon us —

FAL.   And unbound the rest, and then come in the other.

PRINCE.   What, fought you with them all?

FAL.   All! I know not what you call all; but if I fought not with fifty of them, I am a bunch of radish: if there were not two or three and fifty upon poor old Jack, then am I no two-legged creature.

PRINCE.   Pray God you have not murdered some of them.

FAL.   Nay, that's past praying for: I have peppered two of them; two I am sure I have paid, two rogues in buckram suits. I tell thee what, Hal, if I tell thee a lie, spit in my face, call me horse. Thou knowest my old ward;[21] here I lay, and thus I bore my point. Four rogues in buckram let drive at me —

PRINCE.   What, four? thou saidst but two even now.

FAL.   Four, Hal; I told thee four.

---

20. *at half-sword*] at close quarters.
21. *my old ward*] my old guard, my favourite posture of defense.

POINS. Ay, ay, he said four.

FAL. These four came all a-front, and mainly[22] thrust at me. I made me
   no more ado but took all their seven points in my target, thus.

PRINCE. Seven? why, there were but four even now.

FAL. In buckram?

POINS. Ay, four, in buckram suits.

FAL. Seven, by these hilts, or I am a villain else.

PRINCE. Prithee, let him alone; we shall have more anon.

FAL. Dost thou hear me, Hal?

PRINCE. Ay, and mark thee too, Jack.

FAL. Do so; for it is worth the listening to. These nine in buckram that
   I told thee of, —

PRINCE. So, two more already.

FAL. Their points being broken, —

POINS. Down fell their hose.[23]

FAL. Began to give me ground: but I followed me close, came in foot
   and hand; and with a thought seven of the eleven I paid.

PRINCE. O monstrous! eleven buckram men grown out of two!

FAL. But, as the devil would have it, three misbegotten knaves in Kendal
   green came at my back and let drive at me; for it was so dark, Hal,
   that thou couldst not see thy hand.

PRINCE. These lies are like their father that begets them; gross as
   a mountain, open, palpable. Why, thou clay-brained guts, thou
   knotty-pated[24] fool, thou whoreson, obscene, greasy tallow-
   catch,[25] —

FAL. What, art thou mad? art thou mad? is not the truth the truth?

PRINCE. Why, how couldst thou know these men in Kendal green,[26]
   when it was so dark thou couldst not see thy hand? come, tell us
   your reason: what sayest thou to this?

POINS. Come, your reason, Jack, your reason.

FAL. What, upon compulsion? 'Zounds, an I were at the strappado,[27]
   or all the racks in the world, I would not tell you on compulsion.
   Give you a reason on compulsion! if reasons were as plentiful as
   blackberries, I would give no man a reason upon compulsion, I.

PRINCE. I'll be no longer guilty of this sin; this sanguine coward, this
   bed-presser, this horse-back-breaker, this huge hill of flesh, —

FAL. 'Sblood, you starveling, you elf-skin, you dried neat's tongue, you

---

22. *mainly*] violently.
23. *Their points . . . hose*] "Points" has the double meaning of "sword-points" and the "tags"
    or laces, which attached the (trunk) hose to the doublet.
24. *knotty-pated*] blockheaded.
25. *tallow-catch*] apparently a receptacle for tallow-grease.
26. *Kendal green*] green woollen cloth worn by foresters.
27. *strappado*] a kind of torture.

bull's pizzle, you stock-fish! O for breath to utter what is like thee! you tailor's yard, you sheath, you bow-case, you vile standing tuck,[28] —

PRINCE. Well, breathe a while, and then to it again: and when thou hast tired thyself in base comparisons, hear me speak but this.

POINS. Mark, Jack.

PRINCE. We two saw you four set on four and bound them, and were masters of their wealth. Mark now, how a plain tale shall put you down. Then did we two set on you four; and, with a word, out-faced you from your prize, and have it; yea, and can show it you here in the house: and, Falstaff, you carried your guts away as nimbly, with as quick dexterity, and roared for mercy, and still run and roared, as ever I heard bull-calf. What a slave art thou, to hack thy sword as thou hast done, and then say it was in fight! What trick, what device, what starting-hole,[29] canst thou now find out to hide thee from this open and apparent shame?

POINS. Come, let's hear, Jack; what trick hast thou now?

FAL. By the Lord, I knew ye as well as he that made ye. Why, hear you, my masters: was it for me to kill the heir-apparent? should I turn upon the true prince? why, thou knowest I am as valiant as Hercules: but beware instinct; the lion will not touch the true prince. Instinct is a great matter; I was now a coward on instinct. I shall think the better of myself and thee during my life; I for a valiant lion, and thou for a true prince. But, by the Lord, lads, I am glad you have the money. Hostess, clap to the doors: watch to-night, pray to-morrow. Gallants, lads, boys, hearts of gold, all the titles of good fellowship come to you! What, shall we be merry? shall we have a play extempore?

PRINCE. Content; and the argument shall be thy running away.

FAL. Ah, no more of that, Hal, an thou lovest me!

Enter Hostess

HOST. O Jesu, my lord the prince!

PRINCE. How now, my lady the hostess! what sayest thou to me?

HOST. Marry, my lord, there is a nobleman of the court at door would speak with you: he says he comes from your father.

PRINCE. Give him as much as will make him a royal man,[30] and send him back again to my mother.

---

28. *standing tuck*] a rapier standing on end.
29. *starting-hole*] shelter in which a hunted animal takes refuge.
30. *royal*] a pun on the words "noble" and "royal," which were the names of coins. A "noble" was worth 6s. 8d., while the "royal" was of the value of 10s. The prince jestingly suggests that the difference between those two sums defines the interval between a "nobleman" and a "royal man."

FAL. What manner of man is he?

HOST. An old man.

·FAL. What doth gravity out of his bed at midnight? Shall I give him his answer?

PRINCE. Prithee, do, Jack.

FAL. Faith, and I'll send him packing.   [*Exit.*

PRINCE. Now, sirs: by 'r lady, you fought fair; so did you, Peto; so did you, Bardolph: you are lions too, you ran away upon instinct, you will not touch the true prince; no, fie!

BARD. Faith, I ran when I saw others run.

PRINCE. Faith, tell me now in earnest, how came Falstaff's sword so hacked?

PETO. Why, he hacked it with his dagger, and said he would swear truth out of England but he would make you believe it was done in fight, and persuaded us to do the like.

BARD. Yea, and to tickle our noses with spear-grass to make them bleed, and then to beslubber our garments with it and swear it was the blood of true men. I did that I did not this seven year before, I blushed to hear his monstrous devices.

PRINCE. O villain, thou stolest a cup of sack eighteen years ago, and wert taken with the manner,[31] and ever since thou hast blushed extempore. Thou hadst fire[32] and sword on thy side, and yet thou rannest away: what instinct hadst thou for it?

BARD. My lord, do you see these meteors? do you behold these exhalations?[33]

PRINCE. I do.

BARD. What think you they portend?

PRINCE. Hot livers and cold purses.[34]

BARD. Choler, my lord, if rightly taken.

PRINCE. No, if rightly taken, halter.

Re-enter FALSTAFF

Here comes lean Jack, here comes bare-bone. How now, my sweet creature of bombast![35] How long is 't ago, Jack, since thou sawest thine own knee?

FAL. My own knee! when I was about thy years, Hal, I was not an eagle's talon in the waist; I could have crept into any alderman's thumb-ring: a plague of sighing and grief! it blows a man up like a bladder.

---

31. *with the manner*] "in flagrante delicto," in the very act.
32. *Thou hadst fire*] a reference to Bardolph's inflamed countenance.
33. *exhalations*] meteors; here, the red blotches on his face.
34. *Hot livers and cold purses*] Hard drinking and empty purses.
35. *bombast*] stuffing or padding of clothes.

There's villanous news abroad: here was Sir John Bracy from your father; you must to the court in the morning. That same mad fellow of the north, Percy, and he of Wales, that gave Amamon the bastinado,[36] and made Lucifer cuckold, and swore the devil his true liegeman upon the cross of a Welsh hook[37] — what a plague call you him?

POINS. O, Glendower.

FAL. Owen, Owen, the same; and his son-in-law Mortimer, and old Northumberland, and that sprightly Scot of Scots, Douglas, that runs o' horseback up a hill perpendicular, —

PRINCE. He that rides at high speed and with his pistol kills a sparrow flying.

FAL. You have hit it.

PRINCE. So did he never the sparrow.

FAL. Well, that rascal hath good mettle in him; he will not run.

PRINCE. Why, what a rascal art thou then, to praise him so for running!

FAL. O' horseback, ye cuckoo; but afoot he will not budge a foot.

PRINCE. Yes, Jack, upon instinct.

FAL. I grant ye, upon instinct. Well, he is there too, and one Mordake, and a thousand blue-caps[38] more: Worcester is stolen away to-night; thy father's beard is turned white with the news: you may buy land now as cheap as stinking mackerel.

PRINCE. Why, then, it is like, if there come a hot June and this civil buffeting hold, we shall buy maidenheads as they buy hob-nails, by the hundreds.

FAL. By the mass, lad, thou sayest true; it is like we shall have good trading that way. But tell me, Hal, art not thou horrible afeard? thou being heir-apparent, could the world pick thee out three such enemies again as that fiend Douglas, that spirit Percy, and that devil Glendower? art thou not horribly afraid? doth not thy blood thrill at it?

PRINCE. Not a whit, i' faith; I lack some of thy instinct.

FAL. Well, thou wilt be horribly chid to-morrow when thou comest to thy father: if thou love me, practise an answer.

PRINCE. Do thou stand for my father, and examine me upon the particulars of my life.

FAL. Shall I? content: this chair shall be my state,[39] this dagger my sceptre, and this cushion my crown.

---

36. *Amamon . . . bastinado*] the name of an evil spirit . . . a stiff cudgeling.
37. *Welsh hook*] a long-handled weapon with a curved blade.
38. *blue-caps*] the blue bonnets distinctive of Scottish troops.
39. *my state*] my canopied throne.

PRINCE. Thy state is taken for a joined-stool, thy golden sceptre for a leaden dagger, and thy precious rich crown for a pitiful bald crown!

FAL. Well, an the fire of grace be not quite out of thee, now shalt thou be moved. Give me a cup of sack to make my eyes look red, that it may be thought I have wept; for I must speak in passion, and I will do it in King Cambyses' vein.[40]

PRINCE. Well, here is my leg.[41]

FAL. And here is my speech. Stand aside, nobility.

HOST. O Jesu, this is excellent sport, i' faith!

FAL. Weep not, sweet queen; for trickling tears are vain.

HOST. O, the father, how he holds his countenance!

FAL. For God's sake, lords, convey my tristful queen;[42] For tears do stop the flood-gates of her eyes.

HOST. O Jesu, he doth it as like one of these harlotry[43] players as ever I see!

FAL. Peace, good pint-pot; peace, good tickle-brain.[44] Harry, I do not only marvel where thou spendest thy time, but also how thou art accompanied: for though the camomile, the more it is trodden on the faster it grows, yet youth, the more it is wasted the sooner it wears.[45] That thou art my son, I have partly thy mother's word, partly my own opinion, but chiefly a villanous trick of thine eye, and a foolish hanging of thy nether lip, that doth warrant me. If then thou be son to me, here lies the point; why, being son to me, art thou so pointed at? Shall the blessed sun of heaven prove a micher[46] and eat blackberries? a question not to be asked. Shall the son of England prove a thief and take purses? a question to be asked. There is a thing, Harry, which thou hast often heard of, and it is known to many in our land by the name of pitch: this pitch, as ancient writers[47] do report, doth defile; so doth the company thou keepest: for, Harry, now I do not speak to thee in drink but in tears, not in pleasure but in passion, not in words only, but in woes also: and yet there is a virtuous man whom I have often noted in thy company, but I know not his name.

PRINCE. What manner of man, an it like your majesty?

FAL. A goodly portly man, i' faith, and a corpulent; of a cheerful look, a pleasing eye, and a most noble carriage; and, as I think, his age

---

40. *in King Cambyses' vein*] in the ranting style of Thomas Preston's tragedy *Cambises*.

41. *leg*] bow.

42. *convey my tristful queen*] lead away my sorrowful queen.

43. *harlotry*] vagabond.

44. *tickle-brain*] a nickname of strong liquor.

45. *the camomile . . . sooner it wears*] These sentences parody a passage in Lyly's *Euphues*.

46. *a micher*] a truant.

47. *ancient writers*] Cf. *Ecclesiasticus* 13:1: "He that toucheth pitch shall be defiled therewith."

some fifty, or, by 'r lady, inclining to three score; and now I remember me, his name is Falstaff: if that man should be lewdly
given,[48] he deceiveth me; for, Harry, I see virtue in his looks. If then
the tree may be known by the fruit, as the fruit by the tree, then,
peremptorily I speak it, there is virtue in that Falstaff; him keep
with, the rest banish. And tell me now, thou naughty varlet, tell me,
where hast thou been this month?

PRINCE. Dost thou speak like a king? Do thou stand for me, and I'll play
my father.

FAL. Depose me? if thou dost it half so gravely, so majestically, both in
word and matter, hang me up by the heels for a rabbit-sucker or a
poulter's hare.[49]

PRINCE. Well, here I am set.

FAL. And here I stand: judge, my masters.

PRINCE. Now, Harry, whence come you?

FAL. My noble lord; from Eastcheap.

PRINCE. The complaints I hear of thee are grievous.

FAL. 'Sblood, my lord, they are false: nay, I'll tickle ye for a young
prince, i' faith.

PRINCE. Swearest thou, ungracious boy? henceforth ne'er look on me.
Thou art violently carried away from grace: there is a devil haunts
thee in the likeness of an old fat man; a tun of man is thy companion. Why dost thou converse with that trunk of humours, that
bolting-hutch[50] of beastliness, that swollen parcel of dropsies, that
huge bombard[51] of sack, that stuffed cloak-bag of guts, that roasted
Manningtree ox[52] with the pudding in his belly, that reverend vice,
that grey iniquity,[53] that father ruffian, that vanity in years? Wherein
is he good, but to taste sack and drink it? wherein neat and cleanly,
but to carve a capon and eat it? wherein cunning, but in craft?
wherein crafty, but in villany? wherein villanous, but in all things?
wherein worthy, but in nothing?

FAL. I would your grace would take me with you: whom means your
grace?

PRINCE. That villanous abominable misleader of youth, Falstaff, that
old white-bearded Satan.

FAL. My lord, the man I know.

PRINCE. I know thou dost.

---

48. *lewdly given*] inclined to wickedness.
49. *a rabbit-sucker or a poulter's hare*] a sucking rabbit or a poulterer's hare.
50. *bolting-hutch*] flour bin.
51. *bombard*] leather jug or black-jack.
52. *Manningtree ox*] The agricultural town of Manningtree in Essex seems to have been
famous for its breed of fat oxen. A famous fair was held there annually.
53. *vice . . . iniquity*] alternative names of a clownish character in the old morality plays.

FAL.   But to say I know more harm in him than in myself, were to say
more than I know. That he is old, the more the pity, his white hairs
do witness it; but that he is, saving your reverence, a whoremaster,
that I utterly deny. If sack and sugar be a fault, God help the wicked!
if to be old and merry be a sin, then many an old host that I know
is damned: if to be fat be to be hated, then Pharaoh's lean kine[54]
are to be loved. No, my good lord; banish Peto, banish Bardolph,
banish Poins: but for sweet Jack Falstaff, kind Jack Falstaff, true Jack
Falstaff, valiant Jack Falstaff, and therefore more valiant, being, as
he is, old Jack Falstaff, banish not him thy Harry's company, banish
not him thy Harry's company: banish plump Jack, and banish all
the world.

PRINCE.   I do, I will.   [A knocking heard.
                              [Exeunt Hostess, Francis, and Bardolph.

Re-enter BARDOLPH, *running*

BARD.   O, my lord, my lord! the sheriff with a most monstrous watch is
at the door.

FAL.   Out, ye rogue! Play out the play: I have much to say in the behalf
of that Falstaff.

Re-enter the Hostess

HOST.   O Jesu, my lord, my lord! —

PRINCE.   Heigh, heigh! the devil rides upon a fiddlestick:[55] what's the
matter?

HOST.   The sheriff and all the watch are at the door: they are come to
search the house. Shall I let them in?

FAL.   Dost thou hear, Hal? never call a true piece of gold a counterfeit:
thou art essentially mad, without seeming so.[56]

PRINCE.   And thou a natural coward, without instinct.

FAL.   I deny your major:[57] if you will deny the sheriff, so; if not, let him
enter: if I become not a cart[58] as well as another man, a plague on
my bringing up! I hope I shall as soon be strangled with a halter as
another.

---

54. *kine*] cattle. See Exodus 9:3–7.
55. *the devil . . . fiddlestick*] a proverbial phrase; meaning, here's a to-do about nothing.
56. *thou art essentially mad, without seeming so*] you are really mad (by the way you have
been taking me off): there is no need to pretend to be a lunatic.
57. *major*] the major proposition. "Major" being pronounced "mayor" by Falstaff makes the
punning allusion to "the sheriff" clear.
58. *become not a cart*] look not well in the hangman's cart (which takes the criminal to the
scaffold).

PRINCE.   Go, hide thee behind the arras:[59] the rest walk up above. Now, my masters, for a true face and good conscience.

FAL.   Both which I have had; but their date is out, and therefore I'll hide me.

PRINCE.   Call in the sheriff.   [*Exeunt all except the Prince and Peto.*

Enter Sheriff *and the* Carrier

Now, master sheriff, what is your will with me?

SHER.   First, pardon me, my lord. A hue and cry
Hath follow'd certain men unto this house.

PRINCE.   What men?

SHER.   One of them is well known, my gracious lord,
A gross fat man.

CAR.   As fat as butter.

PRINCE.   The man, I do assure you, is not here;
For I myself at this time have employ'd him.
And, sheriff, I will engage my word to thee
That I will, by to-morrow dinner-time,
Send him to answer thee, or any man,
For any thing he shall be charged withal:
And so let me entreat you leave the house.

SHER.   I will, my lord. There are two gentlemen
Have in this robbery lost three hundred marks.

PRINCE.   It may be so: if he have robb'd these men,
He shall be answerable; and so farewell.

SHER.   Good night, my noble lord.

PRINCE.   I think it is good morrow, is it not?

SHER.   Indeed, my lord, I think it be two o'clock.
                                            [*Exeunt Sheriff and Carrier.*

PRINCE.   This oily rascal is known as well as Paul's.[60]
Go, call him forth.

PETO.   Falstaff! — Fast asleep behind the arras, and snorting like a horse.

PRINCE.   Hark, how hard he fetches breath. Search his pockets. [*He searcheth his pockets, and findeth certain papers.*] What hast thou found?

PETO.   Nothing but papers, my lord.

PRINCE.   Let's see what they be: read them.

PETO.   [*reads*] Item, A capon, . . . 2s. 2d.
                    Item, Sauce, . . . 4d.
                    Item, Sack, two gallons, . . . 5s. 8d.

---

59. *arras*] tapestry hanging at some distance from the walls.
60. *Paul's*] St. Paul's Cathedral.

    Item, Anchovies and sack after supper, . . . 2s. 6d.
    Item, Bread, . . . ob.[61]

PRINCE. O monstrous! but one half-pennyworth of bread to this intol-
    erable deal of sack! What there is else, keep close; we'll read it at
    more advantage; there let him sleep till day. I'll to the court in the
    morning. We must all to the wars, and thy place shall be honour-
    able. I'll procure this fat rogue a charge of foot;[62] and I know his
    death will be a march of twelve-score.[63] The money shall be paid
    back again with advantage. Be with me betimes in the morning;
    and so, good morrow, Peto.

PETO.   Good morrow, good my lord.   [*Exeunt.*

---

61. *ob.*] abbreviation of the Latin "obolus," commonly used in England as a symbol for a
     half-penny.
62. *a charge of foot*] command of a company of foot-soldiers.
63. *his death . . . twelve-score*] he will die if he march a distance of twelve-score yards.

ACT III.

SCENE I. *Bangor. The Archdeacon's House.*

Enter HOTSPUR, WORCESTER, MORTIMER, *and* GLENDOWER

MORTIMER.   These promises are fair, the parties sure,
    And our induction[1] full of prosperous hope.
HOT.   Lord Mortimer, and cousin Glendower,
    Will you sit down?
    And uncle Worcester: a plague upon it!
    I have forgot the map.
GLEND.   No, here it is.
    Sit, cousin Percy; sit, good cousin Hotspur.
    For by that name as oft as Lancaster
    Doth speak of you, his cheek looks pale, and with
    A rising sigh he wisheth you in heaven.
HOT.   And you in hell, as oft as he hears Owen Glendower spoke of.
GLEND.   I cannot blame him: at my nativity
    The front of heaven was full of fiery shapes,
    Of burning cressets;[2] and at my birth
    The frame and huge foundation of the earth
    Shaked like a coward.
HOT.   Why, so it would have done at the same season, if your mother's
    cat had but kittened, though yourself had never been born.
GLEND.   I say the earth did shake when I was born.
HOT.   And I say the earth was not of my mind,
    If you suppose as fearing you it shook.
GLEND.   The heavens were all on fire, the earth did tremble.
HOT.   O, then the earth shook to see the heavens on fire,
    And not in fear of your nativity.

---

1. *induction*] opening scene, first move.
2. *cressets*] beacons.

Diseased nature oftentimes breaks forth
In strange eruptions; oft the teeming earth
Is with a kind of colic pinch'd and vex'd
By the imprisoning of unruly wind
Within her womb; which, for enlargement striving,
Shakes the old beldam[3] earth and topples down
Steeples and moss-grown towers. At your birth
Our grandam earth, having this distemperature,
In passion shook.
GLEND.   Cousin, of many men
I do not bear these crossings. Give me leave
To tell you once again that at my birth
The front of heaven was full of fiery shapes,
The goats ran from the mountains, and the herds
Were strangely clamorous to the frighted fields.
These signs have mark'd me extraordinary;
And all the courses of my life do show
I am not in the roll of common men.
Where is he living, clipp'd in with the sea
That chides the banks of England, Scotland, Wales,
Which calls me pupil, or hath read to me?
And bring him out that is but woman's son
Can trace me in the tedious ways of art,
And hold me pace in deep experiments.[4]
HOT.   I think there's no man speaks better Welsh, I'll to dinner.
MORT.   Peace, cousin Percy; you will make him mad.
GLEND.   I can call spirits from the vasty deep.
HOT.   Why, so can I, or so can any man;
But will they come when you do call for them?
GLEND.   Why, I can teach you, cousin, to command
The devil.
HOT.   And I can teach thee, coz, to shame the devil
By telling truth: tell truth, and shame the devil.
If thou have power to raise him, bring him hither,
And I'll be sworn I have power to shame him hence.
O, while you live, tell truth, and shame the devil!
MORT.   Come, come, no more of this unprofitable chat.
GLEND.   Three times hath Henry Bolingbroke made head
Against my power; thrice from the banks of Wye
And sandy-bottom'd Severn have I sent him

---

3. *beldam*] grandmother.
4. *And bring him out . . . experiments*] And produce any one who, being mortal, can follow
   me in tedious ways of learning and keep pace with me in deep experiments.

Bootless home and weather-beaten back.
HOT.   Home without boots, and in foul weather too!
How 'scapes he agues,[5] in the devil's name?
GLEND.   Come, here's the map: shall we divide our right
According to our threefold order ta'en?[6]
MORT.   The archdeacon hath divided it
Into three limits very equally:
England, from Trent and Severn hitherto,
By south and east is to my part assign'd:
All westward, Wales beyond the Severn shore,
And all the fertile land within that bound,
To Owen Glendower: and, dear coz, to you
The remnant northward, lying off from Trent.
And our indentures tripartite are drawn;
Which being sealed interchangeably,
A business that this night may execute,
To-morrow, cousin Percy, you and I
And my good Lord of Worcester will set forth
To meet your father and the Scottish power,
As is appointed us, at Shrewsbury.
My father Glendower is not ready yet,
Nor shall we need his help these fourteen days.
Within that space you may have drawn together
Your tenants, friends, and neighbouring gentlemen.
GLEND.   A shorter time shall send me to you, lords:
And in my conduct shall your ladies come;
From whom you now must steal and take no leave,
For there will be a world of water shed
Upon the parting of your wives and you.
HOT.   Methinks my moiety, north from Burton here,
In quantity equals not one of yours:
See how this river comes me cranking in,[7]
And cuts me from the best of all my land
A huge half-moon, a monstrous cantle[8] out,
I'll have the current in this place damm'd up;
And here the smug and silver Trent shall run
In a new channel, fair and evenly;
It shall not wind with such a deep indent,
To rob me of so rich a bottom here.

---

5. *How 'scapes he agues*] How does he avoid catching cold?
6. *our threefold order ta'en*] our agreement to divide the country in three parts.
7. *comes me cranking in*] comes meandering and twisting about my land.
8. *cantle*] corner, bit (of anything).

GLEND.   Not wind? it shall, it must; you see it doth.
MORT.   Yea, but
     Mark how he bears his course, and runs me up
     With like advantage on the other side;
     Gelding the opposed continent as much
     As on the other side it takes from you.
WOR.   Yea, but a little charge will trench him here,
     And on this north side win this cape of land;
     And then he runs straight and even.
HOT.   I'll have it so: a little charge will do it.
GLEND.   I'll not have it alter'd.
HOT.   Will not you?
GLEND.   No, nor you shall not.
HOT.   Who shall say me nay?
GLEND.   Why, that will I.
HOT.   Let me not understand you, then; speak it in Welsh.
GLEND.   I can speak English, lord, as well as you;
     For I was train'd up in the English court;
     Where, being but young, I framed to the harp
     Many an English ditty lovely well,
     And gave the tongue a helpful ornament,
     A virtue that was never seen in you.
HOT.   Marry,
     And I am glad of it with all my heart:
     I had rather be a kitten and cry mew
     Than one of these same metre ballad-mongers;
     I had rather hear a brazen canstick[9] turn'd,
     Or a dry wheel grate on the axle-tree;
     And that would set my teeth nothing on edge,
     Nothing so much as mincing poetry:
     'Tis like the forced gait of a shuffling nag.
GLEND.   Come, you shall have Trent turn'd.
HOT.   I do not care: I'll give thrice so much land
     To any well-deserving friend;
     But in the way of bargain, mark ye me,
     I'll cavil on[10] the ninth part of a hair.
     Are the indentures drawn? shall we be gone?
GLEND.   The moon shines fair; you may away by night:
     I'll haste the writer,[11] and withal

---

   9. *canstick*] candlestick.
  10. *cavil on*] haggle over.
  11. *the writer*] the copyist of the agreements.

Break with[12] your wives of your departure hence:
I am afraid my daughter will run mad,
So much she doteth on her Mortimer.   [*Exit.*

MORT. Fie, cousin Percy! how you cross my father!
HOT. I cannot choose: sometime he angers me
  With telling me of the moldwarp and the ant,
  Of the dreamer Merlin and his prophecies,
  And of a dragon and a finless fish,
  A clip-wing'd griffin and a moulten raven,
  A couching lion and a ramping[13] cat,[14]
  And such a deal of skimble-skamble stuff[15]
  As puts me from my faith. I tell you what, —
  He held me last night at least nine hours
  In reckoning up the several devils' names
  That were his lackeys: I cried "hum," and "well, go to,"
  But mark'd him not a word. O, he is as tedious
  As a tired horse, a railing wife;
  Worse than a smoky house: I had rather live
  With cheese and garlic in a windmill, far,
  Than feed on cates[16] and have him talk to me
  In any summer-house in Christendom.
MORT. In faith, he is a worthy gentleman,
  Exceedingly well read, and profited
  In strange concealments;[17] valiant as a lion,
  And wondrous affable, and as bountiful
  As mines of India. Shall I tell you, cousin?
  He holds your temper in a high respect,
  And curbs himself even of his natural scope
  When you come 'cross his humour; faith, he does:
  I warrant you, that man is not alive
  Might so have tempted him as you have done,
  Without the taste of danger and reproof:
  But do not use it oft, let me entreat you.
WOR. In faith, my lord, you are too wilful-blame;[18]

---

12. *Break with*] Communicate to.
13. *couching . . . ramping*] lying down . . . rearing; heraldic terms.
14. *of the moldwarp . . . cat*] Hotspur makes impatient and scornfully inexact reference to an old prophecy attributed to Merlin in which Glendower put faith, to the effect that Henry IV, who was likened by Merlin to "a moldwarp" (*i.e.*, a mole), should lose his realm to a band of three assailants, viz., a dragon, a lion, and a wolf.
15. *skimble-skamble stuff*] random nonsense.
16. *cates*] dainties, delicacies.
17. *profited . . . concealments*] skilled in wonderful secrets.
18. *wilful-blame*] wilfully to blame.

And since your coming hither have done enough
To put him quite beside his patience.
You must needs learn, lord, to amend this fault:
Though sometimes it show greatness, courage, blood, —
And that's the dearest grace it renders you, —
Yet oftentimes it doth present harsh rage,
Defect of manners, want of government,
Pride, haughtiness, opinion and disdain:
The least of which haunting a nobleman
Loseth men's hearts, and leaves behind a stain
Upon the beauty of all parts besides,
Beguiling them of commendation.[19]

HOT.   Well, I am school'd: good manners be your speed!
Here come our wives, and let us take our leave.

Re-enter GLENDOWER *with the* ladies

MORT.   This is the deadly spite that angers me;
My wife can speak no English, I no Welsh.

GLEND.   My daughter weeps: she will not part with you;
She'll be a soldier too, she'll to the wars.

MORT.   Good father, tell her that she and my aunt Percy
Shall follow in your conduct speedily.

[*Glendower speaks to her in Welsh, and she answers*
him in the same.

GLEND.   She is desperate here; a peevish self-will'd harlotry, one that no
persuasion can do good upon.   [*The lady speaks in Welsh.*

MORT.   I understand thy looks: that pretty Welsh
Which thou pour'st down from these swelling heavens[20]
I am too perfect in; and, but for shame,
In such a parley should I answer thee.

[*The lady speaks again in Welsh.*

I understand thy kisses and thou mine,
And that's a feeling disputation:[21]
But I will never be a truant, love,
Till I have learn'd thy language; for thy tongue
Makes Welsh as sweet as ditties highly penn'd,
Sung by a fair queen in a summer's bower,
With ravishing division,[22] to her lute.

GLEND.   Nay, if you melt, then will she run mad.

[*The lady speaks again in Welsh.*

---

19. *Beguiling . . . commendation*] Cheating them of the praise due them.
20. *heavens*] i.e., eyes.
21. *a feeling disputation*] a theme of sensibility.
22. *division*] variations on a melody.

MORT. O, I am ignorance itself in this!

GLEND. She bids you on the wanton[23] rushes lay you down
 And rest your gentle head upon her lap,
 And she will sing the song that pleaseth you,
 And on your eyelids crown the god of sleep,
 Charming your blood with pleasing heaviness,
 Making such difference 'twixt wake and sleep
 As is the difference betwixt day and night
 The hour before the heavenly-harness'd team
 Begins his golden progress in the east.

MORT. With all my heart I'll sit and hear her sing:
 By that time will our book, I think, be drawn.[24]

GLEND. Do so;
 And those musicians that shall play to you
 Hang in the air a thousand leagues from hence,
 And straight they shall be here: sit, and attend.

HOT. Come, Kate, thou art perfect in lying down: come, quick, quick,
that I may lay my head in thy lap.

LADY P. Go, ye giddy goose.   *[The music plays.*

HOT. Now I perceive the devil understands Welsh;
 And 'tis no marvel he is so humorous.[25]
 By 'r lady, he is a good musician.

LADY P. Then should you be nothing but musical, for you are altogether
governed by humours. Lie still, ye thief, and hear the lady sing in
Welsh.

HOT. I had rather hear Lady, my brach,[26] howl in Irish.

LADY P. Wouldst thou have thy head broken?

HOT. No.

LADY P. Then be still.

HOT. Neither; 'tis a woman's fault.

LADY P. Now God help thee!

HOT. To the Welsh lady's bed.

LADY P. What's that?

HOT. Peace! she sings.   *[Here the lady sings a Welsh song.*

HOT. Come, Kate, I'll have your song too.

LADY P. Not mine, in good sooth.

HOT. Not yours, in good sooth! Heart! you swear like a comfit-maker's[27]

---

23. *wanton*] soft.
24. *our book . . . be drawn*] our agreements be drawn out.
25. *humorous*] capricious.
26. *brach*] bitch-hound.
27. *comfit-maker's*] confectioner's.

wife. "Not you, in good sooth," and "as true as I live," and "as God
shall mend me," and "as sure as day,"
And givest such sarcenet[28] surety for thy oaths,
As if thou never walk'st further than Finsbury.[29]
Swear me, Kate, like a lady as thou art,
A good mouth-filling oath, and leave "in sooth,"
And such protest of pepper-gingerbread,
To velvet-guards[30] and Sunday-citizens.
Come, sing.
LADY P.   I will not sing.
HOT.   'Tis the next way to turn tailor,[31] or be red-breast teacher. An the
indentures be drawn, I'll away within these two hours; and so, come
in when ye will.   [*Exit.*
GLEND.   Come, come, Lord Mortimer; you are as slow
As hot Lord Percy is on fire to go.
By this our book is drawn; we'll but seal,
And then to horse immediately.
MORT.   With all my heart.   [*Exeunt.*

SCENE II.   *London. The Palace.*

Enter the KING, PRINCE OF WALES, *and others*

KING.   Lords, give us leave;[1] the Prince of Wales and I
Must have some private conference: but be near at hand,
For we shall presently have need of you.   [*Exeunt Lords.*
I know not whether God will have it so,
For some displeasing service I have done,
That, in his secret doom,[2] out of my blood
He'll breed revengement and a scourge for me;

---

28. *sarcenet*] soft, like the silken material known by that name.
29. *Finsbury*] a district where London citizens were wont to promenade.
30. *velvet-guards*] weavers of clothing trimmed with velvet.
31. *turn tailor*] tailors were noted for their singing.

1. *give us leave*] withdraw.
2. *doom*] judgment.

But thou dost in thy passages of life
Make me believe that thou art only mark'd
For the hot vengeance and the rod of heaven
To punish my mistreadings. Tell me else,
Could such inordinate and low desires,
Such poor, such bare, such lewd, such mean attempts,
Such barren pleasures, rude society,
As thou art match'd withal and grafted to,
Accompany the greatness of thy blood,
And hold their level with thy princely heart?

PRINCE.   So please your majesty, I would I could
Quit all offences with as clear excuse
As well as I am doubtless I can purge
Myself of many I am charged withal:
Yet such extenuation let me beg,
As, in reproof of many tales devised,
Which oft the ear of greatness needs must hear,
By smiling pick-thanks[3] and base newsmongers,
I may, for some things true, wherein my youth
Hath faulty wander'd and irregular,
Find pardon on my true submission.

KING.   God pardon thee! yet let me wonder, Harry,
At thy affections, which do hold a wing
Quite from the flight of all thy ancestors.
Thy place in council thou hast rudely lost,
Which by thy younger brother is supplied,
And art almost an alien to the hearts
Of all the court and princes of my blood:
The hope and expectation of thy time
Is ruin'd, and the soul of every man
Prophetically doth forethink thy fall.
Had I so lavish of my presence been,
So common-hackney'd in the eyes of men,
So stale and cheap to vulgar company,
Opinion, that did help me to the crown,
Had still kept loyal to possession,[4]
And left me in reputeless banishment,
A fellow of no mark nor likelihood.
By being seldom seen, I could not stir
But like a comet I was wonder'd at;
That men would tell their children "This is he;"

---

3. *pick-thanks*] parasites, flatterers.
4. *possession*] i.e., to the sovereignty of Richard II.

Others would say "Where, which is Bolingbroke?"
And then I stole all courtesy from heaven,[5]
And dress'd myself in such humility
That I did pluck allegiance from men's hearts,
Loud shouts and salutations from their mouths,
Even in the presence of the crowned king.
Thus did I keep my person fresh and new;
My presence, like a robe pontifical
Ne'er seen but wonder'd at: and so my state,
Seldom but sumptuous, showed like a feast,
And wan by rareness such solemnity.
The skipping[6] king, he ambled up and down,
With shallow jesters and rash bavin[7] wits,
Soon kindled and soon burnt; carded[8] his state,
Mingled his royalty with capering fools,
Had his great name profaned with their scorns,
And gave his countenance, against his name,[9]
To laugh at gibing boys, and stand the push[10]
Of every beardless vain comparative,
Grew a companion to the common streets,
Enfeoff'd[11] himself to popularity;
That, being daily swallow'd by men's eyes,
They surfeited with honey and began
To loathe the taste of sweetness, whereof a little
More than a little is by much too much.
So when he had occasion to be seen,
He was but as the cuckoo is in June,
Heard, not regarded; seen, but with such eyes
As, sick and blunted with community,[12]
Afford no extraordinary gaze,
Such as is bent on sun-like majesty
When it shines seldom in admiring eyes;
But rather drowsed and hung their eyelids down,
Slept in his face and render'd such aspect
As cloudy[13] men use to their adversaries,

---

5. *stole . . . heaven*] assumed a manner of the utmost courtesy.
6. *skipping*] flighty, wanton.
7. *bavin*] brushwood, "soon kindled and soon burnt."
8. *carded*] debased.
9. *name*] dignity.
10. *push*] insolence.
11. *Enfeoff'd*] Gave himself up to.
12. *community*] familiarity.
13. *cloudy*] sullen, morose.

Being with his presence glutted, gorged and full.
And in that very line, Harry, standest thou;
For thou hast lost thy princely privilege
With vile participation:[14] not an eye
But is a-weary of thy common sight,
Save mine, which hath desired to see thee more;
Which now doth that I would not have it do,
Make blind itself with foolish tenderness.

PRINCE. I shall hereafter, my thrice gracious lord,
Be more myself.

KING. For all the world
As thou art to this hour was Richard then
When I from France set foot at Ravenspurgh,
And even as I was then is Percy now.
Now, by my sceptre and my soul to boot,
He hath more worthy interest[15] to the state
Than thou the shadow of succession;[16]
For of no right, nor colour like to right,
He doth fill fields with harness[17] in the realm,
Turns head against the lion's armed jaws,
And, being no more in debt to years than thou,
Leads ancient lords and reverend bishops on
To bloody battles and to bruising arms.
What never-dying honour hath he got
Against renowned Douglas! whose high deeds,
Whose hot incursions and great name in arms
Holds from all soldiers chief majority[18]
And military title capital[19]
Through all the kingdoms that acknowledge Christ:
Thrice hath this Hotspur, Mars in swathling[20] clothes,
This infant warrior, in his enterprizes
Discomfited great Douglas, ta'en him once,
Enlarged him and made a friend of him,
To fill the mouth of deep defiance up,
And shake the peace and safety of our throne.
And what say you to this? Percy, Northumberland,
The Archbishop's grace of York, Douglas, Mortimer,

---

14. *vile participation*] low companionship or society.
15. *interest*] claim, title.
16. *shadow of succession*] heir apparent.
17. *harness*] armor; here, armed warriors.
18. *majority*] preeminence.
19. *capital*] principal.
20. *swathling*] swaddling.

        Capitulate[21] against us and are up.
        But wherefore do I tell these news to thee?
        Why, Harry, do I tell thee of my foes,
        Which art my near'st and dearest enemy?
        Thou that art like enough, through vassal fear
        Base inclination and the start of spleen,[22]
        To fight against me under Percy's pay,
        To dog his heels and curtsy at his frowns,
        To show how much thou art degenerate.
PRINCE.   Do not think so; you shall not find it so:
        And God forgive them that so much have sway'd
        Your majesty's good thoughts away from me!
        I will redeem all this on Percy's head,
        And in the closing of some glorious day
        Be bold to tell you that I am your son;
        When I will wear a garment all of blood,
        And stain my favours in a bloody mask,
        Which, wash'd away, shall scour my shame with it:
        And that shall be the day, whene'er it lights,
        That this same child of honour and renown,
        This gallant Hotspur, this all-praised knight,
        And your unthought-of Harry chance to meet.
        For every honour sitting on his helm,
        Would they were multitudes, and on my head
        My shames redoubled! for the time will come,
        That I shall make this northern youth exchange
        His glorious deeds for my indignities.
        Percy is but my factor, good my lord,
        To engross up glorious deeds on my behalf;
        And I will call him to so strict account,
        That he shall render every glory up,
        Yea, even the slightest worship of his time,
        Or I will tear the reckoning from his heart.
        This, in the name of God, I promise here:
        The which if He be pleased I shall perform,
        I do beseech your majesty may salve
        The long-grown wounds of my intemperance:
        If not, the end of life cancels all bands;
        And I will die a hundred thousand deaths
        Ere break the smallest parcel of this vow.

---

21. *Capitulate*] Form a league.
22. *start of spleen*] impulse of anger.

KING.   A hundred thousand rebels die in this:
Thou shalt have charge and sovereign trust herein.

Enter BLUNT

How now, good Blunt? thy looks are full of speed.
BLUNT.   So hath the business that I come to speak of.
Lord Mortimer of Scotland hath sent word
That Douglas and the English rebels met
The eleventh of this month at Shrewsbury:
A mighty and a fearful head they are,
If promises be kept on every hand,
As ever offer'd foul play in a state.
KING.   The Earl of Westmoreland set forth to-day;
With him my son, Lord John of Lancaster;
For this advertisement[23] is five days old:
On Wednesday next, Harry, you shall set forward;
On Thursday we ourselves will march: our meeting
Is Bridgenorth: and, Harry, you shall march
Through Gloucestershire; by which account,
Our business valued, some twelve days hence
Our general forces at Bridgenorth shall meet.
Our hands are full of business: let's away;
Advantage feeds him[24] fat, while men delay.   [*Exeunt.*

SCENE III.   *The Boar's-Head Tavern in Eastcheap.*

Enter FALSTAFF *and* BARDOLPH

FAL.   Bardolph, am I not fallen away vilely since this last action? do I
not bate? do I not dwindle? Why, my skin hangs about me like an
old lady's loose gown; I am withered like an old apple-john.[1] Well,
I'll repent, and that suddenly, while I am in some liking:[2] I shall be
out of heart shortly, and then I shall have no strength to repent. An
I have not forgotten what the inside of a church is made of, I am
a peppercorn, a brewer's horse:[3] the inside of a church! Company,
villanous company, hath been the spoil of me.

---

23. *advertisement*] intelligence, information.
24. *feeds him*] feeds himself, grows.

---

1. *apple-john*] apple, which kept long though the skin shrivelled quickly.
2. *in some liking*] in fairly good condition.
3. *brewer's horse*] a horse that is lank and bony.

BARD. Sir John, you are so fretful, you cannot live long.

FAL. Why, there is it: come sing me a bawdy song; make me merry. I
was as virtuously given as a gentleman need to be; virtuous enough;
swore little; diced not above seven times a week; went to a bawdy-
house not above once in a quarter — of an hour; paid money that
I borrowed, three or four times; lived well, and in good compass:
and now I live out of all order, out of all compass.

BARD. Why, you are so fat, Sir John, that you must needs be out of all
compass, out of all reasonable compass, Sir John.

FAL. Do thou amend thy face, and I'll amend my life: thou art our admiral, thou bearest the lantern in the poop, but 'tis in the nose of
thee; thou art the Knight of the Burning Lamp.

BARD. Why, Sir John, my face does you no harm.

FAL. No, I'll be sworn; I make as good use of it as many a man doth
of a Death's-head or a memento mori:[4] I never see thy face but I
think upon hell-fire, and Dives[5] that lived in purple; for there he is
in his robes, burning, burning. If thou wert any way given to virtue,
I would swear by thy face; my oath should be, "By this fire, that's
God's angel:"[6] but thou art altogether given over; and wert indeed,
but for the light in thy face, the son of utter darkness. When thou
rannest up Gadshill in the night to catch my horse, if I did not
think thou hadst been an ignis fatuus[7] or a ball of wildfire, there's
no purchase in money. O, thou art a perpetual triumph, an ever-
lasting bonfire-light! Thou hast saved me a thousand marks in links
and torches, walking with thee in the night betwixt tavern and tavern: but the sack that thou hast drunk me would have bought me
lights as good cheap[8] at the dearest chandler's in Europe. I have
maintained that salamander of yours with fire any time this two and
thirty years; God reward me for it!

BARD. 'Sblood, I would my face were in your belly!

FAL. God-a-mercy! so should I be sure to be heart-burned.

Enter Hostess

How now, Dame Partlet[9] the hen! have you inquired yet who picked
my pocket?

HOST. Why, Sir John, what do you think, Sir John? do you think I keep
thieves in my house? I have searched, I have inquired, so has my

---

4. *memento mori*] a common term for a skull and crossbones.
5. *Dives*] the rich man in the parable (Luke 16:19).
6. *By . . . angel*] Cf. Exodus 3:2, Psalms 104:4, and Hebrews 1:7.
7. *an ignis fatuus*] a will o' the wisp.
8. *as good cheap*] quite as cheaply.
9. *Dame Partlet*] The name of the hen in the medieval story of Reynard the Fox.

husband, man by man, boy by boy, servant by servant: the tithe of a hair was never lost in my house before.

FAL. Ye lie, hostess: Bardolph was shaved, and lost many a hair; and I'll be sworn my pocket was picked. Go to, you are a woman, go.

HOST. Who, I? no; I defy thee: God's light, I was never called so in mine own house before.

FAL. Go to, I know you well enough.

HOST. No, Sir John; you do not know me, Sir John. I know you, Sir John: you owe me money, Sir John; and now you pick a quarrel to beguile me of it: I bought you a dozen of shirts to your back.

FAL. Dowlas,[10] filthy dowlas: I have given them away to bakers' wives, and they have made bolters[11] of them.

HOST. Now, as I am a true woman, holland[12] of eight shillings an ell. You owe money here besides, Sir John, for your diet and by-drinkings, and money lent you, four and twenty pound.

FAL. He had his part of it; let him pay.

HOST. He? alas, he is poor: he hath nothing.

FAL. How! poor? look upon his face; what call you rich? let them coin his nose, let them coin his cheeks: I'll not pay a denier.[13] What, will you make a younker[14] of me? shall I not take mine ease in mine inn but I shall have my pocket picked? I have lost a seal-ring of my grandfather's worth forty mark.

HOST. O Jesu, I have heard the prince tell him, I know not how oft, that that ring was copper!

FAL. How! the prince is a Jack, a sneak-cup:[15] 'sblood, and he were here, I would cudgel him like a dog, if he would say so.

Enter the PRINCE *and* PETO, *marching, and* FALSTAFF *meets them playing on his truncheon like a fife*

How now, lad! is the wind in that door, i' faith? must we all march?

BARD. Yea, two and two, Newgate[16] fashion.

HOST. My lord, I pray you, hear me.

PRINCE. What sayest thou, Mistress Quickly? How doth thy husband? I love him well; he is an honest man.

HOST. Good my lord, hear me.

FAL. Prithee, let her alone, and list to me.

PRINCE. What sayest thou, Jack?

---

10. *Dowlas*] The coarsest kind of linen.
11. *bolters*] cloth or hair sieves for sifting meal or flour.
12. *holland*] fine linen.
13. *a denier*] a penny, a stiver, from Latin "denarius."
14. *younker*] greenhorn.
15. *sneak-cup*] one who dodges liquor, who slily avoids drinking his share.
16. *Newgate*] a London prison. Prisoners were marched there in pairs.

FAL. The other night I fell asleep here behind the arras, and had my
pocket picked: this house is turned bawdy-house; they pick pockets.

PRINCE. What didst thou lose, Jack?

FAL. Wilt thou believe me, Hal? three or four bonds of forty pound
a-piece, and a seal-ring of my grandfather's.

PRINCE. A trifle, some eight-penny matter.

HOST. So I told him, my lord; and I said I heard your grace say so: and,
my lord, he speaks most vilely of you, like a foul-mouthed man as
he is; and said he would cudgel you.

PRINCE. What! he did not?

HOST. There's neither faith, truth, nor womanhood in me else.

FAL. There's no more faith in thee than in a stewed prune;[17] nor no
more truth in thee than in a drawn fox;[18] and for womanhood,
Maid Marian may be the deputy's wife of the ward to thee. Go, you
thing, go.

HOST. Say, what thing? what thing?

FAL. What thing! why, a thing to thank God on.

HOST. I am no thing to thank God on, I would thou shouldst know it;
I am an honest man's wife: and, setting thy knighthood aside, thou
art a knave to call me so.

FAL. Setting thy womanhood aside, thou art a beast to say otherwise.

HOST. Say, what beast, thou knave, thou?

FAL. What beast! why, an otter.

PRINCE. An otter, Sir John! why an otter?

FAL. Why, she's neither fish nor flesh; a man knows not where to
have her.

HOST. Thou art an unjust man in saying so: thou or any man knows
where to have me, thou knave, thou!

PRINCE. Thou sayest true, hostess; and he slanders thee most grossly.

HOST. So he doth you, my lord; and said this other day you ought[19]
him a thousand pound.

PRINCE. Sirrah, do I owe you a thousand pound?

FAL. A thousand pound, Hal! a million: thy love is worth a million: thou
owest me thy love.

HOST. Nay, my lord, he called you Jack, and said he would cudgel you.

FAL. Did I, Bardolph?

BARD. Indeed, Sir John, you said so.

FAL. Yea, if he said my ring was copper.

PRINCE. I say 'tis copper: darest thou be as good as thy word now?

---

17. *a stewed prune*] commonly eaten in bawdy houses.
18. *a drawn fox*] a fox drawn from cover, and wily in getting back.
19. *ought*] owed.

FAL.   Why, Hal, thou knowest, as thou art but man, I dare: but as thou
      art prince, I fear thee as I fear the roaring of the lion's whelp.
PRINCE.   And why not as the lion?
FAL.   The king himself is to be feared as the lion; dost thou think I'll fear
      thee as I fear thy father? nay, and I do, I pray God my girdle break.
PRINCE.   O, if it should, how would thy guts fall about thy knees! But,
      sirrah, there's no room for faith, truth, nor honesty in this bosom
      of thine; it is all filled up with guts and midriff. Charge an honest
      woman with picking thy pocket! why, thou whoreson, impudent,
      embossed[20] rascal, if there were anything in thy pocket but tavern-
      reckonings, memorandums of bawdy-houses, and one poor penny-
      worth of sugar-candy to make thee long-winded, if thy pocket were
      enriched with any other injuries but these, I am a villain: and yet
      you will stand to it; you will not pocket up wrong:[21] art thou not
      ashamed?
FAL.   Dost thou hear, Hal? thou knowest in the state of innocency Adam
      fell; and what should poor Jack Falstaff do in the days of villany?
      Thou seest I have more flesh than another man; and therefore more
      frailty. You confess then, you picked my pocket?
PRINCE.   It appears so by the story.
FAL.   Hostess, I forgive thee: go, make ready breakfast; love thy husband,
      look to thy servants, cherish thy guests: thou shalt find me tractable
      to any honest reason: thou seest I am pacified still. Nay, prithee, be
      gone. [*Exit Hostess.*] Now, Hal, to the news at court: for the robbery,
      lad, how is that answered?
PRINCE.   O, my sweet beef, I must still be good angel to thee: the money
      is paid back again.
FAL.   O, I do not like that paying back; 'tis a double labour.
PRINCE.   I am good friends with my father, and may do any thing.
FAL.   Rob me the exchequer the first thing thou doest, and do it with
      unwashed hands[22] too.
BARD.   Do, my lord.
PRINCE.   I have procured thee, Jack, a charge of foot.
FAL.   I would it had been of horse. Where shall I find one that can steal
      well? O for a fine thief, of the age of two and twenty or thereabouts!
      I am heinously unprovided. Well, God be thanked for these rebels,
      they offend none but the virtuous: I laud them, I praise them.
PRINCE.   Bardolph!
BARD.   My lord?

---

20. *embossed*] swollen.
21. *pocket up wrong*] bear injury tamely, without resentment.
22. *with unwashed hands*] at once, without waiting (to wash your hands).

PRINCE. Go bear this letter to Lord John of Lancaster, to my brother
     John; this to my Lord of Westmoreland. [*Exit Bardolph.*] Go, Peto,
     to horse, to horse; for thou and I have thirty miles to ride yet ere
     dinner time. [*Exit Peto.*] Jack, meet me to-morrow in the Temple
     hall at two o'clock in the afternoon.
     There shalt thou know thy charge, and there receive
     Money and order for their furniture.23
     The land is burning; Percy stands on high;
     And either we or they must lower lie.   [*Exit.*
FAL.   Rare words! brave world! Hostess, my breakfast, come!
     O, I could wish this tavern were my drum!24   [*Exit.*

---

23. *furniture*] equipment.
24. *my drum*] my headquarters, my rendezvous.

ACT IV.

SCENE I. *The Rebel Camp near Shrewsbury.*

Enter HOTSPUR, WORCESTER, *and* DOUGLAS

HOTSPUR.   Well said, my noble Scot: if speaking truth
    In this fine age were not thought flattery,
    Such attribution[1] should the Douglas have,
    As not a soldier of this season's stamp
    Should go so general current through the world.
    By God, I cannot flatter; I do defy
    The tongues of soothers;[2] but a braver place
    In my heart's love hath no man than yourself:
    Nay, task me to my word; approve me,[3] lord.
DOUG.   Thou art the king of honour:
    No man so potent breathes upon the ground
    But I will beard[4] him.
HOT.   Do so, and 'tis well.

Enter a Messenger *with letters*

    What letters hast thou there? — I can but thank you.
MESS.   These letters come from your father.
HOT.   Letters from him! why comes he not himself?
MESS.   He cannot come, my lord; he is grievous sick.
HOT.   'Zounds! how has he the leisure to be sick
    In such a justling[5] time? Who leads his power?
    Under whose government come they along?
MESS.   His letters bear his mind, not I, my lord.

---

1. *attribution*] credit.
2. *defy . . . soothers*] disdain flattering tongues.
3. *task . . . approve me*] put my word to the proof, try me.
4. *beard*] defy.
5. *justling*] jostling.

WOR. I prithee, tell me, doth he keep his bed?
MESS: He did, my lord, four days ere I set forth;
      And at the time of my departure thence
      He was much fear'd by his physicians.
WOR. I would the state of time had first been whole,
      Ere he by sickness had been visited:
      His health was never better worth than now.
HOT. Sick now! droop now! this sickness doth infect
      The very life-blood of our enterprise;
      'Tis catching hither, even to our camp.
      He writes me here, that inward sickness —
      And that his friends by deputation could not
      So soon be drawn, nor did he think it meet
      To lay so dangerous and dear a trust
      On any soul removed but on his own.
      Yet doth he give us bold advertisement,[6]
      That with our small conjunction we should on,
      To see how fortune is disposed to us;
      For, as he writes, there is no quailing now,
      Because the king is certainly possess'd
      Of all our purposes. What say you to it?
WOR. Your father's sickness is a maim to us.
HOT. A perilous gash, a very limb lopp'd off:
      And yet, in faith, it is not; his present want
      Seems more than we shall find it: were it good
      To set the exact wealth of all our states
      All at one cast? to set so rich a main[7]
      On the nice hazard of one doubtful hour?
      It were not good; for therein should we read
      The very bottom and the soul of hope,
      The very list, the very utmost bound
      Of all our fortunes.
DOUG.   Faith, and so we should;
      Where now remains a sweet reversion:[8]
      We may boldly spend upon the hope of what
      Is to come in:
      A comfort of retirement lives in this.
HOT. A rendezvous, a home to fly unto,
      If that the devil and mischance look big
      Upon the maidenhead of our affairs.

---

6. *advertisement*] admonition.
7. *set so rich a main*] lay so large a stake.
8. *sweet reversion*] some hope in reserve.

WOR. But yet I would your father had been here.
    The quality and hair[9] of our attempt
    Brooks no division: it will be thought
    By some, that know not why he is away,
    That wisdom, loyalty and mere dislike
    Of our proceedings kept the earl from hence:
    And think how such an apprehension
    May turn the tide of fearful faction,
    And breed a kind of question in our cause;
    For well you know we of the offering side[10]
    Must keep aloof from strict arbitrement,[11]
    And stop all sight-holes, every loop from whence
    The eye of reason may pry in upon us:
    This absence of your father's draws a curtain,
    That shows the ignorant a kind of fear
    Before not dreamt of.
HOT.   You strain too far.
    I rather of his absence make this use:
    It lends a lustre and more great opinion,
    A larger dare to our great enterprise,
    Than if the earl were here; for men must think,
    If we without his help can make a head
    To push against a kingdom, with his help
    We shall o'erturn it topsy-turvy down.
    Yet all goes well, yet all our joints are whole.
DOUG. As heart can think: there is not such a word
    Spoke of in Scotland as this term of fear.

Enter SIR RICHARD VERNON

HOT. My cousin Vernon! welcome, by my soul.
VER. Pray God my news be worth a welcome, lord.
    The Earl of Westmoreland, seven thousand strong,
    Is marching hitherwards; with him Prince John.
HOT. No harm: what more?
VER.   And further, I have learn'd,
    The king himself in person is set forth,
    Or hitherwards intended speedily,
    With strong and mighty preparation.
HOT. He shall be welcome too. Where is his son,
    The nimble-footed madcap Prince of Wales,

---

9. *hair*] complexion, character.
10. *the offering side*] the attacking party.
11. *arbitrement*] judicial inquiry.

And his comrades, that daff'd[12] the world aside,
And bid it pass?
VER.   All furnish'd, all in arms;
All plumed like estridges that with the wind
Baited[13] like eagles having lately bathed;
Glittering in golden coats, like images;[14]
As full of spirit as the month of May,
And gorgeous as the sun at midsummer;
Wanton as youthful goats, wild as young bulls.
I saw young Harry, with his beaver[15] on,
His cuisses[16] on his thighs, gallantly arm'd,
Rise from the ground like feather'd Mercury,
And vaulted with such ease into his seat,
As if an angel dropp'd down from the clouds,
To turn and wind a fiery Pegasus,
And witch the world with noble horsemanship.
HOT.   No more, no more: worse than the sun in March,
This praise doth nourish agues. Let them come;
They come like sacrifices in their trim,[17]
And to the fire-eyed maid of smoky war[18]
All hot and bleeding will we offer them:
The mailed Mars shall on his altar sit
Up to the ears in blood. I am on fire
To hear this rich reprisal is so nigh
And yet not ours. Come, let me taste[19] my horse,
Who is to bear me like a thunderbolt
Against the bosom of the Prince of Wales:
Harry to Harry shall, not horse to horse,
Meet and ne'er part till one drop down a corse.
O that Glendower were come!
VER.   There is more news:
I learn'd in Worcester, as I rode along,
He cannot draw his power this fourteen days.
DOUG.   That's the worst tidings that I hear of yet.
WOR.   Ay, by my faith, that bears a frosty sound.
HOT.   What may the king's whole battle reach unto?

---

12. *daff'd*] tossed contemptuously.
13. *Baited*] This should probably read "bated," flapped their wings.
14. *images*] gaudily painted saints' images.
15. *beaver*] visor of the helmet; here also the helmet itself.
16. *cuisses*] a French word for leg or thigh armour.
17. *trim*] fine apparel, trappings.
18. *maid of smoky war*] the goddess Bellona.
19. *taste*] test, try.

VER.   To thirty thousand.
HOT.   Forty let it be:
   My father and Glendower being both away,
   The powers of us may serve so great a day.
   Come, let us take a muster speedily:
   Doomsday is near; die all, die merrily.
DOUG.   Talk not of dying: I am out of fear
   Of death or death's hand for this one half year.   [*Exeunt.*

SCENE II.   *A Public Road near Coventry.*

Enter FALSTAFF *and* BARDOLPH

FAL.   Bardolph, get thee before to Coventry; fill me a bottle of sack: our
   soldiers shall march through; we'll to Sutton Co'fil'[1] to-night.
BARD.   Will you give me money, captain?
FAL.   Lay out, lay out.
BARD.   This bottle makes an angel.[2]
FAL.   An if it do, take it for thy labour; and if it make twenty, take them
   all; I'll answer the coinage. Bid my lieutenant Peto meet me at
   town's end.
BARD.   I will, captain: farewell.   [*Exit.*
FAL.   If I be not ashamed of my soldiers, I am a soused gurnet.[3] I have
   misused the king's press[4] damnably. I have got, in exchange of a
   hundred and fifty soldiers, three hundred and odd pounds. I press
   me none but good householders, yeomen's sons; inquire me out
   contracted bachelors, such as had been asked twice on the banns;
   such a commodity of warm slaves, as had as lieve hear the devil
   as a drum; such as fear the report of a caliver[5] worse than a struck
   fowl or a hurt wild-duck. I pressed me none but such toasts-and-
   butter, with hearts in their bellies no bigger than pins'-heads, and
   they have bought out their services; and now my whole charge
   consists of ancients,[6] corporals, lieutenants, gentlemen of compa-

---

1. *Sutton Co'fil'*] Sutton Coldfield, some twenty-five miles northwest of Coventry.
2. *angel*] coin worth ten shillings.
3. *soused gurnet*] a pickled fish; a term of contempt.
4. *king's press*] the royal commission for impressing soldiers.
5. *caliver*] musket.
6. *ancients*] ensigns.

nies, slaves as ragged as Lazarus in the painted cloth,[7] where the
glutton's dogs licked his sores; and such as indeed were never soldiers, but discarded unjust serving-men, younger sons to younger
brothers, revolted tapsters, and ostlers trade-fallen; the cankers of a
calm world and a long peace, ten times more dishonourable ragged than an old faced ancient: and such have I, to fill up the rooms
of them that have bought out their services, that you would think
that I had a hundred and fifty tattered prodigals lately come from
swine-keeping, from eating draff[8] and husks. A mad fellow met me
on the way and told me I had unloaded all the gibbets[9] and pressed
the dead bodies. No eye hath seen such scarecrows. I'll not march
through Coventry with them, that's flat: nay, and the villains march
wide betwixt the legs, as if they had gyves[10] on; for indeed I had
the most of them out of prison. There's but a shirt and a half in all
my company; and the half shirt is two napkins tacked together and
thrown over the shoulders like a herald's coat without sleeves; and
the shirt, to say the truth, stolen from my host at Saint Alban's, or
the red-nose innkeeper of Daventry.[11] But that's all one; they'll find
linen enough on every hedge.

Enter the PRINCE *and* WESTMORELAND

PRINCE. How now, blown Jack! how now, quilt!
FAL. What, Hal! how now, mad wag! what a devil dost thou in
    Warwickshire? My good Lord of Westmoreland, I cry you mercy: I
    thought your honour had already been at Shrewsbury.
WEST. Faith, Sir John, 'tis more than time that I were there, and you
    too; but my powers are there already. The king, I can tell you, looks
    for us all: we must away all night.
FAL. Tut, never fear me: I am as vigilant as a cat to steal cream.
PRINCE. I think, to steal cream indeed, for thy theft hath already made
    thee butter. But tell me, Jack, whose fellows are these that come
    after?
FAL. Mine, Hal, mine.
PRINCE. I did never see such pitiful rascals.
FAL. Tut, tut; good enough to toss;[12] food for powder, food for powder;
    they'll fill a pit as well as better: tush, man, mortal men, mortal
    men.

---

7. *Lazarus in the painted cloth*] The story of Lazarus and other scriptural tales were often
   depicted in the painted cloths or rough tapestries which adorned middle-class houses.
8. *draff*] refuse.
9. *gibbets*] gallows.
10. *gyves*] shackles, fetters.
11. *Saint Alban's . . . Daventry*] towns on the direct road from London to Coventry.
12. *to toss*] i.e., on a pike.

WEST. Ay, but, Sir John, methinks they are exceeding poor and bare, too beggarly.

FAL. Faith, for their poverty, I know not where they had that; and for their bareness, I am sure they never learned that of me.

PRINCE. No, I'll be sworn; unless you call three fingers on the ribs[13] bare. But, sirrah, make haste: Percy is already in the field.

FAL. What, is the king encamped?

WEST. He is, Sir John: I fear we shall stay too long.

FAL. Well,
To the latter end of a fray and the beginning of a feast
Fits a dull fighter and a keen guest.   [*Exeunt.*

SCENE III. *The Rebel Camp near Shrewsbury.*

Enter HOTSPUR, WORCESTER, DOUGLAS, *and* VERNON

HOT. We'll fight with him to-night.

WOR.   It may not be.

DOUG. You give him then advantage.

VER.   Not a whit.

HOT. Why say you so? looks he not for supply?

VER. So do we.

HOT.   His is certain, ours is doubtful.

WOR. Good cousin, be advised; stir not to-night.

VER. · Do not, my lord.

DOUG.   You do not counsel well:
You speak it out of fear and cold heart.

VER. Do me no slander, Douglas: by my life,
And I dare well maintain it with my life,
If well-respected honour bid me on,
I hold as little counsel with weak fear
As you, my lord, or any Scot that this day lives:
Let it be seen to-morrow in the battle
Which of us fears.

DOUG.   Yea, or to-night.

VER.   Content.

HOT. To-night, say I.

VER. Come, come, it may not be. I wonder much,

---

13. *three fingers . . . ribs*] three fingers' breadth of flesh.

> Being men of such great leading as you are,
> That you foresee not what impediments
> Drag back our expedition: certain horse
> Of my cousin Vernon's are not yet come up:
> Your uncle Worcester's horse came but to-day;
> And now their pride and mettle is asleep,
> Their courage with hard labour tame and dull,
> That not a horse is half the half of himself.

HOT.   So are the horses of the enemy
> In general, journey-bated[1] and brought low:
> The better part of ours are full of rest.

WOR.   The number of the king exceedeth ours:
> For God's sake, cousin, stay till all come in.

> > > > *[The trumpet sounds a parley.*

Enter SIR WALTER BLUNT

BLUNT.   I come with gracious offers from the king,
> If you vouchsafe me hearing and respect.

HOT.   Welcome, Sir Walter Blunt; and would to God
> You were of our determination!
> Some of us love you well; and even those some
> Envy your great deservings and good name,
> Because you are not of our quality,
> But stand against us like an enemy.

BLUNT.   And God defend but still I should stand so,
> So long as out of limit and true rule
> You stand against anointed majesty.
> But to my charge. The king hath sent to know
> The nature of your griefs, and whereupon
> You conjure from the breast of civil peace
> Such bold hostility, teaching his duteous land
> Audacious cruelty. If that the king
> Have any way your good deserts forgot,
> Which he confesseth to be manifold,
> He bids you name your griefs; and with all speed
> You shall have your desires with interest,
> And pardon absolute for yourself and these
> Herein misled by your suggestion.[2]

HOT.   The king is kind; and well we know the king
> Knows at what time to promise, when to pay.
> My father and my uncle and myself

---

1. *journey-bated*] exhausted with travel.
2. *by your suggestion*] at your prompting, instigation.

Did give him that same royalty he wears;
And when he was not six and twenty strong,
Sick in the world's regard, wretched and low,
A poor unminded outlaw sneaking home,
My father gave him welcome to the shore;
And when he heard him swear and vow to God
He came but to be Duke of Lancaster,
To sue his livery[3] and beg his peace,
With tears of innocency and terms of zeal,
My father, in kind heart and pity moved,
Swore him assistance and perform'd it too.
Now when the lords and barons of the realm
Perceived Northumberland did lean to him,
The more and less came in with cap and knee;
Met him in boroughs, cities, villages,
Attended him on bridges, stood in lanes,
Laid gifts before him, proffer'd him their oaths,
Gave him their heirs, as pages follow'd him
Even at the heels in golden multitudes.
He presently, as greatness knows itself,
Steps me a little higher than his vow
Made to my father, while his blood was poor,[4]
Upon the naked shore of Ravenspurgh;
And now, forsooth, takes on him to reform
Some certain edicts and some strait decrees
That lie too heavy on the commonwealth,
Cries out upon abuses, seems to weep
Over his country's wrongs; and by this face,
This seeming brow of justice, did he win
The hearts of all that he did angle for;
Proceeded further; cut me off the heads
Of all the favourites that the absent king
In deputation left behind him here,
When he was personal[5] in the Irish war.

BLUNT.   Tut, I came not to hear this.
HOT.   Then to the point.
In short time after, he deposed the king;
Soon after that, deprived him of his life;
And in the neck of that,[6] task'd the whole state;

---

3. *sue his livery*] sue for the return of his lands.
4. *while his blood was poor*] while he was in poor, dispirited condition.
5. *was personal*] was present in person.
6. *in the neck of that*] following quick on that.

> To make that worse, suffer'd his kinsman March,
> Who is, if every owner were well placed,
> Indeed his king, to be engaged[7] in Wales,
> There without ransom to lie forfeited;
> Disgraced me in my happy victories,
> Sought to entrap me by intelligence;[8]
> Rated mine uncle from the council-board;
> In rage dismiss'd my father from the court;
> Broke oath on oath, committed wrong on wrong,
> And in conclusion drove us to seek out
> This head of safety,[9] and withal to pry
> Into his title, the which we find
> Too indirect for long continuance.

BLUNT.   Shall I return this answer to the king?

HOT.   Not so, Sir Walter: we'll withdraw a while.
> Go to the king; and let there be impawn'd
> Some surety for a safe return again,
> And in the morning early shall mine uncle
> Bring him our purposes: and so farewell.

BLUNT.   I would you would accept of grace and love.

HOT.   And may be so we shall.

BLUNT.   Pray God you do.   [*Exeunt.*

SCENE IV. *York. The Archbishop's Palace.*

Enter the ARCHBISHOP OF YORK *and* SIR MICHAEL

ARCH.   Hie, good Sir Michael; bear this sealed brief[1]
> With winged haste to the lord marshal;
> This to my cousin Scroop, and all the rest
> To whom they are directed. If you knew
> How much they do import, you would make haste.

SIR M.   My good lord,
> I guess their tenour.

---

7. *engaged*] pledged as a hostage.
8. *by intelligence*] by means of spies.
9. *head of safety*] armed force for our self-protection.

---

1. *brief*] letter.

ARCH.   Like enough you do.
    To-morrow, good Sir Michael, is a day
    Wherein the fortune of ten thousand men
    Must bide the touch;[2] for, sir, at Shrewsbury,
    As I am truly given to understand,
    The king with mighty and quick-raised power
    Meets with Lord Harry: and, I fear, Sir Michael,
    What with the sickness of Northumberland,
    Whose power was in the first proportion,
    And what with Owen Glendower's absence thence,
    Who with them was a rated sinew[3] too
    And comes not in, o'er-ruled by prophecies,
    I fear the power of Percy is too weak
    To wage an instant trial with the king.
SIR M.   Why, my good lord, you need not fear;
    There is Douglas and Lord Mortimer.
ARCH.   No, Mortimer is not there.
SIR M.   But there is Mordake, Vernon, Lord Harry Percy,
    And there is my Lord of Worcester and a head
    Of gallant warriors, noble gentlemen.
ARCH.   And so there is: but yet the king hath drawn
    The special head of all the land together:
    The Prince of Wales, Lord John of Lancaster,
    The noble Westmoreland and warlike Blunt;
    And many mo corrivals[4] and dear men
    Of estimation and command in arms.
SIR M.   Doubt not, my lord, they shall be well opposed.
ARCH.   I hope no less, yet needful 'tis to fear;
    And, to prevent the worst, Sir Michael, speed:
    For if Lord Percy thrive not, ere the king
    Dismiss his power, he means to visit us,
    For he hath heard of our confederacy,
    And 'tis but wisdom to make strong against him:
    Therefore make haste. I must go write again
    To other friends; and so farewell, Sir Michael.   [*Exeunt.*

---

2. *bide the touch*] stand the test.
3. *a rated sinew*] an anticipated source of strength.
4. *mo corrivals*] more partners in the enterprise.

ACT V

SCENE I. *The King's Camp near Shrewsbury.*

Enter the KING, PRINCE OF WALES, LORD JOHN OF LANCASTER,
SIR WALTER BLUNT, *and* FALSTAFF

KING. How bloodily the sun begins to peer
    Above yon busky[1] hill! the day looks pale
    At his distemperature.[2]
PRINCE.   The southern wind
    Doth play the trumpet to his purposes,
    And by his hollow whistling in the leaves
    Foretells a tempest and a blustering day.
KING. Then with the losers let it sympathise,
    For nothing can seem foul to those that win. [*The trumpet sounds.*

Enter WORCESTER *and* VERNON

    How now, my Lord of Worcester! 'tis not well
    That you and I should meet upon such terms
    As now we meet. You have deceived our trust,
    And made us doff our easy robes of peace.
    To crush our old limbs in ungentle steel:
    This is not well, my lord, this is not well.
    What say you to it? will you again unknit
    This churlish knot of all-abhorred war?
    And move in that obedient orb[3] again
    Where you did give a fair and natural light,
    And be no more an exhaled meteor,[4]

---

1. *busky*] bushy, wooded.
2. *distemperature*] inclemency.
3. *obedient orb*] orbit of obedience.
4. *an exhaled meteor*] meteors were supposed to be formed of vapours drawn out of the earth
   by the sun, and were regarded as ill omens.

        A prodigy of fear, and a portent
        Of broached mischief to the unborn times?
WOR.   Hear me, my liege:
        For mine own part, I could be well content
        To entertain the lag-end of my life
        With quiet hours; for, I do protest
        I have not sought the day of this dislike.
KING.   You have not sought it! how comes it, then?
FAL.   Rebellion lay in his way, and he found it.
PRINCE.   Peace, chewet,[5] peace!
WOR.   It pleased your majesty to turn your looks
        Of favour from myself and all our house;
        And yet I must remember you,[6] my lord,
        We were the first and dearest of your friends.
        For you my staff of office did I break
        In Richard's time; and posted day and night
        To meet you on the way, and kiss your hand,
        When yet you were in place and in account
        Nothing so strong and fortunate as I.
        It was myself, my brother, and his son,
        That brought you home, and boldly did outdare
        The dangers of the time. You swore to us,
        And you did swear that oath at Doncaster,
        That you did nothing purpose 'gainst the state;
        Nor claim no further than your new-fall'n right,
        The seat of Gaunt, dukedom of Lancaster:
        To this we swore our aid. But in short space
        It rain'd down fortune showering on your head;
        And such a flood of greatness fell on you,
        What with our help, what with the absent king,
        What with the injuries of a wanton time,
        The seeming sufferances[7] that you had borne,
        And the contrarious winds that held the king
        So long in his unlucky Irish wars
        That all in England did repute him dead;
        And from this swarm of fair advantages
        You took occasion to be quickly woo'd
        To gripe the general sway into your hand;
        Forgot your oath to us at Doncaster;
        And being fed by us you used us so

---

5. *chewet*] a kind of pie, made of minced meat.
6. *remember you*] remind you.
7. *sufferances*] sufferings.

As that ungentle gull, the cuckoo's bird,
Useth the sparrow;[8] did oppress our nest;
Grew by our feeding to so great a bulk
That even our love durst not come near your sight
For fear of swallowing; but with nimble wing
We were enforced, for safety sake, to fly
Out of your sight and raise this present head;
Whereby we stand opposed by such means
As you yourself have forged against yourself,
By unkind usage, dangerous countenance,
And violation of all faith and troth
Sworn to us in your younger enterprise.

KING.   These things indeed you have articulate,[9]
Proclaim'd at market-crosses, read in churches,
To face[10] the garment of rebellion
With some fine colour that may please the eye
Of fickle changelings and poor discontents,
Which gape and rub the elbow[11] at the news
Of hurlyburly innovation:
And never yet did insurrection want
Such water-colours to impaint his cause;
Nor moody beggars, starving for a time
Of pellmell havoc and confusion.

PRINCE.   In both your armies there is many a soul
Shall pay full dearly for this encounter,
If once they join in trial. Tell your nephew,
The Prince of Wales doth join with all the world
In praise of Henry Percy: by my hopes,
This present enterprise set off his head,[12]
I do not think a braver gentleman,
More active-valiant or more valiant-young,
More daring or more bold, is now alive
To grace this latter age with noble deeds.
For my part, I may speak it to my shame,
I have a truant been to chivalry;
And so I hear he doth account me too;
Yet this before my father's majesty —
I am content that he shall take the odds

---

8. *cuckoo's bird . . . sparrow*] the cuckoo was thought to lay its eggs in the sparrow's nest, and the young cuckoo would eat its host as soon as it was old enough.

9. *articulate*] set out in articles, formally defined.

10. *face*] trim, give plausible edge to.

11. *rub the elbow*] a gesture of satisfaction.

12. *set off his head*] struck off his record.

Of his great name and estimation,
And will, to save the blood on either side,
Try fortune with him in a single fight.

KING. And, Prince of Wales, so dare we venture thee,
Albeit considerations infinite
Do make against it. No, good Worcester, no,
We love our people well; even those we love
That are misled upon your cousin's part;
And, will they take the offer of our grace,
Both he and they and you, yea, every man
Shall be my friend again and I'll be his:
So tell your cousin, and bring me word
What he will do: but if he will not yield,
Rebuke and dread correction wait on us
And they shall do their office. So, be gone;
We will not now be troubled with reply:
We offer fair; take it advisedly. [*Exeunt Worcester and Vernon.*

PRINCE. It will not be accepted, on my life:
The Douglas and the Hotspur both together
Are confident against the world in arms.

KING. Hence, therefore, every leader to his charge;
For, on their answer, will we set on them:
And God befriend us, as our cause is just!
[*Exeunt all but the Prince of Wales and Falstaff.*

FAL. Hal, if thou see me down in the battle, and bestride me, so; 'tis a point of friendship.

PRINCE. Nothing but a colossus can do thee that friendship. Say thy prayers, and farewell.

FAL. I would 'twere bed-time, Hal, and all well.

PRINCE. Why, thou owest God a death. [*Exit.*

FAL. 'Tis not due yet; I would be loath to pay him before his day. What need I be so forward with him that calls not on me? Well, 'tis no matter; honour pricks me on. Yea, but how if honour prick me off when I come on? how then? Can honour set to a leg? no: or an arm? no: or take away the grief of a wound? no. Honour hath no skill in surgery, then? no. What is honour? a word. What is in that word honour? what is that honour? air. A trim reckoning! Who hath it? he that died o' Wednesday. Doth he feel it? no. Doth he hear it? no. 'Tis insensible, then? yea, to the dead. But will it not live with the living? no. Why? detraction will not suffer it. Therefore I'll none of it. Honour is a mere scutcheon:[13] and so ends my catechism. [*Exit.*

---

13. *a mere scutcheon*] mere heraldic blazonry.

SCENE II. *The Rebel Camp.*

Enter WORCESTER *and* VERNON

WOR.   O, no, my nephew must not know, Sir Richard,
    The liberal and kind offer of the king.
VER.   'T were best he did.
WOR.   Then are we all undone.
    It is not possible, it cannot be,
    The king should keep his word in loving us;
    He will suspect us still, and find a time
    To punish this offence in other faults:
    Suspicion all our lives shall be stuck full of eyes;
    For treason is but trusted like the fox,
    Who, ne'er so tame, so cherish'd and lock'd up,
    Will have a wild trick of his ancestors.
    Look how we can, or sad or merrily,
    Interpretation will misquote[1] our looks,
    And we shall feed like oxen at a stall,
    The better cherish'd, still the nearer death.
    My nephew's trespass may be well forgot;
    It hath the excuse of youth and heat of blood;
    And an adopted name of privilege,
    A hare-brain'd Hotspur,[2] govern'd by a spleen:
    All his offences live upon my head
    And on his father's; we did train him on,
    And, his corruption being ta'en from us,
    We, as the spring of all, shall pay for all.
    Therefore, good cousin, let not Harry know,
    In any case, the offer of the king.
VER.   Deliver what you will; I'll say 'tis so.
    Here comes your cousin.

Enter HOTSPUR *and* DOUGLAS

HOT.   My uncle is return'd:
    Deliver up my Lord of Westmoreland.
    Uncle, what news?

---

1. *misquote*] misread, misunderstand.
2. *an adopted . . . Hotspur*] the assumed name of Hotspur may serve to justify his rash acts.

WOR.   The king will bid you battle presently.
DOUG.   Defy him by the Lord of Westmoreland.
HOT.   Lord Douglas, go you and tell him so.
DOUG.   Marry, and shall, and very willingly.   [*Exit.*
WOR.   There is no seeming mercy in the king.
HOT.   Did you beg any? God forbid!
WOR.   I told him gently of our grievances,
　　　Of his oath-breaking; which he mended thus,
　　　By now forswearing that he is forsworn:
　　　He calls us rebels, traitors; and will scourge
　　　With haughty arms this hateful name in us.

Re-enter DOUGLAS

DOUG.   Arm, gentlemen; to arms! for I have thrown
　　　A brave defiance in King Henry's teeth,
　　　And Westmoreland, that was engaged, did bear it;
　　　Which cannot choose but bring him quickly on.
WOR.   The Prince of Wales stepp'd forth before the king,
　　　And, nephew, challenged you to single fight.
HOT.   O, would the quarrel lay upon our heads,
　　　And that no man might draw short breath to-day
　　　But I and Harry Monmouth! Tell me, tell me,
　　　How show'd his tasking?[3] seem'd it in contempt?
VER.   No, by my soul; I never in my life
　　　Did hear a challenge urged more modestly,
　　　Unless a brother should a brother dare
　　　To gentle exercise and proof of arms.
　　　He gave you all the duties of a man;
　　　Trimm'd up your praises with a princely tongue,
　　　Spoke your deservings like a chronicle,
　　　Making you ever better than his praise
　　　By still dispraising praise valued with you;
　　　And, which became him like a prince indeed,
　　　He made a blushing cital[4] of himself;
　　　And chid his truant youth with such a grace
　　　As if he master'd there a double spirit
　　　Of teaching and of learning instantly.
　　　There did he pause: but let me tell the world,
　　　If he outlive the envy of this day,
　　　England did never owe so sweet a hope,
　　　So much misconstrued in his wantonness.

---

3. *tasking*] challenge.
4. *cital*] impeachment.

HOT.   Cousin, I think thou art enamoured
          On his follies: never did I hear
          Of any prince so wild a libertine.
          But be he as he will, yet once ere night
          I will embrace him with a soldier's arm,
          That he shall shrink under my courtesy.
          Arm, arm with speed: and, fellows, soldiers, friends,
          Better consider what you have to do
          Than I, that have not well the gift of tongue,
          Can lift your blood up with persuasion.

Enter a Messenger

MESS.   My lord, here are letters for you.
HOT.   I cannot read them now.
          O gentlemen, the time of life is short!
          To spend that shortness basely were too long,
          If life did ride upon a dial's point,
          Still ending at the arrival of an hour.
          An if we live, we live to tread on kings;
          If die, brave death, when princes die with us!
          Now, for our consciences, the arms are fair,
          When the intent of bearing them is just.

Enter another Messenger

MESS.   My lord, prepare; the king comes on apace.
HOT.   I thank him, that he cuts me from my tale,
          For I profess not talking; only this —
          Let each man do his best: and here draw I
          A sword, whose temper I intend to stain
          With the best blood that I can meet withal
          In the adventure of this perilous day.
          Now, Esperance! Percy! and set on.
          Sound all the lofty instruments of war,
          And by that music let us all embrace;
          For, heaven to earth, some of us never shall
          A second time do such a courtesy.
                    [*The trumpets sound. They embrace and exeunt.*

SCENE III. *Plain between the Camps.*

The King enters with his power. Alarum to the battle. Then enter
DOUGLAS *and* SIR WALTER BLUNT

BLUNT. What is thy name, that in the battle thus
   Thou crossest me? what honour dost thou seek
   Upon my head?
DOUG.   Know then, my name is Douglas;
   And I do haunt thee in the battle thus,
   Because some tell me that thou art a king.
BLUNT. They tell thee true.
DOUG. The Lord of Stafford dear to-day hath bought
   Thy likeness; for instead of thee, King Harry,
   This sword hath ended him: so shall it thee,
   Unless thou yield thee as my prisoner.
BLUNT. I was not born a yielder, thou proud Scot;
   And thou shalt find a king that will revenge
   Lord Stafford's death.   *[They fight. Douglas kills Blunt.*

Enter HOTSPUR

HOT. O Douglas, hadst thou fought at Holmedon thus,
   I never had triumph'd upon a Scot.
DOUG. All's done, all's won; here breathless lies the king.
HOT. Where?
DOUG. Here.
HOT. This, Douglas? no: I know this face full well:
   A gallant knight he was, his name was Blunt;
   Semblably furnish'd[1] like the king himself.
DOUG. A fool go with thy soul, whither it goes!
   A borrowed title hast thou bought too dear:
   Why didst thou tell me that thou wert a king?
HOT. The king hath many marching in his coats.
DOUG. Now, by my sword, I will kill all his coats;
   I'll murder all his wardrobe, piece by piece,
   Until I meet the king.
HOT.   Up, and away!
   Our soldiers stand full fairly for the day.   *[Exeunt.*

---

1. *Semblably furnish'd*] Similarly equipped.

Alarum. Enter FALSTAFF, *solus*

FAL. Though I could 'scape shot-free[2] at London, I fear the shot here;
here's no scoring[3] but upon the pate. Soft! who are you? Sir Walter
Blunt: there's honour for you! here's no vanity! I am as hot as molten
lead, and as heavy too: God keep lead out of me! I need no more
weight than mine own bowels. I have led my ragamuffins where
they are peppered: there's not three of my hundred and fifty left
alive; and they are for the town's end, to beg during life. But who
comes here?

Enter the PRINCE

PRINCE.   What, stand'st thou idle here? lend me thy sword:
Many a nobleman lies stark and stiff
Under the hoofs of vaunting enemies,
Whose deaths are yet unrevenged: I prithee, lend me thy sword.

FAL. O Hal, I prithee, give me leave to breathe a while. Turk Gregory[4]
never did such deeds in arms as I have done this day. I have paid
Percy, I have made him sure.

PRINCE.   He is, indeed; and living to kill thee. I prithee, lend me thy
sword.

FAL. Nay, before God, Hal, if Percy be alive, thou get'st not my sword;
but take my pistol, if thou wilt.

PRINCE.   Give it me: what, is it in the case?

FAL. Ay, Hal; 'tis hot, 'tis hot; there's that will sack a city.
[*The Prince draws it out, and finds it to be a bottle of sack.*

PRINCE.   What, is it a time to jest and dally now?
[*He throws the bottle at him. Exit.*

FAL. Well, if Percy be alive, I'll pierce him. If he do come in my way, so:
if he do not, if I come in his willingly, let him make a carbonado[5]
of me. I like not such grinning honour as Sir Walter hath: give me
life: which if I can save, so; if not, honour comes unlooked for, and
there's an end.   [*Exit.*

---

2. *shot-free*] without paying the bill.
3. *scoring*] marking up of charges.
4. *Turk Gregory*] A reference to the militant pope Gregory VII.
5. *carbonado*] piece of meat slashed for broiling.

SCENE IV.   *Another Part of the Field.*

Alarum. Excursions. Enter the KING, *the* PRINCE, LORD JOHN OF
LANCASTER, *and* EARL OF WESTMORELAND

KING.   I prithee,
    Harry, withdraw thyself; thou bleed'st too much.
    Lord John of Lancaster, go you with him.
LAN.   Not I, my lord, unless I did bleed too.
PRINCE.   I beseech your majesty, make up,[1]
    Lest your retirement do amaze[2] your friends.
KING.   I will do so.
    My Lord of Westmoreland, lead him to his tent.
WEST.   Come, my lord, I'll lead you to your tent.
PRINCE.   Lead me, my lord? I do not need your help:
    And God forbid a shallow scratch should drive
    The Prince of Wales from such a field as this,
    Where stain'd nobility lies trodden on,
    And rebels' arms triumph in massacres!
LAN.   We breathe too long: come, cousin Westmoreland,
    Our duty this way lies; for God's sake, come.
                       [Exeunt Prince John and Westmoreland.
PRINCE.   By God, thou hast deceived me, Lancaster;
    I did not think thee lord of such a spirit:
    Before, I loved thee as a brother, John;
    But now, I do respect thee as my soul.
KING.   I saw him hold Lord Percy at the point,[3]
    With lustier maintenance than I did look for
    Of such an ungrown warrior.
PRINCE.   O, this boy
    Lends mettle to us all!   *[Exit.*

Enter DOUGLAS

DOUG.   Another king! they grow like Hydra's heads:
    I am the Douglas, fatal to all those
    That wear those colours on them: what art thou,
    That counterfeit'st the person of a king?
KING.   The king himself; who, Douglas, grieves at heart
    So many of his shadows thou hast met

---

1. *make up*] advance.
2. *amaze*] bewilder, strike with panic.
3. *hold Lord Percy at the point*] parry Lord Percy's blows.

And not the very king. I have two boys
Seek Percy and thyself about the field:
But, seeing thou fall'st on me so luckily,
I will assay thee: so, defend thyself.

DOUG.   I fear thou art another counterfeit;
And yet, in faith, thou bear'st thee like a king:
But mine I am sure thou art, whoe'er thou be,
And thus I win thee.   [*They fight; the King being in danger,*
re-enter Prince of Wales.

PRINCE.   Hold up thy head, vile Scot, or thou art like
Never to hold it up again! the spirits
Of valiant Shirley, Stafford, Blunt, are in my arms:
It is the Prince of Wales that threatens thee;
Who never promiseth but he means to pay.
[*They fight: Douglas flies.*
Cheerly, my lord; how fares your grace?
Sir Nicholas Gawsey hath for succour sent,
And so hath Clifton: I'll to Clifton straight.

KING.   Stay, and breathe a while:
Thou hast redeem'd thy lost opinion,
And show'd thou makest some tender of⁴ my life,
In this fair rescue thou hast brought to me.

PRINCE.   O God! they did me too much injury
That ever said I hearken'd for⁵ your death.
If it were so, I might have let alone
The insulting hand of Douglas over you,
Which would have been as speedy in your end
As all the poisonous potions in the world,
And saved the treacherous labour of your son.

KING.   Make up to Clifton: I'll to Sir Nicholas Gawsey.   [*Exit.*

Enter HOTSPUR

HOT.   If I mistake not, thou art Harry Monmouth.
PRINCE.   Thou speak'st as if I would deny my name.
HOT.   My name is Harry Percy.
PRINCE.   Why, then I see
A very valiant rebel of the name.
I am the Prince of Wales; and think not, Percy,
To share with me in glory any more:
Two stars keep not their motion in one sphere;
Nor can one England brook a double reign,

----

4. *makest some tender of*] showest some regard for.
5. *hearken'd for*] waited for.

Of Harry Percy and the Prince of Wales.

HOT.   Nor shall it, Harry; for the hour is come
To end the one of us; and would to God
Thy name in arms were now as great as mine!

PRINCE.   I'll make it greater ere I part from thee;
And all the budding honours on thy crest
I'll crop, to make a garland for my head.

HOT.   I can no longer brook thy vanities.   [*They fight.*

Enter FALSTAFF

FAL.   Well said, Hal! to it, Hal! Nay, you shall find no boy's play here, I
can tell you.

Re-enter DOUGLAS; *he fights with* FALSTAFF, *who falls down as if he
were dead, and exit* DOUGLAS. HOTSPUR *is wounded, and falls*

HOT.   O, Harry, thou hast robb'd me of my youth!
I better brook the loss of brittle life
Than those proud titles thou hast won of me;
They wound my thoughts worse than thy sword my flesh:
But thought's the slave of life, and life time's fool;
And time, that takes survey of all the world,
Must have a stop.[6] O, I could prophesy,
But that the earthy and cold hand of death
Lies on my tongue: no, Percy, thou art dust,
And food for —   [*Dies.*

PRINCE.   For worms, brave Percy: fare thee well, great heart!
Ill-weaved ambition, how much art thou shrunk!
When that this body did contain a spirit,
A kingdom for it was too small a bound;
But now two paces of the vilest earth
Is room enough: this earth that bears thee dead
Bears not alive so stout a gentleman.
If thou wert sensible of courtesy,
I should not make so dear a show of zeal:
But let my favours[7] hide thy mangled face;
And, even in thy behalf, I'll thank myself
For doing these fair rites of tenderness.
Adieu, and take thy praise with thee to heaven!
Thy ignominy sleep with thee in the grave,
But not remember'd in thy epitaph!

[*He spieth Falstaff on the ground.*

---

6. *thought's . . . stop*] thought depends on life; life obeys the caprice of time, and time, that
embraces all the world in its sway, must have an end.

7. *favours*] ribbons worn as a scarf.

What, old acquaintance! could not all this flesh
Keep in a little life? Poor Jack, farewell!
I could have better spared a better man:
O, I should have a heavy miss of thee,
If I were much in love with vanity!
Death hath not struck so fat a deer to-day,
Though many dearer, in this bloody fray.
Embowell'd[8] will I see thee by and by:
Till then in blood by noble Percy lie.   [*Exit.*

FAL.   [*Rising up*] Embowelled! if thou embowel me to-day, I'll give you
leave to powder[9] me and eat me too to-morrow. 'Sblood, 'twas time
to counterfeit, or that hot termagant Scot had paid me scot and
lot[10] too. Counterfeit? I lie, I am no counterfeit: to die, is to be a
counterfeit; for he is but the counterfeit of a man who hath not the
life of a man: but to counterfeit dying, when a man thereby liveth,
is to be no counterfeit, but the true and perfect image of life indeed.
The better part of valour is discretion; in the which better part I
have saved my life. 'Zounds, I am afraid of this gunpowder Percy,
though he be dead: how, if he should counterfeit too, and rise? by
my faith, I am afraid he would prove the better counterfeit. Therefore I'll make him sure; yea, and I'll swear I killed him. Why may
he not rise as well as I? Nothing confutes me but eyes, and nobody
sees me. Therefore, sirrah [*stabbing him*], with a new wound in
your thigh, come you along with me.

                                   [*Takes up Hotspur on his back.*

Re-enter the PRINCE OF WALES *and* LORD JOHN OF LANCASTER

PRINCE.   Come, brother John; full bravely hast thou flesh'd[11]
         Thy maiden sword.
LAN.   But, soft! whom have we here?
         Did you not tell me this fat man was dead?
PRINCE.   I did; I saw him dead,
         Breathless and bleeding on the ground. Art thou alive?
         Or is it fantasy that plays upon our eyesight?
         I prithee, speak; we will not trust our eyes
         Without our ears: thou art not what thou seem'st.
FAL.   No, that's certain; I am not a double man: but if I be not Jack
Falstaff, then am I a Jack.[12] There is Percy [*throwing the body*

---

8. *Embowell'd*] Embowelled for burial.
9. *powder*] pickle or salt.
10. *scot and lot*] used figuratively to denote complete payment.
11. *fleshed*] initiated.
12. *a Jack*] a Jackanapes.

down]: if your father will do me any honour, so; if not, let him
kill the next Percy himself. I look to be either earl or duke, I can
assure you.

PRINCE.   Why, Percy I killed myself, and saw thee dead.

FAL.   Didst thou? Lord, Lord, how this world is given to lying! I grant
you I was down and out of breath; and so was he: but we rose both
at an instant, and fought a long hour by Shrewsbury clock. If I may
be believed, so; if not, let them that should reward valour bear the
sin upon their own heads. I'll take it upon my death,[13] I gave him
this wound in the thigh: if the man were alive, and would deny it,
'zounds, I would make him eat a piece of my sword.

LAN.   This is the strangest tale that ever I heard.

PRINCE.   This is the strangest fellow, brother John.
Come, bring your luggage nobly on your back:
For my part, if a lie may do thee grace,
I'll gild it with the happiest terms I have.   [A *retreat is sounded.*
The trumpet sounds retreat; the day is ours.
Come, brother, let us to the highest of the field,
To see what friends are living, who are dead.
                              [*Exeunt Prince of Wales and Lancaster.*

FAL.   I'll follow, as they say, for reward. He that rewards me, God reward
him! If I do grow great, I'll grow less; for I'll purge, and leave sack,
and live cleanly as a nobleman should do.   [*Exit.*

SCENE V.   *Another Part of the Field.*

The trumpets sound. Enter the KING, PRINCE OF WALES,
LORD JOHN OF LANCASTER, EARL OF WESTMORELAND,
with WORCESTER *and* VERNON *prisoners*

KING.   Thus ever did rebellion find rebuke.
Ill-spirited[1] Worcester! did not we send grace,
Pardon and terms of love to all of you?
And wouldst thou turn our offers contrary?
Misuse the tenour of thy kinsman's trust?
Three knights upon our party slain to-day,

---

13. *I'll take it upon my death*] I'll stake my life on it.

---

1. *Ill-spirited*] Of evil disposition.

A noble earl and many a creature else
Had been alive this hour,
If like a Christian thou hadst truly borne
Betwixt our armies true intelligence.
WOR.   What I have done my safety urged me to;
And I embrace this fortune patiently,
Since not to be avoided it falls on me.
KING.   Bear Worcester to the death, and Vernon too:
Other offenders we will pause upon.

> [*Exeunt Worcester and Vernon, guarded.*

How goes the field?
PRINCE.   The noble Scot, Lord Douglas, when he saw
The fortune of the day quite turn'd from him,
The noble Percy slain, and all his men
Upon the foot of fear,[2] fled with the rest;
And falling from a hill, he was so bruised
That the pursuers took him. At my tent
The Douglas is; and I beseech your grace
I may dispose of him.
KING.   With all my heart.
PRINCE.   Then, brother John of Lancaster, to you
This honourable bounty shall belong:
Go to the Douglas, and deliver him
Up to his pleasure, ransomless and free:
His valour shown upon our crests to-day
Hath taught us how to cherish such high deeds
Even in the bosom of our adversaries.
LAN.   I thank your grace for this high courtesy,
Which I shall give away immediately.
KING.   Then this remains, that we divide our power.
You, son John, and my cousin Westmoreland
Towards York shall bend you with your dearest speed,[3]
To meet Northumberland and the prelate Scroop,
Who, as we hear, are busily in arms:
Myself and you, son Harry, will towards Wales,
To fight with Glendower and the Earl of March.
Rebellion in this land shall lose his sway,
Meeting the check of such another day:
And since this business so fair is done,
Let us not leave till all our own be won.   [*Exeunt.*

---

2. *Upon the foot of fear*] Rushing off in fear.
3. *the devil . . . fiddlestick*] a proverbial phrase; meaning; here's a to-do about nothing.

Henry IV, Part 2

Henry IV, Part 2

In *Henry IV, Part 2*, Shakespeare completes the cycle of violence and interrupted rule set in motion in *Richard II*. In that play, Henry of Bolingbroke broke the royal succession by forcing the abdication of Richard, his cousin—as well as facilitating his murder—and ascending to the throne. It is made clear in *Henry IV, Part 2* that the king's vow to make a pilgrimage to the Holy Land to atone for his part in the intrigue is not destined to be fulfilled. However, balance will be restored to the kingdom through other means.

Inheriting the theme of usurpation and its consequences from *Richard II* and *Henry IV, Part 1*, the second part of *Henry IV* similarly derives its source material from Raphael Holinshed's *Chronicles of England, Scotland and Ireland* (1587). The play is believed to have been written and presented in the late 1590s, along with Shakespeare's other history plays. The setting is early fifteenth-century England. Following the Battle of Shrewsbury at the close of *Henry IV, Part 1*, the king faces two distinct rebellions. First, although victorious in quelling the rebellion of his Scottish and Welsh subjects, he must prepare for further troubles: the disgruntled Earl of Northumberland has not received all that he believed was promised to him by Henry; he is further inflamed by the death of his son, Henry Percy (Hotspur) at Shrewsbury. Second, King Henry is concerned with the rebellious behavior and carousing of his eldest son, Prince Harry, whose would-be mentor, the disreputable, flamboyant, highly entertaining nobleman and soldier, Sir John Falstaff (reprising his performance from *Part 1*), seems sure to keep Harry from a path suitable to preparing him to inherit the crown.

Henry, in failing health, laments his failure to reach the Holy Land; the unlawful means by which he became king has lain heavily upon his conscience, and in passing the crown to his son, Henry observes, "for what in me was purchased/Falls upon thee in a more fairer sort;/So thou the garland wear'st successively." Harry's reign will restore the rule of law to a throne that was built on a flawed foundation.

The king finally does reach a satisfying reconciliation with his son, who appears ready to rise to the challenge of providing leadership to a divided land. And a challenge is at hand: France is now marked as a target for invasion. After Harry assumes the crown to become Henry V, he distances himself from the corrupting influence of Falstaff. Replying to the scoundrel's plea, "My king! My Jove! I speak to thee, my heart!," the new king states, "I know thee not, old man" and, "Presume me not that I am the thing I was . . . I have turned away my former self." Taken aback by Harry's transformation from a dissipated youth to a sober ruler, Falstaff is skeptical of Henry's admonitions. He is nevertheless banished from the vicinity of the newly crowned king. Finally, Henry's clarity of purpose draws in the disparate noblemen, and the land appears to be unified—for the time being.

JANET BAINE KOPITO

Dramatis Personæ*

RUMOUR, the Presenter.
KING HENRY the Fourth.
HENRY, PRINCE OF WALES, afterwards King Henry V.,
THOMAS, DUKE OF CLARENCE,
PRINCE JOHN OF LANCASTER,
PRINCE HUMPHREY OF GLOUCESTER, } his sons.
EARL OF WARWICK.
EARL OF WESTMORELAND.
EARL OF SURREY.
GOWER.
HARCOURT.
BLUNT.
Lord Chief Justice of the King's Bench.
A Servant of the Chief Justice.
EARL OF NORTHUMBERLAND.
SCROOP, Archbishop of York.
LORD MOWBRAY.
LORD HASTINGS.
LORD BARDOLPH.
SIR JOHN COLVILLE.
TRAVERS and MORTON, retainers of Northumberland.
SIR JOHN FALSTAFF.
His Page.
BARDOLPH.
PISTOL.
POINS.
PETO.
SHALLOW,
SILENCE, } country justices.
DAVY, Servant to Shallow.
MOULDY, SHADOW, WART, FEEBLE, and BULLCALF, recruits.
FANG and SNARE, sheriff's officers.

*This play was first printed in a Quarto volume published in 1600. The text of the First
Folio supplies several passages which the Quarto omits. The Folio first gave a list of
"The Actors' Names" at the extreme end of the piece, and indicated the divisions of
the text into both Acts and Scenes.

LADY NORTHUMBERLAND.
LADY PERCY.
MISTRESS QUICKLY, hostess of a tavern in Eastcheap.
DOLL TEARSHEET.

Lords and Attendants; Porter, Drawers, Beadles, Grooms, &c.
A Dancer, speaker of the epilogue.

SCENE: *England.*

INDUCTION

Warkworth. Before the Castle

Enter RUMOUR, *painted full of tongues*[1]

RUMOUR.   Open your ears; for which of you will stop
 The vent of hearing[2] when loud Rumour speaks?
 I, from the orient to the drooping west,
 Making the wind my post-horse, still unfold
 The acts commenced on this ball of earth:
 Upon my tongues continual slanders ride,
 The which in every language I pronounce,
 Stuffing the ears of men with false reports.
 I speak of peace, while covert enmity
 Under the smile of safety wounds the world:
 And who but Rumour, who but only I,
 Make fearful musters and prepared defence,
 Whiles the big year, swoln with some other grief,
 Is thought with child by the stern tyrant war,
 And no such matter? Rumour is a pipe
 Blown by surmises, jealousies, conjectures,
 And of so easy and so plain a stop[3]
 That the blunt monster with uncounted heads,
 The still-discordant wavering multitude,
 Can play upon it. But what need I thus
 My well-known body to anatomize
 Among my household? Why is Rumour here?

---

[1]stage direction) *Enter Rumour . . . tongues*] The description of this allegorical personage is mainly derived from Virgil's account of Fama, *Aeneid,* iv, 173–188. "Rumour"
figured in many Elizabethan pageants and masques, arrayed symbolically as in the present text.

[2]*The vent of hearing*] The aperture of the ears.

[3]*a stop*] the finger holes which regulate the sound of a pipe or flute.

I run before King Harry's victory;[4]
Who in a bloody field by Shrewsbury
Hath beaten down young Hotspur and his troops,
Quenching the flame of bold rebellion
Even with the rebels' blood. But what mean I
To speak[5] so true at first? my office is
To noise abroad that Harry Monmouth[6] fell
Under the wrath of noble Hotspur's sword,
And that the king before the Douglas' rage
Stoop'd his anointed head as low as death.
This have I rumour'd through the peasant towns[7]
Between that royal field of Shrewsbury
And this worm-eaten hold of ragged stone,[8]
Where Hotspur's father, old Northumberland,
Lies crafty-sick: the posts come tiring on,[9]
And not a man of them brings other news
Than they have learn'd of me: from Rumour's tongues
They bring smooth comforts false, worse than true wrongs.[10]

[*Exit.*

---

[4]*I run . . . victory*] The events of the play are represented as following without any interval the battle of Shrewsbury, which was fought on July 1, 1403, and news of which
is now brought to Hotspur's father, the Duke of Northumberland. The episodes with
which the play deals cover the period of ten years intervening between the battle of
Shrewsbury and King Henry IV's death in 1413.
[5]*To speak*] By speaking.
[6]*Harry Monmouth*] Prince Henry (afterwards King Henry V), so called from
Monmouth, his birthplace.
[7]*the peasant towns*] the villages.
[8]*hold of ragged stone*] stronghold of rugged stone, the castle at Warkworth.
[9]*Lies crafty-sick: . . . tiring on*] Feigns illness: the messengers come riding their hardest.
[10]*true wrongs*] genuine disasters.

ACT I.

Scene I. *The Same*

Enter LORD BARDOLPH

LORD BARDOLPH.   Who keeps the gate here, ho?

The Porter *opens the gate*

    Where is the earl?
PORT.   What shall I say you are?
L. BARD.   Tell thou the earl
    That the Lord Bardolph doth attend him here.
PORT.   His lordship is walk'd forth into the orchard:
    Please if your honour, knock but at the gate,
    And he himself will answer.

Enter NORTHUMBERLAND

L. BARD.   Here comes the earl.   [*Exit* Porter.
NORTH.   What news, Lord Bardolph? every minute now
    Should be the father of some stratagem:[1]
    The times are wild; contention, like a horse
    Full of high feeding, madly hath broke loose
    And bears down all before him.
L. BARD.   Noble earl,
    I bring you certain news from Shrewsbury.
NORTH.   Good, an God will!
L. BARD.   As good as heart can wish:
    The king is almost wounded to the death;
    And, in the fortune of my lord your son,
    Prince Harry slain outright; and both the Blunts
    Kill'd by the hand of Douglas; young Prince John
    And Westmoreland and Stafford fled the field;
    And Harry Monmouth's brawn,[2] the hulk Sir John,

---

[1]*stratagem*] crisis.
[2]*brawn*] roll of fat.

101

Is prisoner to your son: O, such a day,
So fought, so follow'd and so fairly won,
Came not till now to dignify the times,
Since Cæsar's fortunes!

NORTH.   How is this derived?
    Saw you the field? came you from Shrewsbury?

L. BARD.   I spake with one, my lord, that came from thence,
    A gentleman well bred and of good name,
    That freely render'd me these news for true.

NORTH.   Here comes my servant Travers, whom I sent
    On Tuesday last to listen after news.

Enter TRAVERS

L. BARD.   My lord, I over-rode him on the way;
    And he is furnish'd with no certainties
    More than he haply may retail from me.

NORTH.   Now, Travers, what good tidings comes with you?

TRA.   My lord, Sir John Umfrevile turn'd me back
    With joyful tidings; and, being better horsed,
    Out-rode me. After him came spurring hard
    A gentleman, almost forspent[3] with speed,
    That stopp'd by me to breathe his bloodied horse.
    He ask'd the way to Chester; and of him
    I did demand what news from Shrewsbury:
    He told me that rebellion had bad luck,
    And that young Harry Percy's spur was cold.
    With that, he gave his able horse the head,
    And bending forward struck his armed heels
    Against the panting sides of his poor jade
    Up to the rowel-head, and starting so
    He seem'd in running to devour the way,[4]
    Staying no longer question.

NORTH.   Ha! Again:
    Said he young Harry Percy's spur was cold?
    Of Hotspur Coldspur? that rebellion
    Had met ill luck?

L. BARD.   My lord, I'll tell you what;
    If my young lord your son have not the day,

---

[3]*forspent*] exhausted.
[4]*to devour the way*] This figure for extreme speed is common in all literature.

Upon mine honour, for a silken point[5]
I'll give my barony: never talk of it.
NORTH.   Why should that gentleman that rode by Travers
Give then such instances of loss?
L. BARD.   Who, he?
He was some hilding fellow[6] that had stolen
The horse he rode on, and, upon my life,
Spoke at a venture. Look, here comes more news.

Enter MORTON

NORTH.   Yea, this man's brow, like to a title-leaf,
Foretells the nature of a tragic volume:
So looks the strond[7] whereon the imperious flood
Hath left a witness'd usurpation.[8]
Say, Morton, didst thou come from Shrewsbury?
MOR.   I ran from Shrewsbury, my noble lord;
Where hateful death put on his ugliest mask
To fright our party.
NORTH.   How doth my son and brother?
Thou tremblest; and the whiteness in thy cheek
Is apter than thy tongue to tell thy errand.
Even such a man, so faint, so spiritless,
So dull, so dead[9] in look, so woe-begone,
Drew[10] Priam's curtain in the dead of night,
And would have told him half his Troy was burnt;
Bur Priam found the fire ere he his tongue,
And I my Percy's death ere thou report'st it,
This thou wouldst say, "Your son did thus and thus;
Your brother thus: so fought the noble Douglas:"
Stopping my greedy ear with their bold deeds:
But in the end, to stop my ear indeed,
Thou hast a sigh to blow away this praise,
Ending with "Brother, son, and all are dead."
MOR.   Douglas is living, and your brother, yet;
But, for my lord your son,—
NORTH.   Why, he is dead.
See what a ready tongue suspicion hath!

---

[5]*a silken point*] a silk tag or lace fastening clothes together.
[6]*hilding fellow*] base fellow.
[7]*strond*] a variant spelling of "strand."
[8]*a witness'd usurpation*] evidence of encroachment.
[9]*dead*] sullen.
[10]*Drew*] Drew aside, withdrew.

He that but fears the thing he would not know
Hath by instinct knowledge from others' eyes
That what he fear'd is chanced. Yet speak, Morton;
Tell thou an earl his divination lies,
And I will take it as a sweet disgrace,
And make thee rich for doing me such wrong.

MOR.   You are too great to be by me gainsaid:
Your spirit[11] is too true, your fears too certain.

NORTH.   Yet, for all this, say not that Percy's dead.
I see a strange confession in thine eye:
Thou shakest thy head, and hold'st it fear[12] or sin
To speak a truth. If he be slain, say so;
The tongue offends not that reports his death:
And he doth sin that doth belie the dead,
Not he which says the dead is not alive.
Yet the first bringer of unwelcome news
Hath but a losing office, and his tongue
Sounds ever after as a sullen bell,[13]
Remember'd tolling a departing friend.

L. BARD.   I cannot think, my lord, your son is dead.

MOR.   I am sorry I should force you to believe
That which I would to God I had not seen;
But these mine eyes saw him in bloody state,
Rendering faint quittance,[14] wearied and outbreathed,
To Harry Monmouth; whose swift wrath beat down
The never-daunted Percy to the earth,
From whence with life he never more sprung up.
In few, his death, whose spirit lent a fire
Even to the dullest peasant in his camp,
Being bruited once, took fire and heat away
From the best-temper'd courage in his troops;
For from his metal was his party steel'd;[15]
Which once in him abated, all the rest
Turn'd on themselves, like dull and heavy lead:
And as the thing that's heavy in itself,
Upon enforcement flies with greatest speed,
So did our men, heavy in Hotspur's loss,
Lend to this weight such lightness with their fear

---

[11]*spirit*] intuition.
[12]*fear*] danger, cause of fear.
[13]*sullen bell*] dismally tolling bell.
[14]*Rendering faint quittance*] Making a faint return (of blows).
[15]*his party steel'd*] his side emboldened or nerved.

That arrows fled not swifter toward their aim
Than did our soldiers, aiming at their safety,
Fly from the field. Then was that noble Worcester
Too soon ta'en prisoner; and that furious Scot,
The bloody Douglas, whose well-labouring sword
Had three times slain the appearance of the king,
'Gan vail his stomach[16] and did grace the shame
Of those that turn'd their backs, and in his flight,
Stumbling in fear, was took. The sum of all
Is that the king hath won, and hath sent out
A speedy power to encounter you, my lord,
Under the conduct of young Lancaster
And Westmoreland. This is the news at full.

NORTH.   For this I shall have time enough to mourn.
In poison there is physic; and these news,
Having been well,[17] that would have made me sick,
Being sick, have in some measure made me well:
And as the wretch, whose fever-weaken'd joints,
Like strengthless hinges, buckle[18] under life,
Impatient of his fit, breaks like a fire
Out of his keeper's arms, even so my limbs,
Weaken'd with grief, being now enraged with grief,[19]
Are thrice themselves. Hence, therefore, thou nice[20] crutch!
A scaly gauntlet now with joints of steel
Must glove this hand: and hence, thou sickly quoif![21]
Thou art a guard too wanton for the head
Which princes, flesh'd with conquest,[22] aim to hit.
Now bind my brows with iron; and approach
The ragged'st[23] hour that time and spite dare bring
To frown upon the enraged Northumberland!
Let heaven kiss earth! now let not Nature's hand
Keep the wild flood confined! let order die!
And let this world no longer be a stage
To feed contention in a lingering act;

---

[16]*vail his stomach*] abate his pride.
[17]*Having been well*] Had I been in good health.
[18]*buckle*] bend.
[19]*grief . . . grief*] The word in the first place means "bodily pain," and in the second has the ordinary sense of "mental pain" or "sorrow."
[20]*nice*] effeminate.
[21]*sickly quoif*] invalid's scarf, handkerchief.
[22]*flesh'd with conquest*] stimulated by taste of conquest.
[23]*ragged'st*] roughest.

But let one spirit of the first-born Cain
Reign in all bosoms, that, each heart being set
On bloody courses, the rude scene may end,
And darkness be the burier of the dead![24]

TRA.   This strained passion doth you wrong, my lord.[25]

L. BARD.   Sweet earl, divorce not wisdom from your honour.

MOR.   The lives of all your loving complices
Lean on your health; the which, if you give o'er
To stormy passion, must perforce decay.
You cast the event of war, my noble lord,
And summ'd the account of chance, before you said
"Let us make head."[26] It was your presurmise,
That, in the dole of blows,[27] your son might drop:
You knew he walk'd o'er perils, on an edge,
More likely to fall in than to get o'er;
You were advised his flesh was capable
Of wounds and scars, and that his forward spirit
Would lift him where most trade of danger[28] ranged:
Yet did you say "Go forth;" and none of this,
Though strongly apprehended, could restrain
The stiff-borne[29] action: what hath then befallen,
Or what hath this bold enterprise brought forth,
More than that being which was like to be?

L. BARD.   We all that are engaged to[30] this loss
Knew that we ventured on such dangerous seas
That if we wrought out life 't was ten to one;
And yet we ventured, for the gain proposed
Choked the respect[31] of likely peril fear'd;
And since we are o'erset, venture again.
Come, we will all put forth, body and goods.

MOR.   'T is more than time: and, my most noble lord,
I hear for certain, and do speak the truth,
The gentle Archbishop of York is up

---

[24]*And darkness . . . dead*] The speaker invokes chaos to come again, and bury the victims of an universal strife, which shall extirpate mankind.

[25]*This strained . . . lord*] The Folios omit this line. The Quarto assigns it to Sir John Umfrevile.

[26]*Let us make head*] Let us rise in rebellion.

[27]*in the dole of blows*] in the distribution of blows.

[28]*most trade of danger*] busiest traffic, greatest press of danger.

[29]*stiff-borne*] obstinately maintained.

[30]*engaged to*] involved in.

[31]*the respect*] the consideration.

With well-appointed[32] powers: he is a man
Who with a double surety binds his followers.
My lord your son had only but the corpse,
But shadows and the shows of men, to fight;
For that same word, rebellion, did divide
The action of their bodies from their souls;
And they did fight with queasiness,[33] constrain'd,
As men drink potions, that their weapons only
Seem'd on our side; but, for their spirits and souls,
This word, rebellion, it had froze them up,
As fish are in a pond. But now the bishop
Turns insurrection to religion:
Supposed sincere and holy in his thoughts,
He's followed both with body and with mind;
And doth enlarge his rising with the blood
Of fair King Richard,[34] scraped from Pomfret stones;
Derives from heaven his quarrel and his cause;
Tells them he doth bestride[35] a bleeding land,
Gasping for life under great Bolingbroke;
And more and less do flock to follow him.

NORTH.   I knew of this before; but, to speak truth,
This present grief had wiped it from my mind.
Go in with me; and counsel every man
The aptest way for safety and revenge:
Get posts and letters, and make friends with speed:
Never so few, and never yet more need.   [*Exeunt.*

Scene II.   *London. A Street*

Enter FALSTAFF, *with his* Page *bearing his sword and buckler*

FAL.   Sirrah, you giant,[1] what says the doctor to my water?[2]

PAGE.   He said, sir, the water itself was a good healthy water; but, for
the party that owed it, he might have moe diseases than he knew
for.

---

[32]*well-appointed*] well equipped.
[33]*queasiness*] squeamishness, disgust, qualm.
[34]*enlarge . . . Richard*] augments the number of his rebel following by carrying about
drops of the blood of King Richard as a hallowed relic.
[35]*bestride*] stand over so as to protect.

---

[1]*you giant*] an ironical reference to the page's diminutive stature.
[2]*what says the doctor . . . water*] A reference to a common mode of medical diagnosis.

FAL.   Men of all sorts take a pride to gird at me: the brain of this fool-
ish-compounded clay, man, is not able to invent any thing that
tends to laughter, more than I invent or is invented on me: I am
not only witty in myself, but the cause that wit is in other men. I
do here walk before thee like a sow that hath overwhelmed all her
litter but one. If the prince put thee into my service for any other
reason than to set me off,[3] why then I have no judgement. Thou
whoreson mandrake,[4] thou art fitter to be worn in my cap than to
wait at my heels. I was never manned with an agate[5] till now: but
I will inset you neither in gold nor silver, but in vile apparel, and
send you back again to your master, for a jewel,—the juvenal,[6] the
prince your master, whose chin is not yet fledged. I will sooner
have a beard grow in the palm of my hand than he shall get one
on his cheek; and yet he will not stick to say his face is a face-royal:
God may finish it when he will, 't is not a hair amiss yet: he may
keep it still at a face-royal, for a barber shall never earn sixpence
out of it; and yet he'll be crowing as if he had writ man ever since
his father was a bachelor. He may keep his own grace, but he's almost out of mine, I can assure him. What said Master Dombledon
about the satin for my short cloak and my slops?[7]

PAGE.   He said, sir, you should procure him better assurance than
Bardolph: he would not take his band[8] and yours; he liked not the
security.

FAL.   Let him be damned, like the glutton! pray God his tongue be
hotter![9] A whoreson Achitophel![10] a rascally yea-forsooth knave![11]
to bear a gentleman in hand,[12] and then stand upon security! The
whoreson smooth-pates[13] do now wear nothing but high shoes,
and bunches of keys at their girdles; and if a man is through with
them in honest taking up, then they must stand upon security. I
had as lief they would put ratsbane in my mouth as offer to stop it
with security. I looked a' should have sent me two and twenty

---

[3]*set me off*] i.e., by way of contrast or foil.
[4]*mandrake*] a small plant with a root, thought to resemble the human figure.
[5]*agate*] A reference to the miniature figures or heads engraved on agate stones, set in
  rings and brooches.
[6]*juvenal*] youth.
[7]*slops*] broad breeches.
[8]*band*] bond.
[9]*the glutton . . . hotter*] an allusion to the parable of Dives and Lazarus, *Luke*, xvi, 24,
  where the rich glutton in the torments of hell-fire begs for water to cool his tongue.
[10]*Achitophel*] a scriptural type of a false counsellor.
[11]*yea-forsooth knave*] smooth-spoken, oily-mouthed fellow.
[12]*bear . . . in hand*] delude with false promises.
[13]*smooth-pates*] sleek-headed men.

yards of satin, as I am a true knight, and he sends me security. Well, he may sleep in security; for he hath the horn of abundance, and the lightness of his wife shines through it:[14] and yet cannot he see, though he have his own lanthorn to light him. Where's Bardolph?

PAGE.   He's gone into Smithfield to buy your worship a horse.

FAL.   I bought him in Paul's,[15] and he'll buy me a horse in Smithfield: an I could get me but a wife in the stews, I were manned, horsed, and wived.

Enter the LORD CHIEF JUSTICE *and* Servant

PAGE.   Sir, here comes the nobleman that committed the prince for striking him about Bardolph.

FAL.   Wait close;[16] I will not see him.

CH. JUST.   What's he that goes there?

SERV.   Falstaff, an 't please your lordship.

CH. JUST.   He that was in question for the robbery?

SERV.   He, my lord: but he hath since done good service at Shrewsbury; and, as I hear, is now going with some charge[17] to the Lord John of Lancaster.

CH. JUST.   What, to York? Call him back again.

SERV.   Sir John Falstaff!

FAL.   Boy, tell him I am deaf.

PAGE.   You must speak louder; my master is deaf.

CH. JUST.   I am sure he is, to the hearing of any thing good. Go, pluck him by the elbow; I must speak with him.

SERV.   Sir John!

FAL.   What! a young knave, and begging! Is there not wars? is there not employment? doth not the king lack subjects? do not the rebels need soldiers? Though it be a shame to be on any side but one, it is worse shame to beg than to be on the worst side, were it worse than the name of rebellion can tell how to make it.

SERV.   You mistake me, sir.

FAL.   Why, sir, did I say you were an honest man? setting my knighthood and my soldiership aside, I had lied in my throat, if I had said so.

---

[14]*horn of abundance . . . shines through it*] a punning allusion to three kinds of horns, viz., to the "cornucopia" or horn of plenty, to the transparent horned case of a lantern, and to the horns which were believed to grow on dishonoured husbands' heads.

[15]*bought him in Paul's*] hired him in the nave of St. Paul's cathedral, then a crowded promenade for the citizens of London and men seeking employment.

[16]*Wait close*] keep out of sight.

[17]*some charge*] some commission, in charge of a company of soldiers.

SERV.   I pray you, sir, then set your knighthood and your soldiership
aside; and give me leave to tell you, you lie in your throat, if you
say I am any other than an honest man.

FAL.   I give thee leave to tell me so! I lay aside that which grows to
me![18] If thou gettest any leave of me, hang me; if thou takest leave,
thou wert better be hanged. You hunt counter:[19] hence! avaunt!

SERV.   Sir, my lord would speak with you.

CH. JUST.   Sir John Falstaff, a word with you.

FAL.   My good lord! God give your lordship good time of day. I am
glad to see your lordship abroad: I heard say your lordship was
sick: I hope your lordship goes abroad by advice. Your lordship,
though not clean past your youth, hath yet some smack of age in
you, some relish of the saltness[20] of time; and I most humbly beseech your lordship to have a reverend care of your health.

CH. JUST.   Sir John, I sent for you before your expedition to Shrewsbury.

FAL.   An 't please your lordship, I hear his majesty is returned with
some discomfort[21] from Wales.

CH. JUST.   I talk not of his majesty: you would not come when I sent
for you.

FAL.   And I hear, moreover, his highness is fallen into this same
whoreson apoplexy.

CH. JUST.   Well, God mend him! I pray you, let me speak with you.

FAL.   This apoplexy is, as I take it, a kind of lethargy, an 't please your
lordship; a kind of sleeping in the blood, a whoreson tingling.

CH. JUST.   What tell you me of it? be it as it is.

FAL.   It hath it original from much grief, from study and perturbation
of the brain: I have read the cause of his effects in Galen: it is a
kind of deafness.

CH. JUST.   I think you are fallen into the disease; for you hear not what
I say to you.

FAL.   Very well, my lord, very well: rather, an 't please you, it is the disease of not listening, the malady of not marking, that I am troubled withal.

CH. JUST.   To punish you by the heels[22] would amend the attention of
your ears; and I care not if I do become your physician.

FAL.   I am as poor as Job, my lord, but not so patient: your lordship
may minister the potion of imprisonment to me in respect of

---

[18]*that which grows to me*] the knighthood and soldiership, which adhere to me.
[19]*You hunt counter*] You are on the wrong scent.
[20]*saltness*] seasoning.
[21]*discomfort*] anxiety.
[22]*To punish you by the heels*] To set you in the stocks.

poverty; but how I should be your patient to follow your prescriptions, the wise may make some dram of a scruple, or indeed a scruple itself.

CH. JUST.   I sent for you, when there were matters against you for your life, to come speak with me.

FAL.   As I was then advised by my learned counsel in the laws of this land-service,[23] I did not come.

CH. JUST.   Well, the truth is, Sir John, you live in great infamy.

FAL.   He that buckles him in my belt cannot live in less.

CH. JUST.   Your means are very slender, and your waste is great.

FAL.   I would it were otherwise; I would my means were greater, and my waist slenderer.

CH. JUST.   You have misled the youthful prince.

FAL.   The young prince hath misled me: I am the fellow with the great belly, and he my dog.[24]

CH. JUST.   Well, I am loath to gall a new-healed wound: your day's service at Shrewsbury hath a little gilded over your night's exploit on Gadshill: you may thank the unquiet time for your quiet o'er-posting[25] that action.

FAL.   My lord?

CH. JUST.   But since all is well, keep it so: wake not a sleeping wolf.

FAL.   To wake a wolf is as bad as to smell a fox.

CH. JUST.   What! you are as a candle, the better part burnt out.

FAL.   A wassail candle,[26] my lord, all tallow: if I did say of wax,[27] my growth would approve the truth.

CH. JUST.   There is not a white hair on your face but should have his effect of gravity.

FAL.   His effect of gravy, gravy, gravy.

CH. JUST.   You follow the young prince up and down, like his ill angel.

FAL.   Not so, my lord; your ill angel is light;[28] but I hope he that looks upon me will take me without weighing: and yet, in some re-

---

[23]*my learned counsel . . . land-service*] one well acquainted with the annoying conditions or procedure of lawsuits of this kind.

[24]*fellow . . . dog*] a dog commonly led about helpless old men, but there may be a reference to some well known beggar of the day—notably fat and blind—who was led about by a dog.

[25]*your quiet o'er-posting*] your quietly getting clear of.

[26]*A wassail candle*] A large candle used at festivals.

[27]*of wax*] a pun on the word in the sense of "increase."

[28]*your ill angel is light*] a quibble on the use of the word "angel" in the sense of the familiar coin (worth ten shillings); there is also a quibble on the word "light," which means not only "light in weight" (applied especially to bad coins) but "wanton."

spects, I grant, I cannot go: I cannot tell.[29] Virtue is of so little regard in these costermonger times[30] that true valor is turned bear-
herd:[31] pregnancy[32] is made a tapster, and hath his quick wit
wasted in giving reckonings: all the other gifts appertinent to man,
as the malice of this age shapes them, are not worth a gooseberry.
You that are old consider not the capacities of us that are young;
you do measure the heat of our livers[33] with the bitterness of your
galls:[34] and we that are in the vaward[35] of our youth, I must confess, are wags too.

CH. JUST. Do you set down your name in the scroll of youth, that are
written down old with all the characters[36] of age? Have you not a
moist eye? a dry hand? a yellow cheek? a white beard? a decreas-
ing leg? an increasing belly? is not your voice broken? your wind
short? your chin double? your wit single?[37] and every part about
you blasted with antiquity? and will you yet call yourself young?
Fie, fie, fie, Sir John!

FAL. My lord, I was born about three of the clock in the afternoon,
with a white head and something a round belly. For my voice, I
have lost it with halloing and singing of anthems. To approve my
youth further, I will not: the truth is, I am only old in judgement
and understanding; and he that will caper with me for a thousand
marks, let him lend me the money, and have at him. For the box
of the ear that the prince gave you, he gave it like a rude prince,
and you took it like a sensible lord. I have checked him for it, and
the young lion repents; marry, not in ashes and sackcloth, but in
new silk and old sack.

CH. JUST. Well, God send the prince a better companion!

FAL. God send the companion a better prince! I cannot rid my hands
of him.

CH. JUST. Well, the king hath severed you and Prince Harry: I hear
you are going with Lord John of Lancaster against the Archbishop
and the Earl of Northumberland.

FAL. Yea; I thank your pretty sweet wit for it. But look you pray, all

---

[29]*I cannot go . . . tell*] A continuation of the jest on the lightness of a bad coin: I cannot
pass current: I cannot count as good weight.

[30]*in these costermonger times*] in these mercenary times.

[31]*bear-herd*] keeper of a tame bear.

[32]*pregnancy*] readiness of intellect, mental cleverness.

[33]*livers*] passions: the liver was believed to be the seat of the passions.

[34]*with the bitterness of your galls*] with your bilious asperities.

[35]*vaward*] van, heyday.

[36]*characters*] characteristics, marks.

[37]*your wit single?*] your wit feeble?

you that kiss my lady Peace at home, that our armies join[38] not in a hot day; for, by the Lord, I take but two shirts out with me, and I mean not to sweat extraordinarily: if it be a hot day, and I brandish any thing but a bottle, I would I might never spit white again.[39] There is not a dangerous action can peep out his head, but I am thrust upon it: well, I cannot last ever: but it was alway yet the trick of our English nation, if they have a good thing, to make it too common. If ye will needs say I am an old man, you should give me rest. I would to God my name were not so terrible to the enemy as it is: I were better to be eaten to death with a rust than to be scoured to nothing with perpetual motion.

CH. JUST.   Well, be honest, be honest; and God bless your expedition!

FAL.   Will your lordship lend me a thousand pound to furnish me forth?

CH. JUST.   Not a penny, not a penny; you are too impatient to bear crosses.[40] Fare you well: commend me to my cousin Westmoreland.   [*Exeunt* CHIEF JUSTICE *and* Servant.

FAL.   If I do, fillip me with a three-man beetle.[41] A man can no more separate age and covetousness than a' can part young limbs and lechery: but the gout galls the one, and the pox pinches the other; and so both the degrees prevent my curses.[42] Boy!

PAGE.   Sir?

FAL.   What money is in my purse?

PAGE.   Seven groats and two pence.

FAL.   I can get no remedy against this consumption of the purse: borrowing only lingers and lingers it out,[43] but the disease is incurable. Go bear this letter to my Lord of Lancaster; this to the prince; this to the Earl of Westmoreland; and this to old Mistress Ursula, whom I have weekly sworn to marry since I perceived the first white hair on my chin. About it: you know where to find me.

---

[38]*join*] come into action.

[39]*never spit white again*] To spit white was reckoned by some Elizabethan writers as a sign of health, by others as a mark of thirst. But the phrase is now commonly applied to the effects on the palate of excessive drinking, and it is probable that Falstaff is threatening to forego further opportunity of free potations.

[40]*to bear crosses*] For the quibble on the two meanings of the phrase, viz., "endure hardship" and "carry coins," specifically known as "crosses."

[41]*fillip me . . . beetle*] kill me outright; jerk or flip me with the heaviest of mallets. A three-man beetle was a large mallet or rammer with three handles, used for pile driving.

[42]*both the degrees . . . curses*] both the steps or stages of life (age and youth) anticipate or justify my curses.

[43]*lingers and lingers it out*] prolongs the malady unconscionably.

[*Exit* Page.] A pox of this gout! or, a gout of this pox! for the one or the other plays the rogue with my great toe. 'T is no matter if I do halt; I have the wars for my colour, and my pension shall seem the more reasonable. A good wit will make use of any thing: I will turn diseases to commodity.[44]   [*Exit.*

Scene III.   *York. The Archbishop's Palace*

Enter the ARCHBISHOP, *the* LORDS HASTINGS, MOWBRAY, *and* BARDOLPH

ARCH.   Thus have you heard our cause and known our means;
          And, my most noble friends, I pray you all,
          Speak plainly your opinions of our hopes:
          And first, lord marshal, what say you to it?
MOWB.   I well allow the occasion of our arms;
          But gladly would be better satisfied
          How in our means we should advance ourselves
          To look with forehead bold and big enough
          Upon the power and puissance of the king.
HAST.   Our present musters grow upon the file[1]
          To five and twenty thousand men of choice;
          And our supplies live largely in the hope
          Of great Northumberland, whose bosom burns
          With an incensed fire of injuries.[2]
L. BARD.   The question then, Lord Hastings, standeth thus;
          Whether our present five and twenty thousand
          May hold up head[3] without Northumberland?
HAST.   With him, we may.
L. BARD.   Yea, marry, there's the point:
          But if without him we be thought too feeble,
          My judgement is, we should not step too far
          Till we had his assistance by the hand;
          For in a theme so bloody-faced as this
          Conjecture, expectation, and surmise
          Of aids incertain should not be admitted.
ARCH.   'T is very true, Lord Bardolph; for indeed
          It was young Hotspur's case at Shrewsbury.

---

[44]*commodity*] profit.

---

[1]*upon the file*] on the roll.
[2]*an incensed fire of injuries*] a fire kindled by wrongs.
[3]*hold up head*] maintain an attack.

L. BARD.   It was, my lord; who lined[4] himself with hope,
     Eating the air on promise of supply,
     Flattering himself in project of a power
     Much smaller than the smallest of his thoughts:
     And so, with great imagination
     Proper to madmen, led his powers to death,
     And winking leap'd into destruction.
HAST.   But, by your leave, it never yet did hurt
     To lay down likelihoods and forms of hope.
L. BARD.   Yes, if this present quality of war,
     Indeed the instant action: a cause on foot,
     Lives so in hope, as in an early spring
     We see the appearing buds; which to prove fruit,
     Hope gives not so much warrant as despair
     That frosts will bite them. When we mean to build,
     We first survey the plot, then draw the model;[5]
     And when we see the figure of the house,
     Then must we rate the cost of the erection;
     Which if we find outweighs ability,
     What do we then but draw anew the model
     In fewer offices,[6] or at least desist
     To build at all? Much more, in this great work,
     Which is almost to pluck a kingdom down
     And set another up, should we survey
     The plot of situation and the model,
     Consent[7] upon a sure foundation,
     Question surveyors, know our own estate,[8]
     How able such a work to undergo,
     To weigh against his opposite;[9] or else[10]
     We fortify in paper and in figures,
     Using the names of men instead of men:
     Like one that draws the model of a house
     Beyond his power to build it; who, half through,
     Gives o'er and leaves his part-created cost

---

[4]*lined*] stiffened, strengthened; the figure is drawn from the lining of a garment.
[5]*plot . . . model*] site . . . plan.
[6]*In fewer offices*] with fewer apartments.
[7]*Consent*] Agree.
[8]*estate*] means.
[9]*To weigh . . . opposite*] Taking into consideration both sides of the question; setting the likelihood that we are able to go through with the undertaking against the possibility of failing in it.
[10]*or else*] otherwise.

A naked subject to[11] the weeping clouds,
And waste for churlish winter's tyranny.
HAST.   Grant that our hopes, yet likely of fair birth,
    Should be still-born, and that we now possess'd
    The utmost man of expectation,
    I think we are a body strong enough,
    Even as we are, to equal with the king.
L. BARD.   What, is the king but five and twenty thousand?
HAST.   To us[12] no more; nay, not so much, Lord Bardolph.
    For his divisions, as the times do brawl,
    Are in three heads: one power against the French,[13]
    And one against Glendower; perforce a third
    Must take up[14] us: so is the unfirm king
    In three divided; and his coffers sound
    With hollow poverty and emptiness.
ARCH.   That he should draw his several strengths together
    And come against us in full puissance,
    Need not be dreaded.
HAST.   If he should do so,
    He leaves his back unarm'd, the French and Welsh
    Baying him at the heels: never fear that.
L. BARD.   Who is it like should lead his forces hither?
HAST.   The Duke of Lancaster[15] and Westmoreland;
    Against the Welsh, himself and Harry Monmouth:
    But who is substituted 'gainst the French,
    I have no certain notice.
ARCH.   Let us on,
    And publish the occasion of our arms.
    The commonwealth is sick of their own choice;
    Their over-greedy love hath surfeited:
    An habitation giddy and unsure
    Hath he that buildeth on the vulgar heart.
    O thou fond many,[16] with what loud applause

---

[11]*A naked subject to*] a subject exposed to.

[12]*To us*] As far as we know.

[13]*against the French*] During Glendower's rebellion a French army of twelve thousand men landed at Milford Haven in his support.

[14]*take up*] cope with.

[15]*The Duke of Lancaster*] This is an inaccuracy. The reference is to Prince John of Lancaster, Prince Henry's younger brother, who was created Duke of Bedford long after these events, in the second year of Henry V's reign. Prince Henry ("Harry Monmouth") was the Duke of Lancaster of this period.

[16]*fond many*] foolish multitude.

Didst thou beat heaven[17] with blessing Bolingbroke,
Before he was what thou wouldst have him be!
And being now trimm'd in thine own desires,[18]
Thou, beastly feeder, art so full of him,
That thou provokest thyself to cast him up.
So, so, thou common dog, didst thou disgorge
Thy glutton bosom of the royal Richard;
And now thou wouldst eat thy dead vomit up,
And howl'st to find it. What trust is in these times?
They that, when Richard lived, would have him die,
And now become enamour'd on his grave:
Thou, that threw'st dust upon his goodly head
When through proud London he came sighing on
After the admired heels of Bolingbroke,
Criest now "O earth, yield us that king again,
And take thou this!" O thoughts of men accursed!
Past and to come seems best; things present, worst.

MOWB.   Shall we go draw our numbers,[19] and set on?
HAST.   We are time's subjects, and time bids be gone.   [*Exeunt.*

---

[17]*beat heaven*] shout to the vault of heaven.
[18]*trimm'd . . . desires*] decked out, equipped as you wished.
[19]*draw our numbers*] assemble our forces.

ACT II.

Scene I.   *London. A Street*

Enter HOSTESS, FANG *and his* Boy *with her, and* SNARE *following*

HOSTESS.   Master Fang, have you entered the action?

FANG.   It is entered.

HOST.   Where's your yeoman?[1]
  Is 't a lusty yeoman? will a' stand to 't?

FANG.   Sirrah, where's Snare?

HOST.   O Lord, ay! good Master Snare.

SNARE.   Here, here.

FANG.   Snare, we must arrest Sir John Falstaff.

HOST.   Yea, good Master Snare; I have entered him and all.

SNARE.   It may chance cost some of us our lives, for he will stab.

HOST.   Alas the day! take heed of him; he stabbed me in mine own
  house, and that most beastly: in good faith, he cares not what mischief he does, if his weapon be out: he will foin[2] like any devil; he
  will spare neither man, woman, nor child.

FANG.   If I can close with him, I care not for his thrust.

HOST.   No, nor I neither: I'll be at your elbow.

FANG.   An I but fist him once; an a' come but within my vice,[3] —

HOST.   I am undone by his going;[4] I warrant you, he's an infinitive[5]
  thing upon my score. Good Master Fang, hold him sure: good
  Master Snare, let him not 'scape. A' comes continuantly to Pie-cor-
  ner — saving your manhoods[6] — to buy a saddle; and he is indited[7]

---

[1]*yeoman*] attendant on the sheriff's officer, the bailiff's man.
[2]*foin*] thrust.
[3]*vice*] grip, clutch.
[4]*going*] procedure.
[5]*infinitive*] a blunder for infinite, *i.e.*, endless.
[6]*saving your manhoods*] a farcical apology for mentioning so humble a locality.
[7]*indited*] a blunder for invited.

118

to dinner to the Lubber's-head in Lumbert street,[8] to Master
Smooth's the silkman: I pray ye, since my exion[9] is entered and my
case so openly known to the world, let him be brought in to his answer. A hundred mark is a long one[10] for a poor lone woman to
bear: and I have borne, and borne, and borne; and have been
fubbed off,[11] and fubbed off, and fubbed off, from this day to that
day, that it is a shame to be thought on. There is no honesty in such
dealing; unless a woman should be made an ass and a beast, to bear
every knave's wrong. Yonder he comes; and that arrant malmsey-
nose[12] knave, Bardolph, with him. Do your offices, do your offices:
Master Fang and Master Snare, do me, do me, do me your offices.

Enter FALSTAFF, Page, and BARDOLPH

FAL. How now! whose mare's dead?[13] what's the matter?

FANG. Sir John, I arrest you at the suit of Mistress Quickly.

FAL. Away, varlets! Draw, Bardolph: cut me off the villain's head:
throw the quean in the channel.[14]

HOST. Throw me in the channel! I'll throw thee in the channel. Wilt
thou? wilt thou? thou bastardly[15] rogue! Murder, murder! Ah,
thou honey-suckle[16] villain! wilt thou kill God's officers and the
king's? Ah, thou honey-seed rogue! thou art a honey-seed, a man-
queller,[17] and a woman-queller.

FAL. Keep them off, Bardolph.

FANG. A rescue! a rescue!

HOST. Good people, bring a rescue or two. Thou wo't, wo't thou?
thou wo't, wo't ta?[18] do, do, thou rogue! do, thou hemp-seed![19]

PAGE. Away, you scullion! you rampallian![20] you fustilarian! I'll tickle
your catastrophe.[21]

Enter the LORD CHIEF JUSTICE, and his men

---

[8]*Lubber's-head in Lumbert street*] Leopard's-head in Lombard street.

[9]*exion*] blunder for action (at law).

[10]*A hundred mark . . . one*] An unpaid bill of a hundred marks is a long reckoning.

[11]*fubbed off*] put off with excuses.

[12]*malmsey-nose*] a nose reddened with drinking malmsey wine.

[13]*whose mare's dead?*] a comic colloquialism for "what's up?"

[14]*quean . . . channel*] jade . . . gutter.

[15]*bastardly*] blunder for "dastardly."

[16]*honey-suckle*] blunder for "homicidal."

[17]*a man-queller*] a man-killer.

[18]*thou wo't, wo't ta?*] you will, will you?

[19]*hemp-seed*] gallows-bird.

[20]*rampallian*] riotous strumpet; a term of abuse employed by other writers of the day.

[21]*catastrophe*] posterior.

CH. JUST.   What is the matter? keep the peace here, ho!

HOST.   Good my lord, be good to me. I beseech you, stand to me.

CH. JUST.   How now, Sir John! what are you brawling here?
Doth this become your place, your time and business?
You should have been well on your way to York.
Stand from him, fellow: wherefore hang'st upon him?

HOST.   O my most worshipful lord, an 't please your grace, I am a
poor widow of Eastcheap, and he is arrested at my suit.

CH. JUST.   For what sum?

HOST.   It is more than for some, my lord; it is for all, all I have. He
hath eaten me out of house and home; he hath put all my substance into that fat belly of his: but I will have some of it out again,
or I will ride thee o' nights like the mare.

FAL.   I think I am as like to ride the mare,[22] if I have any vantage of
ground to get up.

CH. JUST.   How comes this, Sir John? Fie! what man of good temper
would endure this tempest of exclamation? Are you not ashamed
to enforce a poor widow to so rough a course to come by her own?

FAL.   What is the gross sum that I owe thee?

HOST.   Marry, if thou wert an honest man, thyself and the money too.
Thou didst swear to me upon a parcel-gilt[23] goblet, sitting in my
Dolphin-chamber, at the round table, by a sea-coal fire, upon
Wednesday in Wheeson[24] week, when the prince broke thy head
for liking[25] his father to a singing-man of Windsor, thou didst
swear to me then, as I was washing thy wound, to marry me and
make me my lady thy wife. Canst thou deny it? Did not goodwife
Keech,[26] the butcher's wife, come in then and call me gossip
Quickly? coming in to borrow a mess[27] of vinegar; telling us she
had a good dish of prawns; whereby thou didst desire to eat some;
whereby I told thee they were ill for a green wound? And didst
thou not, when she was gone down stairs, desire me to be no more
so familiarity with such poor people; saying that ere long they
should call me madam? And didst thou not kiss me and bid me

---

[22]*like the mare . . . ride the mare*] The hostess means by mare "nightmare." Falstaff's obscene retort takes cognizance of the circumstance that "to ride the mare" was a slang
term for "to ascend the gallows."

[23]*parcel-gilt*] gilt in parts. The embossed portions of a goblet of silver, pewter, or other
metal were often gilded.

[24]*Wheeson*] blunder for "Whitsun."

[25]*liking*] blunder for "likening."

[26]*goodwife Keech*] "Keech" is the technical term of a roll of tallow prepared by butchers
for the chandler.

[27]*mess*] small quantity.

fetch thee thirty shillings? I put thee now to thy book-oath:[28] deny it, if thou canst.

FAL.   My lord, this is a poor mad soul; and she says up and down the town that her eldest son is like you: she hath been in good case,[29] and the truth is, poverty hath distracted her. But for these foolish officers, I beseech you I may have redress against them.

CH. JUST.   Sir John, Sir John, I am well acquainted with your manner of wrenching the true cause the false way. It is not a confident brow, nor the throng of words that come with such more than impudent sauciness from you, can thrust me from a level consideration:[30] you have, as it appears to me, practised upon the easy-yielding spirit of this woman, and made her serve your uses both in purse and in person.

HOST.   Yea, in truth, my lord.

CH. JUST.   Pray thee, peace. Pay her the debt you owe her, and unpay the villany you have done her: the one you may do with sterling money, and the other with current repentance.

FAL.   My lord, I will not undergo this sneap[31] without reply. You call honourable boldness impudent sauciness: if a man will make courtesy[32] and say nothing, he is virtuous: no, my lord, my humble duty remembered, I will not be your suitor. I say to you, I do desire deliverance from these officers, being upon hasty employment in the king's affairs.

CH. JUST.   You speak as having power to do wrong: but answer in the effect of your reputation,[33] and satisfy the poor woman.

FAL.   Come hither, hostess.

Enter GOWER

CH. JUST.   Now, Master Gower, what news?

GOW.   The king, my lord, and Harry Prince of Wales
Are near at hand: the rest the paper tells.

FAL.   As I am a gentleman.

HOST.   Faith, you said so before.

FAL.   As I am a gentleman. Come, no more words of it.

HOST.   By this heavenly ground I tread on, I must be fain[34] to pawn both my plate and the tapestry of my dining-chambers.

---

[28]*book-oath*] bible-oath, oath sworn on the bible.
[29]*in good case*] in a good position, well off.
[30]*a level consideration*] an impartial point of view.
[31]*undergo this sneap*] submit to this rebuke.
[32]*make courtesy*] make signs of subservience.
[33]*in the effect of your reputation*] in the manner suitable to your position.
[34]*I must be fain*] I must be content.

FAL.   Glasses, glasses, is the only drinking:[35] and for thy walls, a pretty
         slight drollery, or the story of the Prodigal, or the German hunting
         in water-work, is worth a thousand of these bed-hangings[36] and
         these fly-bitten tapestries. Let it be ten pound, if thou canst.
         Come, an 't were not for thy humours, there's not a better wench
         in England. Go, wash thy face, and draw[37] the action. Come, thou
         must not be in this humour with me; dost not know me? come,
         come, I know thou wast set on to this.

HOST.   Pray thee, Sir John, let it be but twenty nobles: i' faith, I am
         loath to pawn my plate, so God save me, la!

FAL.   Let it alone; I'll make other shift: you'll be a fool still.

HOST.   Well, you shall have it, though I pawn my gown. I hope you'll
         come to supper. You'll pay me all together?

FAL.   Will I live?[38] [*To* BARDOLPH] Go, with her, with her; hook on,
         hook on.[39]

HOST.   Will you have Doll Tearsheet meet you at supper?

FAL.   No more words; let's have her.

                    [*Exeunt* HOSTESS, BARDOLPH, Officers, *and* Boy.

CH. JUST.   I have heard better news.

FAL.   What's the news, my lord?

CH. JUST.   Where lay the king last night?

GOW.   At Basingstoke, my lord.

FAL.   I hope, my lord, all's well: what is the news, my lord?

CH. JUST.   Come all his forces back?

GOW.   No; fifteen hundred foot, five hundred horse,
         Are march'd up to my Lord of Lancaster,
         Against Northumberland and the Archbishop.

FAL.   Comes the king back from Wales, my noble lord?

CH. JUST.   You shall have letters of me presently:
         Come, go along with me, good Master Gower.

FAL.   My lord!

CH. JUST.   What's the matter?

FAL.   Master Gower, shall I entreat you with me to dinner?

---

[35]*Glasses . . . drinking*] Persons of fashion at the time only used cups or tankards of glass;
   metal drinking cups had gone out of vogue.

[36]*a pretty . . . bed-hangings*] Falstaff is extolling a new and light fashion of decorating the
   walls of rooms and deprecating the old-fashioned heavy tapestry. By "water-work" is
   meant (as opposed to "oil painting") "water colours" or distemper, which might be
   wrought either on canvas or on wood. "Drollery" is a humorous incident; "the story of
   the Prodigal" means a sketch of that scriptural tale; "the German hunting" would
   mean the presentation of a boar hunt.

[37]*draw*] withdraw.

[38]*Will I live?*] As sure as life.

[39]*hook on*] hold fast to her.

GOW.   I must wait upon my good lord here; I thank you, good Sir John.

CH. JUST.   Sir John, you loiter here too long, being you are to take soldiers up in counties as you go.

FAL.   Will you sup with me, Master Gower?

CH. JUST.   What foolish master taught you these manners, Sir John?

FAL.   Master Gower, if they become me not, he was a fool that taught
them me. This is the right fencing grace, my lord; tap for tap, and
so part fair.

CH. JUST.   Now the Lord lighten[40] thee! thou art a great fool.

[*Exeunt.*

Scene II.   *London. Another Street*

Enter PRINCE HENRY *and* POINS

PRINCE.   Before God, I am exceeding weary.

POINS.   Is 't come to that? I had thought weariness durst not have attached[1] one of so high blood.

PRINCE.   Faith, it does me; though it discolours the complexion of my
greatness to acknowledge it. Doth it not show vilely in me to desire small beer?

POINS.   Why, a prince should not be so loosely studied[2] as to remember so weak a composition.

PRINCE.   Belike then my appetite was not princely got; for, by my troth,
I do now remember the poor creature, small beer. But, indeed,
these humble considerations make me out of love with my greatness. What a disgrace is it to me to remember thy name! or to know
thy face to-morrow! or to take note how many pair of silk stockings
thou hast, viz. these, and those that were thy peach-coloured ones!
or to bear the inventory of thy shirts; as, one for superfluity, and another for use! But that the tennis-court-keeper knows better than I;
for it is a low ebb of linen with thee when thou keepest not racket[3]
there; as thou hast not done a great while, because the rest of thy
low countries have made a shift to eat up thy holland:[4] and God

---

[40]*lighten*] enlighten.

[1]*attached*] seized.

[2]*loosely studied*] frivolously disposed.

[3]*racket*] a pun on a tennis "racquet," and a "racket" in the sense of "disorder."

[4]*low countries . . . holland*] a popular geographical jest; "the Netherlands," or "low countries," was jocose slang for the lower part of the body or the posteriors. The general
sense of the passage would appear to be that Poins's sensual indulgences have cost him
his linen underclothes.

knows, whether those that bawl out the ruins of thy linen shall inherit his kingdom: but the midwives say the children[5] are not in the fault; whereupon the world increases, and kindreds[6] are mightily strengthened.

POINS. How ill it follows, after you have laboured so hard, you should talk so idly! Tell me, how many good young princes would do so, their father's being so sick as yours at this time is?

PRINCE. Shall I tell thee one thing, Poins?

POINS. Yes, faith; and let it be an excellent good thing.

PRINCE. It shall serve among wits of no higher breeding than thine.

POINS. Go to; I stand the push[7] of your one thing that you will tell.

PRINCE. Marry, I tell thee, it is not meet that I should be sad, now my father is sick: albeit I could tell to thee, as to one it pleases me, for fault of a better, to call my friend, I could be sad, and sad indeed too.

POINS. Very hardly upon such a subject.

PRINCE. By this hand, thou thinkest me as far in the devil's book[8] as thou and Falstaff for obduracy and persistency: let the end try the man. But I tell thee, my heart bleeds inwardly that my father is so sick: and keeping such vile company as thou art hath in reason taken from me all ostentation[9] of sorrow.

POINS. The reason?

PRINCE. What wouldst thou think of me, if I should weep?

POINS. I would think thee a most princely hypocrite.

PRINCE. It would be every man's thought; and thou art a blessed fellow to think as every man thinks: never a man's thought in the world keeps the road-way[10] better than thine: every man would think me an hypocrite indeed. And what accites[11] your most worshipful thought to think so?

POINS. Why, because you have been so lewd, and so much engraffed[12] to Falstaff.

PRINCE. And to thee.

POINS. By this light, I am well spoke on; I can hear it with mine own

---

[5]*children*] a somewhat incoherent allusion to bastard children with whom the prince jestingly credits Poins. The babies' yells direct attention to their ragged covering.

[6]*kindreds*] families.

[7]*stand the push*] am equal to the thrust.

[8]*in the devil's book*] in the devil's good books.

[9]*ostentation*] show or manifestation. The word in Elizabethan literature lacked the notion of boastfulness, now attaching to the word.

[10]*road-way*] beaten track.

[11]*accites*] an unusual form of "excites."

[12]*engraffed*] attached.

ears: the worst that they can say of me is that I am a second brother,
and that I am a proper fellow of my hands;[13] and those two things,
I confess, I cannot help. By the mass, here comes Bardolph.

Enter BARDOLPH *and* Page

PRINCE.   And the boy that I gave Falstaff: a' had him from me
Christian; and look, if the fat villain have not transformed him
ape.

BARD.   God save your grace!

PRINCE.   And yours, most noble Bardolph!

BARD.   Come, you virtuous ass, you bashful fool, must you be blushing? wherefore blush you now? What a maidenly man-at-arms are
you become! Is 't such a matter to get a pottle-pot's maidenhead?

PAGE.   A' calls me e'en now, my lord, through a red lattice,[14] and I
could discern no part of his face from the window: at last I spied
his eyes; and methought he had made two holes in the ale-wife's
new petticoat and so peeped through.

PRINCE.   Has not the boy profited?

BARD.   Away, you whoreson upright rabbit, away!

PAGE.   Away, you rascally Althæa's dream, away!

PRINCE.   Instruct us, boy; what dream, boy?

PAGE.   Marry, my lord, Althæa dreamed she was delivered of a firebrand; and therefore I call him her dream.[15]

PRINCE.   A crown's worth of good interpretation: there 't is, boy.

POINS.   O, that this good blossom could be kept from cankers![16] Well,
there is sixpence to preserve thee.

BARD.   An you do not make him hanged among you, the gallows shall
have wrong.

PRINCE.   And how doth thy master, Bardolph?

BARD.   Well, my lord. He heard of your grace's coming to town:
there's a letter for you.

POINS.   Delivered with good respect. And how doth the martlemas,[17]
your master?

---

[13]*a proper . . . hands*] a handsome fellow of my inches.

[14]*a red lattice*] a tavern window. Here there is a jest on Bardolph's red nose.

[15]*Althæa's dream . . . her dream*] Two mythological fables are confused here. Hecuba
(not Althæa) dreamt just before the birth of her son Paris that she was delivered of a
firebrand which should consume Troy. Althæa's firebrand belongs to a different myth;
on the preservation of a certain firebrand from fire depended the continuance of the
life of Althæa's son Meleager of Calydon.

[16]*cankers*] canker-worms, caterpillars.

[17]*the martlemas*] Martinmas: a reference to the warm summer weather which occasionally distinguishes the date of St. Martin's day, 11 November. Falstaff's gaiety in the
winter of his age has already been likened to "Allhallown summer."

BARD.   In bodily health, sir.

POINS.   Marry, the immortal part needs a physician; but that moves not him: though that be sick, it dies not.

PRINCE.   I do allow this wen[18] to be as familiar with me as my dog; and he holds his place; for look you how he writes.

POINS.   [*Reads*] "John Falstaff, knight,"—every man must know that, as oft as he has occasion to name himself: even like those that are kin to the king; for they never prick their finger but they say, "There's some of the king's blood spilt." "How comes that?" says he, that takes upon him not to conceive. The answer is as ready as a borrower's cap,[19] "I am the king's poor cousin, sir."

PRINCE.   Nay, they will be kin to us, or they will fetch it from Japhet. But to the letter:

POINS.   [*Reads*] "Sir John Falstaff, knight, to the son of the king, nearest his father, Harry Prince of Wales, greeting." Why, this is a certificate.

PRINCE.   Peace!

POINS.   [*Reads*] "I will imitate the honourable Romans in brevity:"[20] he sure means brevity in breath, short-winded. "I commend me to thee, I commend thee, and I leave thee. Be not too familiar with Poins; for he misuses thy favours so much, that he swears thou art to marry his sister Nell. Repent at idle times as thou mayest; and so, farewell.

"Thine, by yea and no, which is as much as to say, as thou usest him, JACK FALSTAFF with my familiars, JOHN with my brothers and sisters, and SIR JOHN with all Europe."

My lord, I'll steep this letter in sack, and make him eat it.

PRINCE.   That's to make him eat twenty of his words. But do you use me thus, Ned? must I marry your sister?

POINS.   God send the wench no worse fortune! But I never said so.

PRINCE.   Well, thus we play the fools with the time; and the spirits of the wise sit in the clouds and mock us. Is your master here in London?

BARD.   Yea, my lord.

PRINCE.   Where sups he? doth the old boar feed in the old frank?[21]

BARD.   At the old place, my lord, in Eastcheap.

PRINCE.   What company?

PAGE.   Ephesians,[22] my lord, of the old church.

PRINCE.   Sup any women with him?

---

[18]*this wen*] this swollen excrescence of a man.
[19]*a borrower's cap*] a borrower's salutation.
[20]*I will imitate . . . brevity*] A reference to Cæsar's famous despatch, "veni, vidi, vici."
[21]*frank*] pigsty.
[22]*Ephesians*] bloods, men of mettle.

PAGE.   None, my lord, but old Mistress Quickly and Mistress Doll
    Tearsheet.

PRINCE.   What pagan may that be?

PAGE.   A proper gentlewoman, sir, and a kinswoman of my master's.

PRINCE.   Even such kin as the parish heifers are to the town bull.
    Shall we steal upon them, Ned, at supper?

POINS.   I am your shadow, my lord; I'll follow you.

PRINCE.   Sirrah, you boy, and Bardolph, no word to your master that
    I am yet come to town: there's for your silence.

BARD.   I have no tongue, sir.

PAGE.   And for mine, sir, I will govern it.

PRINCE.   Fare you well; go. [*Exeunt* BARDOLPH *and* Page.]
    This Doll Tearsheet should be some road.[23]

POINS.   I warrant you, as common as the way between Saint Alban's
    and London.

PRINCE.   How might we see Falstaff bestow himself[24] to-night in his
    true colours, and not ourselves be seen?

POINS.   Put on two leathern jerkins and aprons, and wait upon him at
    his table as drawers.

PRINCE.   From a god to a bull? a heavy descension![25] it was Jove's case.
    From a prince to a prentice? a low transformation! that shall be
    mine; for in every thing the purpose must weigh with the folly.[26]
    Follow me, Ned.   [*Exeunt.*

Scene III.   *Warkworth. Before the Castle*

Enter NORTHUMBERLAND, LADY NORTHUMBERLAND, *and* LADY PERCY

NORTH.   I pray thee, loving wife, and gentle daughter,
    Give even way unto my rough affairs:
    Put not you on the visage of the times,
    And be like them to Percy troublesome.

LADY N.   I have given over, I will speak no more:
    Do what you will; your wisdom be your guide.

NORTH.   Alas, sweet wife, my honour is at pawn;
    And, but my going, nothing can redeem it.

---

[23]*road*] prostitute.

[24]*bestow himself*] Deport himself, behave.

[25]*descension*] There is an obvious reference to the story of Jupiter's surprise of Europa in
the shape of a bull, which is told at length in Ovid's *Metamorphoses,* and is many times
referred to by Shakespeare.

[26]*the purpose . . . folly*] the plan must be governed by the levity inspiring it.

LADY P.   O yet, for God's sake, go not to these wars!
    The time was, father, that you broke your word,
    When you were more endear'd[1] to it than now;
    When your own Percy, when my heart's dear Harry,
    Threw many a northward look to see his father
    Bring up his powers; but he did long in vain.
    Who then persuaded you to stay at home?
    There were two honours lost, yours and your son's.
    For yours, the God of heaven brighten it!
    For his, it stuck upon him as the sun
    In the grey vault of heaven, and by his light
    Did all the chivalry of England move
    To do brave acts: he was indeed the glass
    Wherein the noble youth did dress themselves:
    He had no legs that practised not his gait;
    And speaking thick,[2] which nature made his blemish,
    Became the accents of the valiant;
    For those that could speak low and tardily
    Would turn their own perfection to abuse,
    To seem like him: so that in speech, in gait,
    In diet, in affections of delight,
    In military rules, humours of blood,
    He was the mark and glass,[3] copy and book,
    That fashioned others. And him, O wondrous him!
    O miracle of men! him did you leave,
    Second to none, unseconded by you,
    To look upon the hideous god of war
    In disadvantage; to abide a field
    Where nothing but the sound of Hotspur's name
    Did seem defensible:[4] so you left him.
    Never, O never, do his ghost the wrong
    To hold your honour more precise and nice[5]
    With others than with him! let them alone:
    The marshal and the archbishop are strong:
    Had my sweet Harry had but half their numbers,
    To-day might I, hanging on Hotspur's neck,
    Have talk'd of Monmouth's grave.[6]

---

[1]*more endear'd*] more seriously bound.
[2]*speaking thick*] crowding words together.
[3]*the mark and glass*] the example and mirror.
[4]*defensible*] able to furnish means of defence, able to meet attack.
[5]*To hold . . . nice*] To be more scrupulous in keeping your word.
[6]*Monmouth's grave*] Prince Harry's grave.

NORTH.   Beshrew your heart,
　　Fair daughter, you do draw my spirits from me
　　With new lamenting ancient oversights.
　　But I must go and meet with danger there,
　　Or it will seek me in another place
　　And find me worse provided.
LADY N.   O, fly to Scotland,
　　Till that the nobles and the armed commons
　　Have of their puissance made a little taste.[7]
LADY P.　　If they get ground and vantage[8] of the king,
　　Then join you with them, like a rib of steel,
　　To make strength stronger; but, for all our loves,
　　First let them try themselves. So did your son;
　　He was so suffer'd: so came I a widow;
　　And never shall have length of life enough
　　To rain upon remembrance with mine eyes,[9]
　　That it may grow and sprout as high as heaven,
　　For recordation to my noble husband.
NORTH.　　Come, come, go in with me. 'T is with my mind
　　As with the tide swell'd up unto his height,
　　That makes a still-stand, running neither way:
　　Fain would I go to meet the archbishop,
　　But many thousand reasons hold me back.
　　I will resolve for Scotland: there am I,
　　Till time and vantage crave my company.   [*Exeunt.*

Scene IV.　*London. The Boar's-head Tavern in Eastcheap*

Enter two Drawers

FIRST DRAW.　　What the devil hast thou brought there? apple-johns?[1]
　　thou knowest Sir John cannot endure an apple-john.
SEC. DRAW.　　Mass, thou sayest true. The prince once set a dish of
　　apple-johns before him, and told him there were five more Sir
　　Johns; and, putting off his hat, said, "I will now take my leave of
　　these six dry, round, old, withered knights." It angered him to the
　　heart: but he hath forgot that.

---

[7]*Have . . . taste*] Have made some little test or trial of their power.
[8]*get ground and vantage*] gain ground and advantage, get the better.
[9]*To rain . . . eyes*] To water his memory.

---

[1]*apple-johns*] apples with shrivelled skins.

FIRST DRAW.   Why, then, cover,[2] and set them down: and see if thou
canst find out Sneak's noise;[3] Mistress Tearsheet would fain hear
some music. Dispatch: the room where they supped is too hot;
they'll come in straight.

SEC. DRAW.   Sirrah, here will be the prince and Master Poins anon;
and they will put on two of our jerkins and aprons; and Sir John
must not know of it: Bardolph hath brought word.

FIRST DRAW.   By the mass, here will be old utis:[4] it will be an excellent stratagem.

SEC. DRAW.   I'll see if I can find out Sneak.   [*Exit.*

Enter HOSTESS *and* DOLL TEARSHEET

HOST.   I' faith, sweetheart, methinks now you are in an excellent good
temperality: your pulsidge[5] beats as extraordinarily as heart would
desire; and your colour, I warrant you, is as red as any rose, in good
truth, la! But, i' faith, you have drunk too much canaries; and
that's a marvellous searching wine, and it perfumes the blood ere
one can say "What's this?" How do you now?

DOL.   Better than I was: hem!

HOST.   Why, that's well said; a good heart's worth gold. Lo, here
comes Sir John.

Enter FALSTAFF

FAL.   [*Singing*] "When Arthur first in court"—Empty the jordan. [*Exit*
First Drawer.]—[*Singing*] "And was a worthy king."[6] How now,
Mistress Doll!

HOST.   Sick of a calm;[7] yea, good faith.

FAL.   So is all her sect;[8] an they be once in a calm, they are sick.

DOL.   You muddy rascal, is that all the comfort you give me?

FAL.   You make fat rascals, Mistress Doll.

DOL.   I make them! gluttony and diseases make them; I make them
not.

---

[2]*cover*] lay the table.

[3]*noise*] company of musicians.

[4]*old utis*] fine fun or sport. "Utis" is said to be a form of the French "huitas," *i.e.*, "oc-
tave," the eighth day after a church festival, which was often devoted to wild merriment. "Old" is a colloquial intensitive.

[5]*temperality . . . pulsidge*] temperature . . . pulse; both words belong to the Hostess's peculiar dialect.

[6]*When Arthur . . . king*] The first two lines of a popular Arthurian ballad, *Sir Launcelot
du Lake*, which opens in Percy's *Reliques*: "When Arthur first in court began And was
approved king."

[7]*calm*] qualm.

[8]*sect*] sex.

FAL.   If the cook help to make the gluttony, you help to make the diseases, Doll: we catch of you, Doll, we catch of you; grant that, my
poor virtue, grant that.

DOL.   Yea, joy, our chains and our jewels.

FAL.   "Your brooches, pearls, and ouches:"[9] for to serve bravely is to
come halting off, you know; to come off the breach with his pike
bent bravely, and to surgery bravely; to venture upon the charged
chambers[10] bravely, —

DOL.   Hang yourself, you muddy conger,[11] hang yourself!

HOST.   By my troth, this is the old fashion; you two never meet but
you fall to some discord: you are both, i' good truth, as rheumatic[12]
as two dry toasts; you cannot one bear with another's confirmities.[13] What the good-year![14] one must bear, and that must be you:
you are the weaker vessel, as they say, the emptier vessel.

DOL.   Can a weak empty vessel bear such a huge full hogshead?
there's a whole merchant's venture of Bourdeaux stuff in him; you
have not seen a hulk better stuffed in the hold. Come, I'll be
friends with thee, Jack: thou art going to the wars; and whether I
shall ever see thee again or no, there is nobody cares.

Re-enter First Drawer

FIRST DRAW.   Sir, Ancient[15] Pistol's below, and would speak with you.

DOL.   Hang him, swaggering rascal! let him not come hither: it is the
foul-mouthedst rogue in England.

HOST.   If he swagger, let him not come here: no, by my faith; I must
live among my neighbours; I'll no swaggerers: I am in good name
and fame with the very best: shut the door; there comes no swaggerers here: I have not lived all this while, to have swaggering
now: shut the door, I pray you.

FAL.   Dost thou hear, hostess?

HOST.   Pray ye, pacify yourself, Sir John: there comes no swaggerers
here.

FAL.   Dost thou hear? it is mine ancient.

---

[9]*"Your brooches . . . ouches"*] A quotation from some popular song. "Ouches" were rich
jewelled trinkets.
[10]*charged chambers*] loaded pieces of ordnance. There is much obscene quibbling here.
[11]*conger*] fat conger-eel.
[12]*rheumatic*] blunder for choleric, splenetic.
[13]*confirmities*] blunder for infirmities.
[14]*What the good-year*] What in good fortune? "Good-year" has been interpreted without
authority as a corruption of a French word "goujère," the venereal disease.
[15]*Ancient*] here the colloquial corruption of "Ensign."

HOST.　Tilly-fally,[16] Sir John, ne'er tell me: your ancient swaggerer comes not in my doors. I was before Master Tisick, the debuty,[17] t' other day; and, as he said to me, 't was no longer ago than Wednesday last, "I' good faith, neighbour Quickly," says he; Master Dumbe,[18] our minister, was by then; "neighbour Quickly," says he, "receive those that are civil; for," said he, "you are in an ill name:" now a' said so, I can tell whereupon; "for," says he, "you are an honest woman, and well thought on; therefore take heed what guests you receive: receive," says he, "no swaggering companions." There comes none here: you would bless you to hear what he said: no, I'll no swaggerers.

FAL.　He's no swaggerer, hostess; a tame cheater,[19] i' faith; you may stroke him as gently as a puppy greyhound: he'll not swagger with a Barbary hen, if her feathers turn back in any show of resistance. Call him up, drawer.　　　　　　　　　　　　　[*Exit* First Drawer.

HOST.　Cheater, call you him? I will bar no honest man my house, nor no cheater: but I do not love swaggering, by my troth; I am the worse, when one says swagger: feel, master, how I shake; look you, I warrant you.

DOL.　So you do, hostess.

HOST.　Do I? yea, in very truth, do I, an 't were an aspen leaf: I cannot abide swaggerers.

Enter PISTOL, BARDOLPH, *and* Page

PIST.　God save you, Sir John!

FAL.　Welcome, Ancient Pistol. Here, Pistol, I charge you with a cup of sack: do you discharge upon mine hostess.

PIST.　I will discharge upon her, Sir John, with two bullets.

FAL.　She is pistol-proof, sir; you shall hardly offend her.

HOST.　Come, I'll drink no proofs nor no bullets: I'll drink no more than will do me good, for no man's pleasure, I.

---

[16]*Tilly-fally*] Hoity-toity, fiddle-faddle.

[17]*Master Tisick, the debuty*] The name implies that the officer (the deputy of the ward) was pursy and short-winded.

[18]*Master Dumbe*] This epithet was commonly applied to the clergy, who forbore to preach, and only read homilies prescribed by authority.

[19]*a tame cheater*] Falstaff is assuring the hostess that Pistol is a harmless fellow. The word "cheater" was often used for a "gamester" without suggestion of dishonesty on his part, but rather for an honest player who was the prey of sharpers. The hostess mistakes the word for "escheater," *i.e.*, revenue-officer.

PIST.   Then to you, Mistress Dorothy; I will charge you.

DOL.   Charge me! I scorn you, scurvy companion. What! you poor, base, rascally, cheating, lack-linen mate! Away, you mouldy rogue, away! I am meat for your master.

PIST.   I know you, Mistress Dorothy.

DOL.   Away, you cut-purse rascal! you filthy bung,[20] away! by this wine, I'll thrust my knife in your mouldy chaps, an you play the saucy cuttle[21] with me. Away, you bottle-ale rascal! you basket-hilt stale juggler,[22] you! Since when,[23] I pray you, sir? God's light, with two points on your shoulder?[24] much!

PIST.   God let me not live, but I will murder your ruff for this.

FAL.   No more, Pistol; I would not have you go off here: discharge yourself of our company, Pistol.

HOST.   No, good Captain Pistol; not here, sweet captain.

DOL.   Captain! thou abominable damned cheater, art thou not ashamed to be called captain? An captains were of my mind, they would truncheon you out, for taking their names upon you before you have earned them. You a captain! you slave, for what? for tearing a poor whore's ruff in a bawdy-house? He a captain! hang him, rogue! he lives upon mouldy stewed prunes and dried cakes.[25] A captain! God's light, these villains will make the word as odious as the word "occupy;"[26] which was an excellent good word before it was ill sorted: therefore captains had need look to 't.

BARD.   Pray thee, go down, good ancient.

FAL.   Hark thee hither, Mistress Doll.

PIST.   Not I: I tell thee what, Corporal Bardolph, I could tear her: I'll be revenged of her.

PAGE.   Pray thee, go down.

PIST.   I'll see her damned first; to Pluto's damned lake, by this hand, to the infernal deep, with Erebus and tortures vile also. Hold hook

---

[20]*bung*] sharper, thief. "To nip a bung" in thieves' language is to "cut a purse" or pick a pocket.

[21]*cuttle*] cutpurse; perhaps a reference to "the cuttle-bung," in thieves' language the knife used for slitting purses.

[22]*basket-hilt stale juggler*] an used-up swordsman.

[23]*Since when*] An exclamation of incredulity.

[24]*two points . . . shoulder*] a reference to the epaulettes or shoulder-knots on Pistol's uniform.

[25]*he lives . . . cakes*] he lives upon the waste provisions of brothels and pastry shops.

[26]*the word "occupy"*] The word had acquired at the time an obscene sense.

and line,[27] say I. Down, down, dogs! down, faitors![28] Have we not
Hiren here?[29]

HOST.   Good Captain Peesel, be quiet; 't is very late, i' faith: I beseek
you now, aggravate your choler.

PIST.   These be good humours, indeed! Shall pack-horses,
And hollow pamper'd jades of Asia,
Which cannot go but thirty mile a day,
Compare with Cæsars, and with Cannibals,[30]
And Trojan Greeks? nay, rather damn them with
King Cerberus; and let the welkin roar.
Shall we fall foul for toys?

HOST.   By my troth, captain, these are very bitter words.

BARD.   Be gone, good ancient: this will grow to a brawl anon.

PIST.   Die men like dogs! give crowns like pins!
Have we not Hiren here?

HOST.   O' my word, captain, there's none such here.
What the good-year! do you think I would deny her?
For God's sake, be quiet.

PIST.   Then feed, and be fat, my fair Calipolis. Come, give's some
sack.
"Si fortune me tormente, sperato me contento."[31]
Fear we broadsides? no, let the fiend give fire:
Give me some sack: and, sweetheart, lie thou there.

                                    [*Laying down his sword.*

Come we to full points here; and are etceteras nothing?[32]

FAL.   Pistol, I would be quiet.

PIST.   Sweet knight, I kiss thy neaf:[33] what! we have seen the seven
stars.[34]

---

[27]*Hold hook and line*] An irrelevant quotation from an old fishing song.

[28]*faitors*] traitors, rascals, evil-doers.

[29]*Have we not Hiren here?*] A slang interrogation frequently met with in the Elizabethan
drama. Here apparently Pistol associates the word "Hiren" with "iron," and touches his
sword. When he repeats the phrase, the hostess interprets the word as "siren," or loose
woman, in which sense it is occasionally found in contemporary literature.

[30]*Cannibals*] Blunder for "Hannibals."

[31]*"Si fortune . . . contento"*] A misreading of an Italian jingling proverb, which should
read, "Si fortuna me tormenta, la speranza me contenta" (If fortune torment me, hope
contents me).

[32]*Come we . . . nothing?*] Shall we finish here and have no supplementary merriment.
"Full points" are full stops.

[33]*neaf*] fist; a north country word.

[34]*we have seen the seven stars*] we have rioted together by starlight. The "seven stars" are
the Pleiades, or Charles' wain.

DOL.   For God's sake, thrust him down stairs: I cannot endure such a
    fustian rascal.[35]
PIST.   Thrust him down stairs! know we not Galloway nags?[36]
FAL.   Quoit him down, Bardolph, like a shove-groat shilling:[37] nay, an
    a' do nothing but speak nothing, a' shall be nothing here.
BARD.   Come, get you down stairs.
PIST.   What! shall we have incision? shall we imbrue?[38]
                            [*Snatching up his sword.*
    Then death rock me asleep,[39] abridge my doleful days!
    Why, then, let grievous, ghastly, gaping wounds
    Untwine the Sisters Three! Come, Atropos, I say![40]
HOST.   Here's goodly stuff toward![41]
FAL.   Give me my rapier, boy.
DOL.   I pray thee, Jack, I pray thee, do not draw.
FAL.   Get you down stairs.   [*Drawing, and driving* PISTOL *out.*
HOST.   Here's a goodly tumult! I'll forswear keeping house, afore I'll
    be in these tirrits[42] and frights. So; murder, I warrant now. Alas,
    alas! put up your naked weapons, put up your naked weapons.
                        [*Exeunt* PISTOL *and* BARDOLPH.
DOL.   I pray thee, Jack, be quiet; the rascal's gone.
    Ah, you whoreson little valiant villain, you!
HOST.   Are you not hurt i' the groin? methought a' made a shrewd[43]
    thrust at your belly.

Re-enter BARDOLPH

FAL.   Have you turned him out o' doors?
BARD.   Yea, sir. The rascal's drunk: you have hurt him, sir, i' the shoul-
    der.
FAL.   A rascal! to brave me!
DOL.   Ah, you sweet little rogue, you! Alas, poor ape, how thou sweat-
    est! come, let me wipe thy face; come on, you whoreson chops:[44]

---

[35]*a fustian rascal*] a ranting rogue.
[36]*Galloway nags*] the poorest breed of hackney horses.
[37]*Quoit him . . . shove-groat shilling*] Pitch him down like a shove-groat shilling, *i.e.*, the
  broad shilling piece which was commonly used in the popular game of shovel-board,
  a rudimentary form of bagatelle.
[38]*imbrue*] draw blood.
[39]*Then death . . . asleep*] a quotation from a popular song, attributed to Anne Boleyn.
[40]*Untwine . . . I say!*] The reference is to the Three Fates, of whom Atropos filled the office of cutting the thread of human life.
[41]*Here's goodly stuff toward!*] Here's fine trouble coming.
[42]*tirrits*] perhaps "terrors;" like "worrits" for worries.
[43]*shrewd*] bad, grievous.
[44]*chops*] fat-chops.

ah, rogue! i' faith, I love thee: thou art as valorous as Hector of Troy, worth five of Agamemnon, and ten times better than the Nine Worthies: ah, villain!

FAL. A rascally slave! I will toss the rogue in a blanket.

DOL. Do, an thou darest for thy heart: an thou dost, I'll canvass thee between a pair of sheets.

Enter Music

PAGE. The music is come, sir.

FAL. Let them play. Play, sirs. Sit on my knee, Doll. A rascal bragging slave! the rogue fled from me like quicksilver.

DOL. I' faith, and thou followedst him like a church. Thou whoreson little tidy Bartholomew boar-pig,[45] when wilt thou leave fighting o' days and foining[46] o' nights, and begin to patch up thine old body for heaven?

Enter, behind, PRINCE HENRY *and* POINS, *disguised*

FAL. Peace, good Doll! do not speak like a death's-head; do not bid me remember mine end.

DOL. Sirrah, what humour's the prince of?

FAL. A good shallow young fellow: a' would have made a good pantler,[47] a' would ha' chipped bread well.

DOL. They say Poins has a good wit.

FAL. He a good wit? hang him, baboon! his wit's as thick as Tewksbury mustard;[48] there's no more conceit in him than is in a mallet.

DOL. Why does the prince love him so, then?

FAL. Because their legs are both of a bigness; and a' plays at quoits well; and eats conger and fennel;[49] and drinks off candles' ends for flap-dragons;[50] and rides the wild-mare[51] with the boys; and jumps upon joined-stools; and swears with a good grace; and wears his boots very smooth, like unto the sign of the leg; and breeds no bate

---

[45]*tidy Bartholomew boar-pig*] a goodly sort of pig, such as was roasted whole at Bartholomew's fair, the great annual fair of London. "Tidy" is found in the various senses of "timely" (*i.e.*, ripe), "fat," and "neat" (*i.e.*, dapper).

[46]*foining*] thrusting.

[47]*pantler*] pantry-man.

[48]*Tewksbury mustard*] Tewkesbury in Gloucestershire was long famed for the manufacture of mustard.

[49]*conger and fennel*] conger eel and fennel sauce. The dish was regarded as an aphrodisiac.

[50]*drinks off . . . flap-dragons*] a reference to the game of snap-dragon. Raisins were usually thrown into burning spirit to be rescued from the flames and eaten by the players. "Candles' ends" ludicrously misrepresents the ordinary procedure.

[51]*rides the wild-mare*] plays see-saw.

with telling of discreet stories;[52] and such other gambol faculties[53] a' has, that show a weak mind and an able body, for the which the prince admits him: for the prince himself is such another; the weight of a hair will turn the scales between their avoirdupois.

PRINCE.   Would not this nave of a wheel[54] have his ears cut off?

POINS.   Let's beat him before his whore.

PRINCE.   Look, whether the withered elder[55] hath not his poll clawed like a parrot.[56]

POINS.   Is it not strange that desire should so many years outlive performance?

FAL.   Kiss me, Doll.

PRINCE.   Saturn and Venus[57] this year in conjunction! what says the almanac to that?

POINS.   And, look, whether the fiery Trigon, his man, be not lisping to his master's old tables, his note-book, his counsel-keeper.[58]

FAL.   Thou dost give me flattering busses.

DOL.   By my troth, I kiss thee with a most constant heart.

FAL.   I am old, I am old.

DOL.   I love thee better than I love e'er a scurvy young boy of them all.

FAL.   What stuff wilt have a kirtle[59] of? I shall receive money o' Thursday: shalt have a cap to-morrow. A merry song, come: it grows late; we'll to bed. Thou'lt forget me when I am gone.

DOL.   By my troth, thou'lt set me a-weeping, an thou sayest so: prove that ever I dress myself handsome till thy return: well, hearken at the end.

FAL.   Some sack, Francis.

PRINCE. ⎤
POINS. ⎦ Anon, anon, sir.   [Coming forward.

---

[52]*breeds no bate . . . stories*] breeds no quarrelling or dissatisfaction by telling modest stories; in other words, his indecencies satisfy all demands.

[53]*gambol faculties*] skittish capacities.

[54]*this nave of a wheel*] this round wheel, in allusion to Falstaff's rotundity.

[55]*the withered elder*] a punning allusion to the elder tree.

[56]*his poll . . . parrot*] his head scratched as the parrots are wont to have their heads scratched.

[57]*Saturn and Venus*] These planets are most rarely in conjunction, according to astronomical observation.

[58]*the fiery Trigon . . . counsel-keeper*] Poins means that Bardolph is courting the Hostess, Falstaff's old mistress. "Fiery Trigon" is an astrological term; the three "fiery" signs of the zodiac, Aries, Leo, and Sagittarius, were supposed to form in certain planetary conditions of the heavens "trigonum igneum," *i.e.*, the fiery triangle. "Tables" means tablets, memorandum-books, account-books.

[59]*kirtle*] petticoat.

FAL.   Ha! a bastard son of the king's? And art not thou Poins his
       brother?
PRINCE.   Why, thou globe of sinful continents, what a life dost thou
       lead!
FAL.   A better than thou: I am a gentleman; thou art a drawer.
PRINCE.   Very true, sir; and I come to draw you out by the ears.
HOST.   O, the Lord preserve thy good grace! by my troth, welcome to
       London. Now, the Lord bless that sweet face of thine! O Jesu, are
       you come from Wales?
FAL.   Thou whoreson mad compound of majesty, by this light flesh
       and corrupt blood, thou art welcome.
DOL.   How, you fat fool! I scorn you.
POINS.   My lord, he will drive you out of your revenge and turn all to
       a merriment, if you take not the heat.[60]
PRINCE.   You whoreson candle-mine,[61] you, how vilely did you speak
       of me even now before this honest, virtuous, civil gentlewoman!
HOST.   God's blessing of your good heart! and so she is, by my troth.
FAL.   Didst thou hear me?
PRINCE.   Yea, and you knew me, as you did when you ran away by
       Gadshill: you knew I was at your back, and spoke it on purpose to
       try my patience.
FAL.   No, no, no; not so; I did not think thou wast within hearing.
PRINCE.   I shall drive you then to confess the wilful abuse; and then I
       know how to handle you.
FAL.   No abuse, Hal, o' mine honour; no abuse.
PRINCE.   Not to dispraise me,[62] and call me pantler and bread-chipper
       and I know not what?
FAL.   No abuse, Hal.
POINS.   No abuse?
FAL.   No abuse, Ned, i' the world; honest Ned, none. I dispraised him
       before the wicked, that the wicked might not fall in love with him;
       in which doing, I have done the part of a careful friend and a true
       subject, and thy father is to give me thanks for it. No abuse, Hal:
       none, Ned, none: no, faith, boys, none.
PRINCE.   See now, whether pure fear and entire cowardice doth not
       make thee wrong this virtuous gentlewoman to close with us.[63] Is
       she of the wicked? is thine hostess here of the wicked? or is thy boy

---

[60]*take . . . the heat*] strike while the iron's hot.
[61]*candle-mine*] mine or pit of tallow.
[62]*Not to dispraise me*] (Is it) not (abuse) to dispraise me?
[63]*to close with us*] in order to humour us, to rebut our charges.

of the wicked? or honest Bardolph, whose zeal burns in his nose,
of the wicked?

POINS.　Answer, thou dead elm,[64] answer.

FAL.　The fiend hath pricked down Bardolph irrecoverable; and his
face is Lucifer's privy-kitchen, where he doth nothing but roast
malt-worms. For the boy, there is a good angel about him; but the
devil outbids him too.

PRINCE.　For the women?

FAL.　For one of them, she is in hell already, and burns poor souls.[65]
For the other, I owe her money; and whether she be damned for
that, I know not.

HOST.　No, I warrant you.

FAL.　No, I think thou art not; I think thou art quit for that. Marry,
there is another indictment upon thee, for suffering flesh to be
eaten in thy house,[66] contrary to the law; for the which I think
thou wilt howl.

HOST.　All victuallers do so: what's a joint of mutton or two in a whole
Lent?

PRINCE.　You, gentlewoman,—

DOL.　What says your grace?

FAL.　His grace[67] says that which his flesh rebels against.

[Knocking within.

HOST.　Who knocks so loud at door? Look to the door there, Francis.

Enter PETO

PRINCE.　Peto, how now! what news?

PETO.　The king your father is at Westminster;
And there are twenty weak and wearied posts
Come from the north; and, as I came along,
I met and overtook a dozen captains,
Bare-headed, sweating, knocking at the taverns,
And asking every one for Sir John Falstaff.

PRINCE.　By heaven, Poins, I feel me much to blame,
So idly to profane the precious time;
When tempest of commotion, like the south[68]

---

[64]*dead elm*] The allusion is to the poor support Falstaff gives Doll Tearsheet, who is im-
plicitly likened to a vine.

[65]*burns poor souls*] gives the burning fever of (venereal) disease to poor souls.

[66]*suffering flesh . . . house*] The law forbade victuallers to sell flesh during Lent.

[67]*His grace*] A pun on the word in its theological meaning of spiritual grace; *i.e.*, the spiritual state essential to the soul's salvation.

[68]*the south*] the south wind, which, according to Shakespeare, invariably denoted rain
and tempest.

Borne with[69] black vapour, doth begin to melt,
And drop upon our bare unarmed heads.
Give me my sword and cloak. Falstaff, good night.
              [*Exeunt* PRINCE HENRY, POINS, PETO, *and* BARDOLPH.

FAL.   Now comes in the sweetest morsel of the night, and we must
hence, and leave it unpicked. [*Knocking within.*] More knocking
at the door!

Re-enter BARDOLPH

How now! what's the matter?

BARD.   You must away to court, sir, presently;
A dozen captains stay at door for you.

FAL.   [*To the* Page] Pay the musicians, sirrah. Farewell, hostess;
farewell, Doll. You see, my good wenches, how men of merit are
sought after: the undeserver may sleep, when the man of action is
called on. Farewell, good wenches: if I be not sent away post, I will
see you again ere I go.

DOL.   I cannot speak; if my heart be not ready to burst,—well, sweet
Jack, have a care of thyself.

FAL.   Farewell, farewell.   [*Exeunt* FALSTAFF *and* BARDOLPH.

HOST.   Well, fare thee well: I have known thee these twenty-nine
years, come peascod-time; but an honester and truer-hearted
man,—well, fare thee well.

BARD.   [*Within*] Mistress Tearsheet!

HOST.   What's the matter?

BARD.   [*Within*] Bid Mistress Tearsheet come to my master.

HOST.   O, run, Doll, run; run, good Doll: come. [*She comes blub-
bered.*] Yea, will you come, Doll?   [*Exeunt.*

---

[69]*Borne with*] Burdened with.

ACT III.

Scene I.   *Westminster. The Palace*

Enter the KING *in his nightgown, with a* Page[1]

KING.   Go call the Earls of Surrey and of Warwick;
    But, ere they come, bid them o'er-read these letters,
    And well consider of them: make goodspeed.   [*Exit* Page.
    How many thousand of my poorest subjects
    Are at this hour asleep! O sleep, O gentle sleep,
    Nature's soft nurse, how have I frighted thee,
    That thou no more wilt weigh my eyelids down,
    And steep my senses in forgetfulness?
    Why rather, sleep, liest thou in smoky cribs,[2]
    Upon uneasy pallets stretching thee,
    And hush'd with buzzing night-flies to thy slumber,
    Than in the perfumed chambers of the great,
    Under the canopies of costly state,
    And lull'd with sound of sweetest melody?
    O thou dull god, why liest thou with the vile
    In loathsome beds, and leavest the kingly couch
    A watch-case or a common 'larum-bell?[3]
    Wilt thou upon the high and giddy mast
    Seal up the ship-boy's eyes, and rock his brains
    In cradle of the rude imperious surge,
    And in the visitation of the winds,
    Who take the ruffian billows by the top,
    Curling their monstrous heads, and hanging them

---

[1]Act III, Scene I.   The whole of this scene is omitted from most copies of the Quarto;
but it is found in a few, on two inserted leaves.
[2]*cribs*] hovels.
[3]*and leavest . . . 'larum bell?*] The kingly couch becomes in the absence of sleep the post
of a watchful sentry, or a bell ready to give the alarm in case of danger. "Watch-case" is
a watchman's box, a sentry box.

With deafening clamour in the slippery clouds,[4]
That, with the hurly,[5] death itself awakes?
Canst thou, O partial sleep, give thy repose
To the wet sea-boy in an hour so rude;
And in the calmest and most stillest night,
With all appliances and means to boot,
Deny it to a king? Then happy low, lie down![6]
Uneasy lies the head that wears a crown.

Enter WARWICK *and* SURREY

WAR.   Many good morrows to your majesty!
KING.   Is it good morrow, lords?
WAR.   'T is one o'clock, and past.
KING.   Why, then, good morrow to you all, my lords.
    Have you read o'er the letters that I sent you?
WAR.   We have, my liege.
KING.   Then you perceive the body of our kingdom
    How foul it is; what rank diseases grow,
    And with what danger, near the heart of it.
WAR.   It is but as a body yet distemper'd;[7]
    Which to his former strength may be restored
    With good advice and little medicine:
    My Lord Northumberland will soon be cool'd.
KING.   O God! that one might read the book of fate,
    And see the revolution of the times
    Make mountains level, and the continent,
    Weary of solid firmness, melt itself
    Into the sea! and, other times, to see
    The beachy girdle of the ocean
    Too wide for Neptune's hips; how chances mock,
    And changes fill the cup of alteration
    With divers liquors! O, if this were seen,
    The happiest youth, viewing his progress through,
    What perils past, what crosses to ensue,[8]
    Would shut the book, and sit him down and die.
    'T is not ten years gone

---

[4]*slippery clouds*] The clouds give the waves no griphold.
[5]*hurly*] uproar.
[6]*happy low, lie down*] The meaning is "ye who are happy in your humble lots, sleep in peace."
[7]*distemper'd*] out of condition.
[8]*What perils past . . . ensue*] Surveying the perils, however great, through which he has passed, and foreseeing the amount of crosses that are likely to follow.

Since Richard and Northumberland, great friends,
Did feast together, and in two years after
Were they at wars: it is but eight years since[9]
This Percy was the man nearest my soul;
Who like a brother toil'd in my affairs,
And laid his love and life under my foot;
Yea, for my sake, even to the eyes of Richard
Gave him defiance. But which of you was by—
You, cousin Nevil,[10] as I may remember—   [To WARWICK.
When Richard, with his eye brimful of tears,
Then check'd and rated by Northumberland,
Did speak these words, now proved a prophecy?
"Northumberland, thou ladder by the which
My cousin Bolingbroke ascends my throne;"
Though then, God knows, I had no such intent,[11]
But that necessity so bow'd the state,
That I and greatness were compell'd to kiss:
"The time shall come," thus did he follow it,
"The time will come, that foul sin, gathering head,
Shall break into corruption:" so went on,
Foretelling this same time's condition,
And the division of our amity.
WAR.   There is a history in all men's lives,
Figuring the nature of the times deceased;
The which observed, a man may prophesy,
With a near aim, of the main chance of things
As yet not come to life, which in their seeds
And weak beginnings lie intreasured.[12]
Such things become the hatch and brood[13] of time;

---

[9]*eight years since*] The period referred to must be sometime in 1399. Hence this scene
would take place in 1407. But the report of Glendower's death is dated by Holinshed
in 1409.

[10]*cousin Nevil*] There is confusion here. The king is addressing Richard Beauchamp,
Earl of Warwick. No member of the Neville family at the time bore that title. The contemporary head of the Neville family was Ralph Neville, Earl of Westmoreland, who
figures in this play along with Richard Beauchamp, Earl of Warwick. It was the Earl
of Westmoreland's grandson, Richard Neville, the "kingmaker," who was the first Earl
of Warwick of the Neville family.

[11]*I had no such intent*] I should have had no such intent. As a matter of fact, Bolingbroke
had already ascended the throne before this interview of Northumberland with King
Richard.

[12]*intreasured*] stored up.

[13]*hatch and brood*] offspring and progeny.

And by the necessary form of this[14]
King Richard might create a perfect guess
That great Northumberland, then false to him,
Would of that seed grow to a greater falseness;
Which should not find a ground to root upon,
Unless on you.

KING.   Are these things then necessities?
Then let us meet them like necessities:
And that same word even now cries out on us:
They say the bishop and Northumberland
Are fifty thousand strong.

WAR.   It cannot be, my lord;
Rumour doth double, like the voice and echo,
The numbers of the fear'd. Please it your grace
To go to bed. Upon my soul, my lord,
The powers that you already have sent forth
Shall bring this prize in very easily.
To comfort you the more, I have received
A certain instance[15] that Glendower is dead.
Your majesty hath been this fortnight ill;
And these unseason'd[16] hours perforce must add
Unto your sickness.

KING.   I will take your counsel:
And were these inward wars once out of hand,
We would, dear lords, unto the Holy Land.   [*Exeunt.*

Scene II.   *Gloucestershire. Before Justice Shallow's House*

Enter SHALLOW *and* SILENCE, *meeting*; MOULDY, SHADOW, WART,
FEEBLE, BULLCALF, *a* Servant *or two with them*

SHAL.   Come on, come on, come on, sir; give me your hand, sir, give
me your hand, sir: an early stirrer, by the rood![1] And how doth my
good cousin Silence?

SIL.   Good morrow, good cousin Shallow.

SHAL.   And how doth my cousin, your bedfellow? and your fairest
daughter and mine, my god-daughter Ellen?

---

[14]*necessary form of this*] inevitable course of this.
[15]*instance*] proof.
[16]*unseason'd*] unseasonable.

---

[1]*by the rood*] by the holy cross.

SIL.   Alas, a black ousel,[2] cousin Shallow!

SHAL.   By yea and nay,[3] sir, I dare say my cousin William is become a
     good scholar: he is at Oxford still, is he not?

SIL.   Indeed, sir, to my cost.

SHAL.   A' must, then, to the inns o' court shortly: I was once of
     Clement's Inn, where I think they will talk of mad Shallow yet.

SIL.   You were called "lusty Shallow" then, cousin.

SHAL.   By the mass, I was called any thing; and I would have done any
     thing indeed too, and roundly[4] too. There was I, and little John
     Doit of Staffordshire, and black George Barnes, and Francis
     Pickbone, and Will Squele, a Cotswold[5] man; you had not four
     such swingebucklers[6] in all the inns o' court again: and I may say
     to you, we knew where the bona-robas[7] were, and had the best of
     them all at commandment. Then was Jack Falstaff, now Sir John,
     a boy, and page to Thomas Mowbray, Duke of Norfolk.[8]

SIL.   This Sir John, cousin, that comes hither anon about soldiers?

SHAL.   The same Sir John, the very same. I see him break Skogan's[9]
     head at the court-gate, when a' was a crack[10] not thus high: and
     the very same day did I fight with one Sampson Stockfish, a
     fruiterer, behind Gray's Inn. Jesu, Jesu, the mad days that I have
     spent! and to see how many of my old acquaintance are dead!

SIL.   We shall all follow, cousin.

SHAL.   Certain, 't is certain; very sure, very sure: death, as the Psalmist
     saith, is certain to all; all shall die. How[11] a good yoke of bullocks
     at Stamford fair?

SIL.   By my troth, I was not there.

SHAL.   Death is certain. Is old Double of your town living yet?

SIL.   Dead, sir.

SHAL.   Jesu, Jesu, dead! a' drew a good bow; and dead! a' shot a fine
     shoot: John a Gaunt loved him well, and betted much money on

---

[2]*ousel*] blackbird. The speaker civilly deprecates praise of his daughter.

[3]*By yea and nay*] Without question.

[4]*roundly*] bluntly, unceremoniously.

[5]*Cotswold*] Shakespeare shows familiarity with the district of the Cotswold hills, where
     wrestling, coursing, and other sports and athletic exercises were especially practised.

[6]*swingebucklers*] swashbucklers, roisterers.

[7]*bona-robas*] courtesans.

[8]*Falstaff . . . Norfolk*] This was true of Sir John Oldcastle, whose name the character of
     Falstaff bore in Shakespeare's first draft.

[9]*Skogan*] probably an anachronistic reference to John Scogan, Edward IV's fool, of
     whose exploits many traditions survived to Shakespeare's day.

[10]*a crack*] a pert boy.

[11]*How*] How much, what is the price of?

his head. Dead! a would have clapped i' the clout[12] at twelve score; and carried you a forehand shaft[13] a fourteen and fourteen and a half,[14] that it would have done a man's heart good to see. How a score of ewes now?

SIL.   Thereafter as they be:[15] a score of good ewes may be worth ten pounds.

SHAL.   And is old Double dead?

SIL.   Here come two of Sir John Falstaff's men, as I think.

Enter BARDOLPH, *and one with him*

BARD.   Good morrow, honest gentlemen: I beseech you, which is Justice Shallow?

SHAL.   I am Robert Shallow, sir; a poor esquire of this county, and one of the king's justices of the peace: what is your good pleasure with me?

BARD.   My captain, sir, commends him to you; my captain, Sir John Falstaff, a tall[16] gentleman, by heaven, and a most gallant leader.

SHAL.   He greets me well, sir. I knew him a good back-sword[17] man. How doth the good knight? may I ask how my lady his wife doth?

BARD.   Sir, pardon; a soldier is better accommodated[18] than with a wife.

SHAL.   It is well said, in faith, sir; and it is well said indeed too. Better accommodated! it is good; yea, indeed, is it: good phrases are surely, and ever were, very commendable. Accommodated! it comes of "accommodo:" very good; a good phrase.

BARD.   Pardon me, sir; I have heard the word. Phrase call you it? by this good day, I know not the phrase;[19] but I will maintain the word with my sword to be a soldier-like word, and a word of exceeding good command,[20] by heaven. Accommodated; that is, when a man is, as they say, accommodated; or when a man is, being, whereby a' may be thought to be accommodated; which is an excellent thing.

SHAL.   It is very just.

Enter FALSTAFF

---

[12]*clapped i' the clout*] landed in the bull's-eye of the target at a distance of twelve-score yards.

[13]*forehand shaft*] The heavier class of arrow, especially used for long-distance aim.

[14]*a fourteen and fourteen and a half*] fourteen or even fourteen and a half score of yards.

[15]*Thereafter as they be*] That depends on their condition.

[16]*tall*] fine, valiant.

[17]*back-sword*] single-stick.

[18]*accommodated*] furnished, equipped. The word was regarded as somewhat affected.

[19]*I know not the phrase*] I know not the term "phrase."

[20]*of exceeding good command*] of first-rate authority.

Look, here comes good Sir John. Give me your good hand, give me your worship's good hand: by my troth, you like well[21] and bear your years very well: welcome, good Sir John.

FAL.   I am glad to see you well, good Master Robert Shallow: Master Surecard,[22] as I think?

SHAL.   No, Sir John; it is my cousin Silence, in commission with me.

FAL.   Good Master Silence, it well befits you should be of the peace.

SIL.   Your good worship is welcome.

FAL.   Fie! this is hot weather, gentlemen. Have you provided me here half a dozen sufficient men?

SHAL.   Marry, have we, sir. Will you sit?

FAL.   Let me see them, I beseech you.

SHAL.   Where 's the roll? where 's the roll? where 's the roll? Let me see, let me see, let me see. So, so, so, so, so, so, so: yea, marry, sir: Ralph Mouldy! Let them appear as I call; let them do so, let them do so. Let me see; where is Mouldy?

MOUL.   Here, an 't please you.

SHAL.   What think you, Sir John? a good-limbed fellow; young, strong, and of good friends.[23]

FAL.   Is thy name Mouldy?

MOUL.   Yea, an 't please you.

FAL.   'T is the more time thou wert used.

SHAL.   Ha, ha, ha! most excellent, i' faith! things that are mouldy lack use: very singular good! in faith, well said, Sir John; very well said.

FAL.   Prick him.[24]

MOUL.   I was pricked well enough before, an you could have let me alone: my old dame will be undone now, for one to do her husbandry and her drudgery: you need not to have pricked me; there are other men fitter to go out than I.

FAL.   Go to: peace, Mouldy; you shall go. Mouldy, it is time you were spent.

MOUL.   Spent!

SHAL.   Peace, fellow, peace; stand aside: know you where you are? For the other, Sir John: let me see: Simon Shadow!

FAL.   Yea, marry, let me have him to sit under: he's like to be a cold soldier.

SHAL.   Where's Shadow?

SHAD.   Here, sir.

[21]*you like well*] you are in good condition. "Liking" is frequently found in the sense of "good health."

[22]*Master Surecard*] a colloquial term for a boon companion.

[23]*of good friends*] of a sound stock.

[24]*Prick him*] Mark him, by pricking a hole in the paper against the name.

Fal. Shadow, whose son art thou?

Shad. My mother's son, sir.

Fal. Thy mother's son! like enough, and thy father's shadow: so the son of the female is the shadow of the male: it is often so, indeed; but much of the father's substance!

Shal. Do you like him, Sir John?

Fal. Shadow will serve for summer; prick him, for we have a number of shadows[25] to fill up the musterbook.

Shal. Thomas Wart!

Fal. Where's he?

Wart. Here, sir.

Fal. Is thy name Wart?

Wart. Yea, sir.

Fal. Thou art a very ragged wart.

Shal. Shall I prick him down, Sir John?

Fal. It were superfluous; for his apparel is built upon his back, and the whole frame stands upon pins: prick him no more.

Shal. Ha, ha, ha! you can do it, sir; you can do it: I commend you well. Francis Feeble!

Fee. Here, sir.

Shal. What trade art thou, Feeble?

Fee. A woman's tailor, sir.

Shal. Shall I prick him, sir?

Fal. You may: but if he had been a man's tailor, he 'ld ha' pricked you. Wilt thou make as many holes in an enemy's battle[26] as thou hast done in a woman's petticoat?

Fee. I will do my good will, sir: you can have no more.

Fal. Well said, good woman's tailor! well said, courageous Feeble! thou wilt be as valiant as the wrathful dove or most magnanimous[27] mouse. Prick the woman's tailor: well, Master Shallow; deep, Master Shallow.

Fee. I would Wart might have gone, sir.

Fal. I would thou wert a man's tailor, that thou mightst mend him and make him fit to go. I cannot put him to[28] a private soldier, that is the leader of so many thousands: let that suffice, most forcible Feeble.

Fee. It shall suffice, sir.

Fal. I am bound to thee, reverend Feeble. Who is next?

Shal. Peter Bullcalf o' the green!

---

[25]*a number of shadows*] mere names, fictitious entries.

[26]*battle*] battalion, army.

[27]*magnanimous*] great-souled, heroic.

[28]*put him to*] make of him, turn him into.

FAL.   Yea, marry, let's see Bullcalf.

BULL.   Here, sir.

FAL.   'Fore God, a likely fellow! Come, prick me Bullcalf till he roar
again.

BULL.   O Lord! good my lord captain,—

FAL.   What, dost thou roar before thou art pricked?

BULL.   O Lord, sir! I am a diseased man.

FAL.   What disease hast thou?

BULL.   A whoresome cold, sir, a cough, sir, which I caught with ring-
ing in the king's affairs upon his coronation-day, sir.

FAL.   Come, thou shalt go to the wars in a gown; we will have away
thy cold; and I will take such order[29] that thy friends shall ring for
thee.[30] Is here all?

SHAL.   Here is two more called than your number; you must have but
four here,[31] sir: and so, I pray you, go in with me to dinner.

FAL.   Come, I will go drink with you, but I cannot tarry dinner. I am
glad to see you, by my troth, Master Shallow.

SHAL.   O, Sir John, do you remember since we lay all night in the
windmill in Saint George's field?[32]

FAL.   No more of that, good Master Shallow, no more of that.

SHAL.   Ha! 't was a merry night. And is Jane Nightwork alive?

FAL.   She lives, Master Shallow.

SHAL.   She never could away with[33] me.

FAL.   Never, never; she would always say she could not abide Master
Shallow.

SHAL.   By the mass, I could anger her to the heart. She was then a
bona-roba. Doth she hold her own well?

FAL.   Old, old, Master Shallow.

SHAL.   Nay, she must be old; she cannot choose but be old; certain
she's old; and had Robin Nightwork by old Nightwork before I
came to Clement's Inn.

SIL.   That 's fifty five year ago.

SHAL.   Ha, cousin Silence, that thou hadst seen that that this knight
and I have seen! Ha, Sir John, said I well?

FAL.   We have heard the chimes at midnight, Master Shallow.

---

[29]*order*] measures.

[30]*ring for thee*] toll thy funeral bell.

[31]*Here is two . . . four here*] An apparent oversight on Shakespeare's part. Five recruits
have been named, and if Falstaff only required four, Shallow was in error in saying that
he had summoned *two more* than were needed.

[32]*Saint George's field*] This place—in Southwark—was best known as the muster ground
of the London soldiery.

[33]*away with*] endure.

SHAL.   That we have, that we have, that we have; in faith, Sir John, we
have: our watch-word was "Hem boys!"[34] Come, let's to dinner;
come, let's to dinner: Jesus, the days that we have seen! Come,
come.   [*Exeunt* FALSTAFF *and the* Justices.

BULL.   Good master corporate[35] Bardolph, stand my friend; and here's
four Harry ten shillings[36] in French crowns for you. In very truth,
sir, I had as lief be hanged, sir, as go: and yet, for mine own part,
sir, I do not care; but rather, because I am unwilling, and, for
mine own part, have a desire to stay with my friends; else, sir, I did
not care, for mine own part, so much.

BARD.   Go to; stand aside.

MOUL.   And, good master corporal captain, for my old dame's sake,
stand my friend: she has nobody to do any thing about her when
I am gone; and she is old, and cannot help herself: you shall have
forty,[37] sir.

BARD.   Go to; stand aside.

FEE.   By my troth, I care not; a man can die but once: we owe God a
death: I 'll ne'er bear a base mind: an 't be my destiny, so; an 't be
not, so: no man 's too good to serve 's prince; and let it go which
way it will, he that dies this year is quit for the next.

BARD.   Well said; thou 'rt a good fellow.

FEE.   Faith, I 'll bear no base mind.

Re-enter FALSTAFF *and the* Justices

FAL.   Come, sir, which men shall I have?

SHAL.   Four of which you please.

BARD.   Sir, a word with you: I have three pound[38] to free Mouldy and
Bullcalf.

FAL.   Go to; well.

SHAL.   Come, Sir John, which four will you have?

FAL.   Do you choose for me.

SHAL.   Marry, then, Mouldy, Bullcalf, Feeble and Shadow.

FAL.   Mouldy and Bullcalf: for you, Mouldy, stay at home till you are
past service: and for your part, Bullcalf, grow till you come unto it:
I will none of you.

---

[34]"*Hem boys!*"] Mum's the word.

[35]*corporate*] a blunder for "corporal."

[36]*Harry ten shillings*] An anachronism. Ten shilling pieces were first coined by Henry
VII, and were continued by Henry VIII. Hence their epithet of "Harry." No such coins
were in existence in Henry IV's time.

[37]*forty*] shillings.

[38]*three pound*] Bardolph had actually received four pounds; he was concealing the full
amount from Falstaff.

SHAL.   Sir John, Sir John, do not yourself wrong: they are your likeli-
est men, and I would have you served with the best.

FAL.   Will you tell me, Master Shallow, how to choose a man? Care I
for the limb, the thewes, the stature, bulk, and big assemblance[39]
of a man! Give me the spirit, Master Shallow. Here 's Wart; you
see what a ragged appearance it is: a' shall charge you and discharge you[40] with the motion of a pewterer's hammer, come off
and on swifter than he that gibbets on the brewer's bucket.[41] And
this same half-faced[42] fellow, Shadow; give me this man: he pre-
sents no mark to the enemy; the foeman may with as great aim
level at the edge of a penknife. And for a retreat; how swiftly will
this Feeble the woman's tailor run off! O, give me the spare men,
and spare me the great ones. Put me a caliver[43] into Wart's hand,
Bardolph.

BARD.   Hold, Wart, traverse;[44] thus, thus, thus.

FAL.   Come, manage me your caliver. So: very well: go to: very good,
exceeding good. O, give me always a little, lean, old, chapt,[45] bald
shot.[46] Well said, i' faith, Wart; thou 'rt a good scab:[47] hold, there's
a tester[48] for thee.

SHAL.   He is not his craft's-master; he doth not do it right. I remember
at Mile-end Green,[49] when I lay[50] at Clement's Inn,—I was then
Sir Dagonet in Arthur's show,[51]—there was a little quiver[52] fellow,
and a' would manage you his piece thus; and a' would about and

---

[39]*big assemblance*] "large make."

[40]*charge you and discharge you*] advance and retire.

[41]*he that gibbets on . . . bucket*] he that hangs (barrels) on the yoke of the brewers' men.
"Gibbets" means "hangs"; "bucket" is found in the sense of "beam" or "yoke," on
which a barrel may be hung and carried. The reference is to the practice of hauling
about barrels of beer by attaching them to chains depending from a beam borne on
the shoulders of the brewers' men. The attribution of swiftness to this method of
haulage is ironical.

[42]*half-faced*] wizened, a face in profile, like that stamped on a coin.

[43]*caliver*] light musket.

[44]*traverse*] march; a military term.

[45]*chapt*] The original reading is *chopt*. "Chopt" is often found in the sense of wrinkled.

[46]*shot*] shooter, marksman.

[47]*scab*] a disagreeable pun on Wart's name.

[48]*tester*] sixpence.

[49]*Mile-end Green*] a parade ground for the citizen soldiery of London.

[50]*lay*] resided.

[51]*Sir Dagonet in Arthur's show*] a reference to an Elizabethan archery society, which
bore the fantastic title of "The Fellowship of Prince Arthur's Knights." Each member
assumed the name of a personage of Arthurian romance. Sir Dagonet figures in some
of the Arthurian stories as a fool at King Arthur's court.

[52]*quiver*] quick, nimble.

about, and come you in and come you in: "rah, tah, tah," would
a' say; "bounce"[53] would a' say; and away again would a' go, and
again would a' come: I shall ne'er see such a fellow.

FAL. These fellows will do well, Master Shallow. God keep you,
Master Silence: I will not use many words with you. Fare you well,
gentlemen both: I thank you: I must a dozen mile to-night.
Bardolph, give the soldiers coats.

SHAL. Sir John, the Lord bless you! God prosper your affairs! God
send us peace! At your return visit our house; let our old acquaintance be renewed: per-adventure I will with ye to the court.

FAL. 'Fore God, I would you would, Master Shallow.

SHAL. Go to; I have spoke at a word.[54] God keep you.

FAL. Fare you well, gentle gentlemen. [*Exeunt* Justices.] On,
Bardolph; lead the men away. [*Exeunt* BARDOLPH, Recruits, &c.]
As I return, I will fetch off[55] these justices: I do see the bottom of
Justice Shallow. Lord, Lord, how subject we old men are to this
vice of lying! This same starved justice hath done nothing but
prate to me of the wildness of his youth, and the feats he hath
done about Turnbull Street;[56] and every third word a lie, duer
paid to the hearer than the Turk's tribute. I do remember him at
Clement's Inn like a man made after supper of a cheese-paring:
when a' was naked, he was, for all the world, like a forked radish,
with a head fantastically carved upon it with a knife: a' was so for-
lorn, that his dimensions to any thick sight were invisible: a' was
the very genius of famine; yet lecherous as a monkey, and the
whores called him mandrake:[57] a' came ever in the rearward of[58]
the fashion, and sung those tunes to the overscutched huswives[59]
that he heard the carmen whistle, and sware they were his fancies
or his good-nights.[60] And now is this Vice's dagger[61] become a
squire, and talks as familiarly of John a Gaunt as if he had been
sworn brother to him; and I'll be sworn a' ne'er saw him but once

---

[53]*bounce*] bang.

[54]*at a word*] for talking's sake. Shallow has no intention of going to court. The expression usually means "in a word," or "to come to the point."

[55]*fetch off*] get level with, get a rise out of.

[56]*Turnbull Street*] Turnmill Street, near Clerkenwell, the haunt of bad characters.

[57]*mandrake*] a plant, of which the root was deemed to resemble the lower part of the
human anatomy.

[58]*in the rearward of*] behind.

[59]*overscutched huswives*] wornout strumpets.

[60]*fancies or good-nights*] Such titles were often bestowed on short lyrics.

[61]*this Vice's dagger*] The character called the Vice in the old moralities invariably carried about with him a thin "dagger of lath." The Vice was a farcical servant of the devil.

in the Tilt-yard;[62] and then he burst[63] his head for crowding among the marshal's men. I saw it, and told John a Gaunt he beat his own name;[64] for you might have thrust him and all his apparel into an eel-skin; the case of a treble hautboy[65] was a mansion for him, a court: and now has he land and beefs. Well, I 'll be acquainted with him, if I return; and it shall go hard but I will make him a philosopher's two stones[66] to me: if the young dace be a bait for the old pike, I see no reason in the law of nature but I may snap at him.[67] Let time shape, and there an end.   [*Exit.*

---

[62]*Tilt-yard*] The ground at Westminster where royal tournaments were held.

[63]*burst*] broke.

[64]*beat his own name*] belaboured a *gaunt* creature; Shakespeare's favourite pun on the name "gaunt."

[65]*a treble hautboy*] a flute-like instrument playing treble.

[66]*a philosopher's two stones*] a jocosely exaggerated and coarse reference to the alchemist's stone, which was assumed to be capable of transmuting base metals into gold.

[67]*if the young dace . . . snap at him*] Fishermen employed "dace," a very small fish, as bait for catching overgrown pike. Falstaff, rather confusing the metaphor, means that he will play the part of the decoy, and get Justice Shallow into difficulties.

ACT IV.

Scene I.   *Yorkshire. Gaultree Forest*

Enter the ARCHBISHOP OF YORK, MOWBRAY, HASTINGS, *and others*

ARCHBISHOP.   What is this forest call'd?
HAST.   'T is Gaultree Forest,[1] an 't shall please your grace.
ARCH.   Here stand, my lords; and send discoverers forth
 To know the numbers of our enemies.
HAST.   We have sent forth already.
ARCH.   'T is well done.
 My friends and brethren in these great affairs,
 I must acquaint you that I have received
 New-dated letters from Northumberland;
 Their cold intent, tenour and substance, thus:
 Here doth he wish his person, with such powers
 As might hold sortance with[2] his quality,
 The which he could not levy; whereupon
 He is retired, to ripe[3] his growing fortunes,
 To Scotland: and concludes in hearty prayers
 That your attempts may overlive the hazard
 And fearful meeting of their opposite.[4]
MOWB.   Thus do the hopes we have in him touch ground
 And dash themselves to pieces.

Enter a Messenger

HAST.   Now, what news?
MESS.   West of this forest, scarcely off a mile,

---

[1]*Gaultree Forest*] the great forest of Galtres, which once covered 100,000 acres to the
 north of the city of York.
[2]*hold sortance with*] sort with, suit.
[3]*ripe*] ripen, mature.
[4]*their opposite*] the foe.

    In goodly form comes on the enemy;
    And, by the ground they hide, I judge their number
    Upon or near the rate of thirty thousand.
MOWB.   The just proportion that we gave them out.[5]
    Let us sway on[6] and face them in the field.
ARCH.   What well-appointed leader fronts us here?

Enter WESTMORELAND

MOWB.   I think it is my Lord of Westmoreland.
WEST.   Health and fair greeting from our general,
    The prince, Lord John and Duke of Lancaster.
ARCH.   Say on, my Lord of Westmoreland, in peace:
    What doth concern your coming?
WEST.   Then, my lord,
    Unto your grace do I in chief address
    The substance on my speech. If that rebellion
    Came like itself, in base and abject routs,[7]
    Led on by bloody[8] youth, guarded with rags,[9]
    And countenanced by boys and beggary;
    I say, if damn'd commotion[10] so appear'd,
    In his true, native and most proper shape,
    You, reverend father, and these noble lords
    Had not been here, to dress the ugly form
    Of base and bloody insurrection
    With your fair honours. You, lord Archbishop,
    Whose see is by a civil[11] peace maintain'd,
    Whose beard the silver hand of peace hath touch'd,
    Whose learning and good letters peace hath tutor'd,
    Whose white investments[12] figure innocence,
    The dove and very blessed spirit of peace,
    Wherefore do you so ill translate yourself
    Out of the speech of peace that bears such grace,
    Into the harsh and boisterous tongue of war;

---

[5]*The just proportion . . . out*] The very number that we announced.
[6]*Let us sway on*] Let us sweep on or advance.
[7]*abject routs*] beggarly mobs.
[8]*bloody*] full blooded.
[9]*rags*] The original reading is *rage*: "guarded" means "trimmed," hence "dressed."
[10]*commotion*] insurrection.
[11]*civil*] well-ordered.
[12]*white investments*] white vestures; the ordinary episcopal dress.

Turning your books to graves,[13] your ink to blood,
Your pens to lances, and your tongue divine
To a loud trumpet and a point[14] of war?
ARCH.   Wherefore do I this? so the question stands.
Briefly to this end: we are all diseased,
And with our surfeiting and wanton hours
Have brought ourselves into a burning fever,
And we must bleed for it; of which disease
Our late king, Richard, being infected, died.
But, my most noble Lord of Westmoreland,
I take not on me here as a physician,
Nor do I as an enemy to peace
Troop in the throngs of military men;
But rather show a while like fearful war,
To diet rank minds[15] sick of happiness,
And purge the obstructions which begin to stop
Our very veins of life. Hear me more plainly.
I have in equal balance justly weigh'd
What wrongs our arms may do, what wrongs we suffer,
And find our griefs[16] heavier than our offences.
We see which way the stream of time doth run,
And are enforced from our most quiet there[17]
By the rough torrent of occasion;
And have the summary of all our griefs,
When time shall serve, to show in articles;
Which long ere this we offer'd to the king,
And might by no suit gain our audience:
When we are wrong'd and would unfold our griefs,
We are denied access unto his person
Even by those men that most have done us wrong.
The dangers of the days but newly gone,
Whose memory is written on the earth
With yet appearing blood, and the examples

---

[13]*Turning your books to graves*] Thus the original reading, which makes harsh sense. Modern editors change the word *graves* to *greaves*, *i.e.*, leg armour, which was often of leather, like the binding of books. If *graves* be retained, the phrase may be explained as meaning that books are converted into the paraphernalia of death.

[14]*point*] signal.

[15]*To diet rank minds*] So as to put on a medicinal regimen, or prescribe for minds that are overgorged with happiness.

[16]*griefs*] grievances.

[17]*our most quiet there*] our greatest quietness in the stream of time.

      Of every minute's instance,[18] present now,
      Hath put us in these ill-beseeming arms,
      Not to break peace or any branch of it,
      But to establish here a peace indeed,
      Concurring both in name and quality.
WEST.   When ever yet was your appeal denied?
      Wherein have you been galled by the king?
      What peer hath been suborn'd to grate on you,[19]
      That you should seal this lawless bloody book
      Of forged rebellion with a seal divine,
      And consecrate commotion's bitter edge?[20]
ARCH.   My brother general, the commonwealth,
      To brother born an household cruelty,
      I make my quarrel in particular.[21]
WEST.   There is no need of any such redress;
      Or if there were, it not belongs to you.[22]
MOWB.   Why not to him in part, and to us all
      That feel the bruises of the days before,
      And suffer the condition of these times
      To lay a heavy and unequal hand
      Upon our honours?
WEST.   O, my good Lord Mowbray,
      Construe the times to their necessities,[23]
      And you shall say indeed, it is the time,
      And not the king, that doth you injuries.
      Yet for your part, it not appears to me
      Either from the king or in the present time[24]
      That you should have an inch of any ground
      To build a grief[25] on: were you not restored

---

[18]*examples . . . instance*] examples which every minute presses on our notice.
[19]*suborn'd to grate on you*] bribed to harass you.
[20]*commotion's bitter edge*] the cruel sword of insurrection.
[21]*My brother . . . particular*] This passage seems corrupt. Some words have probably been accidentally dropped by the printer. The archbishop seems to mean that the injured commonwealth is his brother in a general sense, while the death of his own born brother, Lord Scrope, who had been executed by King Henry, was a cruel wrong to his family, and both public and private grounds (but private grounds in particular) impel him to take up arms.
[22]*There is no need . . . belongs to you*] The archbishop is not called upon to redress the wrongs either of the commonwealth or of his own brother.
[23]*to their necessities*] according to the exigencies of affairs.
[24]*Either from the king . . . time*] Whether the defects of the government are to be imputed to the king or to pressure of circumstance.
[25]*a grief*] a grievance.

To all the Duke of Norfolk's signories,
Your noble and right well remember'd father's?
MOWB.   What thing, in honour, had my father lost,
That need to be revived and breathed in me?[26]
The king that loved him, as the state stood then,
Was force perforce[27] compell'd to banish him:
And then that Henry Bolingbroke and he,
Being mounted and both roused in their seats,
Their neighing coursers daring of the spur,
Their armed staves in charge, their beavers down,[28]
Their eyes of fire sparkling through sights of steel[29]
And the loud trumpet blowing them together,
Then, then, when there was nothing could have stay'd
My father from the breast of Bolingbroke,
O, when the king did throw his warder[30] down,
His own life hung upon the staff he threw;
Then threw he down himself and all their lives
That by indictment and by dint of sword
Have since miscarried[31] under Bolingbroke.
WEST.   You speak, Lord Mowbray, now you know not what.
The Earl of Hereford[32] was reputed then
In England the most valiant gentleman:
Who knows on whom fortune would then have smiled?
But if your father had been victor there,
He ne'er had borne it out of Coventry:[33]
For all the country in a general voice
Cried hate upon him; and all their prayers and love
Were set on Hereford, whom they doted on
And bless'd and graced indeed, more than the king.
But this is mere digression from my purpose.
Here come I from our princely general
To know your griefs; to tell you from his grace
That he will give you audience; and wherein
It shall appear that your demands are just,

---

[26]*breathed in me*] invested with new breath or life in me.
[27]*force perforce*] of absolute necessity.
[28]*Their armed staves . . . down*] Their lances ready for the charge, the front pieces of their helmets let down.
[29]*sights of steel*] the perforated eyeholes of their helmets.
[30]*warder*] staff.
[31]*miscarried*] been ruined, perished.
[32]*The Earl of Hereford*] Bolingbroke was really *Duke* of Hereford.
[33]*borne it out of Coventry*] ridden out of, escaped from, Coventry.

You shall enjoy them, every thing set off
That might so much as think you enemies.[34]

MOWB.   But he hath forced us to compel this offer;
And it proceeds from policy, not love.

WEST.   Mowbray, you overween[35] to take it so;
This offer comes from mercy, not from fear:
For, lo! within a ken[36] our army lies,
Upon mine honour, all too confident
To give admittance to a thought of fear.
Our battle is more full of names[37] than yours,
Our men more perfect in the use of arms,
Our armour all as strong, our cause the best;
Then reason will[38] our hearts should be as good:
Say you not then our offer is compell'd.

MOWB.   Well, by my will we shall admit no parley.

WEST.   That argues but the shame of your offence:
A rotten case abides no handling.

HAST.   Hath the Prince John a full commission,
In very ample virtue of his father,
To hear and absolutely to determine
Of what conditions we shall stand upon?

WEST.   That is intended in the general's name:[39]
I muse you make so slight a question.

ARCH.   Then take, my Lord of Westmoreland, this schedule,
For this contains our general grievances:
Each several article herein redress'd,
All members of our cause, both here and hence,
That are insinewed to[40] this action,
Acquitted by a true substantial form,[41]
And present execution of our wills
To us and to our purposes confined,[42]

---

[34]*every thing set off . . . enemies*] everything ignored or set aside that might so much as give cause to make you thought to be enemies.

[35]*you overween*] you are arrogant.

[36]*within a ken*] within sight.

[37]*Our battle . . . names*] Our army is richer in men of note.

[38]*reason will*] may reason direct, or determine that.

[39]*intended . . . name*] implied in his title of general.

[40]*insinewed to*] bound to, involved in.

[41]*Acquitted . . . form*] Accorded a pardon of legal validity.

[42]*to our purposes confined*] limited to, or defined by, our explicit demands. This is the original reading, which hardly seems to strengthen the archbishop's position. But no quite satisfactory change has been suggested.

We come within our awful banks[43] again,
And knit our powers to the arm of peace.
WEST.　This will I show the general. Please you, lords,
　　In sight of both our battles[44] we may meet;
　　And either end in peace, which God so frame!
　　Or to the place of difference[45] call the swords
　　Which must decide it.
ARCH.　　　　　　　My lord, we will do so.　　　[*Exit* WEST.
MOWB.　There is a thing within my bosom tells me
　　That no conditions of our peace can stand.
HAST.　Fear you not that: if we can make our peace
　　Upon such large terms and so absolute
　　As our conditions shall consist upon,[46]
　　Our peace shall stand as firm as rocky mountains.
MOWB.　Yea, but our valuation[47] shall be such
　　That every slight and false-derived cause,
　　Yea, every idle, nice and wanton reason[48]
　　Shall to the king taste of this action;
　　That, were our royal faiths martyrs in love,[49]
　　We shall be winnow'd with so rough a wind
　　That even our corn shall seem as light as chaff
　　And good from bad find no partition.[50]
ARCH.　No, no, my lord. Note this; the king is weary
　　Of dainty and such picking[51] grievances:
　　For he hath found to end one doubt by death
　　Revives two greater in the heirs of life,
　　And therefore will he wipe his tables clean,[52]
　　And keep no tell-tale to his memory
　　That may repeat and history his loss[53]
　　To new remembrance; for full well he knows
　　He cannot so precisely weed this land
　　As his misdoubts present occasion:

---

[43]*awful banks*] limits of due reverence.
[44]*battles*] armies.
[45]*place of difference*] point of disagreement.
[46]*consist upon*] consist of, or rest upon.
[47]*our valuation*] the esteem in which we are held.
[48]*nice and wanton reason*] trivial and frivolous affair.
[49]*were our royal . . . love*] did our fidelity to the king make us ready to die in our affection for his cause.
[50]*partition*] separation, mark of distinction.
[51]*dainty and such picking*] capricious and such paltry.
[52]*wipe his tables clean*] clean the slate; "tables" were tablets of slate or ivory.
[53]*history his loss*] record, chronicle his loss.

His foes are so enrooted with his friends
That, plucking to unfix an enemy,
He doth unfasten so and shake a friend.
So that this land, like an offensive wife
That hath enraged him on[54] to offer strokes,
As he is striking, holds his infant up,
And hangs resolved correction[55] in the arm
That was uprear'd to execution.

HAST.   Besides, the king hath wasted all his rods
On late offenders, that he now doth lack
The very instruments of chastisement:
So that his power, like to a fangless lion,
May offer, but not hold.[56]

ARCH.   'T is very true:
And therefore be assured, my good lord marshal,
If we do now make our atonement well,
Our peace will, like a broken limb united,
Grow stronger for the breaking.

MOWB.   Be it so.
Here is return'd my lord of Westmoreland.

Re-enter WESTMORELAND

WEST.   The prince is here at hand: pleaseth your lordship
To meet his grace just distance 'tween our armies.

MOWB.   Your grace of York, in God's name, then, set forward.

ARCH.   Before, and greet his grace: my lord, we come.   [Exeunt.

Scene II.   *Another Part of the Forest*

Enter, from one side, MOWBRAY, *attended; afterwards, the* ARCHBISHOP,
HASTINGS, *and others: from the other side,* PRINCE JOHN OF
LANCASTER, *and* WESTMORELAND; *Officers, and others with them*

LAN.   You are well encounter'd here, my cousin Mowbray:
Good day to you, gentle lord archbishop;
And so to you, Lord Hastings, and to all.
My Lord of York, it better show'd with you
When that your flock, assembled by the bell,

---

[54]*enraged him on*] driven him (*i.e.*, the husband) on by anger.

[55]*hangs resolved correction*] suspends, arrests his resolve to give correction. The purposed
  stroke is not delivered.

[56]*May offer . . . hold*] May offer to strike, but not persist in his purpose.

Encircled you to hear with reverence
Your exposition on the holy text,
Than now to see you here an iron man,[1]
Cheering a rout of rebels with your drum,
Turning the word to sword and life to death.
That man that sits within a monarch's heart,
And ripens in the sunshine of his favour,
Would he abuse the countenance of the king,
Alack, what mischiefs might he set abroach
In shadow of such greatness! With you, lord bishop,
It is even so. Who hath not heard it spoken
How deep you were within the books of God?
To us the speaker in his parliament;
To us the imagined voice of God himself;
The very opener and intelligencer[2]
Between the grace, the sanctities of heaven
And our dull workings. O, who shall believe
But you misuse the reverence of your place,
Employ the countenance and grace of heaven,
As a false favourite doth his prince's name,
In deeds dishonourable? You have ta'en up,[3]
Under the counterfeited zeal of God,
The subjects of his substitute, my father,
And both against the peace of heaven and him
Have here up-swarm'd them.[4]

ARCH.   Good my Lord of Lancaster,
I am not here against your father's peace;
But, as I told my Lord of Westmoreland,
The time misorder'd doth, in common sense,[5]
Crowd us and crush us to this monstrous form,
To hold our safety up. I sent your grace
The parcels and particulars of our grief,[6]
The which hath been with scorn shoved from the court,
Whereon this Hydra son of war is born;

---

[1]*an iron man*] a man in armour.
[2]*intelligencer*] go-between, conveyer of news.
[3]*ta'en up*] raised in arms.
[4]*up-swarm'd*] made them to swarm (like bees).
[5]*in common sense*] owing to the dictates of ordinary reason.
[6]*parcels . . . of our grief*] specific details of our grievance.

Whose dangerous eyes may well be charm'd asleep[7]
With grant of our most just and right desires,
And true obedience, of this madness cured,
Stoop tamely to the foot of majesty.

MOWB.   If not, we ready are to try our fortunes
To the last man.

HAST.   And though we here fall down,
We have supplies to second our attempt:
If they miscarry, theirs shall second them;
And so success of mischief[8] shall be born,
And heir from heir shall hold this quarrel up,
Whiles England shall have generation.

LAN.   You are too shallow, Hastings, much too shallow,
To sound the bottom of the after-times.

WEST.   Pleaseth your grace to answer them directly
How far forth you do like their articles.

LAN.   I like them all, and do allow[9] them well;
And swear here, by the honour of my blood,
My father's purposes have been mistook;
And some about him have too lavishly
Wrested his meaning and authority.
My lord, these griefs shall be with speed redress'd;
Upon my soul, they shall. If this may please you,
Discharge your powers[10] unto their several counties,
As we will ours: and here between the armies
Let's drink together friendly and embrace,
That all their eyes may bear those tokens home
Of our restored love and amity.

ARCH.   I take your princely word for these redresses.

LAN.   I give it you, and will maintain my word:
And thereupon I drink unto your grace.

HAST.   Go, captain, and deliver to the army
This news of peace: let them have pay, and part:
I know it will well please them. Hie thee, captain.   [*Exit* Officer.

ARCH.   To you, my noble Lord of Westmoreland.

---

[7]*Hydra son of war . . . charm'd asleep*] Hydra was the many-headed monster, challenged
by Hercules, which, when one of its heads was cut off, supplied its place by another.
The reference here to the creature's dangerous eyes seems due to a confusion of Hydra
with Argus, the hundred-eyed monster, who was "charmed asleep" by Mercury.
[8]*success of mischief*] a continuous succession of disasters.
[9]*allow*] approve.
[10]*Discharge your powers*] According to Holinshed, Westmoreland, not Prince John,
made this treacherous proposal.

WEST.   I pledge your grace; and, if you knew what pains
    I have bestow'd to breed this present peace,
    You would drink freely: but my love to ye
    Shall show itself more openly hereafter.
ARCH.   I do not doubt you.
WEST.   I am glad of it.
    Health to my lord and gentle cousin, Mowbray.
MOWB.   You wish me health in very happy season;
    For I am, on the sudden, something ill.
ARCH.   Against ill chances men are ever merry;
    But heaviness[11] foreruns the good event.
WEST.   Therefore be merry, coz; since sudden sorrow
    Serves to say[12] thus, "some good thing comes to-morrow."
ARCH.   Believe me, I am passing light in spirit.
MOWB.   So much the worse, if your own rule be true. [*Shouts within*.
LAN.   The word of peace is render'd: hark, how they shout!
MOWB.   This had been cheerful after victory.
ARCH.   A peace is of the nature of a conquest;
    For then both parties nobly are subdued,
    And neither party loser.
LAN.   Go, my lord,
    And let our army be discharged too.   [*Exit* WESTMORELAND.
    And, good my lord, so please you, let our trains
    March by us,[13] that we may peruse the men
    We should have coped withal.
ARCH.   Go, good Lord Hastings,
    And, ere they be dismiss'd, let them march by.   [*Exit* HASTINGS.
LAN.   I trust, lords, we shall lie to-night together.

Re-enter WESTMORELAND

    Now, cousin, wherefore stands our army still?
WEST.   The leaders, having charge from you to stand,
    Will not go off until they hear you speak.
LAN.   They know their duties.

Re-enter HASTINGS

HAST.   My lord, our army is dispersed already:
    Like youthful steers unyoked, they take their courses

---

[11]*heaviness*] sadness, anxiety.
[12]*Serves to say*] Has the effect of saying.
[13]*let our trains March by us*] This is the original reading. The meaning is, "Let the forces
    on each side march beside us."

      East, west, north, south; or, like a school broke up,
      Each hurries toward his home and sporting-place.
WEST.   Good tidings, my Lord Hastings; for the which
      I do arrest thee, traitor, of high treason:
      And you, lord archbishop, and you, Lord Mowbray,
      Of capital treason I attach[14] you both.
MOWB.   Is this proceeding just and honourable?
WEST.   Is your assembly so?
ARCH.   Will you thus break your faith?
LAN.   I pawn'd thee none:
      I promised you redress of these same grievances
      Whereof you did complain; which, my mine honour,
      I will perform with a most Christian care.
      But for you, rebels, look to taste the due
      Meet for rebellion and such acts as yours.
      Most shallowly did you these arms commence,
      Fondly brought here and foolishly sent hence.
      Strike up our drums, pursue the scatter'd stray:[15]
      God, and not we, hath safely fought to-day.
      Some guard these traitors to the block of death,
      Treason's true bed and yielder up of breath.   *[Exeunt.*

Scene III.   *Another Part of the Forest*

Alarum. Excursions. Enter FALSTAFF *and* COLEVILE, *meeting*

FAL.   What's your name, sir? of what condition are you, and of what
    place, I pray?
COLE.   I am a knight, sir; and my name is Colevile of the dale.
FAL.   Well, then, Colevile is your name, a knight is your degree, and
    your place the dale: Colevile shall be still your name, a traitor
    your degree, and the dungeon your place, a place deep enough;
    so shall you be still Colevile of the dale.
COLE.   Are not you Sir John Falstaff?
FAL.   As good a man as he, sir, whoe'er I am. Do ye yield, sir? or shall
    I sweat for you? If I do sweat, they are the drops of thy lovers, and
    they weep for thy death: therefore rouse up fear and trembling,
    and do observance[1] to my mercy.

---

[14]*attach*] arrest.
[15]*the scatter'd stray*] the rout, the dispersed force.

---

[1]*do observance*] make obeisance.

COLE. I think you are Sir John Falstaff, and in that thought yield me.

FAL. I have a whole school of tongues in this belly of mine, and not a tongue of them all speaks any other word but my name. An I had but a belly of any indifferency,[2] I were simply the most active fellow in Europe: my womb, my womb, my womb, undoes me. Here comes our general.

Enter PRINCE JOHN OF LANCASTER, WESTMORELAND, BLUNT, *and others*

LAN. The heat is past;[3] follow no further now:
Call in the powers, good cousin Westmoreland.
                        [*Exit* WESTMORELAND.
Now, Falstaff, where have you been all this while?
When every thing is ended, then you come:
These tardy tricks of yours will, on my life,
One time or other break some gallows' back.

FAL. I would be sorry, my lord, but it should be thus: I never knew yet but rebuke and check was the reward of valour. Do you think me a swallow, an arrow, or a bullet? have I, in my poor and old motion, the expedition of thought? I have speeded hither with the very extremest inch of possibility; I have foundered nine score and odd posts: and here, travel-tainted as I am, have, in my pure and immaculate valour, taken Sir John Colevile of the dale, a most furious knight and valorous enemy. But what of that? he saw me, and yielded; that I may justly say, with the hook-nosed fellow of Rome, "I came, saw, and overcame."

LAN. It was more of his courtesy than your deserving.

FAL. I know not: here he is, and here I yield him: and I beseech your grace, let it be booked with the rest of this day's deeds; or, by the Lord, I will have it in a particular ballad else, with mine own picture on the top on 't, Colevile kissing my foot: to the which course if I be enforced, if you do not all show like gilt two-pences to me, and I in the clear sky of fame o'ershine you as much as the full moon doth the cinders of the element,[4] which show like pins' heads to her, believe not the word of the noble: therefore let me have right, and let desert mount.

LAN. Thine's too heavy to mount.

FAL. Let it shine, then.

LAN. Thine's too thick to shine.

---

[2]*of any indifferency*] of any moderate size.
[3]*The heat is past*] The violence of resentment is over.
[4]*cinders of the element*] stars.

FAL.   Let it do something, my good lord, that may do me good, and
       call it what you will.
LAN.   Is thy name Colevile?
COLE. It is, my lord.
LAN.   A famous rebel art thou, Colevile.
FAL.   And a famous true subject took him.
COLE. I am, my lord, but as my betters are
       That led me hither: had they been ruled by me,
       You should have won them dearer than you have.
FAL.   I know not how they sold themselves: but thou, like a kind fel-
       low, gavest thyself away gratis; and I thank thee for thee.

                    Re-enter WESTMORELAND

LAN.   Now, have you left pursuit?
WEST. Retreat is made and execution stay'd.
LAN.   Send Colevile with his confederates
       To York, to present execution:
       Blunt, lead him hence; and see you guard him sure.
                              [*Exeunt* BLUNT *and others with* COLEVILE.
       And now dispatch we toward the court, my lords:
       I hear the king my father is sore sick:
       Our news shall go before us to his majesty,
       Which, cousin, you shall bear to comfort him;
       And we with sober speed will follow you.
FAL.   My lord, I beseech you, give me leave to go
       Through Gloucestershire: and, when you come to court,
       Stand my good lord, pray, in your good report.[5]
LAN.   Fare you well, Falstaff: I, in my condition,[6]
       Shall better speak of you than you deserve.
                              [*Exeunt all except* FALSTAFF.
FAL.   I would you had but the wit: 't were better than your dukedom.
       Good faith, this same young sober-blooded boy doth not love me;
       nor a man cannot make him laugh; but that's no marvel, he drinks
       no wine. There's never none of these demure boys come to any
       proof;[7] for thin drink doth so over-cool their blood, and making
       many fish-meals, that they fall into a kind of male green-sickness;[8]
       and then, when they marry, they get wenches: they are generally
       fools and cowards; which some of us should be too, but for in-

---

[5]*Stand my good lord . . . report*] Be my benefactor in the good account you give of me.
[6]*in my condition*] in my position as general, in my official capacity.
[7]*come to any proof*] give any proof of ability.
[8]*green-sickness*] chlorosis; a malady incident to girls.

flammation. A good sherris-sack[9] hath a two-fold operation in it. It ascends me into the brain; dries me there all the foolish and dull and crudy vapours which environ it; makes it apprehensive, quick, forgetive,[10] full of nimble, fiery and delectable shapes; which, delivered o'er to the voice, the tongue, which is the birth, becomes excellent wit. The second property of your excellent sherris is, the warming of the blood; which, before cold and settled, left the liver white and pale, which is the badge of pusillanimity and cowardice; but the sherris warms it and makes it course from the inwards to the parts extreme: it illumineth the face, which as a beacon gives warning to all the rest of this little kingdom, man, to arm; and then the vital commoners and inland[11] petty spirits muster me all to their captain, the heart, who, great and puffed up with this retinue, doth any deed of courage; and this valour comes of sherris. So that skill in the weapon is nothing without sack, for that sets it a-work; and learning a mere hoard of gold kept by a devil, till sack commences it[12] and sets it in act and use. Hereof comes it that Prince Harry is valiant; for the cold blood he did naturally inherit of his father, he hath, like lean sterile and bare land, manured, husbanded and tilled with excellent endeavour of drinking good and good store of fertile sherris, that he is become very hot and valiant. If I had a thousand sons, the first humane principle I would teach them should be, to forswear thin potations, and to addict themselves to sack.

Enter BARDOLPH

How now, Bardolph?

BARD.   The army is discharged all and gone.

FAL.   Let them go. I'll through Gloucestershire; and there will I visit Master Robert Shallow, esquire: I have him already tempering[13] between my finger and my thumb, and shortly will I seal with him. Come away.   [*Exeunt.*

---

[9]*sherris-sack*] sherry-wine, sack coming from Xeres.

[10]*apprehensive . . . forgetive*] quick to understand . . . able to forge, imaginative.

[11]*inland*] provincial.

[12]*till sack commences it*] The word "commence" was academically used of taking the degree of bachelor of arts, from the Cambridge term "commencement," that is, the ceremony of conferring the degree. Sack is here said to give learning its diploma for active service.

[13]*tempering*] in process of fashioning like wax.

Scene IV.   *Westminster. The Jerusalem Chamber*

Enter the KING, *the* PRINCES THOMAS OF CLARENCE *and*
HUMPHREY OF GLOUCESTER, WARWICK, *and others*

KING.   Now, lords, if God doth give successful end
  To this debate[1] that bleedeth at our doors,
  We will our youth lead on to higher fields[2]
  And draw no swords but what are sanctified.
  Our navy is address'd,[3] our power collected,
  Our substitutes in absence well invested,
  And every thing lies level to our wish:
  Only, we want a little personal strength;
  And pause us, till these rebels, now afoot,
  Come underneath the yoke of government.
WAR.   Both which we doubt not but your majesty
  Shall soon enjoy.
KING.   Humphrey, my son of Gloucester,
  Where is the prince your brother?
GLOU.   I think he's gone to hunt, my lord, at Windsor.
KING.   And how accompanied?
GLOU.   I do not know, my lord.
KING.   Is not his brother, Thomas of Clarence, with him?
GLOU.   No, my good lord; he is in presence here.
CLAR.   What would my lord and father?
KING.   Nothing but well to thee, Thomas of Clarence.
  How chance thou art not with the prince thy brother?
  He loves thee, and thou dost neglect him, Thomas;
  Thou hast a better place in his affection
  Than all thy brothers: cherish it, my boy,
  And noble offices thou mayst effect
  Of mediation, after I am dead,
  Between his greatness and thy other brethren:
  Therefore omit[4] him not; blunt not his love,
  Nor lose the good advantage of his grace
  By seeming cold or careless of his will;
  For he is gracious, if he be observed:[5]

---

[1]*debate*] contention, war, quarrel.
[2]*We will . . . to higher fields*] A reference to the crusade, which Henry IV had promised
  to lead to the Holy Land at the beginning of the reign.
[3]*address'd*] ready, prepared.
[4]*omit*] neglect.
[5]*observed*] treated with attention.

He hath a tear for pity, and a hand
Open as day for melting charity:
Yet notwithstanding, being incensed, he's flint,
As humorous as winter,[6] and as sudden
As flaws congealed in the spring of day.[7]
His temper, therefore, must be well observed:
Chide him for faults, and do it reverently,
When you perceive his blood inclined to mirth;
But, being moody, give him line and scope,
Till that his passions, like a whale on ground,
Confound themselves with working. Learn this, Thomas,
And thou shalt prove a shelter to thy friends,
A hoop of gold to bind thy brothers in,
That the united vessel of their blood,
Mingled with venom of suggestion—[8]
As, force perforce,[9] the age will pour it in—
Shall never leak, though it do work as strong
As aconitum[10] or rash[11] gunpowder.

CLAR.   I shall observe him with all care and love.
KING.   Why art thou not at Windsor with him, Thomas?
CLAR.   He is not there to-day; he dines in London.
KING.   And how accompanied? canst thou tell that?
CLAR.   With Poins,[12] and other his continual followers.
KING.   Most subject is the fattest soil to weeds;
And he, the noble image of my youth,
Is overspread with them: therefore my grief
Stretches itself beyond the hour of death:
The blood weeps from my heart when I do shape,
In forms imaginary, the unguided days
And rotten times that you shall look upon,
When I am sleeping with my ancestors.
For when his headstrong riot hath no curb,
When rage and hot blood are his counsellors,

---

[6]*humorous as winter*] capricious, changeable as the weather of a winter's day.

[7]*flaws . . . day*] sudden gusts of wind, cold as congealed ice, which, blowing up in the sunshine, betoken the approach of spring.

[8]*Mingled with . . . suggestion*] Though their blood be infected by the temptations to which youth is subject.

[9]*force perforce*] of absolute necessity.

[10]*aconitum*] aconite, wolf's bane.

[11]*rash*] explosive.

[12]*With Poins*] Nothing further is heard of this character either in this play or its sequels, *Henry V* and *Merry Wives of Windsor*.

> When means and lavish manners meet together,
> O, with what wings shall his affections[13] fly
> Towards fronting peril and opposed decay!

WAR.   My gracious lord, you look beyond him[14] quite:
> The prince but studies his companions
> Like a strange tongue, wherein, to gain the language,
> 'T is needful that the most immodest word
> Be look'd upon and learn'd; which once attain'd,
> Your highness knows, comes to no further use
> But to be known and hated. So, like gross terms,
> The prince will in the perfectness of time
> Cast off his followers; and their memory
> Shall as a pattern or a measure live,
> By which his grace must mete the lives of others,
> Turning past evils to advantages.

KING.   'T is seldom when the bee doth leave her comb
> In the dead carrion.[15]

Enter WESTMORELAND

> Who's here? Westmoreland?

WEST.   Health to my sovereign, and new happiness
> Added to that that I am to deliver!
> Prince John your son doth kiss your grace's hand:
> Mowbray, the Bishop Scroop, Hastings and all
> Are brought to the correction of your law;
> There is not now a rebel's sword unsheathed,
> But Peace puts forth her olive every where.
> The manner how this action hath been borne
> Here at more leisure may your highness read,
> With every course in his particular.[16]

KING.   O Westmoreland, thou art a summer bird,
> Which ever in the haunch[17] of winter sings
> The lifting up of day.[18]

Enter HARCOURT

---

[13]*affections*] passions.

[14]*look beyond him*] overstate his defects.

[15]*'T is seldom . . . carrion*] The bee having once located her honey-comb in a carcass is unwilling to desert the honey she stores there. The implication is that the man who once finds pleasure in low company will be unwilling to abandon it.

[16]*in his particular*] in its special details.

[17]*haunch*] end.

[18]*sings The lifting up of day*] foretells in song the lengthening-out of day.

                   Look, here's more news.

HAR.   From enemies heaven keep your majesty;
      And, when they stand against you, may they fall
      As those that I am come to tell you of!
      The Earl Northumberland[19] and the Lord Bardolph,
      With a great power of English and of Scots,
      Are by the sheriff of Yorkshire overthrown:
      The manner and true order of the fight,
      This packet, please it you, contains at large.

KING.   And wherefore should these good news make me sick?
      Will Fortune never come with both hands full,
      But write her fair words still in foulest letters?
      She either gives a stomach and no food;
      Such are the poor, in health; or else a feast
      And takes away the stomach; such are the rich,
      That have abundance and enjoy it not.
      I should rejoice now at this happy news;
      And now my sight fails, and my brain is giddy:
      O me! come near me; now I am much ill.

GLOU.   Comfort, your majesty!

CLAR.   O my royal father!

WEST.   My sovereign lord, cheer up yourself, look up.

WAR.   Be patient, princes; you do know, these fits
      Are with his highness very ordinary.
      Stand from him, give him air; he'll straight be well.

CLAR.   No, no, he cannot long hold out these pangs:
      The incessant care and labour of his mind
      Hath wrought the mure,[20] that should confine it in,
      So thin that life looks through and will break out.

GLOU.   The people fear me;[21] for they do observe
      Unfather'd heirs[22] and loathly births of nature:
      The seasons change their manners, as the year
      Had found some months asleep and leap'd them over.

CLAR.   The river hath thrice flow'd, no ebb between;
      And the old folk, time's doting chronicles,

---

[19]*Earl Northumberland*] The defeat and death of Northumberland took place on Bramham Moor on 19 February, 1408. But Shakespeare places the scene in the last days of Henry IV's reign, in 1413.

[20]*wrought the mure*] worn away the wall of flesh.

[21]*fear me*] cause me fear or anxiety; alarm me.

[22]*Unfather'd heirs*] Elves not begotten of mortal men but miraculously created by divine or demoniac powers.

Say it did so a little time before
That our great-grandsire, Edward, sick'd and died.[23]
WAR.   Speak lower, princes, for the king recovers.
GLOU.   This apoplexy will certain be his end.
KING.   I pray you, take me up, and bear me hence
Into some other chamber: softly, pray.   [*Exeunt.*

Scene V.   *Another Chamber*

The KING *lying on a bed:* CLARENCE, GLOUCESTER, WARWICK,
and others in attendance

KING.   Let there be no noise[1] made, my gentle friends;
Unless some dull and favourable hand[2]
Will whisper music to my weary spirit.
WAR.   Call for the music in the other room.
KING.   Set me the crown upon my pillow here.
CLAR.   His eye is hollow, and he changes much.
WAR.   Less noise, less noise!

Enter PRINCE HENRY

PRINCE.   Who saw the Duke of Clarence?
CLAR.   I am here, brother, full of heaviness.
PRINCE.   How now! rain within doors, and none abroad!
How doth the king?
GLOU.   Exceeding ill.
PRINCE.   Heard he the good news yet?
Tell it him.
GLOU.   He alter'd much upon the hearing it.
PRINCE.   If he be sick with joy, he'll recover without physic.
WAR.   Not so much noise, my lords: sweet prince, speak low;
The king your father is disposed to sleep.
CLAR.   Let us withdraw into the other room.

---

[23]*The river . . . died*] Holinshed credits the river Thames with three flood tides on 12
October, 1411, a long period before Henry IV's death. No authority is known for
Shakespeare's account of a similar portent before the death of Edward III.

---

[1]*Let there be no noise*] No new scene is indicated here in the Folios. But it is clear that
the king's swoon took place in the Jerusalem chamber of Westminster Abbey, and that
the royal patient was removed immediately to "some other chamber" in the palace at
Westminster, where the episode which now follows took place.
[2]*dull and favourable hand*] slow, drowsy, and soothing musician's hand.

WAR.   Will 't please your grace to go along with us?
PRINCE.   No; I will sit and watch here by the king.
                          [*Exeunt all except the* PRINCE.
    Why doth the crown lie there upon his pillow,
    Being so troublesome a bedfellow?
    O polish'd perturbation! golden care!
    That keep'st the ports of slumber[3] open wide
    To many a watchful night! sleep with it now!
    Yet not so sound and half so deeply sweet
    As he whose brow with homely biggen[4] bound
    Snores out the watch of night. O majesty!
    When thou dost pinch thy bearer, thou dost sit
    Like a rich armour worn in heat of day,
    That scalds with safety.[5] By his gates of breath
    There lies a downy feather which stirs not:
    Did he suspire,[6] that light and weightless down
    Perforce must move. My gracious lord! my father!
    This sleep is sound indeed; this is a sleep,
    That from this golden rigol[7] hath divorced
    So many English kings. Thy due from me
    Is tears and heavy sorrows of the blood,
    Which nature, love, and filial tenderness,
    Shall, O dear father, pay thee plenteously:
    My due from thee is this imperial crown,
    Which, as immediate from thy place and blood,
    Derives itself to me. Lo, here it sits,
    Which God shall guard: and put the world's whole strength
    Into one giant arm, it shall not force
    This lineal honour from me: this from thee
    Will I to mine leave, as 't is left to me.   [*Exit.*
KING.   Warwick! Gloucester! Clarence!

    Re-enter WARWICK, GLOUCESTER, CLARENCE, *and the rest*

CLAR.   Doth the king call?
WAR.   What would your majesty? How fares your grace?
KING.   Why did you leave me here alone, my lords?
CLAR.   We left the prince my brother here, my liege,
    Who undertook to sit and watch by you.

---

[3]*the ports of slumber*] the gates of slumber, the eyes.
[4]*biggen*] nightcap, head-band of coarse cloth.
[5]*with safety*] while it gives protection.
[6]*suspire*] breathe lightly.
[7]*rigol*] circle; a rare word, derived from the Italian "rigolo," *i.e.*, a little wheel.

KING.   The Prince of Wales! Where is he? let me see him:
  He is not here.
WAR.   This door is open; he is gone this way.
GLOU.   He came not through the chamber where we stay'd.
KING.   Where is the crown? who took it from my pillow?
WAR.   When we withdrew, my liege, we left it here.
KING.   The prince hath ta'en it hence: go, seek him out.
  Is he so hasty that he doth suppose
  My sleep my death?
  Find him, my Lord of Warwick; chide him hither.

                                        [*Exit* WARWICK.

  This part[8] of his conjoins with my disease,
  And helps to end me. See, sons, what things you are!
  How quickly nature falls into revolt
  When gold becomes her object!
  For this the foolish over-careful fathers
  Have broke their sleep with thoughts, their brains with care,
  Their bones with industry;
  For this they have engrossed[9] and piled up
  The canker'd heaps of strange-achieved gold;[10]
  For this they have been thoughtful to invest
  Their sons with arts and martial exercises:
  When, like the bee, culling from every flower
  The virtuous sweets,
  Our thighs pack'd with wax, our mouths with honey,
  We bring it to the hive; and, like the bees,
  Are murder'd for our pains. This bitter taste
  Yield his engrossments to the ending father.[11]

                   Re-enter WARWICK

  Now, where is he that will not stay so long
  Till his friend sickness hath determined me?[12]
WAR.   My lord, I found the prince in the next room,
  Washing with kindly tears[13] his gentle cheeks,
  With such a deep demeanour in great sorrow,
  That tyranny, which never quaff'd but blood,

---

[8]*This part*] This rôle.
[9]*engrossed*] amassed.
[10]*The canker'd . . . gold*] The corrupt stores of gold derived from foreign lands.
[11]*Yield . . . father*] The accumulations of wealth yield to the dying father.
[12]*will not stay so long Till . . . determined me*] will not wait until his friendly ally, my illness, has made an end of me.
[13]*kindly tears*] tears of natural affection.

Would, by beholding him, have wash'd his knife
With gentle eye-drops. He is coming hither.

KING. But wherefore did he take away the crown?

Re-enter PRINCE HENRY

Lo, where he comes. Come hither to me, Harry.
Depart the chamber, leave us here alone.

[*Exeunt* WARWICK *and the rest.*

PRINCE. I never thought to hear you speak again.

KING. Thy wish was father, Harry, to that thought:
I stay too long by thee, I weary thee.
Dost thou so hunger for mine empty chair
That thou wilt needs invest thee with my honours
Before thy hour be ripe? O foolish youth!
Thou seek'st the greatness that will overwhelm thee.
Stay but a little; for my cloud of dignity
Is held from falling with so weak a wind
That it will quickly drop: my day is dim.
Thou hast stolen that which after some few hours
Were thine without offence; and at my death
Thou hast seal'd up[14] my expectation:
Thy life did manifest thou lovedst me not,
And thou wilt have me die assured of it.
Thou hidest a thousand daggers in thy thoughts,
Which thou hast whetted on thy stony heart,
To stab at half an hour of my life.
What! canst thou not forbear me half an hour?
Then get thee gone and dig my grave thyself,
And bid the merry bells ring to thine ear
That thou art crowned, not that I am dead.
Let all the tears that should bedew my hearse
Be drops of balm to sanctify thy head:
Only compound me with forgotten dust;
Give that which gave thee life unto the worms.
Pluck down my officers, break my decrees;
For now a time is come to mock at form:
Harry the fifth is crown'd: up, vanity!
Down, royal state! all you sage counsellors, hence!
And to the English court assemble now,
From every region, apes of idleness!
Now, neighbour confines, purge you of your scum:

---

[14]*at my death . . . seal'd up*] in the hour of my death thou hast confirmed.

Have you a ruffian that will swear, drink, dance,
Revel the night, rob, murder, and commit
The oldest sins the newest kind of ways?
Be happy, he will trouble you no more;
England shall double gild his treble guilt,[15]
England shall give him office, honour, might;
For the fifth Harry from curb'd license plucks
The muzzle of restraint, and the wild dog[16]
Shall flesh his tooth on every innocent.
O my poor kingdom, sick with civil blows!
When that my care could not withhold thy riots,
What wilt thou do when riot is thy care?[17]
O, thou wilt be a wilderness again,
Peopled with wolves, thy old inhabitants!

PRINCE.   O, pardon me, my liege! but for my tears,
The moist impediments unto my speech,
I had forestall'd this dear and deep[18] rebuke,
Ere you with grief had spoke and I had heard
The course of it so far. There is your crown;
And He that wears the crown immortally
Long guard it yours! If I affect it more
Than as your honour and as your renown,
Let me no more from this obedience rise,
Which my most inward true and duteous spirit
Teacheth, this prostrate and exterior bending.[19]
God witness with me, when I here came in,
And found no course of breath within your majesty,
How cold it struck my heart! If I do feign,
O, let me in my present wildness die,
And never live to show the incredulous world
The noble change that I have purposed!
Coming to look on you, thinking you dead,
And dead almost, my liege, to think you were,
I spake unto this crown as having sense,
And thus upbraided it: "The care on thee depending
Hath fed upon the body of my father;

---

[15]*gild . . . guilt*] a very poor and inappropriate pun, but one to which Shakespeare seems
to have been incorrigibly addicted.

[16]*the wild dog*] unmuzzled license.

[17]*thy care*] thy regular business.

[18]*dear and deep*] potent and piercing.

[19]*Let me no more . . . bending*] Let me no more rise from this attitude of obeisance, this
outward act of prostration, which my loyalty and inward sense of duty prompt.

Therefore, thou best of gold art worst of gold:
Other, less fine in carat, is more precious,
Preserving life in medicine potable;[20]
But thou, most fine, most honour'd, most renown'd,
Hast eat thy bearer up." Thus, my most royal liege,
Accusing it, I put it on my head,
To try with it, as with an enemy
That had before my face murder'd my father,
The quarrel of a true inheritor.
But if it did infect my blood with joy,
Or swell my thoughts to any strain of pride;
If any rebel or vain spirit of mine
Did with the least affection of a welcome
Give entertainment to the might of it,
Let God for ever keep it from my head,
And make me as the poorest vassal is,
That doth with awe and terror kneel to it!

KING.   O my son,
God put it in thy mind to take it hence,
That thou mightst win the more thy father's love,
Pleading so wisely in excuse of it!
Come hither, Harry, sit thou by my bed;
And hear, I think, the very latest counsel
That ever I shall breathe. God knows, my son,
By what by-paths and indirect crook'd ways
I met this crown; and I myself know well
How troublesome it sat upon my head.
To thee it shall descend with better quiet,
Better opinion, better confirmation;
For all the soil[21] of the achievement goes
With me into the earth. It seem'd in me
But as an honour snatch'd with boisterous hand,
And I had many living to upbraid
My gain of it by their assistances;
Which daily grew to quarrel and to bloodshed,
Wounding supposed[22] peace: all these bold fears[23]
Thou see'st with peril I have answered;[24]

---

[20]*medicine potable*] an allusion to a liquid solution or tincture of gold, which was regarded of great value as a medicine.
[21]*soil*] stain, reproach.
[22]*supposed*] unreal, imaginary.
[23]*bold fears*] signal dangers (*i.e.*, causes of fear).
[24]*answered*] faced.

For all my reign hath been but as a scene
Acting that argument: and now my death
Changes the mode;[25] for what in me was purchased,
Falls upon thee in a more fairer sort;
So thou the garland wear'st successively.[26]
Yet, though thou stand'st more sure than I could do,
Thou art not firm enough, since griefs are green;
And all my friends,[27] which thou must make thy friends,
Have but their stings and teeth newly ta'en out;
By whose fell working I was first advanced
And by whose power I well might lodge a fear
To be again displaced: which to avoid,
I cut them off;[28] and had a purpose now
To lead out many to the Holy Land,
Lest rest and lying still might make them look
Too near unto my state. Therefore, my Harry,
Be it thy course to busy giddy minds
With foreign quarrels; that action, hence borne out,
May waste the memory of the former days.
More would I, but my lungs are wasted so
That strength of speech is utterly denied me.
How I came by the crown, O God forgive;
And grant it may with thee in true peace live!

PRINCE.   My gracious liege,
You won it, wore it, kept it, gave it me;
Then plain and right must my possession be:
Which I with more than with a common pain
'Gainst all the world will rightfully maintain.

Enter LORD JOHN OF LANCASTER

KING.   Look, look, here comes my John of Lancaster.
LAN.   Health, peace, and happiness to my royal father!
KING.   Thou bring'st me happiness and peace, son John;
But health, alack, with youthful wings is flown
From this bare wither'd trunk: upon thy sight
My worldly business makes a period.
Where is my Lord of Warwick?
PRINCE.   My Lord of Warwick!

---

[25]*mode*] position of affairs.
[26]*successively*] by inheritance, in order of succession.
[27]*all my friends*] a needful correction of the original reading *all thy friends*.
[28]*I cut them off*] I held them aloof from me.

Re-enter WARWICK, *and others*

KING.   Doth any name particular belong
  Unto the lodging[29] where I first did swoon?
WAR.   'T is call'd Jerusalem, my noble lord.
KING.   Laud be to God! even there my life must end.
  It hath been prophesied to me many years,
  I should not die but in Jerusalem;
  Which vainly I supposed the Holy Land:
  But bear me to that chamber; there I'll lie;
  In that Jerusalem shall Harry die.   [*Exeunt.*

---

[29]*the lodging*] the apartment.

ACT V.

Scene I. *Gloucestershire. Shallow's House*

Enter SHALLOW, FALSTAFF, BARDOLPH, *and* Page

SHALLOW. By cock and pie,[1] sir, you shall not away to-night. What,
Davy, I say!

FAL. You must excuse me, Master Robert Shallow.

SHAL. I will not excuse you; you shall not be excused; excuses shall
not be admitted; there is no excuse shall serve; you shall not be excused. Why, Davy!

Enter DAVY

DAVY. Here, sir.

SHAL. Davy, Davy, Davy, Davy, let me see, Davy; let me see, Davy; let
me see: yea, marry, William cook, bid him[2] come hither. Sir John,
you shall not be excused.

DAVY. Marry, sir, thus; those precepts[3] cannot be served: and, again,
sir, shall we sow the headland[4] with wheat?

SHAL. With red wheat,[5] Davy. But for William cook: are there no
young pigeons?

---

[1]*By cock and pie*] A popular petty oath: "cock" seems a corruption of God, while "pie"
was a name given to the Roman Catholic ordinal or service-book. The reference was
vulgarly understood to be to the birds, the cock and the magpie. "The Cock and Pie"
became a common sign for taverns.

[2]*William cook, bid him*] bid William the cook.

[3]*precepts*] writs or summonses, which it was the office of Davy, the justice's factotum, to
serve on debtors or witnesses.

[4]*the headland*] probably here a field on a high ground, a field on a hill. The headland
commonly meant a strip of unploughed or uncultivated land bordering a ploughed
field.

[5]*red wheat*] wheat which was sown in early autumn, and was known in the country of
the Cotswolds as "red lammas wheat." This practice of wheat-sowing appears to have
been almost peculiar to the Cotswold country, a district with which Shakespeare gives
many signs of familiarity.

DAVY.   Yes, sir. Here is now the smith's note[6] for shoeing and plough-irons.

SHAL.   Let it be cast[7] and paid. Sir John, you shall not be excused.

DAVY.   Now, sir, a new link to the bucket must needs be had: and, sir, do you mean to stop any of William's wages, about the sack he lost the other day at Hinckley[8] fair?

SHAL.   A' shall answer it.[9] Some pigeons, Davy, a couple of short-legged hens, a joint of mutton, and any pretty little tiny kick-shaws,[10] tell William cook.

DAVY.   Doth the man of war stay all night, sir?

SHAL.   Yea, Davy. I will use him well: a friend i' the court is better than a penny in purse.[11] Use his men well, Davy; for they are arrant knaves, and will backbite.

DAVY.   No worse than they are backbitten, sir; for they have marvellous foul linen.

SHAL.   Well conceited, Davy: about thy business, Davy.

DAVY.   I beseech you, sir, to countenance William Visor of Woncot against Clement Perkes o' the hill.[12]

SHAL.   There is many complaints, Davy, against that Visor: that Visor is an arrant knave, on my knowledge.

DAVY.   I grant your worship that he is a knave, sir; but yet, God forbid, sir, but a knave should have some countenance at his friend's request. An honest man, sir, is able to speak for himself, when a knave is not. I have served your worship truly, sir, this eight years; and if I cannot once or twice in a quarter bear out[13] a knave against an honest man, I have but a very little credit with your worship. The knave is mine honest friend, sir; therefore, I beseech your worship, let him be countenanced.

SHAL.   Go to; I say he shall have no wrong. Look about, Davy. [*Exit* DAVY.] Where are you, Sir John? Come, come, come, off with your boots. Give me your hand, Master Bardolph.

BARD.   I am glad to see your worship.

---

[6]*smith's note*] blacksmith's account or bill.

[7]*cast*] added up (and verified).

[8]*Hinckley*] a market-town of Warwickshire, northeast of Coventry.

[9]*A' shall answer it*] He shall be answerable for it.

[10]*kickshaws*] fancy dishes, French dishes.

[11]*a friend i' the court . . . purse*] a proverb of antiquity.

[12]*William Visor of Woncot . . . hill*] Woncot is the local pronunciation of Woodmancote, a village in Gloucestershire, where a family of Visor or Vizard has resided from time immemorial, and is still represented. Adjoining the village of Woodmancote is Stinchcombe Hill, known locally as "The Hill," where a family named Perkes is shown by local records to have dwelt for many generations.

[13]*bear out*] stand up for, espouse the cause of.

SHAL.   I thank thee with all my heart, kind Master Bardolph: and wel-
    come, my tall fellow [*to the* Page]. Come, Sir John.
FAL.   I'll follow you, good Master Robert Shallow. [*Exit* SHALLOW.]
    Bardolph, look to our horses. [*Exeunt* BARDOLPH *and* Page.] If I
    were sawed into quantities,[14] I should make four dozen of such
    bearded hermits' staves as Master Shallow. It is a wonderful thing
    to see the semblable coherence[15] of his men's spirits and his: they,
    by observing of him, do bear themselves like foolish justices; he,
    by conversing with them, is turned into a justice-like serving-man:
    their spirits are so married in conjunction with the participation of
    society that they flock together in consent,[16] like so many wild-
    geese. If I had a suit to Master Shallow, I would humour his men
    with the imputation of being near their master:[17] if to his men, I
    would curry with Master Shallow that no man could better com-
    mand his servants. It is certain that either wise bearing or ignorant
    carriage is caught, as men take diseases, one of another: therefore
    let men take heed of their company. I will devise matter enough
    out of this Shallow to keep Prince Harry in continual laughter the
    wearing out of six fashions, which is four terms, or two actions,[18]
    and a' shall laugh without intervallums. O, it is much that a lie
    with a slight oath and a jest with a sad brow[19] will do with a fellow
    that never had the ache in his shoulders![20] O, you shall see him
    laugh till his face be like a wet cloak ill laid up![21]
SHAL.   [*Within*] Sir John!
FAL.   I come, Master Shallow; I come, Master Shallow.   [*Exit.*

Scene II.   *Westminster. The Palace*

Enter WARWICK *and the* LORD CHIEF JUSTICE, *meeting*

WAR.   How now, my lord chief justice! whither away?
CH. JUST.   How doth the king?
WAR.   Exceeding well; his cares are now all ended.

---

[14]*quantities*] fragments, pieces.
[15]*semblable coherence*] close resemblance or identity.
[16]*in consent*] in unison.
[17]*near their master*] on intimate terms with their master.
[18]*four terms, or two actions*] four law terms, or the space of time occupied by the varioius
    stages of two actions at law.
[19]*a jest . . . brow*] a jest told with a serious face.
[20]*a fellow . . . shoulders*] a fellow that never felt a touch of age.
[21]*ill laid up*] ill folded, all tumbled.

CH. JUST.   I hope, not dead.

WAR.   He's walked th' way of nature;
   And to our purposes he lives no more.

CH. JUST.   I would his majesty had call'd me with him:
   The service that I truly did his life
   Hath left me open to all injuries.

WAR.   Indeed I think the young king loves you not.

CH. JUST.   I know he doth not, and do arm myself
   To welcome the condition of the time,
   Which cannot look more hideously upon me
   Than I have drawn it in my fantasy.

   Enter LANCASTER, CLARENCE, GLOUCESTER, WESTMORELAND,
                    and others

WAR.   Here comes the heavy issue[1] of dead Harry:
   O that the living Harry had the temper
   Of him, the worst[2] of these three gentlemen!
   How many nobles then should hold[3] their places,
   That must strike sail to[4] spirits of vile sort!

CH. JUST.   O God, I fear all will be overturn'd!

LAN.   Good morrow, cousin Warwick, good morrow.

GLOU. ⎱
CLAR. ⎰ Good morrow, cousin.

LAN.   We meet like men that had forgot to speak.

WAR.   We do remember; but our argument[5]
   Is all too heavy to admit much talk.

LAN.   Well, peace be with him that hath made us heavy!

CH. JUST.   Peace be with us, lest we be heavier!

GLOU.   O, good my lord, you have lost a friend indeed;
   And I dare swear you borrow not that face
   Of seeming sorrow, it is sure your own.

LAN.   Though no man be assured what grace to find,
   You stand in coldest expectation:
   I am the sorrier; would 't were otherwise.

CLAR.   Well, you must now speak Sir John Falstaff fair;
   Which swims against your stream of quality.[6]

---

[1]*heavy issue*] sorrow-stricken sons.
[2]*Of him, the worst*] Of the one who is the worst.
[3]*hold*] keep.
[4]*strike sail to*] give place to.
[5]*our argument*] the theme of our thought.
[6]*Which swims . . . quality*] Which goes much against the grain in a man of your
 character.

CH. JUST.   Sweet princes, what I did, I did in honour,
  Led by the impartial conduct of my soul;
  And never shall you see that I will beg
  A ragged and forestall'd remission.[7]
  If truth and upright innocency fail me,
  I'll to the king my master that is dead,
  And tell him who hath sent me after him.
WAR.   Here comes the prince.

   Enter KING HENRY *the fifth, attended*

CH. JUST.   Good morrow, and God save your majesty!
KING.   This new and gorgeous garment, majesty,
  Sits not so easy on me as you think.
  Brothers, you mix your sadness with some fear:
  This is the English, not the Turkish court;
  Not Amurath an Amurath[8] succeeds,
  But Harry Harry. Yet be sad, good brothers,
  For, by my faith, it very well becomes you:
  Sorrow so royally in you appears
  That I will deeply put the fashion on,
  And wear it in my heart: why then, be sad;
  But entertain no more of it, good brothers,
  Than a joint burden laid upon us all.
  For me, by heaven, I bid you be assured,
  I'll be your father and your brother too;
  Let me but bear your love, I'll bear your cares:
  Yet weep that Harry's dead; and so will I;
  But Harry lives, that shall convert those tears
  By number[9] into hours of happiness.
PRINCES.   We hope no other from your majesty.
KING.   You all look strangely on me: and you most;
  You are, I think, assured I love you not.
CH. JUST.   I am assured, if I be measured rightly,
  Your majesty hath no just cause to hate me.

---

[7] *A ragged . . . remission*] An ignominious pardon that is preceded by a supplication. The
Chief Justice means that he will only accept a free and unsolicited forgiveness for a
deed that desrved no condemnation.

[8] *Amurath*] A general reference to very recent Turkish history. Amurath, or Mourad III,
sixth Sultan of the Turks, on succeeding to the throne of his father, Selim II, in 1574,
caused all his brothers to be strangled. Amurath III died on 18 January, 1595–96, only
some two or three years before Shakespeare wrote these words, and he was succeeded
by his eldest son Mahomet III, who, following his father's example, caused all his brothers to be done to death.

[9] *By number*] Tear for tear.

KING. No!
> How might a prince of my great hopes forget
> So great indignities you laid upon me?
> What! rate, rebuke, and roughly send to prison
> The immediate heir of England! Was this easy?[10]
> May this be wash'd in Lethe, and forgotten?

CH. JUST. I then did use the person of your father;
> The image of his power lay then in me:
> And, in the administration of his law,
> Whiles I was busy for the commonwealth,
> Your highness pleased to forget my place,
> The majesty and power of law and justice,
> The image of the king whom I presented,
> And struck me in my very seat of judgement;
> Whereon, as an offender to your father,
> I gave bold way to my authority,
> And did commit you. If the deed were ill,
> Be you contented, wearing now the garland,
> To have a son set your decrees at nought,
> To pluck down justice from your awful[11] bench,
> To trip the course of law[12] and blunt the sword
> That guards the peace and safety of your person;
> Nay, more, to spurn at your most royal image
> And mock your workings in a second body.[13]
> Question your royal thoughts, make the case yours;
> Be now the father and propose a son,[14]
> Hear your own dignity so much profaned,
> See your most dreadful laws so loosely slighted,
> Behold yourself so by a son disdain'd;
> And then imagine me taking your part,
> And in your power soft silencing your son:
> After this cold considerance, sentence me;
> And, as you are a king, speak in your state[15]
> What I have done that misbecame my place,
> My person, or my liege's sovereignty.

KING. You are right, justice, and you weigh this well;

---

[10]*Was this easy?*] Was this a slight matter?
[11]*awful*] in the ordinary sense of "reverend."
[12]*trip . . . law*] defeat the process of justice.
[13]*mock . . . body*] treat with scorn acts done in your name by a representative.
[14]*propose a son*] imagine that you have a son.
[15]*in your state*] in your royal character.

Therefore still bear the balance[16] and the sword:
And I do wish your honours may increase,
Till you do live to see a son of mine
Offend you, and obey you, as I did.
So shall I live to speak my father's words:
"Happy am I, that have a man so bold,
That dares do justice on my proper son;[17]
And not less happy, having such a son,
That would deliver up his greatness so
Into the hands of justice." You did commit me:
For which, I do commit into your hand
The unstained sword that you have used to bear;
With this remembrance,[18] that you use the same
With the like bold, just, and impartial spirit
As you have done 'gainst me. There is my hand.
You shall be as a father to my youth:
My voice shall sound as you do prompt mine ear,
And I will stoop and humble my intents
To your well-practised wise directions.
And, princes all, believe me, I beseech you;
My father is gone wild into his grave,[19]
For in his tomb lie my affections;[20]
And with his spirit sadly I survive,[21]
To mock the expectation of the world,
To frustrate prophecies, and to raze out
Rotten opinion,[22] who hath writ me down
After my seeming. The tide of blood in me
Hath proudly flow'd in vanity till now:
Now doth it turn and ebb back to the sea,
Where it shall mingle with the state of floods,[23]
And flow henceforth in formal majesty.
Now call we our high court of parliament:
And let us choose such limbs of noble counsel,

---

[16]*the balance*] the scales of justice.

[17]*my proper son*] my own son.

[18]*remembrance*] admonition.

[19]*is gone wild into his grave*] has gone to his grave carrying my wild disposition there with him.

[20]*affections*] a kind of quibbling is implied here; affections meaning not only affectionate love but also "wild passions."

[21]*And . . . survive*] And his serious spirit only survives in me.

[22]*Rotten opinion*] False, untrustworthy public opinion.

[23]*the state of floods*] the majestic dignity of the ocean.

That the great body of our state may go
In equal rank with the best govern'd nation;
That war, or peace, or both at once, may be
As things acquainted and familiar to us;
In which you, father, shall have foremost hand.
Our coronation done, we will accite,[24]
As I before remember'd, all our state:
And, God consigning to my good intents,[25]
No prince nor peer shall have just cause to say,
God shorten Harry's happy life one day!   [*Exeunt.*

Scene III. *Gloucestershire. Shallow's Orchard*

Enter FALSTAFF, SHALLOW, SILENCE, DAVY, BARDOLPH, *and the* Page

SHAL.   Nay, you shall see my orchard, where, in an arbour, we will eat
    a last year's pippin of my own graffing, with a dish of caraways,[1]
    and so forth: come, cousin Silence: and then to bed.
FAL.   'Fore God, you have here a goodly dwelling and a rich.
SHAL.   Barren, barren, barren; beggars all, beggars all, Sir John: marry,
    good air. Spread, Davy; spread, Davy: well said,[2] Davy.
FAL.   This Davy serves you for good uses; he is your serving-man and
    your husband.
SHAL.   A good varlet, a good varlet, a very good varlet, Sir John: by the
    mass, I have drunk too much sack at supper: a good varlet. Now sit
    down, now sit down: come, cousin.
SIL.   Ah, sirrah! quoth-a, we shall
            Do nothing but eat, and make good cheer,   [*Singing.*
            And praise God for the merry year;
            When flesh is cheap and females dear,
            And lusty lads roam here and there
                    So merrily,
            And ever among[3] so merrily.

FAL.   There's a merry heart! Good Master Silence, I'll give you a
    health for that anon.
SHAL.   Give Master Bardolph some wine, Davy.

---

[24]*accite*] summon.
[25]*consigning to . . . intents*] conforming with my good intentions.

[1]*caraways*] sweetmeats, of which caraway seeds were an important ingredient.
[2]*well said*] well done.
[3]*ever among*] here and there, in and out; an expression of great antiquity.

DAVY.   Sweet sir, sit; I'll be with you anon; most sweet sir, sit. Master
page, good master page, sit. Proface![4] What you want in meat,
we'll have in drink: but you must bear; the heart's all.[5]   [*Exit.*

SHAL.   Be merry, Master Bardolph; and, my little soldier there, be
merry.

SIL.   Be merry, be merry, my wife has all: [*Singing.*
For women are shrews, both short and tall:
'T is merry in hall when beards wag all,[6]
    And welcome merry Shrove-tide.
Be merry, be merry.

FAL.   I did not think Master Silence had been a man of this mettle.
SIL.   Who, I? I have been merry twice and once ere now.

Re-enter DAVY

DAVY.   There's a dish of leather-coats for you.[7]   [*To* BARDOLPH.
SHAL.   Davy!
DAVY.   Your worship! I'll be with you straight [*to* BARDOLPH]. A cup of
wine, sir?

SIL.   A cup of wine that's brisk and fine,   [*Singing.*
And drink unto the leman[8] mine;
    And a merry heart lives long-a.

FAL.   Well said, Master Silence.
SIL.   An we shall be merry, now comes in the sweet o' the night.
FAL.   Health and long life to you, Master Silence.
SIL.   Fill the cup, and let it come;   [*Singing.*
I'll pledge you a mile to the bottom.

SHAL.   Honest Bardolph, welcome: if thou wantest any thing, and wilt
not call, beshrew thy heart. Welcome, my little tiny thief [*to the*
Page], and welcome indeed too. I'll drink to Master Bardolph, and
to all the cavaleros[9] about London.

DAVY.   I hope to see London once ere I die.
BARD.   An I might see you there, Davy,—

---

[4]*Proface!*] Much good may it do you! An invitation to drink, used in much the same way
as "Prosit" in Germany. It comes through the old French "prouface" or the Italian (pro-
faccia" from the Latin "proficiat."
[5]*You must bear; the heart's all*] you must excuse the entertainment; the good intention
is everything.
[6]*'T is merry in hall when beards wag all*] This line often figures as a proverb in contemporary literature before the date of this play, and seems to have been the burden of a
popular song. To "wag beards" is "to talk."
[7]*leather-coats*] a name for russet apples.
[8]*leman*] sweetheart.
[9]*cavaleros*] blades or bucks.

SHAL.   By the mass, you'll crack a quart together, ha! will you not,
    Master Bardolph?

BARD.   Yea, sir, in a pottle-pot.[10]

SHAL.   By God's liggens, I thank thee: the knave will stick by thee, I
    can assure thee that. A' will not out;[11] he is true bred.

BARD.   And I'll stick by him, sir.

SHAL.   Why, there spoke a king. Lack nothing: be merry. [*Knocking
    within.*] Look who's at door there, ho! who knocks?   [*Exit* DAVY.

FAL.   Why, now you have done me right.[12]

                      [*To* SILENCE, *seeing him take off a bumper.*

SIL.   Do me right,   [*Singing.*
        And dub me knight:
           Samingo.[13]

    Is 't not so?

FAL.   'T is so.

SIL.   Is 't so? Why then, say an old man can do somewhat.

Re-enter DAVY

DAVY.   An 't please your worship, there's one Pistol come from the
    court with news.

FAL.   From the court! let him come in.

Enter PISTOL

    How now, Pistol!

PIST.   Sir John, God save you!

FAL.   What wind blew you hither, Pistol?

PIST.   Not the ill wind which blows no man to good. Sweet knight,
    thou art now one of the greatest men in this realm.

SIL.   By 'r lady, I think a' be, but goodman Puff of Barson.[14]

---

[10]*pottle-pot*] a pot holding two quarts.

[11]*A' will not out*] He will not shirk, fail; an expression used of well-bred hounds.

[12]*done me right*] "To do a man right" was a toper's phrase for drinking his health in a
bumper.

[13]*Do me right . . . Samingo*] A fuller version of this popular song is in Nashe's *Summers
Last Will and Testament* (1600); it there begins: "Mounsieur Mingo for quaffing doth
surpass," and it ends, "God Bacchus *doe mee right, And dubbe mee knight Domingo.*"
"Samingo," which in Shakespeare's text takes the place of Nashe's "Domingo" (*i.e.*, St.
Dominic, a reputed patron-saint of topers), is apparently a corruption of San
Domingo. Seeing, however, that the song celebrates the potations of "Mounsieur
Mingo" and invites the honour of knighthood, "*Sir* Mingo" might well be substituted
here for "Samingo."

[14]*but goodman Puff of Barson*] excepting, or save, goodman Puff of Barston (the name
of a village in Warwickshire).

PIST.   Puff!
     Puff in thy teeth, most recreant coward base!
     Sir John, I am thy Pistol and thy friend,
     And helter-skelter have I rode to thee,
     And tidings do I bring and lucky joys
     And golden times and happy news of price.
FAL.   I pray thee now, deliver them like a man of this world.
PIST.   A foutre[15] for the world and worldlings base!
     I speak of Africa and golden joys.
FAL.   O base Assyrian knight, what is thy news?
     Let King Cophetua know the truth thereof.
SIL.   And Robin Hood, Scarlet, and John.[16]   [*Singing.*

PIST.   Shall dunghill curs confront the Helicons?[17]
     And shall good news be baffled?[18]
     Then, Pistol, lay thy head in Furies' lap.
SHAL.   Honest gentleman, I know not your breeding.[19]
PIST.   Why then, lament therefore.
SHAL.   Give me pardon, sir: if, sir, you come with news from the
     court, I take it there's but two ways, either to utter them, or to con-
     ceal them. I am, sir, under the king, in some authority.
PIST.   Under which king, Besonian?[20] speak, or die.
SHAL.   Under King Harry.
PIST.   Harry the fourth? or fifth?
SHAL.   Harry the fourth.
PIST.   A foutre for thine office!
     Sir John, thy tender lambkin now is king;
     Harry the fifth's the man. I speak the truth:
     When Pistol lies, do this; and fig me, like
     The bragging Spaniard.[21]
FAL.   What, is the old king dead?
PIST.   As nail in door:[22] the things I speak are just.

---

[15]*A foutre*] A coarse expression of scorn.
[16]*And Robin Hood . . . John*] a scrap from the ballad of "Robin Hood and the Pinder of
   Wakefield."
[17]*the Helicons*] the Muses. A characteristically slovenly allusion to the mountain which,
   according to Greek mythology, was the special haunt of the Muses. Pistol bombasti-
   cally claims the honour due to a servant of the Muses.
[18]*baffled*] treated with ignominy.
[19]*I know not your breeding*] I don't understand your bringing up. I cannot make out the
   sort of man you are.
[20]*Besonian*] A cant term for beggar.
[21]*fig me, like . . . Spaniard*] "To fig" was to use an insulting gesture, by putting the thumb
   between the fore and middle finger. It was reckoned of Spanish origin.
[22]*As nail in door*] As dead as a door-nail.

FAL.   Away, Bardolph! saddle my horse. Master Robert Shallow, choose what office thou wilt in the land, 't is thine. Pistol, I will double-charge thee with dignities.

BARD.   O joyful day!
   I would not take a knighthood for my fortune.

PIST.   What! I do bring good news.

FAL.   Carry Master Silence to bed. Master Shallow, my Lord Shallow,—be what thou wilt; I am fortune's steward—get on thy boots: we'll ride all night. O sweet Pistol! Away, Bardolph! [*Exit* BARD.] Come, Pistol, utter more to me; and withal devise something to do thyself good. Boot, boot,[23] Master Shallow! I know the young king is sick for me. Let us take any man's horses; the laws of England are at my commandment. Blessed are they that have been my friends; and woe to my lord chief justice!

PIST.   Let vultures vile seize on his lungs also!
   "Where is the life that late I led?" say they:
   Why, here it is; welcome these pleasant days!   [*Exeunt.*

Scene IV.   *London. A Street*

Enter Beadles, *dragging in* HOSTESS QUICKLY *and* DOLL TEARSHEET

HOST.   No, thou arrant knave; I would to God that I might die, that I might have thee hanged: thou hast drawn my shoulder out of joint.

FIRST BEAD.   The constables have delivered her over to me; and she shall have whipping-cheer[1] enough, I warrant her: there hath been a man or two lately killed about her.

DOL.   Nut-hook, nut-hook,[2] you lie. Come on; I'll tell thee what, thou damned tripe-visaged rascal, an the child I now go with do miscarry, thou wert better thou hadst struck thy mother, thou paper-faced villain.

HOST.   O the Lord, that Sir John were come! he would make this a bloody day to somebody. But I pray God the fruit of her womb miscarry!

FIRST BEAD.   If it do, you shall have a dozen of cushions again; you have but eleven now. Come, I charge you both go with me; for the man is dead that you and Pistol beat amongst you.

---

[23]*Boot, boot*] On with your boots!

[1]*whipping-cheer*] whipping fare, plenty of whipping.
[2]*nut-hook*] a cant name for a bailiff or constable.

DOL.   I'll tell you what, you thin man in a censer,[3] I will have you as
    soundly swinged for this,—you blue-bottle rogue,[4] you filthy fam-
    ished correctioner, if you be not swinged, I'll forswear half-kirtles.[5]
FIRST BEAD.   Come, come, you she knight-errant, come.
HOST.   O God, that right should thus overcome might!
    Well, of sufferance comes ease.[6]
DOL.   Come, you rogue, come; bring me to a justice.
HOST.   Ay, come, you starved blood-hound.
DOL.   Goodman death, goodman bones!
HOST.   Thou atomy,[7] thou!
DOL.   Come, you thin thing; come, you rascal.
FIRST BEAD.   Very well.   [*Exeunt.*

Scene V.   *A Public Place near Westminster Abbey*

Enter two Grooms, *strewing rushes*

FIRST GROOM.   More rushes, more rushes.[1]
SEC. GROOM.   The trumpets have sounded twice.
FIRST GROOM.   'T will be two o'clock ere they come from the coro-
    nation: dispatch, dispatch.   [*Exeunt.*

Enter FALSTAFF, SHALLOW, PISTOL, BARDOLPH, *and* Page

FAL.   Stand here by me, Master Robert Shallow; I will make the king
    do you grace: I will leer upon him as a' comes by; and do but mark
    the countenance that he will give me.
PIST.   God bless thy lungs, good knight.
FAL.   Come here, Pistol; stand behind me. O, if I had had time to
    have made new liveries, I would have bestowed the thousand
    pound I borrowed of you. But 't is no matter; this poor show doth
    better: this doth infer the zeal I had to see him.
SHAL.   It doth so.
FAL.   It shows my earnestness of affection,—
SHAL.   It doth so.

---

[3]*you thin man in a censer*] A censer or fire pan for burning perfumes usually had a small
  figure of a man embossed on the pierced cover.
[4]*blue-bottle rogue*] a reference to the blue uniform of beadles.
[5]*half-kirtles*] short petticoats or aprons.
[6]*of sufferance comes ease*] after suffering comes quiet.
[7]*atomy*] anatomy, skeleton.

---

[1]*More rushes*] Rushes were invariably strewn on ceremonial occasions both on the floors
  of houses and about the streets.

FAL.   My devotion,—

SHAL.   It doth, it doth, it doth.

FAL.   As it were, to ride day and night; and not to deliberate, not to remember, not to have patience to shift me,—

SHAL.   It is best, certain.

FAL.   But to stand stained with travel, and sweating with desire to see him; thinking of nothing else, putting all affairs else in oblivion, as if there were nothing else to be done but to see him.

PIST.   'T is "semper idem," for "obsque hoc nihil est:"[2] 't is all in every part.[3]

SHAL.   'T is so, indeed.

PIST.   My knight, I will inflame thy noble liver,
And make thee rage.
Thy Doll, and Helen of thy noble thoughts,
Is in base durance and contagious prison;
Haled thither
By most mechanical and dirty hand:
Rouse up revenge[4] from ebon den with fell Alecto's snake,[5]
For Doll is in.[6] Pistol speaks nought but truth.

FAL.   I will deliver her.   [*Shouts within, and the trumpets sound.*

PIST.   There roar'd the sea, and trumpet-clangor sounds.

Enter the KING *and his train, the* LORD CHIEF JUSTICE *among them*

FAL.   God save thy grace, King Hal! my royal Hal!

PIST.   The heavens thee guard and keep, most royal imp[7] of fame!

FAL.   God save thee, my sweet boy!

KING.   My lord chief justice, speak to that vain man.[8]

CH. JUST.   Have you your wits? know you what 't is you speak?

FAL.   My king! my Jove! I speak to thee, my heart!

KING.   I know thee not, old man: fall to thy prayers;
How ill white hairs become a fool and jester!
I have long dream'd of such a kind of man,
So surfeit-swelled, so old, and so profane;

---

[2]*"semper idem"* . . . *"obsque hoc nihil est"*] always the same . . . without this there is nothing.

[3]*'t is all in every part*] a free rendering of an old English proverb, "All in all, and all in every part," signifying complete identity.

[4]*Rouse up revenge*] A parody of the ghost's reiterated cry in Kyd's *Spanish Tragedy*.

[5]*Alecto's snake*] Alecto was one of the three Furies, who is described as crowned with snakes in Virgil's *Aeneid*.

[6]*Doll is in*] sc. gaol.

[7]*imp*] scion.

[8]*vain man*] foolish man.

But, being awaked, I do despise my dream.
Make less thy body hence, and more thy grace;
Leave gormandizing; know the grave doth gape
For thee thrice wider than for other men.
Reply not to me with a fool-born jest:
Presume not that I am the thing I was;
For God doth know, so shall the world perceive,
That I have turn'd away my former self;
So will I those that kept my company.
When thou dost hear I am as I have been,
Approach me, and thou shalt be as thou wast,
The tutor and the feeder of my riots:
Till then, I banish thee, on pain of death,
As I have done the rest of my misleaders,
Not to come near our person by ten mile.
For competence of life I will allow you,
That lack of means enforce you not to evil:
And, as we hear you do reform yourselves,
We will, according to your strengths and qualities,
Give you advancement. Be it your charge, my lord,
To see perform'd the tenour of our word.
Set on.   [*Exeunt* KING, &c.

FAL.   Master Shallow, I owe you a thousand pound.

SHAL.   Yea, marry, Sir John; which I beseech you to let me have home
with me.

FAL.   That can hardly be, Master Shallow. Do not you grieve at this; I
shall be sent for in private to him: look you, he must seem thus to
the world: fear not your advancements; I will be the man yet that
shall make you great.

SHAL.   I cannot well perceive how unless you should give me your
doublet, and stuff me out with straw. I beseech you, good Sir John,
let me have five hundred of my thousand.

FAL.   Sir, I will be as good as my word: this that you heard was but a
colour.[9]

SHAL.   A colour that I fear you will die in, Sir John.

FAL.   Fear no colours,[10] go with me to dinner: come, Lieutenant
Pistol; come, Bardolph: I shall be sent for soon at night.[11]

Re-enter PRINCE JOHN, *and the* LORD CHIEF JUSTICE;
Officers *with them*

---

[9]*but a colour*] only a pretext, blind, make-believe.

[10]*Fear no colours*] Fear nothing: a proverbial expression.

[11]*soon at night*] as soon as it is night.

CH. JUST. Go, carry Sir John Falstaff to the Fleet:[12]
  Take all his company along with him.
FAL. My lord, my lord,—
CH. JUST. I cannot now speak: I will hear you soon.
  Take them away.
PIST. Si fortuna me tormenta, spero contenta.[13]
                  [*Exeunt all but* PRINCE JOHN *and the* CHIEF JUSTICE.
LAN. I like this fair proceeding of the king's:
  He hath intent his wonted followers
  Shall be all very well provided for;
  But all are banish'd till their conversations[14]
  Appear more wise and modest to the world.
CH. JUST. And so they are.
LAN. The king hath call'd his parliament, my lord.
CH. JUST. He hath.
LAN. I will lay odds that, ere this year expire,
  We bear our civil swords and native fire
  As far as France: I heard a bird so sing,[15]
  Whose music, to my thinking, pleased the king.
  Come, will you hence?   [*Exeunt.*

---

[12]*the Fleet*] one of the chief prisons in the centre of London.
[13]*Si fortuna . . . contenta*] Falstaff has already quoted this Italian proverb.
[14]*conversations*] manners, modes of life.
[15]*I heard a bird so sing*] a familiar reference to the proverbially prophetic powers of the "little bird."

EPILOGUE

Spoken by a Dancer[1]

First my fear; then my courtesy; last my speech. My fear is, your displeasure; my courtesy, my duty; and my speech, to beg your pardons. If you look for a good speech now, you undo me: for what I have to say is of mine own making; and what indeed I should say will, I doubt,[2] prove mine own marring. But to the purpose, and so to the venture. Be it known to you, as it is very well, I was lately here in the end of a displeasing play, to pray your patience for it and to promise you a better. I meant indeed to pay you with this; which, if like an ill venture it come unluckily home, I break,[3] and you, my gentle creditors, lose. Here I promised you I would be, and here I commit my body to your mercies: bate me some, and I will pay you some, and, as most debtors do, promise you infinitely.

If my tongue cannot entreat you to acquit me, will you command me to use my legs? and yet that were but light payment, to dance out of your debt. But a good conscience will make any possible satisfaction, and so would I. All the gentlewomen here have forgiven me: if the gentlemen will not, then the gentlemen do not agree with the gentlewomen, which was never seen before in such an assembly.

One word more, I beseech you. If you be not too much cloyed with fat meat, our humble author will continue the story, with Sir John in it,[4] and make you merry with fair Katharine of France: where, for any thing I know, Falstaff shall die of a sweat,[5] unless already a' be

---

[1]stage direction] *Spoken by a Dancer.*
[2]*I doubt*] I fear.
[3]*I break*] I become bankrupt.
[4]*our humble author . . . with Sir John in it*] This promise was not fulfilled in the sequel to this play, *Henry V*, from which Falstaff is excluded.
[5]*Falstaff shall die of a sweat*] an allusion either to the sweating sickness or to venereal disease.

killed with your hard opinions; for Oldcastle died a martyr, and this is not the man.[6] My tongue is weary; when my legs are too, I will bid you good night: and so kneel down before you; but, indeed, to pray for the queen.[7]

---

[6]*Oldcastle died a martyr . . . man*] In his first draft of the piece Shakespeare bestowed on his fat humourist the name of Sir John Oldcastle, the Lollard leader, who was executed in 1417. In deference to protests, Shakespeare changed the name before the piece was printed to Falstaff, and here, somewhat lightly, calls attention to the alteration.

[7]*pray for the queen*] It was the custom on the Elizabethan stage for the actors at the end of a performance to kneel down and recite a prayer for the queen.

Henry V

Henry V

By the time depicted in this play, Henry has left his riotous youth behind, discarded his drinking companions from the Boar's-Head Tavern, and become a great leader. Though he has retained his common touch and his sense of humor, he has become fiercely focused, brave, modest, and forgiving—but with a sense of justice so strong that when one of his former companions robs a church in France he does not hesitate to have him put to death. He has become the greatest of English kings.

This, at least, was the Elizabethans' estimation of Henry V. The last decade of the sixteenth century, when Shakespeare wrote his history plays, was a time of intense patriotism in England. People had strong memories of the Spanish Armada's bold incursion, in July 1588, into the English Channel, with the intent—fully supported and blessed by the Pope—of deposing Elizabeth and installing a Catholic ruler in her stead. The Armada's defeat was even more earth-shaking than Henry V's unforgettably lopsided victory at Agincourt; it marked the end of Spanish dominance and the rise of England as a world power. In the exuberant patriotism of the following decade, Shakespeare's history plays (which are among the earliest plays he wrote) proved to be resoundingly popular. The first part of *Henry VI* probably was staged the year after the Armada's defeat, when the author was only 25, and he kept the franchise going through the 1590s, following the remaining two parts of *Henry VI* with *Richard III*, *Richard II*, *King John*, and the two parts of *Henry IV* before tackling *Henry V*. *Henry V* was first performed in 1599 and has remained one of the most popular of Shakespeare's history plays ever since.

The historical Henry V was probably quite different from the man Shakespeare portrays. As far as we can tell, he was never the slacker or tavern habitué portrayed in *Henry IV*. Even as a teen-ager, he was in the heart of battles and politics. At least nominally, he was administrator of Wales from the age of 13. Three years later, he was in actual command of the English forces in the battle of Shrewsbury. Even during his memorable though relatively brief kingship,[1] Henry was not

---

[1] Two years after marrying Catherine, when their son (the future Henry VI) was eight months old, Henry, who was longing to mount a new crusade to the Holy Land, died in France of dysentery. He was not quite thirty-five years old. Catherine, who was twenty-one at the time, went on to bear five children to her Welsh squire, Owen Tudor (who may or may not have become her husband); the eldest of these children, Edmund, later fathered Henry VII, the first in the Tudor line that was to end with Elizabeth.

entirely the sort of person portrayed by Shakespeare. He was acknowl-edged to be brave, honorable, and just, but he could also be ruthless, intolerant, and fanatic. As a modern biographer has written, "Henry had none of the more attractive virtues—he had little charm, although a real concern for his soldiers; no sense of humor, and a truly terrifying conviction of his own position as the instrument of God."[2]

But Shakespeare did not have access to modern scholarship, and actually he stayed fairly close to the sources that were available to him—primarily Raphael Holinshed's *Chronicles of England, Scotland, and Ireland* (published in 1587) and Samuel Daniel's poem *The Civile Wars Between the Two Houses of Lancaster and Yorke* (1595). He also picked up a few incidents (such as the Dauphin's gift of tennis balls, Pistol's encounter with Monsieur le Fer, and Henry's wooing of Catherine) from the anonymous chronicle play *The Famous Victories of Henry V* (probably first acted around 1588). These works all acced-ed to the view of Henry's wild youth and sudden conversion that was first promulgated about twenty years after his death—a view that seems to have had its origin in the friendship that the young Henry had had with Sir John Oldcastle.[3] Oldcastle was a leader of the Lollards (who had the misfortune to espouse protestantism a hundred years before Henry VIII gave it the royal imprimatur), and when Prince Hal became king he signed his old friend's death warrant. Though Sir John had paid for his religious beliefs by being burned to death over a slow fire, he was still remembered as a corrupter of youth.

All these historical facts are interesting. But what matters, when you read this play, is not what the "real" Henry V was like, or what Shake-speare's sources said, or what became of Catherine, or any of the other ribbons and bows that, in the guise of introductions or critiques, one can wrap around any of Shakespeare's works. The only important thing is the play itself. Transport yourself into the "wooden O" of the Globe theater in 1599, and find yourself being pulled along inexorably by the astounding dramaturgy, poetry, passion, humor, and human truth that make up this and virtually every other play by Will. Shakespeare, Gent.

T. N. R. ROGERS

---

[2] Margaret Wade Labarge, in *Henry V: The Cautious Conqueror* (London: Secker and Warburg, 1975).

[3] Shakespeare originally gave Oldcastle's name to the character who later turned into Jack Falstaff. He evidently changed the name at the behest of one of Oldcastle's descendants.

Dramatis Personæ[1]

KING HENRY the Fifth.
DUKE OF GLOUCESTER, } brothers to the King.
DUKE OF BEDFORD,
DUKE OF EXETER, uncle to the King.
DUKE OF YORK, cousin to the King.
EARLS OF SALISBURY, WESTMORELAND, and WARWICK.
ARCHBISHOP OF CANTERBURY.
BISHOP OF ELY.
EARL OF CAMBRIDGE.
LORD SCROOP.
SIR THOMAS GREY.
SIR THOMAS ERPINGHAM, GOWER, FLUELLEN, MACMORRIS, JAMY, officers
    in King Henry's army.
BATES, COURT, WILLIAMS, soldiers in the same.
PISTOL, NYM, BARDOLPH.
Boy.
A Herald.

CHARLES the Sixth, King of France.
LEWIS, the Dauphin.
DUKES OF BURGUNDY, ORLEANS, and BOURBON.
The Constable of France.
RAMBURES AND GRANDPRÉ, French Lords.
Governor of Harfleur.
MONTJOY, a French Herald.
Ambassadors to the King of England.

ISABEL, Queen of France.
KATHARINE, daughter to Charles and Isabel.
ALICE, a lady attending on her.
Hostess of a tavern in Eastcheap, formerly Mistress Quickly, and now
    married to Pistol.

Lords, Ladies, Officers, Soldiers, Citizens, Messengers, and Attendants.

Chorus.

SCENE—*England; afterwards France*

---

[1]The full text of this play first appeared in the First Folio of 1623. An imperfect sketch
was issued surreptitiously in 1600 in a Quarto volume, which was reissued in 1602 and
1608. The First Folio divides the piece into Acts only, although the opening heading
runs "Actus Primus Scœna Prima." Pope first supplied scenic subdivisions.

PROLOGUE

Enter Chorus

CHORUS. O for a muse of fire, that would ascend
    The brightest heaven of invention,
    A kingdom for a stage, princes to act
    And monarchs to behold the swelling scene!
    Then should the warlike Harry, like himself,
    Assume the port of Mars; and at his heels,
    Leash'd in like hounds, should famine, sword and fire
    Crouch for employment. But pardon, gentles all,
    The flat unraised spirits that have dared
    On this unworthy scaffold to bring forth   10
    So great an object: can this cockpit hold
    The vasty fields of France? or may we cram
    Within this wooden O the very casques
    That did affright the air at Agincourt?
    O, pardon! since a crooked figure may
    Attest in little place a million;
    And let us, ciphers to this great accompt,
    On your imaginary forces work.
    Suppose within the girdle of these walls
    Are now confined two mighty monarchies,   20
    Whose high upreared and abutting fronts

6 *port*] carriage.
9 *unraised*] humble, lowly.
10 *scaffold*] stage.
11 *cockpit*] place appointed for cock-fighting matches, a reference to the confined area
    of the theatre.
13 *this wooden O*] A reference to the newly-erected Globe Theatre with its circular in-
    terior. This play was one of the first pieces produced there.
    casques] helmets.
17 *accompt*] account.
18 *imaginary forces*] powers of imagination.
21 *abutting fronts*] the cliffs of Dover and Calais.

The perilous narrow ocean parts asunder:
Piece out our imperfections with your thoughts;
Into a thousand parts divide one man,
And make imaginary puissance;
Think, when we talk of horses, that you see them
Printing their proud hoofs i' the receiving earth;
For 't is your thoughts that now must deck our kings,
Carry them here and there; jumping o'er times,
Turning the accomplishment of many years   30
Into an hour-glass: for the which supply,
Admit me Chorus to this history;
Who prologue-like your humble patience pray,
Gently to hear, kindly to judge, our play.

                                                     [*Exit.*

23 *Piece out*] Make up.
24 *Into a thousand . . . man*] Suppose one man to represent a thousand.
25 *puissance*] armed might, army.
31 *an hour-glass*] A rough estimate of the time occupied by a theatrical performance.
32 *Chorus*] Interpreter.

ACT I.

SCENE I. *London. An Ante-Chamber in the King's Palace.*

Enter the ARCHBISHOP of CANTERBURY, *and the* BISHOP of ELY

CANTERBURY.　My Lord, I'll tell you; that self bill is urged,
　　Which in the eleventh year of the last king's reign
　　Was like, and had indeed against us pass'd,
　　But that the scambling and unquiet time
　　Did push it out of farther question.
ELY.　But how, my lord, shall we resist it now?
CANT.　It must be thought on. If it pass against us,
　　We lose the better half of our possession:
　　For all the temporal lands, which men devout
　　By testament have given to the church,　　　　　　　　　10
　　Would they strip from us; being valued thus:
　　As much as would maintain, to the king's honour,
　　Full fifteen earls and fifteen hundred knights,
　　Six thousand and two hundred good esquires;
　　And, to relief of lazars and weak age,
　　Of indigent faint souls past corporal toil,
　　A hundred almshouses right well supplied;
　　And to the coffers of the king beside,
　　A thousand pounds by the year: thus runs the bill.
ELY.　This would drink deep.　　　　　　　　　　　　　　20
CANT.　　　　　　　　　'T would drink the cup and all.
ELY.　But what prevention?
CANT.　The king is full of grace and fair regard.
ELY.　And a true lover of the holy church.

---

1 CANTERBURY] The speaker is Henry Chichele, Archbishop of Canterbury, founder of All Souls College, Oxford. Shakespeare makes him the leader of the plot against Henry IV's bill for confiscating church property.
　　self] same.
4 *scambling*] bustling, turbulent.
15 *lazars*] lepers.

CANT.   The courses of his youth promised it not.
        The breath no sooner left his father's body,
        But that his wildness, mortified in him,
        Seem'd to die too; yea, at that very moment,
        Consideration like an angel came
        And whipp'd the offending Adam out of him,   30
        Leaving his body as a paradise,
        To envelope and contain celestial spirits.
        Never was such a sudden scholar made;
        Never came reformation in a flood,
        With such a heady currance, scouring faults;
        Nor never Hydra-headed wilfulness
        So soon did lose his seat, and all at once,
        As in this king.
ELY.   We are blessed in the change,
CANT.   Hear him but reason in divinity,   40
        And all-admiring with an inward wish
        You would desire the king were made a prelate:
        Hear him debate of commonwealth affairs,
        You would say it hath been all in all his study:
        List his discourse of war, and you shall hear
        A fearful battle render'd you in music:
        Turn him to any cause of policy,
        The Gordian knot of it he will unloose,
        Familiar as his garter: that, when he speaks,
        The air, a charter'd libertine, is still,   50
        And the mute wonder lurketh in men's ears,
        To steal his sweet and honey'd sentences;
        So that the art and practic part of life
        Must be the mistress to this theoric:
        Which is a wonder how his grace should glean it,
        Since his addiction was to courses vain,
        His companies unletter'd, rude and shallow,

27 *mortified*] killed.
29 *Consideration*] Reflection, repentance.
30 *offending Adam*] original sin.
35 *heady currance*] impetuous flow.
36 *Hydra-headed wilfulness*] many headed, infinitely varied, waywardness.
37 *his seat*] throne.
42 *prelate*] a high-ranking church dignitary.
47 *cause of policy*] question of state affairs.
53 *art and practic part of life*] practical experience of life.
54 *mistress to this theoric*] the inspirer or teacher of this theoretical knowledge.
57 *companies*] companions, associates.

His hours fill'd up with riots, banquets, sports,
And never noted in him any study,
Any retirement, any sequestration   60
From open haunts and popularity.

ELY.   The strawberry grows underneath the nettle,
And wholesome berries thrive and ripen best
Neighbour'd by fruit of baser quality:
And so the prince obscured his contemplation
Under the veil of wildness; which, no doubt,
Grew like the summer grass, fastest by night,
Unseen, yet crescive in his faculty.

CANT.   It must be so; for miracles are ceased;
And therefore we must needs admit the means   70
How things are perfected.

ELY.   But, my good lord,
How now for mitigation of this bill
Urged by the commons? Doth his majesty
Incline to it, or no?

CANT.   He seems indifferent,
Or rather swaying more upon our part
Than cherishing the exhibiters against us;
For I have made an offer to his majesty,
Upon our spiritual convocation   80
And in regard of causes now in hand,
Which I have open'd to his grace at large,
As touching France, to give a greater sum
Than ever at one time the clergy yet
Did to his predecessors part withal.

ELY.   How did this offer seem received, my lord?

CANT.   With good acceptance of his majesty;
Save that there was not time enough to hear,
As I perceived his grace would fain have done,
The severals and unhidden passages   90
Of his true titles to some certain dukedoms,
And generally to the crown and seat of France,
Derived from Edward, his great-grandfather.

ELY.   What was the impediment that broke this off?

CANT.   The French ambassador upon that instant

---

61 *popularity*] intercourse with the common people.
65 *obscured his contemplation*] concealed his devotion to study.
68 *crescive in his faculty*] increasing in strength.
77 *swaying*] inclining.
90 *The severals . . . passages*] The details and clear or undoubted steps in the lineage.

    Craved audience; and the hour, I think, is come
    To give him hearing: is it four o'clock?

ELY.   It is.

CANT.   Then go we in, to know his embassy;
    Which I could with a ready guess declare,   100
    Before the Frenchman speak a word of it.

ELY.   I'll wait upon you, and I long to hear it.   [*Exeunt.*

SCENE II. *The Same—The Presence Chamber.*

Enter KING HENRY, GLOUCESTER, BEDFORD, EXETER, WARWICK,
   WESTMORELAND, *and* Attendants

K. HEN.   Where is my gracious Lord of Canterbury?

EXE.   Not here in presence.

K. HEN.   Send for him, good uncle.

WEST.   Shall we call in the ambassador, my liege?

K. HEN.   Not yet, my cousin: we would be resolved,
    Before we hear him, of some things of weight
    That task our thoughts, concerning us and France.

Enter the ARCHBISHOP *of* CANTERBURY *and the* BISHOP *of* ELY

CANT.   God and his angels guard your sacred throne
    And make you long become it!

K. HEN.   Sure, we thank you.   10
    My learned lord, we pray you to proceed
    And justly and religiously unfold
    Why the law Salique that they have in France
    Or should, or should not, bar us in our claim:
    And God forbid, my dear and faithful lord,
    That you should fashion, wrest, or bow your reading,
    Or nicely charge your understanding soul
    With opening titles miscreate, whose right
    Suits not in native colours with the truth;
    For God doth know how many now in health   20
    Shall drop their blood in approbation
    Of what your reverence shall incite us to.

---

5 *resolved*] satisfied.
13 *the law Salique*] the Salic law against the succession of females.
17 *nicely charge . . . soul*] by subtlety or sophistry oppress or injure your conscience,
   which knows the truth.
18 *With . . . miscreate*] By setting forth spurious titles.
21–22 *in approbation Of*] in making good, in actively carrying out.

Therefore take heed how you impawn our person,
How you awake our sleeping sword of war:
We charge you, in the name of God, take heed;
For never two such kingdoms did contend
Without much fall of blood; whose guiltless drops
Are every one a woe, a sore complaint
'Gainst him whose wrongs give edge unto the swords
That make such waste in brief mortality.   30
Under this conjuration speak, my lord;
For we will hear, note and believe in heart'
That what you speak is in your conscience wash'd
As pure as sin with baptism.
CANT.   Then hear me, gracious sovereign, and you peers,
That owe yourselves, your lives and services
To this imperial throne. There is no bar
To make against your highness' claim to France
But this, which they produce from Pharamond,
"In terram Salicam mulieres ne succedant":   40
"No woman shall succeed in Salique land":
Which Salique land the French unjustly gloze
To be the realm of France, and Pharamond
The founder of this law and female bar.
Yet their own authors faithfully affirm
That the land Salique is in Germany,
Between the floods of Sala and of Elbe;
Where Charles the Great, having subdued the Saxons,
There left behind and settled certain French;
Who, holding in disdain the German women   50
For some dishonest manners of their life,
Establish'd then this law; to wit, no female
Should be inheritrix in Salique land:
Which Salique, as I said, 'twixt Elbe and Sala,
Is at this day in Germany call'd Meisen.
Then doth it well appear the Salique law
Was not devised for the realm of France;
Nor did the French possess the Salique land
Until four hundred one and twenty years
After defunction of King Pharamond,   60
Idly supposed the founder of this law;
Who died within the year of our redemption

42 *gloze*] explain, interpret.
51 *dishonest*] unchaste.
60 *defunction*] death of.

Four hundred twenty-six; and Charles the Great
Subdued the Saxons, and did seat the French
Beyond the river Sala, in the year
Eight hundred five. Besides, their writers say,
King Pepin, which deposed Childeric,
Did, as heir general, being descended
Of Blithild, which was daughter to King Clothair,
Make claim and title to the crown of France.   70
Hugh Capet also, who usurp'd the crown
Of Charles the duke of Lorraine, sole heir male
Of the true line and stock of Charles the Great,
To find his title with some shows of truth,
Though, in pure truth, it was corrupt and naught,
Convey'd himself as heir to the Lady Lingare,
Daughter to Charlemain, who was the son
To Lewis the emperor, and Lewis the son
Of Charles the Great. Also King Lewis the tenth,
Who was sole heir to the usurper Capet,   80
Could not keep quiet in his conscience,
Wearing the crown of France, till satisfied
That fair Queen Isabel, his grandmother,
Was lineal of the Lady Ermengare,
Daughter to Charles the foresaid duke of Lorraine:
By the which marriage the line of Charles the Great
Was re-united to the crown of France.
So that, as clear as is the summer's sun,
King Pepin's title and Hugh Capet's claim,
King Lewis his satisfaction, all appear   90
To hold in right and title of the female:
So do the kings of France unto this day;
Howbeit they would hold up this Salique law
To bar your highness claiming from the female,
And rather choose to hide them in a net
Than amply to imbar their crooked titles
Usurp'd from you and your progenitors.
K. HEN.   May I with right and conscience make this claim?
CANT.   The sin upon my head, dread sovereign!

---

76 *Convey'd himself*] Represented himself, passed himself off.
84 *lineal of*] lineally descended from.
90 *King Lewis his satisfaction*] the satisfying of King Lewis's scruples.
95 *hide them in a net*] hide the weakness of their argument in a tangle of contradictions.
96 *amply to imbar . . . titles*] fully and frankly to admit the fatal defect in (and so disown)
   their own unjust or false titles.

For in the book of Numbers is it writ,
When the man dies, let the inheritance   100
. Descend unto the daughter. Gracious lord,
Stand for your own; unwind your bloody flag;
Look back into your mighty ancestors:
Go, my dread lord, to your great-grandsire's tomb,
From whom you claim; invoke his warlike spirit,
And your great-uncle's, Edward the Black Prince,
Who on the French ground play'd a tragedy,
Making defeat on the full power of France,
Whiles his most mighty father on a hill   110
Stood smiling to behold his lion's whelp
Forage in blood of French nobility.
O noble English, that could entertain
With half their forces the full pride of France
And let another half stand laughing by,
All out of work and cold for action!

ELY.   Awake remembrance of these valiant dead,
And with your puissant arm renew their feats:
You are their heir; you sit upon their throne;
The blood and courage that renowned them   120
Runs in your veins; and my thrice-puissant liege
Is in the very May-morn of his youth,
Ripe for exploits and mighty enterprises.

EXE.   Your brother kings and monarchs of the earth
Do all expect that you should rouse yourself,
As did the former lions of your blood.

WEST.   They know your grace hath cause and means and might;
So hath your highness; never king of England
Had nobles richer and more loyal subjects,
Whose hearts have left their bodies here in England   130
And lie pavilion'd in the fields of France.

CANT.   O, let their bodies follow, my dear liege,
With blood and sword and fire to win your right;
In aid whereof we of the spiritualty
Will raise your highness such a mighty sum
As never did the clergy at one time
Bring in to any of your ancestors.

103 *your bloody flag*] your flag of war.
108 *Who . . . play'd a tragedy*] A reference to the battle of Crécy in 1346.
116 *cold for action*] cold for want of action, for standing idle.
131 *And lie pavilion'd*] And are already (in imagination) dwelling in tents in preparation
for war.
134 *spiritualty*] clergy.

K. HEN.   We must not only arm to invade the French,
         But lay down our proportions to defend
         Against the Scot, who will make road upon us   140
         With all advantages.
CANT.   They of those marches, gracious sovereign,
         Shall be a wall sufficient to defend
         Our inland from the pilfering borderers.
K. HEN.   We do not mean the coursing snatchers only,
         But fear the main intendment of the Scot,
         Who hath been still a giddy neighbour to us;
         For you shall read that my great-grandfather
         Never went with his forces into France,
         But that the Scot on his unfurnish'd kingdom   150
         Came pouring, like the tide into a breach,
         With ample and brim fulness of his force,
         Galling the gleaned land with hot assays,
         Girding with grievous siege castles and towns;
         That England, being empty of defence,
         Hath shook and trembled at the ill neighbourhood.
CANT.   She hath been then more fear'd than harm'd, my liege;
         For hear her but exampled by herself:
         When all her chivalry hath been in France,
         And she a mourning widow of her nobles,   160
         She hath herself not only well defended,
         But taken and impounded as a stray
         The King of Scots; whom she did send to France,
         To fill King Edward's fame with prisoner kings,
         And make her chronicle as rich with praise,
         As is the ooze and bottom of the sea
         With sunken wreck and sumless treasuries.
WEST.   But there's a saying very old and true,
            "If that you will France win,
            Then with Scotland first begin":   170
         For once the eagle England being in prey,

139 *lay down our proportions*] allocate our forces.
140 *make road . . . advantages*] make inroads at every favorable opportunity.
142 *They of those marches*] The inhabitants of the Scottish border.
145 *coursing snatchers*] scattered, unattached raiders.
146 *the main intendment of the Scot*] the design of the armed forces of Scotland.
147 *giddy*] fickle, untrustworthy.
153 *assays*] assaults.
163 *The King of Scots*] David II, the king of Scotland, was taken prisoner at the battle of
         Neville's Cross, October 17, 1346, and was captive in England for eleven years.
164 *prisoner kings*] John II, king of France, was also one of Edward III's prisoners.

To her unguarded nest the weasel Scot
Comes sneaking and so sucks her princely eggs,
Playing the mouse in absence of the cat,
To tear and havoc more than she can eat.

EXE.   It follows then the cat must stay at home:
Yet that is but a crush'd necessity,
Since we have locks to safeguard necessaries,
And pretty traps to catch the petty thieves.
While that the armed hand doth fight abroad,   180
The advised head defends itself at home;
For government, though high and low and lower,
Put into parts, doth keep in one consent,
Congreeing in a full and natural close,
Like music.

CANT.   Therefore doth heaven divide
The state of man in divers functions,
Setting endeavour in continual motion;
To which is fixed, as an aim or butt,
Obedience: for so work the honey-bees,   190
Creatures that by a rule in nature teach
The act of order to a peopled kingdom.
They have a king and officers of sorts;
Where some, like magistrates correct at home,
Others, like merchants, venture trade abroad,
Others, like soldiers, armed in their stings,
Make boot upon the summer's velvet buds,
Which pillage they with merry march bring home
To the tent-royal of their emperor;
Who, busied in his majesty, surveys   200
The singing masons building roofs of gold,
The civil citizens kneading up the honey,
The poor mechanic porters crowding in
Their heavy burdens at his narrow gate,
The sad-eyed justice, with his surly hum,

---

177 *a crush'd necessity*] a need or condition that is put out of account or rendered
   negligible.
181 *advised*] thoughtful.
183 *in one consent*] in unison.
184 *Congreeing . . . close*] Harmonizing . . . cadence.
189 *butt*] goal or target.
197 *boot*] booty, prey.
202 *civil*] orderly.
205 *sad-eyed*] grave-eyed.

Delivering o'er to executors pale
The lazy yawning drone. I this infer,
That many things, having full reference
To one consent, may work contrariously:
As many arrows, loosed several ways,　　　　　　　　　210
Come to one mark; as many ways meet in one town;
As many fresh streams meet in one salt sea;
As many lines close in the dial's centre;
So may a thousand actions, once afoot,
End in one purpose, and be all well borne
Without defeat. Therefore to France, my liege.
Divide your happy England into four;
Whereof take you one quarter into France,
And you withal shall make all Gallia shake.
If we, with thrice such powers left at home,　　　　　220
Cannot defend our own doors from the dog,
Let us be worried and our nation lose
The name of hardiness and policy.

K. HEN.　　Call in the messengers sent from the Dauphin.

　　　　　　　　　　　　　　　　[*Exeunt some Attendants.*

Now are we well resolved; and, by God's help,
And yours, the noble sinews of our power,
France being ours, we'll bend it to our awe,
Or break it all to pieces: or there we'll sit,
Ruling in large and ample empery
O'er France and all her almost kingly dukedoms,　　230
Or lay these bones in an unworthy urn,
Tombless, with no remembrance over them:
Either our history shall with full mouth
Speak freely of our acts, or else our grave,
Like Turkish mute, shall have a tongueless mouth,
Not worshipp'd with a waxen epitaph.

Enter Ambassadors of France

206 *executors*] executioners.
219 *Gallia*] France.
223 *hardiness and policy*] valor and political wisdom.
224 *Dauphin*] the heir apparent to the French throne.
229 *empery*] dominion.
236 *Not worshipp'd with . . . epitaph*] Not honored even with an inscription in wax.
　　"Waxen" suggests that which can be easily effaced, is not lasting.

Now are we well prepared to know the pleasure
Of our fair cousin Dauphin; for we hear
Your greeting is from him, not from the king.

FIRST AMB.   May't please your majesty to give us leave   240
Freely to render what we have in charge;
Or shall we sparingly show you far off
The Dauphin's meaning and our embassy?

K. HEN.   We are no tyrant, but a Christian king;
Unto whose grace our passion is as subject
As are our wretches fetter'd in our prisons:
Therefore with frank and with uncurbed plainness
Tell us the Dauphin's mind.

FIRST AMB.   Thus, then, in few.
Your highness, lately sending into France,   250
Did claim some certain dukedoms, in the right
Of your great predecessor, King Edward the third.
In answer of which claim, the prince our master
Says that you savour too much of your youth,
And bids you be advised there's nought in France
That can be with a nimble galliard won;
You cannot revel into dukedoms there.
He therefore sends you, meeter for your spirit,
This tun of pleasure; and, in lieu of this,
Desires you let the dukedoms that you claim   260
Hear no more of you. This the Dauphin speaks.

K. HEN.   What treasure, uncle?

EXE.   Tennis-balls, my liege.

K. HEN.   We are glad the Dauphin is so pleasant with us;
His present and your pains we thank you for:
When we have match'd our rackets to these balls,
We will, in France, by God's grace, play a set
Shall strike his father's crown into the hazard.
Tell him he hath made a match with such a wrangler
That all the courts of France will be disturb'd   270

---

256 *galliard*] quick dance.
258 *meeter*] more fitting.
259 *This tun*] This barrel.
    in lieu of this] in exchange for this gift.
267 *play a set*] This play abounds in the technical vocabulary of a game or set at tennis.
268 *the hazard*] a hole in the wall of the tennis court near the ground. A stroke into this
    hole would score a point for the player.
269 *a wrangler*] an opponent.

With chaces. And we understand him well,
How he comes o'er us with our wilder days,
Not measuring what use we made of them.
We never valued this poor seat of England;
And therefore, living hence, did give ourself
To barbarous license; as 't is ever common
That men are merriest when they are from home.
But tell the Dauphin I will keep my state,
Be like a king and show my sail of greatness
When I do rouse me in my throne of France: 280
For that I have laid by my majesty,
And plodded like a man for working-days;
But I will rise there with so full a glory
That I will dazzle all the eyes of France,
Yea, strike the Dauphin blind to look on us.
And tell the pleasant prince this mock of his
Hath turn'd his balls to gun-stones; and his soul
Shall stand sore charged for the wasteful vengeance
That shall fly with them: for many a thousand widows
Shall this his mock mock out of their dear husbands;   290
Mock mothers from their sons, mock castles down;
And some are yet ungotten and unborn
That shall have cause to curse the Dauphin's scorn.
But this lies all within the will of God,
To whom I do appeal; and in whose name
Tell you the Dauphin I am coming on,
To venge me as I may and to put forth
My rightful hand in a well-hallow'd cause.
So get you hence in peace; and tell the Dauphin
His jest will savour but of shallow wit,   300
When thousands weep more than did laugh at it.
Convey them with safe conduct. Fare you well.
                                          [*Exeunt* Ambassadors.
EXE.   This was a merry message.
K. HEN.   We hope to make the sender blush at it.

271 *chaces*] the word has various meanings in tennis, viz., a double bounce or an unsuccessful return.
272 *comes o'er us*] taunts us.
274 *seat of England*] throne of England.
275 *hence*] away from the court.
281 *For that I have laid by*] Despite the fact that I have laid aside or neglected my dignity.
287 *gun-stones*] cannonballs, which were originally made of stone.
288 *sore charged*] sorely burdened with responsibility.

Therefore, my lords, omit no happy hour
That may give furtherance to our expedition;
For we have now no thought in us but France,
Save those to God, that run before our business.
Therefore let our proportions for these wars
Be soon collected, and all things thought upon   310
That may with reasonable swiftness add
More feathers to our wings; for, God before,
We'll chide this Dauphin at his father's door.
Therefore let every man now task his thought,
That this fair action may on foot be brought.

                              [*Exeunt. Flourish.*

309 *proportions*] numbers.
312 *God before*] God guiding us.

ACT II.—PROLOGUE

Enter Chorus

CHORUS.   Now all the youth of England are on fire,
 And silken dalliance in the wardrobe lies:
 Now thrive the armorers, and honour's thought
 Reigns solely in the breast of every man:
 They sell the pasture now to buy the horse,
 Following the mirror of all Christian kings,
 With winged heels, as English Mercuries.
 For now sits Expectation in the air,
 And hides a sword from hilts unto the point
 With crowns imperial, crowns and coronets,   10
 Promised to Harry and his followers.
 The French, advised by good intelligence
 Of this most dreadful preparation,
 Shake in their fear and with pale policy
 Seek to divert the English purposes.
 O England! model to thy inward greatness,
 Like little body with a mighty heart,
 What mightst thou do, that honour would thee do,
 Were all thy children kind and natural!
 But see thy fault! France hath in thee found out   20
 A nest of hollow bosoms, which he fills
 With treacherous crowns; and three corrupted men,
 One, Richard Earl of Cambridge, and the second,
 Henry Lord Scroop of Masham, and the third,
 Sir Thomas Gray, knight, of Northumberland,
 Have, for the gilt of France,—O guilt indeed!—
 Confirm'd conspiracy with fearful France;

2 *silken dalliance*] silk clothes (i.e., luxuries) and idle pleasures are stored away.
16 *model*] model in miniature, pattern.
19 *kind*] filial.
20 *France*] The king of France.

And by their hands this grace of kings must die,
If hell and treason hold their promises,
Ere he take ship for France, and in Southampton.   30
Linger your patience on; and we'll digest
The abuse of distance; force a play:
The sum is paid; the traitors are agreed;
The king is set from London; and the scene
Is now transported, gentles, to Southampton;
There is the playhouse now, there must you sit:
And thence to France shall we convey you safe,
And bring you back, charming the narrow seas
To give you gentle pass; for, if we may,
We'll not offend one stomach with our play.   40
But, till the king come forth, and not till then,
Unto Southampton do we shift our scene.

[*Exit.*

Scene I. *London. A Street.*

Enter Corporal Nym *and* Lieutenant Bardolph

Bard.   Well met, Corporal Nym.
Nym.   Good morrow, Lieutenant Bardolph.
Bard.   What, are Ancient Pistol and you friends yet?
Nym.   For my part, I care not: I say little; but when time shall
        serve, there shall be smiles; but that shall be as it may. I dare
        not fight; but I will wink and hold out mine iron: it is a sim-
        ple one; but what though? it will toast cheese, and it will en-
        dure cold as another man's sword will: and there's an end.
Bard.   I will bestow a breakfast to make you friends; and we'll be

---

31–32 *Linger . . . on . . . force a play*] The meaning may be, "Prolong your patience, and
  we'll set right the awkwardness of the distance between the different places where the
  incidents of the play occur, and compel the sequence of events into the necessary limits of dramatic action."
40 *We'll not offend one stomach*] We'll make nobody seasick.
41–42 *But, till the king . . . scene*] The words very crudely explain that the scene will not
  be shifted from London to Southampton until the king comes onstage again.

1 *Nym*] In thieves' language the word is a verb meaning "to steal."
3 *Ancient*] Ensign.
5 *when time . . . smiles*] probably Nym means that one of them will have the laugh on
  his side, when the time comes for him and Pistol to square accounts.
6 *wink*] shut my eyes.
  iron] sword.

all three sworn brothers to France: let it be so, good Corporal 10
Nym.

NYM. Faith, I will live so long as I may, that's the certain of it;
and when I cannot live any longer, I will do as I may: that is
my rest, that is the rendezvous of it.

BARD. It is certain, corporal, that he is married to Nell Quickly:
and, certainly, she did you wrong; for you were troth-plight
to her.

NYM. I cannot tell: things must be as they may: men may sleep,
and they may have their throats about them at that time; and
some say knives have edges. It must be as it may: though pa- 20
tience be a tired mare, yet she will plod. There must be conclusions. Well, I cannot tell.

Enter PISTOL *and* HOSTESS

BARD. Here comes Ancient Pistol and his wife: good corporal,
be patient here. How now, mine host Pistol!

PIST. Base tike, call'st thou me host?
Now, by this hand, I swear, I scorn the term;
Nor shall my Nell keep lodgers.

HOST. No, by my troth, not long; for we cannot lodge and board
a dozen or fourteen gentlewomen that live honestly by the
prick of their needles, but it will be thought we keep a bawdy 30
house straight. [NYM *and* PISTOL *draw.*] O well a day, Lady,
if he be not drawn now! we shall see wilful adultery and murder committed.

BARD. Good lieutenant! good corporal! offer nothing here.

NYM. Pish!

PIST. Pish for thee, Iceland dog! thou prick-ear'd cur of Iceland!

HOST. Good Corporal Nym, show thy valour, and put up your
sword.

NYM. Will you shog off? I would have you solus.

PIST. "Solus," egregious dog? O viper vile! 40

---

10 *sworn brothers to France*] bosom comrades on our visit to France.
14 *rest*] stake or wager; a term in the game of "primero."
16 *troth-plight*] betrothed.
21–22 *conclusions*] an end to all things.
25 *tike*] ugly dog.
34 *offer nothing*] do not fight.
36 *Iceland dog*] a shaggy, sharp-eared, white-haired dog, in much favor with ladies in
Shakespeare's time.
39 *shog off*] go.
40 *solus*] alone.

The "solus" in thy most mervailous face;
The "solus" in thy teeth, and in thy throat,
And in thy hateful lungs, yea, in thy maw, perdy,
And, which is worse, within thy nasty mouth!
I do retort the "solus" in thy bowels;
For I can take, and Pistol's cock is up,
And flashing fire will follow.

NYM.   I am not Barbason; you cannot conjure me. I have an humour to knock you indifferently well. If you grow foul with me, Pistol, I will scour you with my rapier, as I may, in fair   50
terms: if you would walk off, I would prick your guts a little, in good terms, as I may: and that's the humour of it.

PIST.   O braggart vile, and damned furious wight!
The grave doth gape, and doting death is near;
Therefore exhale.

BARD.   Hear me, hear me what I say: he that strikes the first stroke, I'll run him up to the hilts, as I am a soldier.

                                         [*Draws.*

PIST.   An oath of mickle might; and fury shall abate.
Give me thy fist, thy fore-foot to me give:
Thy spirits are most tall.   60

NYM.   I will cut thy throat, one time or other, in fair terms: that is the humour of it.

PIST.   "Couple a gorge!"
That is the word. I thee defy again.
O hound of Crete, think'st thou my spouse to get?
No; to the spital go,
And from the powdering-tub of infamy
Fetch forth the lazar kite of Cressid's kind,

---

41 *mervailous*] Pistol's affected pronunciation of "marvelous."

43 *perdy*] a corruption of "par Dieu," "by God."

46 *take*] "take fire" or "catch fire"; used of a gun going off. Pistol is talking to himself as if he were a pistol.

48 *Barbason*] a popular name of a fiend of hell.

52 *that's the humour of it*] that's my meaning.

53 *wight*] person.

55 *exhale*] draw swords, in Pistol's vocabulary.

58 *mickle*] great.

63 *"Couple a gorge!"*] Corruption of "Coupe la gorge," cut your throat.

65 *O hound of Crete*] Cretan hounds were credited by classical authors with special excellence.

66–67 *spital . . . powdering-tub*] a reference to the hospital and the treatment accorded there to sufferers from venereal disease.

68 *the lazar kite of Cressid's kind*] the leprous whore.

Doll Tearsheet she by name, and her espouse:
I have, and I will hold, the quondam Quickly   70
For the only she; and—pauca, there's enough.
Go to.

Enter the Boy

BOY.   Mine host Pistol, you must come to my master, and you,
hostess: he is very sick, and would to bed. Good Bardolph,
put thy face between his sheets, and do the office of a
warming-pan. Faith, he's very ill.

BARD.   Away, you rogue!

HOST.   By my troth, he'll yield the crow a pudding one of these
days. The king has killed his heart. Good husband, come
home presently.   [*Exeunt* HOSTESS *and* boy.   80

BARD.   Come, shall I make you two friends? We must to France
together: why the devil should we keep knives to cut one another's throats?

PIST.   Let floods o'erswell, and fiends for food howl on!

NYM.   You'll pay me the eight shillings I won of you at betting?

PIST.   Base is the slave that pays.

NYM.   That now I will have: that's the humour of it.

PIST.   As manhood shall compound: push home.   [*They draw.*

BARD.   By this sword, he that makes the first thrust, I'll kill him;
by this sword, I will.   90

PIST.   Sword is an oath, and oaths must have their course.

BARD.   Corporal Nym, an thou wilt be friends, be friends: an
thou wilt not, why, then, be enemies with me too. Prithee,
put up.

NYM.   I shall have my eight shillings I won of you at betting?

PIST.   A noble shalt thou have, and present pay;
And liquor likewise will I give to thee,
And friendship shall combine, and brotherhood:
I'll live by Nym, and Nym shall live by me;
Is not this just? for I shall sutler be   100

70 *quondam*] former.
71 *pauca*] in brief.
75–76 *do the office of a warming-pan*] A reference to Bardolph's fiery red face.
78 *yield . . . a pudding*] be eaten by crows.
79 *killed*] broken.
88 *As manhood shall compound*] As valor shall settle the issue (in fight).
91 *sword is an oath*] Elizabethans often swore by their swords.
94 *put up*] sheathe thy sword.
96 *A noble*] A coin worth less than eight shillings.
100 *sutler*] one who sells goods to soldiers.

Unto the camp, and profits will accrue.
　　Give me thy hand.
NYM.　I shall have my noble?
PIST.　In cash most justly paid.
NYM.　Well, then, that's the humour of 't.

Re-enter HOSTESS

HOST.　As ever you came of women, come in quickly to Sir
　　John. Ah, poor heart! he is so shaked of a burning quotidian
　　tertian, that it is most lamentable to behold. Sweet men,
　　come to him.
NYM.　The king hath run bad humours on the knight; that's the　　110
　　even of it.
PIST.　Nym, thou hast spoke the right;
　　His heart is fracted and corroborate.
NYM.　The king is a good king: but it must be as it may; he passes
　　some humours and careers.
PIST.　Let us condole the knight; for, lambkins, we will live.

SCENE II. *Southampton—A Council-Chamber.*

Enter EXETER, BEDFORD, *and* WESTMORELAND

BED.　'Fore God, his grace is bold, to trust these traitors.
EXE.　They shall be apprehended by and by.
WEST.　How smooth and even they do bear themselves!
　　As if allegiance in their bosoms sat,
　　Crowned with faith and constant loyalty.
BED.　The king hath note of all that they intend,
　　By interception which they dream not of.
EXE.　Nay, but the man that was his bedfellow,
　　Whom he hath dull'd and cloy'd with gracious favours,
　　That he should, for a foreign purse, so sell　　　　　　　10
　　His sovereign's life to death and treachery.

107–108 *quotidian tertian*] Mrs. Quickly jumbles together two kinds of fever, the "quo-
　　tidian," in which the paroxysms take place every day, and the "tertian," in which they
　　take place every third day.
110 *run bad humours*] let loose evil caprices, or perversities of temper.
110–111 *that's the even of it*] that's the level truth.
113 *corroborate*] a blunder for corrupted.
114–115 *he passes . . . careers*] he indulges in some whims and caprices.
116 *lambkins*] term of endearment.

---

9 *dull'd and cloy'd . . . favours*] rendered inappreciative through excess of generosity.

Trumpets sound. Enter KING HENRY, SCROOP, CAMBRIDGE,
   GREY, *and* Attendants

K. HEN.   Now sits the wind fair, and we will aboard.
   My Lord of Cambridge, and my kind Lord of Masham,
   And you, my gentle knight, give me your thoughts:
   Think you not that the powers we bear with us
   Will cut their passage through the force of France,
   Doing the execution and the act
   For which we have in head assembled them?
SCROOP.   No doubt, my liege, if each man do his best.
K. HEN.   I doubt not that; since we are well persuaded   20
   We carry not a heart with us from hence
   That grows not in a fair consent with ours,
   Nor leave not one behind that doth not wish
   Success and conquest to attend on us.
CAM.   Never was monarch better fear'd and loved
   Than is your majesty: there's not, I think, a subject
   That sits in heart-grief and uneasiness
   Under the sweet shade of your government.
GREY.   True: those that were your father's enemies
   Have steep'd their galls in honey, and do serve you   30
   With hearts create of duty and of zeal.
K. HEN.   We therefore have great cause of thankfulness;
   And shall forget the office of our hand,
   Sooner than quittance of desert and merit
   According to the weight and worthiness.
SCROOP.   So service shall with steeled sinews toil,
   And labour shall refresh itself with hope,
   To do your grace incessant services.
K. HEN.   We judge no less. Uncle of Exeter,
   Enlarge the man committed yesterday,   40
   That rail'd against our person: we consider
   It was excess of wine that set him on;
   And on his more advice we pardon him.
SCROOP.   That's mercy, but too much security:
   Let him be punish'd, sovereign, lest example

15 *powers*] armed forces.
18 *in head*] in force.
22 *in a fair consent*] in unison, in friendly concord.
31 *create*] composed, made up.
40 *Enlarge*] Set free.
43 *on his more advice*] on his return to better judgment.
44 *security*] confidence.

Breed, by his sufferance, more of such a kind.

K. HEN.   O, let us yet be merciful.

CAM.   So may your highness, and yet punish too.

GREY.   Sir,
You show great mercy, if you give him life,   50
After the taste of much correction.

K. HEN.   Alas, your too much love and care of me
Are heavy orisons 'gainst this poor wretch!
If little faults, proceeding on distemper,
Shall not be wink'd at, how shall we stretch our eye
When capital crimes, chew'd, swallow'd and digested,
Appear before us? We'll yet enlarge that man,
Though Cambridge, Scroop and Grey, in their dear care
And tender preservation of our person,
Would have him punish'd. And now to our French causes: 60
Who are the late commissioners?

CAM.   I one, my lord:
Your highness bade me ask for it to-day.

SCROOP.   So did you me, my liege.

GREY.   And I, my royal sovereign.

K. HEN.   Then, Richard Earl of Cambridge, there is yours;
There yours, Lord Scroop of Masham; and, sir knight,
Grey of Northumberland, this same is yours:
Read them; and know, I know your worthiness.
My Lord of Westmoreland, and uncle Exeter,   70
We will aboard to-night. Why, how now, gentlemen!
What see you in those papers that you lose
So much complexion? Look ye, how they change!
Their cheeks are paper. Why, what read you there,
That hath so cowarded and chased your blood
Out of appearance?

CAM.   I do confess my fault;
And do submit me to your highness' mercy.

GREY.   } To which we all appeal.
SCROOP. }

---

46 *sufferance*] being pardoned.
53 *orisons*] prayers, pleas.
54 *proceeding on distemper*] resulting from sudden outbursts of passion (in this case from excess of drink).
56 *chew'd . . . digested*] premeditated.
61 *late*] lately or recently appointed.
63 *ask for it*] ask for my warrant as commissioner.

K. HEN.   The mercy that was quick in us but late,   80
  By your own counsel is suppress'd and kill'd:
  You must not dare, for shame, to talk of mercy;
  For your own reasons turn into your bosoms,
  As dogs upon their masters, worrying you.
  See you, my princes and my noble peers,
  These English monsters! My Lord of Cambridge here,
  You know how apt our love was to accord
  To furnish him with all appertinents
  Belonging to his honour; and this man
  Hath, for a few light crowns, lightly conspired,   90
  And sworn unto the practices of France,
  To kill us here in Hampton: to the which
  This knight, no less for bounty bound to us
  Than Cambridge is, hath likewise sworn. But, O,
  What shall I say to thee, Lord Scroop? thou cruel,
  Ingrateful, savage and inhuman creature!
  Thou that didst bear the key of all my counsels,
  That knew'st the very bottom of my soul,
  That almost mightst have coin'd me into gold,
  Wouldst thou have practised on me for thy use,   100
  May it be possible, that foreign hire
  Could out of thee extract one spark of evil
  That might annoy my finger? 't is so strange,
  That, though the truth of it stands off as gross
  As black and white, my eye will scarcely see it.
  Treason and murder ever kept together,
  As two yoke-devils sworn to either's purpose,
  Working so grossly in a natural cause,
  That admiration did not hoop at them:
  But thou, 'gainst all proportion, didst bring in   110

80 *quick*] alive.
87 *accord*] consent.
88 *appertinents*] accessories.
91 *sworn unto the practices*] sworn to engage in the plots.
93 *This knight*] i.e., Grey.
100 *practised on*] plotted against.
104 *stands off as gross*] stands out as palpable.
107 *yoke-devils*] partners in a diabolical cause.
108–109 *Working so grossly in . . . hoop at them*] Working toward a purpose that suits
  them so naturally that they provoked no outcry of wonder.
110 *'gainst all proportion*] against all the fitness of things.

Wonder to wait on treason and on murder:
And whatsoever cunning fiend it was
That wrought upon thee so preposterously
Hath got the voice in hell for excellence:
All other devils that suggest by treasons
Do botch and bungle up damnation
With patches, colours, and with forms being fetch'd
From glistering semblances of piety;
But he that temper'd thee bade thee stand up,
Gave thee no instance why thou shouldst do treason,   120
Unless to dub thee with the name of traitor.
If that same demon that hath gull'd thee thus
Should with his lion gait walk the whole world,
He might return to vasty Tartar back,
And tell the legions "I can never win
A soul so easy as that Englishman's."
O, how hast thou with jealousy infected
The sweetness of affiance! Show men dutiful?
Why, so didst thou: seem they grave and learned?
Why, so didst thou: come they of noble family?   130
Why, so didst thou: seem they religious?
Why, so didst thou: or are they spare in diet,
Free from gross passion or of mirth or anger,
Constant in spirit, not swerving with the blood,
Garnish'd and deck'd in modest complement,
Not working with the eye without the ear,
And but in purged judgement trusting neither?
Such and so finely bolted didst thou seem:
And thus thy fall hath left a kind of blot,

115 *suggest by treasons*] tempt to treasons.
119 *temper'd thee*] fashioned thee.
120 *instance*] reason.
123 *lion gait*] Biblical reference to the Devil, who was said to walk about the world like a lion.
124 *Tartar*] Tartarus, the classical name for hell.
128 *affiance*] trust.
134 *blood*] passionate impulse.
135 *complement*] accomplishment.
136 *Not working . . . ear*] Not judging men merely by appearance, but listening to their talk.
137 *but*] save, except.
138 *bolted*] refined.

To mark the full-fraught man and best indued　　　　140
With some suspicion. I will weep for thee;
For this revolt of thine, methinks, is like
Another fall of man. Their faults are open:
Arrest them to the answer of the law;
And God acquit them of their practices!

EXE.　I arrest thee of high treason, by the name of Richard Earl
　　　of Cambridge.
　　I arrest thee of high treason, by the name of Henry Lord
　　　Scroop of Masham.
　　I arrest thee of high treason, by the name of Thomas Grey,
　　　knight, of Northumberland.

SCROOP.　Our purposes God justly hath discover'd;
　　And I repent my fault more than my death;　　　　150
　　Which I beseech your highness to forgive,
　　Although my body pay the price of it.

CAM.　For me, the gold of France did not seduce;
　　Although I did admit it as a motive
　　The sooner to effect what I intended:
　　But God be thanked for prevention;
　　Which I in sufferance heartily will rejoice,
　　Beseeching God and you to pardon me.

GREY.　Never did faithful subject more rejoice
　　At the discovery of most dangerous treason　　　　160
　　Than I do at this hour joy o'er myself,
　　Prevented from a damned enterprise:
　　My fault, but not my body, pardon, sovereign.

K. HEN.　God quit you in his mercy! Hear your sentence.
　　You have conspired against our royal person,
　　Join'd with an enemy proclaim'd, and from his coffers
　　Received the golden earnest of our death;
　　Wherein you would have sold your king to slaughter,
　　His princes and his peers to servitude,
　　His subjects to oppression and contempt,　　　　170
　　And his whole kingdom into desolation.
　　Touching our person seek we no revenge;

---

140 *the full-fraught man*] the truly virtuous man.
145 *God acquit them*] God absolve them.
155 *The sooner . . . intended*] Cambridge's object was to obtain the English crown for
　　his brother-in-law, Roger Mortimer, Earl of March, a descendant of Edward III.
157 *in sufferance*] in my suffering (for my sin).
167 *the golden earnest*] advance payment.

But we our kingdom's safety must so tender,
Whose ruin you have sought, that to her laws
We do deliver you. Get you therefore hence,
Poor miserable wretches, to your death:
The taste whereof, God of his mercy give
You patience to endure, and true repentance
Of all your dear offences! Bear them hence.
       [*Exeunt* CAMBRIDGE, SCROOP, *and* GREY, *guarded.*
Now, lords, for France; the enterprise whereof   180
Shall be to you, as us, like glorious.
We doubt not of a fair and lucky war,
Since God so graciously hath brought to light
This dangerous treason lurking in our way
To hinder our beginnings. We doubt not now
But every rub is smoothed on our way.
Then forth, dear countrymen: let us deliver
Our puissance into the hand of God,
Putting it straight in expedition.
Cheerly to sea; the signs of war advance: 190
No king of England, if not king of France.   [*Exeunt.*

SCENE III. *London — Before a Tavern.*

Enter PISTOL, HOSTESS, NYM, BARDOLPH, *and* Boy

HOST.   Prithee, honey-sweet husband, let me bring thee to
    Staines.
PIST.   No; for my manly heart doth yearn.
    Bardolph, be blithe: Nym, rouse thy vaunting veins:
    Boy, bristle thy courage up; for Falstaff he is dead,
    And we must yearn therefore.
BARD.   Would I were with him, wheresome'er he is, either in
    heaven or in hell!
HOST.   Nay, sure, he's not in hell: he's in Arthur's bosom, if ever
    man went to Arthur's bosom. A' made a finer end and went   10
    away an it had been any christom child; a' parted even just

179 *dear*] grievous.
186 *rub*] obstacle.
188 *puissance*] army.

---

  1 *bring*] accompany.
  3 *yearn*] mourn.
  9 *in Arthur's bosom*] Mrs. Quickly's blunder for "in Abraham's bosom."
11 *an . . . christom child*] as if he had been a newly christened child.

between twelve and one, even at the turning o' the tide: for
after I saw him fumble with the sheets, and play with flowers, and smile upon his fingers' ends, I knew there was but
one way; for his nose was as sharp as a pen, and a' babbled
of green fields. "How now, Sir John!" quoth I: "what, man!
be o' good cheer." So a' cried out "God, God, God!" three
or four times. Now I, to comfort him, bid him a' should not
think of God; I hoped there was no need to trouble himself
with any such thoughts yet. So a' bade me lay more clothes   20
on his feet: I put my hand into the bed and felt them, and
they were as cold as any stone; then I felt to his knees, and
they were as cold as any stone, and so upward and upward,
and all was as cold as any stone.

NYM.   They say he cried out of sack.

HOST.   Ay, that a' did.

BARD.   And of women.

HOST.   Nay, that a' did not.

BOY.   Yes, that a' did; and said they were devils incarnate.

HOST.   A' could never abide carnation; 't was a colour he never   30
liked.

BOY.   A' said once, the devil would have him about women.

HOST.   A' did in some sort, indeed, handle women; but then he
was rheumatic, and talked of the whore of Babylon.

BOY.   Do you not remember, a' saw a flea stick upon Bardolph's
nose, and a' said it was a black soul burning in hell-fire?

BARD.   Well, the fuel is gone that maintained that fire: that's all
the riches I got in his service.

NYM.   Shall we shog? the king will be gone from Southampton.

PIST.   Come, let's away. My love, give me thy lips.   40
Look to my chattels and my movables:
Let senses rule; the word is "Pitch and Pay":
Trust none;
For oaths are straws, men's faiths are wafer-cakes,
And hold-fast is the only dog, my duck:
Therefore, Caveto be thy counsellor.

---

25 *cried out of sack*] exclaimed against sack (a Spanish wine).
34 *rheumatic*] her blunder for "lunatic."
37 *fuel*] alcohol.
39 *shog*] be off.
42 *"Pitch and Pay"*] a colloquial phrase for "pay ready money."
45 *hold-fast . . . dog*] Cf. the old proverb "Brag is a good dog, but holdfast a better."
   my duck] my good friend. (A colloquial term of endearment.)
46 *Caveto*] caution.

Go, clear thy crystals. Yoke-fellows in arms,
Let us to France; like horse-leeches, my boys,
To suck, to suck, the very blood to suck!
BOY.   And that's but unwholesome food, they say.   50
PIST.   Touch her soft mouth, and march.
BARD.   Farewell, hostess.   [*Kissing her.*
NYM.   I cannot kiss, that is the humour of it; but, adieu.
PIST.   Let housewifery appear: keep close, I thee command.
HOST.   Farewell; adieu.   [*Exeunt.*

SCENE IV. *France—The King's Palace.*

Flourish. Enter the FRENCH KING, *the* DAUPHIN, *the* DUKES *of*
BERRI *and* BRETAGNE, *the* CONSTABLE, *and others*

FR. KING.   Thus comes the English with full power upon us;
And more than carefully it us concerns
To answer royally in our defences.
Therefore the Dukes of Berri and of Bretagne,
Of Brabant and of Orleans, shall make forth,
And you, Prince Dauphin, with all swift dispatch,
To line and new repair our towns of war
With men of courage and with means defendant;
For England his approaches makes as fierce
As waters to the sucking of a gulf.   10
It fits us then to be as provident
As fear may teach us out of late examples
Left by the fatal and neglected English
Upon our fields.
DAU.   My most redoubted father,
It is most meet we arm us 'gainst the foe;
For peace itself should not so dull a kingdom,
Though war nor no known quarrel were in question,
But that defences, musters, preparations,

47 *clear thy crystals*] dry thine eyes.
54 *keep close*] stay at home.

2 *more than carefully*] with more than common care.
7 *line*] support, strengthen.
10 *As waters . . . gulf*] As waters drawn to a whirlpool.
13 *the fatal and neglected English*] the English whom we have fatally neglected (potentially to our ruin).
16 *most meet*] imperative.
17 *so dull*] make so lazy.

Should be maintain'd, assembled and collected,   20
As were a war in expectation.
Therefore, I say 't is meet we all go forth
To view the sick and feeble parts of France:
And let us do it with no show of fear;
No, with no more than if we heard that England
Were busied with a Whitsun morris-dance:
For, my good liege, she is so idly king'd,
Her sceptre so fantastically borne
By a vain, giddy, shallow, humorous youth,
That fear attends her not.   30

CON.   O peace, Prince Dauphin!
You are too much mistaken in this king:
Question your grace the late ambassadors,
With what great state he heard their embassy,
How well supplied with noble counsellors,
How modest in exception, and withal
How terrible in constant resolution,
And you shall find his vanities forespent
Were but the outside of the Roman Brutus,
Covering discretion with a coat of folly;   40
As gardeners do with ordure hide those roots
That shall first spring and be most delicate.

DAU.   Well, 't is not so, my lord high constable;
But though we think it so, it is no matter:
In cases of defence 't is best to weigh
The enemy more mighty than he seems:
So the proportions of defence are fill'd;
Which of a weak and niggardly projection
Doth, like a miser, spoil his coat with scanting
A little cloth.   50

FR. KING.   Think we King Harry strong;
And, princes, look you strongly arm to meet him.

---

26 *morris-dance*] A vigorous English dance performed by men in costumes and bells.
29 *humorous*] capricious, frolicsome.
36 *modest in exception*] diffident in expressions of dissent.
    withal] in addition.
39–40 *Brutus . . . folly*] Lucius Junius Brutus, the founder of Republican Rome, according to Livy, feigned idiocy to escape ruin at the hands of his foe, King Tarquinius Superbus, whose rule he ultimately brought to an end.
41 *ordure*] manure.
47 *the proportions*] the appropriate needs.
48 *Which . . . projection*] The provision of which on a weak and inadequate plan. (This clause forms the subject of "doth spoil" in the next line.)

The kindred of him hath been flesh'd upon us;
And he is bred out of that bloody strain
That haunted us in our familiar paths:
Witness our too much memorable shame
When Cressy battle fatally was struck,
And all our princes captived by the hand
Of that black name, Edward, Black Prince of Wales;
Whiles that his mountain sire, on mountain standing,   60
Up in the air, crown'd with the golden sun,
Saw his heroical seed, and smiled to see him,
Mangle the work of nature, and deface
The patterns that by God and by French fathers
Had twenty years been made. This is a stem
Of that victorious stock; and let us fear
The native mightiness and fate of him.

Enter a Messenger

MESS.   Ambassadors from Harry King of England
    Do crave admittance to your majesty.
FR. KING.   We'll give them present audience. Go, and bring
    them.   [*Exeunt* Messenger *and certain* Lords.   70
    You see this chase is hotly follow'd, friends.
Dau.   Turn head, and stop pursuit; for coward dogs
    Most spend their mouths when what they seem to threaten
    Runs far before them. Good my sovereign,
    Take up the English short, and let them know
    Of what a monarchy you are the head:
    Self-love, my liege, is not so vile a sin
    As self-neglecting.

Re-enter Lords, *with* EXETER *and train*

FR. KING.   From our brother England?
EXE.   From him; and thus he greets your majesty.   80
    He wills you, in the name of God Almighty,
    That you divest yourself, and lay apart
    The borrow'd glories that by gift of heaven,

---

53 *The kindred . . . upon us*] His family (Edward III was King Henry's great-grandfather,
    and Edward the Black Prince was his great-uncle) gained its first military experience
    in conflict with us. (A hound was said to be "fleshed," when it first tasted blood in
    the chase.)
57 *Cressy battle*] Crécy, a major defeat for the French in 1346. (See above: I, ii, 108.)
60 *mountain sire*] reference to Edward III, who was born in mountainous Wales.
73 *spend their mouths*] bark their loudest.

By law of nature and of nations, 'long
To him and to his heirs; namely, the crown
And all wide-stretched honours that pertain
By custom and the ordinance of times
Unto the crown of France. That you may know
'T is no sinister nor no awkward claim,   90
Pick'd from the worm-holes of long-vanish'd days,
Nor from the dust of old oblivion raked,
He sends you this most memorable line,
In every branch truly demonstrative;
Willing you overlook this pedigree:
And when you find him evenly derived
From his most famed of famous ancestors,
Edward the third, he bids you then resign
Your crown and kingdom, indirectly held
From him the native and true challenger.

FR. KING.   Or else what follows?   100

EXE.   Bloody constraint; for if you hide the crown
Even in your hearts, there will he rake for it:
Therefore in fierce tempest is he coming,
In thunder and in earthquake, like a Jove,
That, if requiring fail, he will compel;
And bids you, in the bowels of the Lord,
Deliver up the crown, and to take mercy
On the poor souls for whom this hungry war
Opens his vasty jaws; and on your head
Turning the widows' tears, and the orphans' cries,   110
The dead men's blood, the pining maidens' groans,
For husbands, fathers and betrothed lovers,
That shall be swallow'd in this controversy.
This is his claim, his threatening, and my message;
Unless the Dauphin be in presence here,
To whom expressly I bring greeting too.

FR. KING.   For us, we will consider of this further:
To-morrow shall you bear our full intent
Back to our brother England.

84 *'long*] belong.
92 *line*] pedigree.
94 *overlook*] look over, examine.
95 *evenly*] directly.
98 *indirectly*] unjustly.
99 *challenger*] claimant.
105 *requiring*] asking.
106 *bowels*] innermost being, mercy.

DAU.　　　　　　　　　　For the Dauphin,　　　　120
　　　I stand here for him: what to him from England?
EXE.　Scorn and defiance; slight regard, contempt,
　　　And any thing that may not misbecome
　　　The mighty sender, doth he prize you at.
　　　Thus says my king; an if your father's highness
　　　Do not, in grant of all demands at large,
　　　Sweeten the bitter mock you sent his majesty,
　　　He'll call you to so hot an answer of it,
　　　That caves and womby vaultages of France
　　　Shall chide your trespass, and return your mock　　130
　　　In second accent of his ordnance.
DAU.　Say, if my father render fair return,
　　　It is against my will; for I desire
　　　Nothing but odds with England: to that end,
　　　As matching to his youth and vanity,
　　　I did present him with the Paris balls.
EXE.　He'll make your Paris Louvre shake for it,
　　　Were it the mistress-court of mighty Europe:
　　　And, be assured, you'll find a difference,
　　　As we his subjects have in wonder found,　　　140
　　　Between the promise of his greener days
　　　And these he masters now: now he weighs time
　　　Even to the utmost grain: that you shall read
　　　In your own losses, if he stay in France.
FR. KING.　To-morrow shall you know our mind at full.
EXE.　Dispatch us with all speed, lest that our king
　　　Come here himself to question our delay;
　　　For he is footed in this land already.
FR. KING.　You shall be soon dispatch'd with fair conditions:
　　　A night is but small breath and little pause　　150
　　　To answer matters of this consequence.

　　　　　　　　　　　　　　[*Flourish. Exeunt.*

---

129 *womby vaultages*] hollow places beneath the soil, the subterranean foundations.
131 *In second accent of his ordnance*] In the echo of his cannon's roar.
136 *balls*] bawdy pun and reference to tennis balls the Dauphin sent to King Henry.
137 *Louvre*] French royal palace.
148 *is footed*] has foothold.
150 *breath*] breathing space.

ACT III. — PROLOGUE

Enter Chorus

CHORUS. Thus with imagined wing our swift scene flies
      In motion of no less celerity
      Than that of thought. Suppose that you have seen
      The well-appointed king at Hampton pier
      Embark his royalty; and his brave fleet
      With silken streamers the young Phœbus fanning:
      Play with your fancies, and in them behold
      Upon the hempen tackle ship-boys climbing;
      Hear the shrill whistle which doth order give
      To sounds confused; behold the threaden sails,   10
      Borne with the invisible and creeping wind,
      Draw the huge bottoms through the furrow'd sea,
      Breasting the lofty surge: O, do but think
      You stand upon the rivage and behold
      A city on the inconstant billows dancing;
      For so appears this fleet majestical,
      Holding due course to Harfleur. Follow, follow:
      Grapple your minds to sternage of this navy,
      And leave your England, as dead midnight still,
      Guarded with grandsires, babies and old women,   20
      Either past or not arrived to pith and puissance;
      For who is he, whose chin is but enrich'd
      With one appearing hair, that will not follow
      These cull'd and choice-drawn cavaliers to France?
      Work, work your thoughts, and therein see a siege;
      Behold the ordnance on their carriages,

1 *with imagined wing*] with the wing of imagination.
2 *celerity*] speed.
8 *hempen tackle*] the ropes that support a ship's masts.
14 *rivage*] French word for "shore."
18 *sternage*] stern, steerage; the rudder was in the stern.

With fatal mouths gaping on girded Harfleur.
Suppose the ambassador from the French comes back;
Tells Harry that the king doth offer him
Katharine his daughter, and with her, to dowry,   30
Some petty and unprofitable dukedoms.
The offer likes not: and the nimble gunner
With linstock now the devilish cannon touches,
                              [*Alarum, and chambers go off.*
And down goes all before them. Still be kind,
And eke out our performance with your mind.   [*Exit.*

SCENE I. *France—Before Harfleur.*

Alarum. Enter KING HENRY, EXETER, BEDFORD, GLOUCESTER,
    and Soldiers, *with scaling-ladders*

K. HEN.   Once more unto the breach, dear friends, once more;
    Or close the wall up with our English dead.
    In peace there's nothing so becomes a man
    As modest stillness and humility:
    But when the blast of war blows in our ears,
    Then imitate the action of the tiger;
    Stiffen the sinews, summon up the blood,
    Disguise fair nature with hard-favour'd rage;
    Then lend the eye a terrible aspect;
    Let it pry through the portage of the head   10
    Like the brass cannon; let the brow o'erwhelm it
    As fearfully as doth a galled rock
    O'erhang and jutty his confounded base,
    Swill'd with the wild and wasteful ocean.
    Now set the teeth and stretch the nostril wide,
    Hold hard the breath and bend up every spirit
    To his full height. On, on, you noblest English,

30 *to dowry*] as dowry.
32 *likes not*] pleases not.
33 *linstock*] the stick to which was attached the match for firing guns.
    chambers] small cannons.

8 *hard-favour'd*] grim-faced.
9 *terrible aspect*] terrifying appearance.
10 *portage*] portholes, eyes.
13 *jutty his confounded base*] hang over its worn-away base.
14 *Swill'd . . . ocean*] Washed over . . . by the desolating ocean.
16 *bend up*] extend.

Whose blood is fet from fathers of war-proof!
Fathers that, like so many Alexanders,
Have in these parts from morn till even fought,   20
And sheathed their swords for lack of argument:
Dishonour not your mothers; now attest
That those whom you call'd fathers did beget you.
Be copy now to men of grosser blood,
And teach them how to war. And you, good yeomen,
Whose limbs were made in England, show us here
The mettle of your pasture; let us swear
That you are worth your breeding; which I doubt not;
For there is none of you so mean and base,
That hath not noble lustre in your eyes.   30
I see you stand like greyhounds in the slips,
Straining upon the start. The game's afoot:
Follow your spirit, and upon this charge
Cry "God for Harry, England, and Saint George!"
                    [*Exeunt. Alarum, and chambers go off.*

SCENE II. *The Same.*

Enter NYM, BARDOLPH, PISTOL, *and* Boy

BARD. On, on, on, on, on! to the breach, to the breach!
NYM. Pray thee, corporal, stay: the knocks are too hot; and, for
         mine own part, I have not a case of lives: the humour of it is
         too hot, that is the very plain-song of it.
PIST. The plain-song is most just; for humours do abound:

              Knocks go and come; God's vassals drop and die;
                       And sword and shield,
                       In bloody field,
                    Doth win immortal fame.

18 *fet*] fetched, drawn.
   war-proof] strength proved in war.
19 *Alexanders*] reference to Alexander the Great.
20 *even*] evening.
21 *argument*] opposition.
24 *copy*] models.
27 *mettle of your pasture*] quality of your breeding.
31 *slips*] leashes, which held the hounds before the game was started.

3–4 *case . . . plain-song*] A "case" is a set of four musical instruments; for the simple
   music of a "plain-song," a case would not be required.
 5 *humours*] whimsicalities, fantasies.

BOY.   Would I were in an alehouse in London! I would give all   10
   my fame for a pot of ale and safety.

PIST.   And I:

> If wishes would prevail with me,
> My purpose should not fail with me,
> But thither would I hie.

BOY.   As duly, but not as truly,
> As bird doth sing on bough.

Enter FLUELLEN

FLU.   Up to the breach, you dogs! avaunt, you cullions!
                    [Driving them forward.

PIST.   Be merciful, great duke, to men of mould.
   Abate thy rage, abate thy manly rage,   20
   Abate thy rage, great duke!
   Good bawcock, bate thy rage; use lenity, sweet chuck!

NYM.   These be good humours! your honour wins bad humours.   *[Exeunt all but* Boy.

BOY.   As young as I am, I have observed these three swashers. I
am boy to them all three: but all they three, though they
would serve me, could not be man to me; for indeed three
such antics do not amount to a man. For Bardolph, he is
white-livered and red-faced; by the means whereof a' faces it
out, but fights not. For Pistol, he hath a killing tongue and a   30
quiet sword; by the means whereof a' breaks words, and
keeps whole weapons. For Nym, he hath heard that men of
few words are the best men; and therefore he scorns to say
his prayers, lest a' should be thought a coward: but his few
bad words are matched with as few good deeds; for a' never
broke any man's head but his own, and that was against a
post when he was drunk. They will steal any thing, and call
it purchase. Bardolph stole a lute-case, bore it twelve

---

18 *cullions*] a coarse term of abuse.
19 *great duke*] Pistol thinks to flatter Captain Fluellen by exaggerating his rank.
   men of mould] men of earth, poor mortal men.
22 *Good bawcock . . . sweet chuck*] terms of playful endearment equivalent to "my fine
   fellow" or "dear old boy."
23–24 *These be good . . . bad humours*] Nym commends Pistol's blandishments. Pistol
   conciliates bad tempers. "Your honour" means "your lordship."
25 *swashers*] swashbucklers, blusterers.
28 *antics*] buffoons.
29–30 *a' faces it out*] he puts on a brave front.
31–32 *a' breaks words, and keeps whole weapons*] he fights using words, not weapons.
38 *purchase*] a colloquial euphemism for theft.

leagues, and sold it for three half-pence. Nym and Bardolph
are sworn brothers in filching, and in Calais they stole a fire- 40
shovel: I knew by that piece of service the men would carry
coals. They would have me as familiar with men's pockets as
their gloves or their handkerchers: which makes much
against my manhood, if I should take from another's pocket
to put into mine; for it is plain pocketing up of wrongs. I
must leave them, and seek some better service: their villany
goes against my weak stomach, and therefore I must cast it
up. [*Exit.*

Re-enter FLUELLEN, GOWER *following*

GOW.   Captain Fluellen, you must come presently to the mines;
the Duke of Gloucester would speak with you.   50
FLU.   To the mines! tell you the duke, it is not so good to come
to the mines; for, look you, the mines is not according to the
disciplines of the war: the concavities of it is not sufficient;
for, look you, th' athversary, you may discuss unto the duke,
look you, is digt himself four yard under the countermines:
by Cheshu, I think a' will plow up all, if there is not better
directions.
GOW.   The Duke of Gloucester, to whom the order of the siege
is given, is altogether directed by an Irishman, a very valiant
gentleman, i' faith.   60
FLU.   It is Captain Macmorris, is it not?
GOW.   I think it be.
FLU.   By Cheshu, he is an ass, as in the world: I will verify as
much in his beard: he has no more directions in the true disciplines of the wars, look you, of the Roman disciplines, than
is a puppy-dog.

Enter MACMORRIS *and* Captain JAMY

GOW.   Here a' comes; and the Scots captain, Captain Jamy,
with him.

40 *brothers in filching*] partners in crime.
41–42 *carry coals*] perform the lowest of all domestic services—hence, submit tamely to
humiliation.
45 *pocketing up of wrongs*] putting up with insults.
49 *the mines*] the tunnels being dug by the English under the city as part of their
planned attack.
54–55 *th' athversary . . . the countermines*] the enemy, you must explain to the Duke, is
digging tunnels four yards under ours.
56 *Cheshu*] Jesu, Jesus.
plow] mispronunciation of "blow."
64 *in his beard*] to his face.

FLU.   Captain Jamy is a marvellous falorous gentleman, that is
       certain; and of great expedition and knowledge in th'   70
       aunchient wars, upon my particular knowledge of his direc-
       tions: by Cheshu, he will maintain his argument as well as
       any military man in the world, in the disciplines of the pris-
       tine wars of the Romans.

JAMY.   I say gud-day, Captain Fluellen.

FLU.   God-den to your worship, good Captain James.

GOW.   How now, Captain Macmorris! have you quit the mines?
       have the pioners given o'er?

MAC.   By Chrish, la! tish ill done: the work ish give over, the
       trompet sound the retreat. By my hand, I swear, and my fa-   80
       ther's soul, the work ish ill done; it ish give over: I would
       have blowed up the town, so Chrish save me, la! in an hour:
       O, tish ill done, tish ill done; by my hand, tish ill done!

FLU.   Captain Macmorris, I beseech you now, will you voutsafe
       me, look you, a few disputations with you, as partly touching
       or concerning the disciplines of the war, the Roman wars, in
       the way of argument, look you, and friendly communica-
       tion; partly to satisfy my opinion, and partly for the satisfac-
       tion, look you, of my mind, as touching the direction of the
       military discipline; that is the point.   90

JAMY.   It sall be vary gud, gud feith, gud captains bath: and I sall
       quit you with gud leve, as I may pick occasion; that sall I,
       marry.

MAC.   It is no time to discourse, so Chrish save me: the day is
       hot, and the weather, and the wars, and the king, and the
       dukes: it is no time to discourse. The town is beseeched, and
       the trumpet call us to the breach; and we talk, and, be
       Chrish, do nothing: 't is shame for us all: so God sa' me, 't is
       shame to stand still; it is shame, by my hand: and there is
       throats to be cut, and works to be done; and there ish noth-   100
       ing done, so Chrish sa' me, la!

JAMY.   By the mess, ere theise eyes of mine take themselves to
       slomber, ay'll de gud service, or ay'll lig i' the grund for it; ay,

---

70 *expedition*] a combination in Fluellen's dialect of "experience" and "erudition."
76 *God-den*] a common colloquial form of "good e'en," "good evening."
78 *pioners*] pioneers, military engineers.
79 *ill*] mispronunciation of "all."
84 *voutsafe*] vouchsafe, permit.
91 *bath*] mispronunciation of "both."
92 *quit you*] requite, answer you.
102 *mess*] mass.
103 *ay 'll lig*] I'll lie.

or go to death; and ay'll pay 't as valorously as I may, that sall
I suerly do, that is the breff and the long. Marry, I wad full
fain hear some question 'tween you tway.

FLU.   Captain Macmorris, I think, look you, under your correction, there is not many of your nation—

MAC.   Of my nation! What ish my nation? Ish a villain, and a
bastard, and a knave, and a rascal. What ish my nation? Who   110
talks of my nation?

FLU.   Look you, if you take the matter otherwise than is meant,
Captain Macmorris, peradventure I shall think you do not
use me with that affability as in discretion you ought to use
me, look you; being as good a man as yourself, both in the
disciplines of war, and in the derivation of my birth, and in
other particularities.

MAC.   I do not know you so good a man as myself: So Chrish
save me, I will cut off your head.

GOW.   Gentlemen both, you will mistake each other.   120

JAMY.   A! that's a foul fault.

                                        [A *parley sounded.*

GOW.   The town sounds a parley.

FLU.   Captain Macmorris, when there is more better opportunity to be required, look you, I will be so bold as to tell you
I know the disciplines of war; and there is an end.

                                        [*Exeunt.*

SCENE III. *The Same—Before the Gates.*

The Governor *and some* Citizens *on the walls; the English forces
below. Enter* KING HENRY *and his train*

K. HEN.   How yet resolves the governor of the town?
This is the latest parle we will admit:
Therefore to our best mercy give yourselves;
Or like to men proud of destruction
Defy us to our worst: for, as I am a soldier,
A name that in my thoughts becomes me best,

105–106 I *wad full fain hear some question*] I would very much like to hear some debate.
109 *What ish my nation?*] Macmorris sarcastically challenges Fluellen to say a word
against Ireland.

---

2 *the latest parle*] i.e., "this is your last chance to surrender." Henry is warning the
governor of Harfleur.

If I begin the battery once again,
I will not leave the half-achieved Harfleur
Till in her ashes she lie buried.
The gates of mercy shall be all shut up,   10
And the flesh'd soldier, rough and hard of heart,
In liberty of bloody hand shall range
With conscience wide as hell, mowing like grass
Your fresh-fair virgins and your flowering infants.
What is it then to me, if impious war,
Array'd in flames like to the prince of fiends,
Do, with his smirch'd complexion, all fell feats
Enlink'd to waste and desolation?
What is 't to me, when you yourselves are cause,
If your pure maidens fall into the hand   20
Of hot and forcing violation?
What rein can hold licentious wickedness
When down the hill he holds his fierce career?
We may as bootless spend our vain command
Upon the enraged soldiers in their spoil
As send precepts to the leviathan
To come ashore. Therefore, you men of Harfleur,
Take pity of your town and of your people,
Whiles yet my soldiers are in my command;
Whiles yet the cool and temperate wind of grace   30
O'erblows the filthy and contagious clouds
Of heady murder, spoil and villany.
If not, why, in a moment look to see
The blind and bloody soldier with foul hand
Defile the locks of your shrill-shrieking daughters;
Your fathers taken by the silver beards,
And their most reverend heads dash'd to the walls,
Your naked infants spitted upon pikes,
Whiles the mad mothers with their howls confused
Do break the clouds, as did the wives of Jewry   40
At Herod's bloody-hunting slaughtermen.
What say you? will you yield, and this avoid,

---

8 *half-achieved*] half-conquered.
11 *the flesh'd soldier*] the soldier who has first tasted blood.
18 *Enlink'd . . . desolation*] Inevitably associated with ruin and destruction.
26 *precepts*] summons.
31 *O'erblows*] Blows away, disperses.
41 *Herod's . . . slaughtermen*] Biblical reference (Matthew 2:16–18) to King Herod's massacre of innocent children.

        Or, guilty in defence, be thus destroy'd?
GOV.   Our expectation hath this day an end:
        The Dauphin, whom of succours we entreated,
        Returns us that his powers are yet not ready
        To raise so great a siege. Therefore, great king,
        We yield our town and lives to thy soft mercy.
        Enter our gates; dispose of us and ours;
        For we no longer are defensible.   50
K. HEN.   Open your gates. Come, uncle Exeter,
        Go you and enter Harfleur; there remain,
        And fortify it strongly 'gainst the French:
        Use mercy to them all. For us, dear uncle,
        The winter coming on, and sickness growing
        Upon our soldiers, we will retire to Calais.
        To-night in Harfleur will we be your guest;
        To-morrow for the march are we addrest.
             [*Flourish.* The KING *and his train enter the town.*

SCENE IV. *The French King's Palace.*

Enter KATHARINE *and* ALICE

KATH.   Alice, tu as été en Angleterre, et tu parles bien le langage.

ALICE.   Un peu, madame.

KATH.   Je te prie, m'enseignez; il faut que j'apprenne à parler. Comment appelez-vous la main en Anglois?

ALICE.   La main? elle est appelée de hand.

KATH.   De hand. Et les doigts?

ALICE.   Les doigts? ma foi, j'oublie les doigts; mais je me souviendrai. Les doigts? je pense qu'ils sont appelés de fingres; oui, de fingres.   10

KATH.   La main, de hand; les doigts, de fingres. Je pense que je suis le bon écolier; j'ai gagné deux mots d'Anglois vitement. Comment appelez-vous les ongles?

---

43 *in defence*] i.e., by not surrendering.
45 *whom of succours*] whose help.
46 *Returns us*] Answers us.
50 *defensible*] capable of defending ourselves.
58 *addrest*] prepared.

SCENE IV] For a translation of this scene into English, see the Appendix.

ALICE.   Les ongles? nous les appelons de nails.

KATH.   De nails. Ecoutez; dites-moi, si je parle bien: de hand, de fingres, et de nails.

ALICE.   C'est bien dit, madame; il est fort bon Anglois.

KATH.   Dites-moi l'Anglois pour le bras.

ALICE.   De arm, madame.

KATH.   Et le coude?

ALICE.   De elbow.

KATH.   De elbow. Je m'en fais la répétition de tous les mots que vous m'avez appris dès à présent.

ALICE.   Il est trop difficile, madame, comme je pense.

KATH.   Excusez-moi, Alice; écoutez: de hand, de fingres, de nails, de arma, de bilbow.

ALICE.   De elbow, madame.

KATH.   O Seigneur Dieu, je m'en oublie! de elbow. Comment appelez-vous le col?

ALICE.   De neck, madame.

KATH.   De nick. Et le menton?

ALICE.   De chin.

KATH.   De sin. Le col, de nick; le menton, de sin.

ALICE.   Oui. Sauf votre honneur, en vérité, vous prononcez les mots aussi droit que les natifs d'Angleterre.

KATH.   Je ne doute point d'apprendre, par la grace de Dieu, et en peu de temps.

ALICE.   N'avez vous pas déjà oublié ce que je vous ai enseigné?

KATH.   Non, je reciterai à vous promptement: de hand, de fingres, de mails,—

ALICE.   De nails, madame.

KATH.   De nails, de arm, de ilbow.

ALICE.   Sauf votre honneur, de elbow.

KATH.   Ainsi dis-je; de elbow, de nick, et de sin. Comment appelez-vous le pied et la robe?

ALICE.   De foot, madame; et de coun.

KATH.   De foot et de coun! O Seigneur Dieu! ce sont mots de son mauvais, corruptible, gros, et impudique, et non pour les dames d'honneur d'user: je ne voudrais prononcer ces mots devant les seigneurs de France pour tout le monde. Foh! le foot et le coun! Néanmoins, je réciterai une autre fois ma leçon ensemble: de hand, de fingres, de nails, de arm, de elbow, de nick, de sin, de foot, de coun.

ALICE.   Excellent, madame!

KATH.   C'est assez pour une fois: allons-nous à dîner.

                              [Exeunt.

Scene V. *The Same.*

Enter the King *of* France, *the* Dauphin, *the* Duke *of* Bourbon,
     the Constable *of* France, *and others*

Fr. King.   'T is certain he hath pass'd the river Somme.
Con.   And if he be not fought withal, my lord,
          Let us not live in France; let us quit all,
          And give our vineyards to a barbarous people.
Dau.   O Dieu vivant! shall a few sprays of us,
          The emptying of our fathers' luxury,
          Our scions, put in wild and savage stock,
          Spirt up so suddenly into the clouds,
          And overlook their grafters?
Bour.   Normans, but bastard Normans, Norman bastards!   10
          Mort de ma vie! if they march along
          Unfought withal, but I will sell my dukedom,
          To buy a slobbery and a dirty farm
          In that nook-shotten isle of Albion.
Con.   Dieu de batailles! where have they this mettle?
          Is not their climate foggy, raw and dull,
          On whom, as in despite, the sun looks pale,
          Killing their fruit with frowns? Can sodden water,
          A drench for sur-rein'd jades, their barley-broth,
          Decoct their cold blood to such valiant heat?   20
          And shall our quick blood, spirited with wine,
          Seem frosty? O, for honour of our land,
          Let us not hang like roping icicles
          Upon our houses' thatch, whiles a more frosty people
          Sweat drops of gallant youth in our rich fields!—
          Poor we may call them in their native lords.

---

3 *quit all*] give up, yield.
5 *sprays*] sprigs or sprouts. Reference is here made to the fact that the English raiders
     are descendants of Frenchmen through William the Conqueror, who was himself
     born out of wedlock.
6 *our fathers' luxury*] our ancestors' lust.
7–9 *Our scions . . . grafters*] The image here is of the branches or scions of a tree (i.e.,
     France) being replanted in "wild and savage stock" (i.e., England) and suddenly over-
     shadowing the "tree" from which they came.
13 *slobbery*] waterlogged.
14 *nook-shotten Isle of Albion*] many-inleted island of England.
19 A *drench for sur-rein'd jades*] Liquid medicine for overworked horses.
20 *Decoct*] Boil, heat. A tonic medicine is often called a "decoction."
26 *Poor we may . . . their native lords*] We may call our *rich* fields *poor* because of the
     feeble character of their native owners.

DAU.   By faith and honour,
    Our madams mock at us, and plainly say
    Our mettle is bred out, and they will give
    Their bodies to the lust of English youth,   30
    To new-store France with bastard warriors.
BOUR.   They bid us to the English dancing-schools,
    And teach lavoltas high and swift corantos;
    Saying our grace is only in our heels,
    And that we are most lofty runaways.
FR. KING.   Where is Montjoy the herald? speed him hence:
    Let him greet England with our sharp defiance.
    Up, princes! and, with spirit of honour edged
    More sharper than your swords, hie to the field:
    Charles Delabreth, high constable of France;   40
    You Dukes of Orleans, Bourbon, and of Berri,
    Alençon, Brabant, Bar, and Burgundy;
    Jaques Chatillon, Rambures, Vaudemont,
    Beaumont, Grandpré, Roussi, and Fauconberg,
    Foix, Lestrale, Bouciqualt, and Charolois;
    High dukes, great princes, barons, lords and knights,
    For your great seats now quit you of great shames.
    Bar Harry England, that sweeps through our land
    With pennons painted in the blood of Harfleur:
    Rush on his host, as doth the melted snow   50
    Upon the valleys, whose low vassal seat
    The Alps doth spit and void his rheum upon:
    Go down upon him, you have power enough,
    And in a captive chariot into Rouen
    Bring him our prisoner.
CON.   This becomes the great.
    Sorry am I his numbers are so few,
    His soldiers sick and famish'd in their march,
    For I am sure, when he shall see our army,
    He'll drop his heart into the sink of fear   60
    And for achievement offer us his ransom.
FR. KING.   Therefore, lord constable, haste on Montjoy,
    And let him say to England that we send

33 *lavoltas and corantos*] Lively dances.
47 *For your great seats . . . you*] For (the protection of) your noble castles now acquit
    yourselves.
49 *pennons*] banners.
52 *rheum*] i.e., waters.
60 *He'll drop his heart . . . fear*] A strong expression for vomiting.
61 *for achievement*] instead of achieving victory over us, of conquering us.

To know what willing ransom he will give.
Prince Dauphin, you shall stay with us in Rouen.
DAU.   Not so, I do beseech your majesty.
FR. KING.   Be patient, for you shall remain with us.
Now forth, lord constable and princes all,
And quickly bring us word of England's fall.   [*Exeunt.*

SCENE VI. *The English Camp in Picardy.*

Enter GOWER *and* FLUELLEN, *meeting*

GOW.   How now, Captain Fluellen! come you from the bridge?
FLU.   I assure you, there is very excellent services committed at
the bridge.
GOW.   Is the Duke of Exeter safe?
FLU.   The Duke of Exeter is as magnanimous as Agamemnon;
and a man that I love and honour with my soul, and my
heart, and my duty, and my life, and my living, and my ut-
termost power: he is not—God be praised and blessed!—any
hurt in the world; but keeps the bridge most valiantly, with
excellent discipline. There is an aunchient lieutenant there   10
at the pridge, I think in my very conscience he is as valiant
a man as Mark Antony; and he is a man of no estimation in
the world; but I did see him do as gallant service.
GOW.   What do you call him?
FLU.   He is called Aunchient Pistol.
GOW.   I know him not.

Enter PISTOL

FLU.   Here is the man.
PIST.   Captain, I thee beseech to do me favours:
The Duke of Exeter doth love thee well.
FLU.   Ay, I praise God; and I have merited some love at his   20
hands.
PIST.   Bardolph, a soldier, firm and sound of heart,
And of buxom valour, hath, by cruel fate,
And giddy Fortune's furious fickle wheel,

---

1 *the bridge*] The bridge over the river Ternoise, which lay on the road of Henry's
march to Calais. The French attempt to demolish it was defeated by the English.
2 *services*] victories.
10 *aunchient lieutenant*] a confused reference to Pistol, whose rank was that of "ancient," i.e., ensign, not "lieutenant."

That goddess blind,
That stands upon the rolling restless stone—
FLU. By your patience, Aunchient Pistol. Fortune is painted
blind, with a muffler afore her eyes, to signify to you that
Fortune is blind; and she is painted also with a wheel, to sig-
nify to you, which is the moral of it, that she is turning, and　　30
inconstant, and mutability, and variation: and her foot, look
you, is fixed upon a spherical stone, which rolls, and rolls,
and rolls: in good truth, the poet makes a most excellent de-
scription of it: Fortune is an excellent moral.
PIST. Fortune is Bardolph's foe, and frowns on him;
For he hath stolen a pax, and hanged must a' be:
A damned death!
Let gallows gape for dog; let man go free
And let not hemp his wind-pipe suffocate:
But Exeter hath given the doom of death　　　　　　　　　　40
For pax of little price.
Therefore, go speak; the duke will hear thy voice;
And let not Bardolph's vital thread be cut
With edge of penny cord and vile reproach:
Speak, captain, for his life, and I will thee requite.
FLU. Aunchient Pistol, I do partly understand your meaning.
PIST. Why then, rejoice therefore.
FLU. Certainly, aunchient, it is not a thing to rejoice at: for if,
look you, he were my brother, I would desire the duke to use
his good pleasure, and put him to execution; for discipline　　50
ought to be used.
PIST. Die and be damn'd! and figo for thy friendship!
FLU. It is well.
PIST. The fig of Spain!　　　　　　　　　　　　　　　[Exit.
FLU. Very good.
GOW. Why, this is an arrant counterfeit rascal; I remember him
now; a bawd, a cutpurse.
FLU. I'll assure you, a' uttered as prave words at the pridge as
you shall see in a summer's day. But it is very well; what he
has spoke to me, that is well, I warrant you, when time is　　60
serve.

28 *muffler*] blindfold.
36 *pax*] a small piece of plate, engraved with the picture of the crucifixion, which was
offered by the priest during Mass.
45 *requite*] repay.
52 *figo*] a fig, any contemptible trifle, a snap of the fingers.
54 *The fig of Spain*] Pistol underlines his insult by specifying the gesture made by thrusting the thumb out between the first and second fingers in semblance of a vulva.

GOW.   Why, 't is a gull, a fool, a rogue, that now and then goes
to the wars, to grace himself at his return into London under
the form of a soldier. And such fellows are perfect in the
great commanders' names: and they will learn you by rote
where services were done; at such and such a sconce, at such
a breach, at such a convoy; who came off bravely, who was
shot, who disgraced, what terms the enemy stood on; and
this they con perfectly in the phrase of war, which they trick
up with new-tuned oaths: and what a beard of the general's   70
cut and a horrid suit of the camp will do among foaming
bottles and ale-washed wits, is wonderful to be thought on.
But you must learn to know such slanders of the age, or else
you may be marvellously mistook.

FLU.   I tell you what, Captain Gower; I do perceive he is not the
man that he would gladly make show to the world he is: if I
find a hole in his coat, I will tell him my mind. [*Drum
heard.*] Hark you, the king is coming, and I must speak with
him from the pridge.

Drum and Colours. Enter KING HENRY, GLOUCESTER, *and*
Soldiers

    God pless your majesty!   80

K. HEN.   How now, Fluellen! camest thou from the bridge?

FLU.   Ay, so please your majesty. The Duke of Exeter has very
gallantly maintained the pridge: the French is gone off, look
you; and there is gallant and most prave passages: marry, th'
athversary was have possession of the pridge; but he is enforced to retire, and the Duke of Exeter is master of the
pridge: I can tell your majesty, the duke is a prave man.

K. HEN.   What men have you lost, Fluellen?

FLU.   The perdition of th' athversary hath been very great, reasonable great: marry, for my part, I think the duke hath lost   90
never a man, but one that is like to be executed for robbing
a church, one Bardolph, if your majesty know the man: his
face is all bubukles, and whelks, and knobs, and flames o'

---

64 *are perfect in*] i.e., can recite perfectly.
66 *sconce*] fortification.
71 *horrid suit*] war-stained uniform.
73 *slanders*] disgraces, slanderers.
78–79 *speak . . . pridge*] tell him what has happened at the bridge.
89 *perdition*] losses.
93 *bubukles*] blotches; a word made up of "buboes" and "carbuncles."
   whelks] pimples.

fire: and his lips blows at his nose, and it is like a coal of fire,
sometimes plue and sometimes red; but his nose is executed, and his fire 's out.

K. HEN.   We would have all such offenders so cut off: and we
give express charge, that in our marches through the country, there be nothing compelled from the villages, nothing
taken but paid for, none of the French upbraided or abused   100
in disdainful language; for when lenity and cruelty play for a
kingdom, the gentler gamester is the soonest winner.

Tucket. Enter MONTJOY

MONT.   You know me by my habit.
K. HEN.   Well then I know thee: what shall I know of thee?
MONT.   My master's mind.
K. HEN.   Unfold it.
MONT.   Thus says my king: Say thou to Harry of England:
Though we seemed dead, we did but sleep: advantage is a
better soldier than rashness. Tell him we could have rebuked
him at Harfleur, but that we thought not good to bruise an   110
injury till it were full ripe: now we speak upon our cue, and
our voice is imperial: England shall repent his folly, see his
weakness, and admire our sufferance. Bid him therefore
consider of his ransom; which must proportion the losses we
have borne, the subjects we have lost, the disgrace we have
digested; which in weight to re-answer, his pettiness would
bow under. For our losses, his exchequer is too poor; for the
effusion of our blood, the muster of his kingdom too faint a
number; and for our disgrace, his own person, kneeling at
our feet, but a weak and worthless satisfaction. To this add   120
defiance: and tell him, for conclusion, he hath betrayed his
followers, whose condemnation is pronounced. So far my
king and master; so much my office.

K. HEN.   What is thy name? I know thy quality.
MONT.   Montjoy.

---

102 *gamester*] player.
   Tucket] Flourish on a trumpet as Montjoy, the French herald, enters.
103 *habit*] The herald's coat, which was inviolable in war.
111 *upon our cue*] in our turn, at the right moment.
112 *England*] i.e., King Henry.
116 *in weight to re-answer*] to repay in full.
117 *exchequer*] treasury.
124 *quality*] rank and profession.

K. HEN.   Thou dost thy office fairly. Turn thee back,
And tell thy king I do not seek him now;
But could be willing to march on to Calais
Without impeachment: for, to say the sooth,
Though 't is no wisdom to confess so much   130
Unto an enemy of craft and vantage,
My people are with sickness much enfeebled,
My numbers lessen'd, and those few I have
Almost no better than so many French;
Who when they were in health, I tell thee, herald,
I thought upon one pair of English legs
Did march three Frenchmen. Yet, forgive me, God,
That I do brag thus! This your air of France
Hath blown that vice in me; I must repent.
Go therefore, tell thy master here I am;   140
My ransom is this frail and worthless trunk,
My army but a weak and sickly guard;
Yet, God before, tell him we will come on,
Though France himself and such another neighbour
Stand in our way. There's for thy labour, Montjoy.
Go, bid thy master well advise himself:
If we may pass, we will; if we be hinder'd,
We shall your tawny ground with your red blood
Discolour: and so, Montjoy, fare you well.
The sum of all our answer is but this: 150
We would not seek a battle, as we are;
Nor, as we are, we say we will not shun it:
So tell your master.

MONT.   I shall deliver so. Thanks to your highness.   [*Exit.*

GLOU.   I hope they will not come upon us now.

K. HEN.   We are in God's hand, brother, not in theirs.
March to the bridge; it now draws toward night:
Beyond the river we'll encamp ourselves,
And on to-morrow bid them march away.   [*Exeunt.*

129 *Without impeachment*] Without hindrance.
   sooth] truth.
131 *craft and vantage*] cunning and superior numbers.
141 *trunk*] body.
143 *God before*] God guiding us, with God for guide.

SCENE VII. *The French Camp, near Agincourt.*

Enter the CONSTABLE *of France, the* LORD RAMBURES, ORLEANS,
   DAUPHIN, *with others*

CON.   Tut! I have the best armour of the world. Would it were
   day!

ORL.   You have an excellent armour; but let my horse have his
   due.

CON.   It is the best horse of Europe.

ORL.   Will it never be morning?

DAU.   My Lord of Orleans, and my lord high constable, you talk
   of horse and armour?

ORL.   You are as well provided of both as any prince in the
   world.   10

DAU.   What a long night is this! I will not change my horse with
   any that treads but on four pasterns. Ça, ha! he bounds from
   the earth, as if his entrails were hairs; le cheval volant, the
   Pegasus, chez les narines de feu! When I bestride him, I
   soar, I am a hawk: he trots the air; the earth sings when he
   touches it; the basest horn of his hoof is more musical than
   the pipe of Hermes.

ORL.   He's of the colour of the nutmeg.

DAU.   And of the heat of the ginger. It is a beast for Perseus: he
   is pure air and fire; and the dull elements of earth and water   20
   never appear in him, but only in patient stillness while his
   rider mounts him: he is indeed a horse; and all other jades
   you may call beasts.

CON.   Indeed, my lord, it is a most absolute and excellent horse.

DAU.   It is the prince of palfreys; his neigh is like the bidding of
   a monarch, and his countenance enforces homage.

ORL.   No more, cousin.

DAU.   Nay, the man hath no wit that cannot, from the rising of
   the lark to the lodging of the lamb, vary deserved praise on
   my palfrey: it is a theme as fluent as the sea: turn the sands   30

---

12 *pasterns*] i.e., hooves.

13 *as if his entrails were hairs*] a reference to the elasticity of tennis balls, which were
   stuffed with hair.

13–14 *le cheval volant . . . de feu!*] the flying horse, Pegasus, with nostrils of fire!

17 *the pipe of Hermes*] According to Ovid's *Metamorphoses*, Mercury (or Hermes) puts
   the monster Argus to sleep by the music of his pipe.

22 *jades*] a pejorative word for horses.

25 *palfreys*] saddle horses.

29 *lodging*] lying down, resting.

into eloquent tongues, and my horse is argument for them
all: 't is a subject for a sovereign to reason on, and for a sovereign's sovereign to ride on; and for the world, familiar to us
and unknown, to lay apart their particular functions and
wonder at him. I once writ a sonnet in his praise, and began
thus: "Wonder of nature," —

ORL. I have heard a sonnet begin so to one's mistress.

DAU. Then did they imitate that which I composed to my
courser, for my horse is my mistress.

ORL. Your mistress bears well.   40

DAU. Me well; which is the prescript praise and perfection of a
good and particular mistress.

CON. Nay, for methought yesterday your mistress shrewdly
shook your back.

DAU. So perhaps did yours.

CON. Mine was not bridled.

DAU. O then belike she was old and gentle; and you rode, like
a kern of Ireland, your French hose off, and in your strait
strossers.

CON. You have good judgement in horsemanship.   50

DAU. Be warned by me, then: they that ride so, and ride not
warily, fall into foul bogs. I had rather have my horse to my
mistress.

CON. I had as lief have my mistress a jade.

DAU. I tell thee, constable, my mistress wears his own hair.

CON. I could make as true a boast as that, if I had a sow to my
mistress.

DAU. "Le chien est retourné à son propre vomissement, et la
truie lavée au bourbier:" thou makest use of any thing.

CON. Yet do I not use my horse for my mistress, or any such   60
proverb so little kin to the purpose.

---

39 *my horse is my mistress*] This line begins a bawdy conversation comparing horses to
mistresses. The scene emphasizes the vanity and overconfidence of the French, especially when compared to the more sober and profound sentiments on war expressed by King Henry.

41 *prescript*] prescribed, appropriate.

48–49 *a kern of Ireland . . . strossers*] An Irish kern was a lightly clad foot soldier, but here
seems used in the sense of one half-naked. "French hose" were loose and wide
breeches; "strait strossers" were tight breeches. The Dauphin suggests that the constable rode very lightly clad, or without wearing any clothes at all.

54 *lief*] happily.

55 *my mistress . . . hair*] a hit at the practice of wearing wigs.

58–59 *"Le chien . . . bourbier"*] A verbatim quotation from the French translation of the
Bible, from 2 Peter, ii, 22, "The dog is turned to his own vomit again; and the sow
that was washed to her wallowing in the mire."

RAM. My lord constable, the armour that I saw in your tent to-
night, are those stars or suns upon it?

CON. Stars, my lord.

DAU. Some of them will fall to-morrow, I hope.

CON. And yet my sky shall not want.

DAU. That may be, for you bear a many superfluously, and 't
were more honour some were away.

CON. Even as your horse bears your praises; who would trot as
well, were some of your brags dismounted.   70

DAU. Would I were able to load him with his desert! Will it
never be day? I will trot to-morrow a mile, and my way shall
be paved with English faces.

CON. I will not say so, for fear I should be faced out of my way:
but I would it were morning; for I would fain be about the
ears of the English.

RAM. Who will go to hazard with me for twenty prisoners?

CON. You must first go yourself to hazard, ere you have them.

DAU. 'T is midnight; I'll go arm myself.   [*Exit.*

ORL. The Dauphin longs for morning.   80

RAM. He longs to eat the English.

CON. I think he will eat all he kills.

ORL. By the white hand of my lady, he's a gallant prince.

CON. Swear by her foot, that she may tread out the oath.

ORL. He is simply the most active gentleman of France.

CON. Doing is activity; and he will still be doing.

ORL. He never did harm, that I heard of.

CON. Nor will do none to-morrow: he will keep that good name
still.

ORL. I know him to be valiant.   90

CON. I was told that by one that knows him better than you.

ORL. What's he?

CON. Marry, he told me so himself; and he said he cared not
who knew it.

ORL. He needs not; it is no hidden virtue in him.

CON. By my faith, sir, but it is; never any body saw it but his

---

74   *faced out*] bluffed out; an expression used in card games.

75–76 *fain be about the ears of*] gladly be striking the heads of.

77 *go to hazard*] gamble. (In the next line the same phrase means "put yourself in danger.")

84 *tread out the oath*] attest the oath by dancing. This suggestion is that the prince's gal-
lantry has more concern with dancing than with military prowess.

lackey: 't is a hooded valour; and when it appears, it will
bate.

ORL. Ill will never said well.

CON. I will cap that proverb with "There is flattery in friend-   100
ship."

ORL. And I will take up that with "Give the devil his due."

CON. Well placed: there stands your friend for the devil: have
at the very eye of that proverb with "A pox of the devil."

ORL. You are the better at proverbs, by how much "A fool's bolt
is soon shot."

CON. You have shot over.

ORL. 'T is not the first time you were overshot.

Enter a Messenger

MESS. My lord high constable, the English lie within fifteen
hundred paces of your tents.   110

CON. Who hath measured the ground?

MESS. The Lord Grandpré.

CON. A valiant and most expert gentleman. Would it were day!
Alas, poor Harry of England! he longs not for the dawning as
we do.

ORL. What a wretched and peevish fellow is this. King of
England, to mope with his fat-brained followers so far out of
his knowledge!

CON. If the English had any apprehension, they would run
away.   120

ORL. That they lack; for if their heads had any intellectual armour, they could never wear such heavy head-pieces.

RAM. That island of England breeds very valiant creatures; their
mastiffs are of unmatchable courage.

ORL. Foolish curs, that run winking into the mouth of a
Russian bear and have their heads crushed like rotten

97–98 *'t is a hooded valour . . . bate*] The language belongs to the sport of falconry. The
falcon's head was covered with a hood until the falconer wanted it to fly. To "bate"
is to flutter the wings (instead of going after prey). The constable suggests that the
Dauphin's valor is all talk and bluster.

105 *bolt*] short, blunt arrow.

107 *shot over*] missed the mark.

108 *overshot*] The word had two meanings: "put to shame" and "intoxicated" or
"drunk."

119 *apprehension*] sense, intelligence.

124 *mastiffs*] a breed of large dogs.

125 *winking*] with their eyes closed.

apples! You may as well say, that's a valiant flea that dare eat
his breakfast on the lip of a lion.

CON.　Just, just; and the men do sympathize with the mastiffs in
robustious and rough coming on, leaving their wits with 130
their wives: and then give them great meals of beef, and iron
and steel, they will eat like wolves, and fight like devils.

ORL.　Ay, but these English are shrewdly out of beef.

CON.　Then shall we find to-morrow they have only stomachs to
eat and none to fight. Now is it time to arm: come, shall we
about it?

ORL.　It is now two o'clock: but, let me see, by ten
We shall have each a hundred Englishmen.　　　[Exeunt.

130 *robustious*] boisterous.

ACT IV. — PROLOGUE

Enter Chorus

CHORUS.   Now entertain conjecture of a time
    When creeping murmur and the poring dark
    Fills the wide vessel of the universe.
    From camp to camp through the foul womb of night
    The hum of either army stilly sounds,
    That the fix'd sentinels almost receive
    The secret whispers of each other's watch:
    Fire answers fire, and through their paly flames
    Each battle sees the other's umber'd face;
    Steed threatens steed, in high and boastful neighs   10
    Piercing the night's dull ear; and from the tents
    The armourers, accomplishing the knights,
    With busy hammers closing rivets up,
    Give dreadful note of preparation:
    The country cocks do crow, the clocks do toll,
    And the third hour of drowsy morning name.
    Proud of their numbers and secure in soul,
    The confident and over-lusty French
    Do the low-rated English play at dice;
    And chide the cripple tardy-gaited night   20
    Who, like a foul and ugly witch, doth limp
    So tediously away. The poor condemned English,
    Like sacrifices, by their watchful fires
    Sit patiently and inly ruminate
    The morning's danger, and their gesture sad
    Investing lank-lean cheeks and war-worn coats

2 *poring*] in which one must strain to see.
9 *umber'd*] shadowed.
12 *accomplishing*] equipping.
17 *secure in soul*] overconfident.
25–26 *their gesture sad . . . coats*] the sadness of their gesture, which communicates it-
    self to their lank-lean cheeks and to their ragged coats.

Presenteth them unto the gazing moon
So many horrid ghosts. O now, who will behold
The royal captain of this ruin'd band
Walking from watch to watch, from tent to tent,　　　30
Let him cry "Praise and glory on his head!"
For forth he goes and visits all his host,
Bids them good morrow with a modest smile,
And calls them brothers, friends and countrymen.
Upon his royal face there is no note
How dread an army hath enrounded him;
Nor doth he dedicate one jot of colour
Unto the weary and all-watched night,
But freshly looks and over-bears attaint
With cheerful semblance and sweet majesty;　　　40
That every wretch, pining and pale before,
Beholding him, plucks comfort from his looks:
A largess universal like the sun
His liberal eye doth give to every one,
Thawing cold fear, that mean and gentle all
Behold, as may unworthiness define,
A little touch of Harry in the night.
And so our scene must to the battle fly;
Where—O for pity!—we shall much disgrace
With four or five most vile and ragged foils,　　　50
Right ill-disposed in brawl ridiculous,
The name of Agincourt. Yet sit and see,
Minding true things by what their mockeries be.　　　[*Exit.*

SCENE I. *The English Camp at Agincourt.*

Enter KING HENRY, BEDFORD, *and* GLOUCESTER

K. HEN.　Gloucester, 't is true that we are in great danger;
　　　The greater therefore should our courage be.
　　　Good morrow, brother Bedford. God Almighty!
　　　There is some soul of goodness in things evil,

---

36 *enrounded*] surrounded.
39 *over-bears attaint*] overcomes the effects of fatigue.
46 *as may unworthiness define*] i.e., as we can describe to you only imperfectly.
53 *mockeries*] inadequate imitations.

Would men observingly distil it out.
For our bạd neighbour makes us early stirrers,
Which is both healthful and good husbandry:
Besides, they are our outward consciences,
And preachers to us all, admonishing
That we should dress us fairly for our end.   10
Thus may we gather honey from the weed,
And make a moral of the devil himself.

Enter ERPINGHAM

Good morrow, old Sir Thomas Erpingham:
A good soft pillow for that good white head
Were better than a churlish turf of France.
ERP.   Not so, my liege: this lodging likes me better,
Since I may say "Now lie I like a king."
K. HEN.   'T is good for men to love their present pains
Upon example; so the spirit is eased:
And when the mind is quicken'd, out of doubt,   20
The organs, though defunct and dead before,
Break up their drowsy grave and newly move,
With casted slough and fresh legerity.
Lend me thy cloak, Sir Thomas. Brothers both,
Commend me to the princes in our camp;
Do my good morrow to them, and anon
Desire them all to my pavilion.
GLOU.   We shall, my liege.
ERP.   Shall I attend your grace?
K. HEN.   No, my good knight;   30
Go with my brothers to my lords of England:
I and my bosom must debate a while,
And then I would no other company.
ERP.   The Lord in heaven bless thee, noble Harry!
                              [*Exeunt all but* KING.
K. HEN.   God-a-mercy, old heart! thou speak'st cheerfully.

Enter PISTOL

PIST.   Qui va là?

5 *observingly*] observantly.
7 *husbandry*] economy, thrift.
10 *dress us*] address, prepare ourselves.
15 *churlish*] rough, hard.
23 *casted slough*] as though having shed old skin, like a snake.
    legerity] nimbleness.
36 *Qui va là?*] Who goes there?

K. HEN.   A friend.
PIST.   Discuss unto me; art thou officer?
    Or art thou base, common, and popular?
K. HEN.   I am a gentleman of a company.   40
PIST.   Trail'st thou the puissant pike?
K. HEN.   Even so. What are you?
PIST.   As good a gentleman as the emperor.
K. HEN.   Then you are a better than the king.
PIST.   The king's a bawcock, and a heart of gold,
    A lad of life, an imp of fame;
    Of parents good, of fist most valiant:
    I kiss his dirty shoe, and from heart-string
    I love the lovely bully. What is thy name?
K. HEN.   Harry le Roy.   50
PIST.   Le Roy! a Cornish name: art thou of Cornish crew?
K. HEN.   No, I am a Welshman.
PIST.   Know'st thou Fluellen?
K. HEN.   Yes.
PIST.   Tell him, I'll knock his leek about his pate
    Upon Saint Davy's day.
K. HEN.   Do not you wear your dagger in your cap that day, lest
    he knock that about yours.
PIST.   Art thou his friend?
K. HEN.   And his kinsman too.   60
PIST.   The figo for thee, then!
K. HEN.   I thank you: God be with you!
PIST.   My name is Pistol call'd.   [*Exit.*
K. HEN.   It sorts well with your fierceness.

Enter FLUELLEN *and* GOWER

GOW.   Captain Fluellen!
FLU.   So! in the name of Jesu Christ, speak lower. It is the great-
    est admiration in the universal world, when the true and
    aunchient prerogatifes and laws of the wars is not kept: if you
    would take the pains but to examine the wars of Pompey the
    Great, you shall find, I warrant you, that there is no tiddle   70

41 *Trail'st . . . pike?*] i.e., are you in the infantry?
45 *bawcock*] a good fellow.
46 *imp*] scion, sprout.
49 *bully*] fine chap.
55 *leek*] a plant worn by Welshmen to commemorate a victory over the Saxons.
    pate] head.
61 *figo*] insulting gesture. (See above, III, vi, 54.)
68 *aunchient prerogatifes*] old rules.

taddle nor pibble pabble in Pompey's camp; I warrant you,
you shall find the ceremonies of the wars, and the cares of it,
and the forms of it, and the sobriety of it, and the modesty of
it, to be otherwise.

GOW.   Why, the enemy is loud; you hear him all night.

FLU.   If the enemy is an ass and a fool and a prating coxcomb, is
it meet, think you, that we should also, look you, be an ass
and a fool and a prating coxcomb? in your own conscience,
now?

GOW.   I will speak lower.   80

FLU.   I pray you and beseech you that you will.

                              [*Exeunt* GOWER *and* FLUELLEN.

K. HEN.   Though it appear a little out of fashion,
There is much care and valour in this Welshman.

Enter three soldiers, JOHN BATES, ALEXANDER COURT, *and*
MICHAEL WILLIAMS

COURT.   Brother John Bates, is not that the morning which
breaks yonder?

BATES.   I think it be: but we have no great cause to desire the approach of day.

WILL.   We see yonder the beginning of the day, but I think we
shall never see the end of it. Who goes there?

K. HEN.   A friend.   90

WILL.   Under what captain serve you?

K. HEN.   Under Sir Thomas Erpingham.

WILL.   A good old commander and a most kind gentleman: I
pray you, what thinks he of our estate?

K. HEN.   Even as men wrecked upon a sand, that look to be
washed off the next tide.

BATES.   He hath not told his thought to the king?

K. HEN.   No; nor it is not meet he should. For, though I speak it
to you, I think the king is but a man, as I am: the violet
smells to him as it doth to me; the element shows to him as   100
it doth to me; all his senses have but human conditions: his
ceremonies laid by, in his nakedness he appears but a man;
and though his affections are higher mounted than ours, yet,

---

76 *prating coxcomb*] loud, chattering fool.
94 *our estate*] our situation.
95 *wrecked*] shipwrecked.
100 *the element*] the sky.
103 *are higher mounted*] soar higher.

when they stoop, they stoop with the like wing. Therefore
when he sees reason of fears, as we do, his fears, out of
doubt, be of the same relish as ours are: yet, in reason, no
man should possess him with any appearance of fear, lest he,
by showing it, should dishearten his army.

BATES.   He may show what outward courage he will; but I believe, as cold a night as 't is, he could wish himself in   110
Thames up to the neck; and so I would he were, and I by
him, at all adventures, so we were quit here.

K. HEN.   By my troth, I will speak my conscience of the king: I
think he would not wish himself any where but where he is.

BATES.   Then I would he were here alone; so should he be sure
to be ransomed, and a many poor men's lives saved.

K. HEN.   I dare say you love him not so ill, to wish him here
alone, howsoever you speak this to feel other men's minds:
methinks I could not die any where so contented as in the
king's company; his cause being just and his quarrel hon-   120
ourable.

WILL.   That's more than we know.

BATES.   Ay, or more than we should seek after; for we know
enough, if we know we are the king's subjects: if his cause be
wrong, our obedience to the king wipes the crime of it out
of us.

WILL.   But if the cause be not good, the king himself hath a
heavy reckoning to make, when all those legs and arms and
heads, chopped off in a battle, shall join together at the latter day and cry all "We died at such a place"; some swearing,   130
some crying for a surgeon, some upon their wives left poor
behind them, some upon the debts they owe, some upon
their children rawly left. I am afeard there are few die well
that die in a battle; for how can they charitably dispose of any
thing, when blood is their argument? Now, if these men do
not die well, it will be a black matter for the king that led
them to it; whom to disobey were against all proportion of
subjection.

K. HEN.   So, if a son that is by his father sent about merchandise

---

112 *at all adventures*] no matter what happens.
   quit here] gone from here.
129–130 *at the latter day*] at the last day, at the day of judgment.
133 *rawly left*] left young and helpless.
135 *when blood . . . argument*] when shedding of blood is the subject of their thought,
   their business in hand.
137–138 *proportion of subjection*] proper duty of a subject.

do sinfully miscarry upon the sea, the imputation of his   140
wickedness, by your rule, should be imposed upon his father
that sent him: or if a servant, under his master's command
transporting a sum of money, be assailed by robbers and die
in many irreconciled iniquities, you may call the business of
the master the author of the servant's damnation: but this is
not so: the king is not bound to answer the particular end-
ings of his soldiers, the father of his son, nor the master of his
servant; for they purpose not their death, when they purpose
their services. Besides, there is no king, be his cause never so
spotless, if it come to the arbitrement of swords, can try it out   150
with all unspotted soldiers: some peradventure have on them
the guilt of premeditated and contrived murder; some, of beguiling virgins with the broken seals of perjury; some, making the wars their bulwark, that have before gored the gentle
bosom of peace with pillage and robbery. Now, if these men
have defeated the law and outrun native punishment,
though they can outstrip men, they have no wings to fly from
God: war is His beadle, war is His vengeance; so that here
men are punished for before-breach of the king's laws in now
the king's quarrel: where they feared the death, they have   160
borne life away; and where they would be safe, they perish:
then if they die unprovided, no more is the king guilty of
their damnation than he was before guilty of those impieties
for the which they are now visited. Every subject's duty is the
king's; but every subject's soul is his own. Therefore should
every soldier in the wars do as every sick man in his bed,
wash every mote out of his conscience: and dying so, death
is to him advantage; or not dying, the time was blessedly lost
wherein such preparation was gained: and in him that es-
capes, it were not sin to think that, making God so free an   170
offer, He let him outlive that day to see His greatness and to
teach others how they should prepare.

140 *sinfully miscarry*] perish in sin; die without repenting their sins.
148 *purpose*] intend.
150 *arbitrement*] arbitration, settling of a dispute.
151 *peradventure*] perhaps.
152 *contrived*] actually committed.
156 *native*] at home.
158 *beadle*] parish officer who punishes petty offenders.
162 *unprovided*] unprepared spiritually.
167 *mote*] small impurity.

WILL.   'T is certain, every man that dies ill, the ill upon his own
        head, the king is not to answer it.
BATES.   I do not desire he should answer for me; and yet I de-
        termine to fight lustily for him.
K. HEN.   I myself heard the king say he would not be ransomed.
WILL.   Ay, he said so, to make us fight cheerfully: but when our
        throats are cut, he may be ransomed, and we ne'er the wiser.
K. HEN.   If I live to see it, I will never trust his word after.   180
WILL.   You pay him then. That's a perilous shot out of an elder-
        gun, that a poor and a private displeasure can do against a
        monarch! you may as well go about to turn the sun to ice
        with fanning in his face with a peacock's feather. You'll
        never trust his word after! come, 't is a foolish saying.
K. HEN.   Your reproof is something too round: I should be angry
        with you, if the time were convenient.
WILL.   Let it be a quarrel between us, if you live.
K. HEN.   I embrace it.
WILL.   How shall I know thee again?   190
K. HEN.   Give me any gage of thine, and I will wear it in my
        bonnet: then, if ever thou darest acknowledge it, I will make
        it my quarrel.
WILL.   Here's my glove: give me another of thine.
K. HEN.   There.
WILL.   This will I also wear in my cap: if ever thou come to me
        and say, after to-morrow, "This is my glove," by this hand, I
        will take thee a box on the ear.
K. HEN.   If ever I live to see it, I will challenge it.
WILL.   Thou darest as well be hanged.   200
K. HEN.   Well, I will do it, though I take thee in the king's com-
        pany.
WILL.   Keep thy word: fare thee well.
BATES.   Be friends, you English fools, be friends: we have
        French quarrels enow, if you could tell how to reckon.
K. HEN.   Indeed, the French may lay twenty French crowns to
        one, they will beat us; for they bear them on their shoulders:

173 *dies ill*] dies in sin.
181–182 *an elder-gun*] a toy gun made of elder word.
186 *round*] blunt, outspoken.
191 *gage*] pledge.
192 *bonnet*] military headgear.
198 *take*] give, strike.

but it is no English treason to cut French crowns, and to-
morrow the king himself will be a clipper.

[*Exeunt* Soldiers.

Upon the king! let us our lives, our souls,   210
Our debts, our careful wives,
Our children and our sins lay on the king!
We must bear all. O hard condition,
Twin-born with greatness, subject to the breath
Of every fool, whose sense no more can feel
But his own wringing! What infinite heart's-ease
Must kings neglect, that private men enjoy!
And what have kings, that privates have not too,
Save ceremony, save general ceremony?
And what art thou, thou idol ceremony?   220
What kind of god art thou, that suffer'st more
Of mortal griefs than do thy worshippers?
What are thy rents? what are thy comings in?
O ceremony, show me but thy worth!
What is thy soul of adoration?
Art thou aught else but place, degree and form,
Creating awe and fear in other men?
Wherein thou art less happy being fear'd
Than they in fearing.
What drink'st thou oft, instead of homage sweet,   230
But poison'd flattery? O, be sick, great greatness,
And bid thy ceremony give thee cure!
Think'st thou the fiery fever will go out
With titles blown from adulation?
Will it give place to flexure and low bending?
Canst thou, when thou command'st the beggar's knee,
Command the health of it? No, thou proud dream,
That play'st so subtly with a king's repose;
I am a king that find thee, and I know
'T is not the balm, the sceptre and the ball,   240

208 *cut French crowns*] an allusion to the felonious practice of cutting pieces off coins,
    with a pun on crowns in the sense of heads.
211 *careful*] anxious.
215–216 *whose sense . . . wringing*] who has no feeling for any suffering save that which
    wrings his own heart, that which he endures himself.
225 *thy soul of adoration*] the essential virtue which men adore in thee.
234 *blown from adulation*] blown from the lips of flatterers.
235 *flexure*] bending.
238 *repose*] rest, sleep.
239 *balm*] oil used at the king's coronation.

The sword, the mace, the crown imperial,
The intertissued robe of gold and pearl,
The farced title running 'fore the king,
The throne he sits on, nor the tide of pomp
That beats upon the high shore of this world,
No, not all these, thrice-gorgeous ceremony,
Not all these, laid in bed majestical,
Can sleep so soundly as the wretched slave,
Who with a body fill'd and vacant mind
Gets him to rest, cramm'd with distressful bread;   250
Never sees horrid night, the child of hell,
But, like a lackey, from the rise to set
Sweats in the eye of Phœbus and all night
Sleeps in Elysium; next day after dawn,
Doth rise and help Hyperion to his horse,
And follows so the ever-running year,
With profitable labour, to his grave:
And, but for ceremony, such a wretch,
Winding up days with toil and nights with sleep,
Had the fore-hand and vantage of a king.   260
The slave, a member of the country's peace,
Enjoys it; but in gross brain little wots
What watch the king keeps to maintain the peace,
Whose hours the peasant best advantages.

Re-enter ERPINGHAM

ERP.   My lord, your nobles, jealous of your absence,
    Seek through your camp to find you.
K. HEN.   Good old knight,
    Collect them all together at my tent:
    I'll be before thee.
ERP.   I shall do't, my lord.   [*Exit.*   270
K. HEN.   O God of battles! steel my soldiers' hearts;
    Possess them not with fear; take from them now

243 *farced*] swollen, pompous.
250 *distressful*] earned by the pain of hard work.
252 *a lackey*] constant attendant, servant.
253 *Phœbus*] the sun god.
254 *Elysium*] in Greek mythology, resting place for the blessed.
255 *Hyperion*] the charioteer who pulls the sun across the sky.
260 *fore-hand and vantage*] upper hand and advantage.
262 *wots*] knows.
264 *best advantages*] applies to best advantage.
265 *jealous of*] anxious about.

The sense of reckoning, if the opposed numbers
Pluck their hearts from them. Not to-day, O Lord,
O, not to-day, think not upon the fault
My father made in compassing the crown!
I Richard's body have interred new;
And on it have bestow'd more contrite tears
Than from it issued forced drops of blood:
Five hundred poor I have in yearly pay,   280
Who twice a-day their wither'd hands hold up
Toward heaven, to pardon blood; and I have built
Two chantries, where the sad and solemn priests
Sing still for Richard's soul. More will I do;
Though all that I can do is nothing worth,
Since that my penitence comes after all,
Imploring pardon.

Re-enter GLOUCESTER

GLOU.   My liege!
K. HEN.   My brother Gloucester's voice? Ay;
I know thy errand, I will go with thee: 290
The day, my friends and all things stay for me.   [*Exeunt.*

SCENE II. *The French Camp.*

Enter DAUPHIN, ORLEANS, RAMBURES, *and others*

ORL.   The sun doth gild our armour; up, my lords!
DAU.   Montez à cheval! My horse! varlet! laquais! ha!
ORL.   O brave spirit!
DAU.   Via! les eaux et la terre.
ORL.   Rien puis? l'air et le feu.
DAU.   Ciel, cousin Orleans.

Enter CONSTABLE

Now, my lord constable!

273–274 *The sense of . . . hearts from them*] their ability to count, if the enemy are so
    many as to make them fearful.
275–276 *the fault . . . the crown*] reference to the murder of King Richard II.
283 *chantries*] chapels in which masses for the dead are held.

---

2 *Montez . . . laquais!*] Mount your horses! My horse! page! footman!
4 *Via! . . . terre.*] Away with water and earth! (See above, III, vii, 20.)
5 *Rien . . . feu.*] Nothing left but air and fire?
6 *Ciel*] Sky, heaven.

CON.   Hark, how our steeds for present service neigh!
DAU.   Mount them, and make incision in their hides,
     That their hot blood may spin in English eyes,
     And dout them with superfluous courage, ha!   10
RAM.   What, will you have them weep our horses' blood?
     How shall we then behold their natural tears?

Enter MESSENGER

MESS.   The English are embattled, you French peers.
CON.   To horse, you gallant princes! straight to horse!
     Do but behold yon poor and starved band,
     And your fair show shall suck away their souls,
     Leaving them but the shales and husks of men.
     There is not work enough for all our hands;
     Scarce blood enough in all their sickly veins   20
     To give each naked curtle-axe a stain,
     That our French gallants shall to-day draw out,
     And sheathe for lack of sport: let us but blow on them,
     The vapour of our valour will o'erturn them.
     'T is positive 'gainst all exceptions, lords,
     That our superfluous lackeys and our peasants,
     Who in unnecessary action swarm
     About our squares of battle, were enow
     To purge this field of such a hilding foe,
     Though we upon this mountain's basis by   30
     Took stand for idle speculation:
     But that our honours must not. What's to say?
     A very little little let us do,
     And all is done. Then let the trumpets sound
     The tucket sonance and the note to mount;
     For our approach shall so much dare the field
     That England shall couch down in fear and yield.

---

9 *incision*] i.e., with spurs.
11 *dout*] put out
16 *poor and starved band*] the English army, which is low on provisions and vastly out-
     numbered by the French.
18 *shales*] shells or pods.
21 *curtle-axe*] broad, curving sword.
29 *hilding*] worthless, base.
31 *Took . . . speculation*] Merely stood idly looking on.
35 *The tucket sonance*] The trumpet blast.
36 *dare the field*] a term in falconry, used of the hawk when, rising in the air, it terrifies
     birds on the ground. The French believe the very size of their forces will scare the
     English into retreat.

Enter GRANDPRÉ

GRAND.   Why do you stay so long, my lords of France?
      Yon island carrions, desperate of their bones,
      Ill-favouredly become the morning field: 40
      Their ragged curtains poorly are let loose,
      And our air shakes them passing scornfully:
      Big Mars seems bankrupt in their beggar'd host
      And faintly through a rusty beaver peeps:
      The horsemen sit like fixed candlesticks,
      With torch-staves in their hand; and their poor jades
      Lob down their heads, dropping the hides and hips,
      The gum down-roping from their pale-dead eyes,
      And in their pale dull mouths the gimmal bit
      Lies foul with chew'd grass, still and motionless;   50
      And their executors, the knavish crows,
      Fly o'er them, all impatient for their hour.
      Description cannot suit itself in words
      To demonstrate the life of such a battle
      In life so lifeless as it shows itself.
CON.   They have said their prayers, and they stay for death.
DAU.   Shall we go send them dinners and fresh suits
      And give their fasting horses provender,
      And after fight with them?
CON.   I stay but for my guidon: to the field!   60
      I will the banner from a trumpet take,
      And use it for my haste. Come, come, away!
      The sun is high, and we outwear the day.   [*Exeunt.*

---

40 *Ill-favouredly become the . . . field*] Make a poor show on the field.
41 *curtains*] flags, pennats.
43 *Mars*] god of war.
44 *beaver*] face-guard of the helmet.
48 *down-roping*] hanging down in rope-like fashion.
49 *gimmal bit*] bit formed of a chain or interlinked rings.
51 *the knavish crows*] the birds of prey, circling overhead.
52 *their hour*] their hour of death.
54 *a battle*] the English army.
60 *guidon*] standard or ensign.
61 *the banner from a trumpet*] the banner or small flag held by the trumpeter.

SCENE III. *The English Camp.*

Enter GLOUCESTER, BEDFORD, EXETER, ERPINGHAM, *with all his*
     host: SALISBURY *and* WESTMORELAND

GLOU.   Where is the king?
BED.   The king himself is rode to view their battle.
WEST.   Of fighting men they have full three score thousand.
EXE.   There's five to one; besides, they all are fresh.
SAL.   God's arm strike with us! 't is a fearful odds.
     God be wi' you, princes all; I'll to my charge:
     If we no more meet till we meet in heaven,
     Then, joyfully, my noble Lord of Bedford,
     My dear Lord Gloucester, and my good Lord Exeter,
     And my kind kinsman, warriors all, adieu!   10
BED.   Farewell, good Salisbury; and good luck go with thee!
EXE.   Farewell, kind lord; fight valiantly to-day:
     And yet I do thee wrong to mind thee of it,
     For thou art framed of the firm truth of valour.

                                        [*Exit* SALISBURY.

BED.   He is as full of valour as of kindness;
     Princely in both.

Enter the KING

WEST.   O that we now had here
     But one ten thousand of those men in England
     That do no work to-day!
K. HEN.   What's he that wishes so?   20
     My cousin Westmoreland? No, my fair cousin:
     If we are mark'd to die, we are enow
     To do our country loss; and if to live,
     The fewer men, the greater share of honour.
     God's will! I pray thee, wish not one man more.
     By Jove, I am not covetous for gold,
     Nor care I who doth feed upon my cost;
     It yearns me not if men my garments wear;
     Such outward things dwell not in my desires:

4 *five to one*] the amount by which the French force is estimated to outnumber the
   English.
20 *What's he*] Who is he.
22 *enow*] enough.
27 *upon my cost*] at my expense.
28 *yearns*] grieves.

But if it be a sin to covet honour,   30
I am the most offending soul alive.
No, faith, my coz, wish not a man from England:
God's peace! I would not lose so great an honour
As one man more, methinks, would share from me
For the best hope I have. O, do not wish one more!
Rather proclaim it, Westmoreland, through my host,
That he which hath no stomach to this fight,
Let him depart; his passport shall be made
And crowns for convoy put into his purse:
We would not die in that man's company   40
That fears his fellowship to die with us.
This day is call'd the feast of Crispian:
He that outlives this day, and comes safe home,
Will stand a tip-toe when this day is named,
And rouse him at the name of Crispian.
He that shall live this day, and see old age,
Will yearly on the vigil feast his neighbours,
And say, "To-morrow is Saint Crispian":
Then will he strip his sleeve and show his scars,
And say "These wounds I had on Crispin's day."
Old men forget; yet all shall be forgot,
But he'll remember with advantages
What feats he did that day: then shall our names,
Familiar in his mouth as household words,
Harry the king, Bedford and Exeter,
Warwick and Talbot, Salisbury and Gloucester,
Be in their flowing cups freshly remember'd.
This story shall the good man teach his son;
And Crispin Crispian shall ne'er go by,
From this day to the ending of the world,   60
But we in it shall be remembered;
We few, we happy few, we band of brothers;
For he to-day that sheds his blood with me
Shall be my brother; be he ne'er so vile,
This day shall gentle his condition:

32 *coz*] cousin.
41 *That fears . . . with us*] That fears to be our comrade in death.
42 *the feast of Crispian*] October 25 was the day of two brothers, Crispin and Crispian,
    who suffered martyrdom for their fidelity to Christianity at Soissons, about 300 A.D.
47 *the vigil*] the eve of the festival.
52 *with advantages*] with embellishments.
64 *vile*] lowly.
65 *gentle his condition*] raise him to rank of gentleman.

And gentlemen in England now a-bed
Shall think themselves accursed they were not here,
And hold their manhoods cheap whiles any speaks
That fought with us upon Saint Crispin's day.

Re-enter SALISBURY

SAL.   My sovereign lord, bestow yourself with speed: 70
    The French are bravely in their battles set,
    And will with all expedience charge on us.
K. HEN.   All things are ready, if our minds be so.
WEST.   Perish the man whose mind is backward now!
K. HEN.   Thou dost not wish more help from England, coz?
WEST.   God's will! my liege, would you and I alone,
    Without more help, could fight this royal battle!
K. HEN.   Why, now thou hast unwish'd five thousand men;
    Which likes me better than to wish us one.
    You know your places: God be with you all!   80

Tucket. Enter MONTJOY

MONT.   Once more I come to know of thee, King Harry,
    If for thy ransom thou wilt now compound,
    Before thy most assured overthrow:
    For certainly thou art so near the gulf,
    Thou needs must be englutted. Besides, in mercy,
    The constable desires thee thou wilt mind
    Thy followers of repentance; that their souls
    May make a peaceful and a sweet retire
    From off these fields, where, wretches, their poor bodies
    Must lie and fester.
K. HEN.   Who hath sent thee now?   90
MONT.   The Constable of France.
K. HEN.   I pray thee, bear my former answer back:
    Bid them achieve me and then sell my bones.
    Good God! why should they mock poor fellows thus?
    The man that once did sell the lion's skin

70 *bestow yourself*] prepare battle positions.
71 *in their battles set*] lined up in their battalions.
72 *expedience*] speed.
74 *backward*] hesitant, afraid.
84 *gulf*] whirlpool.
85 *englutted*] engulfed, swallowed up.
86 *thou wilt mind*] that you will remind.
88 *retire*] retreat, withdrawal.
94 *achieve*] conquer, finish off.

While the beast lived, was killed with hunting him.
A many of our bodies shall no doubt
Find native graves; upon the which, I trust,
Shall witness live in brass of this day's work: 100
And those that leave their valiant bones in France,
Dying like men, though buried in your dunghills,
They shall be famed; for there the sun shall greet them,
And draw their honours reeking up to heaven;
Leaving their earthly parts to choke your clime,
The smell whereof shall breed a plague in France.
Mark then abounding valour in our English,
That being dead, like to the bullet's grazing,
Break out into a second course of mischief,
Killing in relapse of mortality.   110
Let me speak proudly: tell the constable
We are but warriors for the working-day;
Our gayness and our gilt are all besmirch'd
With rainy marching in the painful field;
There's not a piece of feather in our host—
Good argument, I hope, we will not fly—
And time hath worn us into slovenry:
But, by the mass, our hearts are in the trim;
And my poor soldiers tell me, yet ere night
They'll be in fresher robes, or they will pluck   120
The gay new coats o'er the French soldiers' heads
And turn them out of service. If they do this,—
As, if God please, they shall,—my ransom then
Will soon be levied. Herald, save thou thy labour;
Come thou no more for ransom, gentle herald:
They shall have none, I swear, but these my joints;
Which if they have as I will leave 'em them,
Shall yield them little, tell the constable.
MONT.   I shall, King Harry. And so fare thee well:
Thou never shalt hear herald any more.   [*Exit.*   130
K. HEN.   I fear thou'lt once more come again for ransom.

Enter YORK

---

107 *abounding*] abundant.
108 *the bullet's grazing*] the bullet's ricocheting after grazing.
110 *Killing . . . mortality*] Killing when they are at the point of death.
113 *gilt*] gilding, outward brilliance.
116 *slovenry*] appearing unclean.
118 *in the trim*] prepared.

YORK.   My lord, most humbly on my knee I beg
    The leading of the vaward.
K. HEN.   Take it, brave York. Now, soldiers, march away:
    And how thou pleasest, God, dispose the day!   [*Exeunt.*

SCENE IV. *The Field of Battle.*

Alarum. Excursions. Enter PISTOL, French Soldier, *and* Boy

PIST.   Yield, cur!
FR. SOL.   Je pense que vous êtes gentilhomme de bonne qualité.
PIST.   Qualtitie calmie custure me! Art thou a gentleman? what
    is thy name? discuss.
FR. SOL.   O Seigneur Dieu!
PIST.   O, Signieur Dew should be a gentleman:
    Perpend my words, O Signieur Dew, and mark;
    O Signieur Dew, thou diest on point of fox,
    Except, O signieur, thou do give to me
    Egregious ransom.
FR. SOL.   O, prenez miséricorde! ayez pitié de moi!   10
PIST.   Moy shall not serve; I will have forty moys;
    Or I will fetch thy rim out at thy throat
    In drops of crimson blood.
FR. SOL.   Est-il impossible d'échapper la force de ton bras?
PIST.   Brass, cur!
    Thou damned and luxurious mountain goat,
    Offer'st me brass?

133 *vaward*] vanguard.

---

  2 *Je . . . qualité.*] I think that you're a gentleman of noble lineage.
  3 *calmie custure me*] This gibberish seems suggested by a favorite Irish air of the day,
    called "Calen o custure me," meaning "I am a girl from beside the [river] Suir."
  5 *O . . . Dieu!*] O Lord God!
  7 *Perpend*] Consider.
  8 *fox*] sword.
10 *Egregious*] Enormous.
11 *O, prenez . . . moi!*] O, have mercy! take pity on me!
12 *Moy*] a bushel of corn.
13 *rim*] rim, or membrane, of the belly.
15 *Est-il . . . bras?*] Is it impossible to escape the strength of your arm?
17 *luxurious*] lascivious.

FR. SOL.   O pardonnez moi!

PIST.   Say'st thou me so? is that a ton of moys?   20
    Come hither, boy: ask me this slave in French
    What is his name.

BOY.   Écoutez: comment êtes-vous appelé?

FR. SOL.   Monsieur le Fer.

BOY.   He says his name is Master Fer.

PIST.   Master Fer! I'll fer him, and firk him, and ferret him: discuss the same in French unto him.

BOY.   I do not know the French for fer, and ferret, and firk.

PIST.   Bid him prepare; for I will cut his throat.

FR. SOL.   Que dit-il, monsieur?   30

BOY.   Il me commande de vous dire que vous faites vous prêt;
car ce soldat ici est disposé tout à cette heure de couper votre
gorge.

PIST.   Owy, cuppele gorge, permafoy,
    Peasant, unless thou give me crowns, brave crowns;
    Or mangled shalt thou be by this my sword.

FR. SOL.   O, je vous supplie, pour l'amour de Dieu, me pardonner! Je suis gentilhomme de bonne maison: gardez ma
vie, et je vous donnerai deux cents écus.

PIST.   What are his words?   40

BOY.   He prays you to save his life: he is a gentleman of a good
house; and for his ransom he will give you two hundred
crowns.

PIST.   Tell him my fury shall abate, and I
    The crowns will take.

FR. SOL.   Petit monsieur, que dit-il?

---

19 *O . . . moi!*] O, pardon me!

23 *Écoutez . . . appelé?*] Listen: what's your name?

26 *Master Fer! I'll fer him*] Pistol plays aimlessly on the Frenchman's name.
   firk] beat, thrash.
   ferret him] treat him as the ferret tortures the rabbit.

30 *Que . . . monsieur?*] What is he saying, sir?

31–33 *Il . . . gorge.*] He commands me to tell you to prepare yourself; because this soldier intends to cut your throat right away.

34 *Owy . . . permafoy,*] Yes, cut the throat, by my faith.

37–39 *O, . . . écus.*] O, I beg you to pardon me, for the love of God! I'm a gentleman of
a good breeding: save my life, and I'll give you two hundred crowns.

46 *Petit . . . dit-il?*] Young man, what does he say?

BOY.   Encore qu'il est contre son jurement de pardonner aucun prisonnier, néanmoins, pour les écus que vous l'avez promis, il est content de vous donner la liberté, le franchisement.

FR. SOL.   Sur mes genoux je vous donne mille remercîmens; et   50
je m'estime heureux que je suis tombé entre les mains d'un chevalier, je pense, le plus brave, vaillant, et très distingué seigneur d'Angleterre.

PIST.   Expound unto me, boy.

BOY.   He gives you, upon his knees, a thousand thanks; and he esteems himself happy that he hath fallen into the hands of one, as he thinks, the most brave, valorous, and thrice-worthy signieur of England.

PIST.   As I suck blood, I will some mercy show.
Follow me!   60

BOY.   Suivez-vous le grand capitaine. [*Exeunt* PISTOL, *and* French Soldier.] I did never know so full a voice issue from so empty a heart: but the saying is true, "The empty vessel makes the greatest sound." Bardolph and Nym had ten times more valour than this roaring devil i' the old play, that every one may pare his nails with a wooden dagger; and they are both hanged; and so would this be, if he durst steal any thing adventurously. I must stay with the lackeys, with the luggage of our camp: the French might have a good prey of us, if he knew of it; for there is none to guard it but boys.   [*Exit*.

SCENE V. *Another Part of the Field.*

Enter CONSTABLE, ORLEANS, BOURBON, DAUPHIN, *and* RAMBURES

CON.   O diable!

ORL.   O Seigneur! le jour est perdu, tout est perdu!

DAU.   Mort de ma vie! all is confounded, all!

47–49 *Encore . . . franchisement.*] Again that it is against his policy to pardon any prisoner. Nonetheless, for the crowns that you've promised, he agrees to give you your liberty, to set you free.

50–53 *Sur . . . d'Angleterre.*] On my knees I give you a thousand thanks; and I count myself lucky to have fallen into the hands of a knight who, I think, is the bravest, most valiant, and most distinguished lord of England.

61 *Suivez . . . capitaine.*] Follow the great captain.

65 *devil . . . dagger*] a reference to the Devil (who often carried a wooden dagger) in old morality plays.

---

2 *O . . . perdu!*] O lord! the day is lost, all is lost!

      Reproach and everlasting shame
      Sits mocking in our plumes. O méchante fortune!
      Do not run away.   [*A short alarum.*

CON.   Why, all our ranks are broke.

DAU.   O perdurable shame! let's stab ourselves.
      Be these the wretches that we play'd at dice for?

ORL.   Is this the king we sent to for his ransom?   10

BOUR.   Shame and eternal shame, nothing but shame!
      Let us die in honour: once more back again;
      And he that will not follow Bourbon now,
      Let him go hence, and with his cap in hand,
      Like a base pandar, hold the chamber-door
      Whilst by a slave, no gentler than my dog,
      His fairest daughter is contaminated.

CON.   Disorder, that hath spoil'd us, friend us now!
      Let us on heaps go offer up our lives.

ORL.   We are enow yet living in the field   20
      To smother up the English in our throngs,
      If any order might be thought upon.

BOUR.   The devil take order now! I'll to the throng:
      Let life be short; else shame will be too long.   [*Exeunt.*

SCENE VI. *Another Part of the Field.*

Alarum. Enter KING HENRY *and forces,* EXETER, *and others*

K. HEN.   Well have we done, thrice valiant countrymen:
      But all's not done; yet keep the French the field.

EXE.   The Duke of York commends him to your majesty.

K. HEN.   Lives he, good uncle? thrice within this hour
      I saw him down; thrice up again, and fighting;
      From helmet to the spur all blood he was.

EXE.   In which array, brave soldier, doth he lie,
      Larding the plain; and by his bloody side,

---

  8 *perdurable*] lasting, eternal.
 15 *pandar*] pimp.
 16 *no gentler*] of no higher rank.
 19 *on heaps*] in crowds, altogether.
 20 *enow*] enough.

---

  7 *In which array*] In that manner (bloodied "from helmet to spur").
  8 *Larding the plain*] Fattening the earth.

Yoke-fellow to his honour-owing wounds,
The noble Earl of Suffolk also lies.   10
Suffolk first died: and York, all haggled over,
Comes to him, where in gore he lay insteep'd,
And takes him by the beard; kisses the gashes
That bloodily did yawn upon his face;
And cries aloud "Tarry, dear cousin Suffolk!
My soul shall thine keep company to heaven;
Tarry, sweet soul, for mine, then fly abreast,
As in this glorious and well-foughten field
We kept together in our chivalry!"
Upon these words I came and cheer'd him up: 20
He smiled me in the face, raught me his hand,
And, with a feeble gripe, says "Dear my lord,
Commend my service to my sovereign."
So did he turn, and over Suffolk's neck
He threw his wounded arm and kiss'd his lips;
And so espoused to death, with blood he seal'd
A testament of noble-ending love.
The pretty and sweet manner of it forced
Those waters from me which I would have stopp'd;
But I had not so much of man in me,   30
And all my mother came into mine eyes
And gave me up to tears.
K. HEN.   I blame you not;
For, hearing this, I must perforce compound
With mistful eyes, or they will issue too.   [*Alarum.*
But, hark! what new alarum is this same?
The French have reinforced their scatter'd men:
Then every soldier kill his prisoners;
Give the word through.   [*Exeunt.*

---

9 *honour-owing*] honor-owning, honorable.
11 *haggled*] hacked.
21 *raught*] reached.
31 *my mother*] i.e., the more sensitive part of me.
35 *mistful*] growing dim with coming tears.
37 *The French . . . men*] According to some accounts, a few French horsemen suddenly
   raided unguarded tents of the English camp, while the main army was in the field,
   and killed many of the servants; some of the survivors, seized with panic, spread the
   report, which had small foundation, that the French army was regrouping for attack,
   whereupon Henry V gave the order for the slaughter of his French prisoners. In the
   next scene, Gower and Fluellen, upon hearing the rumor that English servant boys
   were killed, express their disgust at the French.

SCENE VII. *Another Part of the Field.*

Enter FLUELLEN *and* GOWER

FLU. Kill the poys and the luggage! 't is expressly against the law
of arms: 't is as arrant a piece of knavery, mark you now, as
can be offer't; in your conscience, now, is it not?

GOW. 'T is certain there's not a boy left alive; and the cowardly
rascals that ran from the battle ha' done this slaughter: besides, they have burned and carried away all that was in the
king's tent; wherefore the king, most worthily, hath caused
every soldier to cut his prisoner's throat. O, 't is a gallant
king!

FLU. Ay, he was porn at Monmouth, Captain Gower. What call 10
you the town's name where Alexander the Pig was born?

GOW. Alexander the Great.

FLU. Why, I pray you, is not pig great? the pig, or the great, or
the mighty, or the huge, or the magnanimous, are all one
reckonings, save the phrase is a little variations.

GOW. I think Alexander the Great was born in Macedon: his father was called Philip of Macedon, as I take it.

FLU. I think it is in Macedon where Alexander is porn. I tell
you, captain, if you look in the maps of the 'orld, I warrant
you sall find, in the comparisons between Macedon and 20
Monmouth, that the situations, look you, is both alike.
There is a river in Macedon; and there is also moreover a
river at Monmouth: it is called Wye at Monmouth; but it is
out of my prains what is the name of the other river; but 't is
all one, 't is alike as my fingers is to my fingers, and there is
salmons in both. If you mark Alexander's life well, Harry of
Monmouth's life is come after it indifferent well; for there is
figures in all things. Alexander, God knows, and you know,
in his rages, and his furies, and his wraths, and his cholers,
and his moods, and his displeasures, and his indignations, 30
and also being a little intoxicates in his prains, did, in his ales
and his angers, look you, kill his best friend, Cleitus.

GOW. Our king is not like him in that: he never killed any of his
friends.

FLU. It is not well done, mark you now, to take the tales out of
my mouth, ere it is made and finished. I speak but in the

---

10 *Monmouth*] in Wales, Fluellen's native land.
11 *Pig*] Fluellen's mispronunciation, due to his Welsh accent, of "Big."

figures and comparisons of it: as Alexander killed his friend
Cleitus, being in his ales and his cups; so also Harry Monmouth, being in his right wits and his good judgements,
turned away the fat knight with the great-belly doublet: he   40
was full of jests, and gipes, and knaveries, and mocks; I have
forgot his name.

GOW.   Sir John Falstaff.

FLU.   That is he: I'll tell you there is good men porn at
Monmouth.

GOW.   Here comes his majesty.

Alarum. Enter KING HENRY *and forces;* WARWICK, GLOUCESTER,
EXETER, *and others*

K. HEN.   I was not angry since I came to France
Until this instant. Take a trumpet, herald;
Ride thou unto the horsemen on yon hill:
If they will fight with us, bid them come down,   50
Or void the field; they do offend our sight:
If they'll do neither, we will come to them,
And make them skirr away, as swift as stones
Enforced from the old Assyrian slings:
Besides, we'll cut the throats of those we have,
And not a man of them that we shall take
Shall taste our mercy. Go and tell them so.

Enter MONTJOY

EXE.   Here comes the herald of the French, my liege.

GLOU.   His eyes are humbler than they used to be.

K. HEN.   How now! what means this, herald? know'st thou not   60
That I have fined these bones of mine for ransom?
Comest thou again for ransom?

MONT.   No, great king:
I come to thee for charitable license,
That we may wander o'er this bloody field
To book our dead, and then to bury them;
To sort our nobles from our common men.
For many of our princes — woe the while! —
Lie drown'd and soak'd in mercenary blood;

---

53 *skirr*] scurry.
61 *fined*] agreed to pay as fine.
66 *book*] register.

So do our vulgar drench their peasant limbs   70
In blood of princes; and their wounded steeds
Fret fetlock deep in gore, and with wild rage
Yerk out their armed heels at their dead masters,
Killing them twice. O, give us leave, great king,
To view the field in safety and dispose
Of their dead bodies!

K. HEN.   I tell thee truly, herald,
I know not if the day be ours or no;
For yet a many of your horsemen peer
And gallop o'er the field.   80

MONT.   The day is yours.

K. HEN.   Praised be God, and not our strength, for it!
What is this castle call'd that stands hard by?

MONT.   They call it Agincourt.

K. HEN.   Then call we this the field of Agincourt,
Fought on the day of Crispin Crispianus.

FLU.   Your grandfather of famous memory, an 't please your
majesty, and your great-uncle Edward the Plack Prince of
Wales, as I have read in the chronicles, fought a most prave
pattle here in France.   90

K. HEN.   They did, Fluellen.

FLU.   Your majesty says very true: if your majesties is remembered of it, the Welshmen did good service in a garden
where leeks did grow, wearing leeks in their Monmouth
caps; which, your majesty know, to this hour is an honourable badge of the service; and I do believe your majesty
takes no scorn to wear the leek upon Saint Tavy's day.

K. HEN.   I wear it for a memorable honour;
For I am Welsh, you know, good countryman.

FLU.   All the water in Wye cannot wash your majesty's Welsh   100
plood out of your pody, I can tell you that: God pless it and
preserve it, as long as it pleases his grace, and his majesty
too!

K. HEN.   Thanks, good my countryman.

FLU.   By Jeshu, I am your majesty's countryman, I care not who

70 *vulgar*] commoners.
73 *Yerk*] Jerk, kick.
83 *hard by*] nearby.
86 *Crispin Crispianus*] See IV, iii, 42.
87 *an 't*] if it.
94–95 *Monmouth caps*] Caps made at Monmouth were considered to be of the best
quality.

know it; I will confess it to all the 'orld: I need not to be
ashamed of your majesty, praised be God, so long as your
majesty is an honest man.

K. HEN.   God keep me so! Our heralds go with him:
Bring me just notice of the numbers dead   110
On both our parts. Call yonder fellow hither.

[*Points to* WILLIAMS. *Exeunt* Heralds *with* MONTJOY.

EXE.   Soldier, you must come to the king.

K. HEN.   Soldier, why wearest thou that glove in thy cap?

WILL.   An 't please your majesty, 't is the gage of one that I
should fight withal, if he be alive.

K. HEN.   An Englishman?

WILL.   An 't please your majesty, a rascal that swaggered with me
last night; who, if alive and ever dare to challenge this glove,
I have sworn to take him a box o' th' ear: or if I can see my
glove in his cap, which he swore, as he was a soldier, he   120
would wear if alive, I will strike it out soundly.

K. HEN.   What think you, Captain Fluellen? is it fit this soldier
keep his oath?

FLU.   He is a craven and a villain else, an 't please your majesty,
in my conscience.

K. HEN.   It may be his enemy is a gentleman of great sort, quite
from the answer of his degree.

FLU.   Though he be as good a gentleman as the devil is, as
Lucifer and Belzebub himself, it is necessary, look your
grace, that he keep his vow and his oath: if he be perjured,   130
see you now, his reputation is as arrant a villain and a
Jacksauce, as ever his black shoe trod upon God's ground
and his earth, in my conscience, la!

K. HEN.   Then keep thy vow, sirrah, when thou meetest the fellow.

WILL.   So I will, my liege, as I live.

K. HEN.   Who servest thou under?

---

113 *Soldier . . . cap*] See IV, i, 186–199, for the quarrel between Williams and King
Henry, who was disguised as a commoner. Williams still does not realize that he
made the challenge to his king.

126–127 *a gentleman . . . degree*] a gentleman of such high rank as not to allow him to
answer a challenge from one of the soldiers of low degree.

132 *a Jacksauce*] a saucy Jack; a common term of contempt.

WILL.   Under Captain Gower, my liege.

FLU.   Gower is a good captain, and is good knowledge and liter-
atured in the wars.   140

K. HEN.   Call him hither to me, soldier.

WILL.   I will, my liege.   [*Exit.*

K. HEN.   Here, Fluellen; wear thou this favour for me and stick
it in thy cap: when Alençon and myself were down together,
I plucked this glove from his helm: if any man challenge
this, he is a friend to Alençon, and an enemy to our person;
if thou encounter any such, apprehend him, an thou dost
me love.

FLU.   Your grace doo's me as great honours as can be desired in
the hearts of his subjects: I would fain see the man, that has   150
but two legs, that shall find himself aggriefed at this glove;
that is all; but I would fain see it once, an 't please God of
his grace that I might see.

K. HEN.   Knowest thou Gower?

FLU.   He is my dear friend, an 't please you.

K. HEN.   Pray thee, go seek him, and bring him to my tent.

FLU.   I will fetch him.   [*Exit.*

K. HEN.   My Lord of Warwick, and my brother Gloucester,
Follow Fluellen closely at the heels:
The glove which I have given him for a favour   160
May haply purchase him a box o' th' ear;
It is the soldier's; I by bargain should
Wear it myself. Follow, good cousin Warwick:
If that the soldier strike him, as I judge
By his blunt bearing he will keep his word,
Some sudden mischief may arise of it;
For I do know Fluellen valiant,
And, touch'd with choler, hot as gunpowder,
And quickly will return an injury:
Follow, and see there be no harm between them.   170
Go you with me, uncle of Exeter.   [*Exeunt.*

---

144 *Alençon*] This alludes to a legendary encounter between the king and the Duke of
Alençon in the course of the battle of Agincourt. The king was almost felled by the
duke, but he succeeded in striking the Frenchman down, and in killing two of the
duke's companions. The duke himself was killed by the king's guard.

145 *helm*] helmet.

150 *fain*] willingly.

168 *touch'd with choler*] hot-tempered.

SCENE VIII. *Before King Henry's Pavilion.*

Enter GOWER *and* WILLIAMS

WILL.   I warrant it is to knight you, captain.

Enter FLUELLEN

FLU.   God's will and his pleasure, captain, I beseech you now,
    come apace to the king: there is more good toward you per-
    adventure than is in your knowledge to dream of.

WILL.   Sir, know you this glove?

FLU.   Know the glove! I know the glove is a glove.

WILL.   I know this; and thus I challenge it.   [*Strikes him.*

FLU.   'Sblood! an arrant traitor as any is in the universal world,
    or in France, or in England!

GOW.   How now, sir! you villain!   10

WILL.   Do you think I'll be forsworn?

FLU.   Stand away, Captain Gower; I will give treason his pay-
    ment into plows, I warrant you.

WILL.   I am no traitor.

FLU.   That's a lie in thy throat. I charge you in his majesty's
    name, apprehend him: he's a friend of the Duke Alençon's.

Enter WARWICK *and* GLOUCESTER

WAR.   How now, how now! what's the matter?

FLU.   My Lord of Warwick, here is—praised be God for it!—a
    most contagious treason come to light, look you, as you shall
    desire in a summer's day. Here is his majesty.   20

Enter KING HENRY *and* EXETER

K. HEN.   How now! what's the matter?

FLU.   My liege, here is a villain and a traitor, that, look your
    grace, has struck the glove which your majesty is take out of
    the helmet of Alençon.

WILL.   My liege, this was my glove; here is the fellow of it; and
    he that I gave it to in change promised to wear it in his cap:
    I promised to strike him, if he did: I met this man with my
    glove in his cap, and I have been as good as my word.

FLU.   Your majesty hear now, saving your majesty's manhood,

---

3 *apace*] at once.
13 *into plows*] in blows, punches.
19 *contagious*] blunder for "outrageous."
26 *in change*] in exchange.

what an arrant, rascally, beggarly, lousy knave it is: I hope　30
your majesty is pear me testimony and witness, and will
avouchment, that this is the glove of Alençon, that your
majesty is give me; in your conscience, now.

K. HEN.　Give me thy glove, soldier: look, here is the fellow of
it.
'T was I, indeed, thou promised'st to strike;
And thou hast given me most bitter terms.

FLU.　And please your majesty, let his neck answer for it, if there
is any martial law in the world.

K. HEN.　How canst thou make me satisfaction?　40

WILL.　All offences, my lord, come from the heart: never came
any from mine that might offend your majesty.

K. HEN.　It was ourself thou didst abuse.

WILL.　Your majesty came not like yourself: you appeared to me
but as a common man; witness the night, your garments,
your lowliness; and what your highness suffered under that
shape, I beseech you to take it for your own fault and not
mine: for had you been as I took you for, I made no offence;
therefore, I beseech your highness, pardon me.

K. HEN.　Here, uncle Exeter, fill this glove with crowns,　50
And give it to this fellow. Keep it, fellow;
And wear it for an honour in thy cap
Till I do challenge it. Give him the crowns:
And, captain, you must needs be friends with him.

FLU.　By this day and this light, the fellow has mettle enough in
his belly. Hold, there is twelve pence for you; and I pray you
to serve God, and keep you out of prawls, and prabbles, and
quarrels, and dissensions, and, I warrant you, it is the better
for you.

WILL.　I will none of your money.　60

FLU.　It is with a good will; I can tell you, it will serve you to
mend your shoes: come, wherefore should you be so pash-
ful? your shoes is not so good: 't is a good silling, I warrant
you, or I will change it.

Enter an English Herald

K. HEN.　Now, herald, are the dead number'd?

HER.　Here is the number of the slaughter'd French.

K. HEN.　What prisoners of good sort are taken, uncle?

31 *is pear*] will bear.
32 *avouchment*] avouch, affirm.
46 *lowliness*] humble appearance.

EXE.   Charles Duke of Orleans, nephew to the king;
      John Duke of Bourbon, and Lord Bouciqualt:
      Of other lords and barons, knights and squires,   70
      Full fifteen hundred, besides common men.
K. HEN.   This note doth tell me of ten thousand French
      That in the field lie slain: of princes, in this number,
      And nobles bearing banners, there lie dead
      One hundred twenty six: added to these,
      Of knights, esquires, and gallant gentlemen,
      Eight thousand and four hundred; of the which,
      Five hundred were but yesterday dubb'd knights:
      So that, in these ten thousand they have lost,
      There are but sixteen hundred mercenaries;   80
      The rest are princes, barons, lords, knights, squires,
      And gentlemen of blood and quality.
      The names of those their nobles that lie dead:
      Charles Delabreth, high constable of France;
      Jaques of Chatillon, admiral of France;
      The master of the cross-bows, Lord Rambures;
      Great Master of France, the brave Sir Guichard Dolphin,
      John Duke of Alençon, Anthony Duke of Brabant,
      The brother to the Duke of Burgundy,
      And Edward Duke of Bar: of lusty earls,   90
      Grandpré and Roussi, Fauconberg and Foix,
      Beaumont and Marle, Vaudemont and Lestrale.
      Here was a royal fellowship of death!
      Where is the number of our English dead?
                   [Herald *shews him another paper.*
      Edward the Duke of York, the Earl of Suffolk,
      Sir Richard Ketly, Davy Gam, esquire:
      None else of name; and of all other men
      But five and twenty. O God, thy arm was here;
      And not to us, but to thy arm alone,
      Ascribe we all! When, without stratagem,   100
      But in plain shock and even play of battle,
      Was ever known so great and little loss
      On one part and on th' other? Take it, God,
      For it is none but thine!

---

96 *Davy Gam*] David Gam or Ab Llewelyn, a Welsh warrior who, it is recorded, was
     ordered to discover the strength of the enemy and reported to the king "There are
     enough to be killed, enough to take prisoners, and enough to run away."
101 *shock*] confrontation.
     even] equal.

EXE.   'T is wonderful!

K. HEN.   Come, go we in procession to the village:
     And be it death proclaimed through our host
     To boast of this or take that praise from God
     Which is his only.

FLU.   Is it not lawful, an 't please your majesty, to tell how many   110
     is killed?

K. HEN.   Yes, captain; but with this acknowledgement,
     That God fought for us.

FLU.   Yes, my conscience, he did us great good.

K. HEN.   Do we all holy rites;
     Let there be sung "Non nobis" and "Te Deum";
     The dead with charity enclosed in clay:
     And then to Calais; and to England then;
     Where ne'er from France arrived more happy men.

                                      [*Exeunt.*

---

116 *Non nobis*] reference to Psalm 115, which begins, "Not unto us, O Lord, not unto
     us, but unto thy name give glory."
   Te Deum] a hymn of thanksgiving, which begins "We praise thee O God."

ACT V.—PROLOGUE

Enter Chorus

CHORUS. Vouchsafe to those that have not read the story,
  That I may prompt them: and of such as have,
  I humbly pray them to admit the excuse
  Of time, of numbers and due course of things,
  Which cannot in their huge and proper life
  Be here presented. Now we bear the king
  Toward Calais: grant him there; there seen,
  Heave him away upon your winged thoughts
  Athwart the sea. Behold, the English beach
  Pales in the flood with men, with wives and boys,   10
  Whose shouts and claps out-voice the deep-mouth'd sea,
  Which like a mighty whiffler 'fore the king
  Seems to prepare his way: so let him land,
  And solemnly see him set on to London.
  So swift a pace hath thought, that even now
  You may imagine him upon Blackheath;
  Where that his lords desire him to have borne
  His bruised helmet and his bended sword
  Before him through the city: he forbids it,
  Being free from vainness and self-glorious pride;   20
  Giving full trophy, signal and ostent
  Quite from himself to God. But now behold,

3–6 *admit the excuse . . . presented*] excuse, in the interests of time, that we cannot tell
  the entire story.
10 *Pales in the flood*] surrounds the sea.
12 *whiffler*] an officer who marches at the head of a procession to clear the way.
14 *solemnly . . . set on*] in solemn state . . . set forth.
16 *Blackheath*] area just outside of London.
21–22 *Giving full trophy . . . to God*] Transferring all credit for the trophies, signs, and
  outward show of the victory from himself to God.

In the quick forge and working-house of thought,
How London doth pour out her citizens!
The mayor and all his brethren in best sort,
Like to the senators of the antique Rome,
With the plebeians swarming at their heels,
Go forth and fetch their conquering Cæsar in:
As, by a lower but loving likelihood,
Were now the general of our gracious empress,   30
As in good time he may, from Ireland coming,
Bringing rebellion broached on his sword,
How many would the peaceful city quit,
To welcome him! much more, and much more cause,
Did they this Harry. Now in London place him;
As yet the lamentation of the French
Invites the King of England's stay at home;
The emperor's coming in behalf of France,
To order peace between them; and omit
All the occurrences, whatever chanced,   40
Till Harry's back return again to France:
There must we bring him; and myself have play'd
The interim, by remembering you 't is past.
Then brook abridgement, and your eyes advance,
After your thoughts, straight back again to France.   [*Exit.*

25 *in best sort*] in best array.
29 *by a lower . . . likelihood*] to take a similar event, of inferior importance, but exciting no less affectionate emotion.
30–32 *Were now . . . his sword*] This is a reference to Robert Devereux, second earl of Essex, Queen Elizabeth's favorite, who was at the time of the production of this play lord deputy of Ireland and was engaged in repressing a native rebellion. He had passed through London on 27 March 1599, on his way to Ireland, and had been accorded a great popular ovation. Shakespeare's anticipation of his triumphant return was not realized. His government of Ireland proved a failure, and he came home in September in disgrace.
32 *broached*] spitted, transfixed.
38–39 *The emperor's coming . . . between them*] The Holy Roman Emperor came to England in May 1416 to mediate between England and France. The emperor was unsuccessful, the war between the French and English continued, and King Henry traveled once again back to France.

SCENE I. *France—The English Camp.*

Enter FLUELLEN *and* GOWER

GOW.   Nay, that's right; but why wear you your leek to-day?
Saint Davy's day is past.

FLU.   There is occasions and causes why and wherefore in all
things: I will tell you, asse my friend, Captain Gower: the
rascally, scauld, beggarly, lousy, pragging knave, Pistol,
which you and yourself and all the world know to be no petter than a fellow, look you now, of no merits, he is come to
me and prings me pread and salt yesterday, look you, and bid
me eat my leek: it was in a place where I could not breed no
contention with him; but I will be so bold as to wear it in my   10
cap till I see him once again, and then I will tell him a little
piece of my desires.

Enter PISTOL

GOW.   Why, here he comes, swelling like a turkey-cock.

FLU.   'T is no matter for his swellings nor his turkey-cocks. God
pless you, Aunchient Pistol! you scurvy, lousy knave, God
pless you.

PIST.   Ha! art thou bedlam? dost thou thirst, base Trojan,
To have me fold up Parca's fatal web?
Hence! I am qualmish at the smell of leek.

FLU.   I peseech you heartily, scurvy, lousy knave, at my desires,   20
and my requests, and my petitions, to eat, look you, this leek:
because, look you, you do not love it, nor your affections and
your appetites and your digestions doo's not agree with it, I
would desire you to eat it.

PIST.   Not for Cadwallader and all his goats.

FLU.   There is one goat for you. [*Strikes him.*] Will you be so
good, scauld knave, as eat it?

---

4 *asse*] mispronounciation of "as."
5 *scauld*] scabby; a low word of contempt, implying filth.
6–7 *petter*] mispronunciation of "better."
17 *art thou bedlam*] art thou a madman.
    Trojan] i.e., rascal.
18 *fold up Parca's fatal web*] end thy life.
19 *qualmish*] squeamish, nauseated.
25 *Cadwallader*] a former king of Wales.
    all his goats] Pistol insults Fluellen with the English taunt that the Welsh are no
    more than common goatherders.

PIST. Base Trojan, thou shalt die.

FLU. You say very true, scauld knave, when God's will is: I will
desire you to live in the mean time, and eat your victuals: 30
come, there is sauce for it. [*Strikes him.*] You called me yesterday mountain-squire; but I will make you to-day a squire
of low degree. I pray you, fall to: if you can mock a leek, you
can eat a leek.

GOW. Enough, captain: you have astonished him.

FLU. I say, I will make him eat some part of my leek, or I will
peat his pate four days. Bite, I pray you; it is good for your
green wound and your ploody coxcomb.

PIST. Must I bite?

FLU. Yes, certainly, and out of doubt and out of question too,   40
and ambiguities.

PIST. By this leek, I will most horribly revenge: I eat and eat, I
swear—

FLU. Eat, I pray you: will you have some more sauce to your
leek? there is not enough leek to swear by.

PIST. Quiet thy cudgel; thou dost see I eat.

FLU. Much good do you, scauld knave, heartily. Nay, pray you,
throw none away; the skin is good for your broken coxcomb.
When you take occasions to see leeks hereafter, I pray you,
mock at 'em; that is all.   50

PIST. Good.

FLU. Ay, leeks is good: hold you, there is a groat to heal your
pate.

PIST. Me a groat!

FLU. Yes, verily and in truth, you shall take it; or I have another
leek in my pocket, which you shall eat.

PIST. I take thy groat in earnest of revenge.

FLU. If I owe you any thing, I will pay you in cudgels: you shall
be a woodmonger, and buy nothing of me but cudgels. God
b' wi' you, and keep you, and heal your pate.   [*Exit.*   60

PIST. All hell shall stir for this.

GOW. Go, go; you are a counterfeit cowardly knave. Will you
mock at an ancient tradition, begun upon an honourable
respect, and worn as a memorable trophy of predeceased

---

35 *astonished him*] put him into a panic.
37 *peat his pate*] beat his head.
38 *coxcomb*] fool's head.
46 *Quiet thy cudgel*] Put down your weapon, stop with your threats.
52 *groat*] coin of little value.
59 *a woodmonger*] a dealer in wood.

valour, and dare not avouch in your deeds any of your
words? I have seen you gleeking and galling at this gentleman twice or thrice. You thought, because he could not
speak English in the native garb, he could not therefore handle an English cudgel: you find it otherwise; and henceforth
let a Welsh correction teach you a good English condition.   70
Fare ye well.

[*Exit.*

PIST.   Doth Fortune play the huswife with me now?
        News have I, that my Doll is dead i' the spital
        Of malady of France;
        And there my rendezvous is quite cut off.
        Old I do wax; and from my weary limbs
        Honour is cudgelled. Well, bawd I'll turn,
        And something lean to cutpurse of quick hand.
        To England will I steal, and there I'll steal:
        And patches will I get unto these cudgell'd scars,   80
        And swear I got them in the Gallia wars.   [*Exit.*

SCENE II. *France—A Royal Palace.*

Enter, at one door, KING HENRY, EXETER, BEDFORD,
    GLOUCESTER, WARWICK, WESTMORELAND, *and other* Lords;
    at another, the FRENCH KING, QUEEN ISABEL, *the* PRINCESS
    KATHARINE, ALICE *and other* Ladies; *the* DUKE OF
    BURGUNDY, *and his train*

K. HEN.   Peace to this meeting, wherefore we are met!
        Unto our brother France, and to our sister,
        Health and fair time of day; joy and good wishes
        To our most fair and princely cousin Katharine;
        And, as a branch and member of this royalty,

66 *gleeking and galling*] gibing or sneering and mocking.
70 *condition*] behavior, manners.
72 *huswife*] hussy, jilt.
73–74 News . . . *of France*] Pistol has learned that his wife died in the hospital of a vene-
    real disease. "Doll" is Shakespeare's error for "Nell," Mrs. Quickly's first name. (See
    above, II, i, 15.)
75 *rendezvous*] refuge.
76 *wax*] become.
78 *something lean to cutpurse*] become a pickpocket.
81 *Gallia*] French.

1 *Peace . . . met*] Peace, for making which we have met, be to this meeting.

      By whom this great assembly is contrived,
      We do salute you, Duke of Burgundy;
      And, princes French, and peers, health to you all!

FR. KING.   Right joyous are we to behold your face,
      Most worthy brother England; fairly met: 10
      So are you, princes English, every one.

Q. ISA.   So happy be the issue, brother England,
      Of this good day and of this gracious meeting,
      As we are now glad to behold your eyes;
      Your eyes, which hitherto have borne in them
      Against the French, that met them in their bent,
      The fatal balls of murdering basilisks:
      The venom of such looks, we fairly hope,
      Have lost their quality, and that this day
      Shall change all griefs and quarrels into love.   20

K. HEN.   To cry amen to that, thus we appear.

Q. ISA.   You English princes all, I do salute you.

BUR.   My duty to you both, on equal love,
      Great Kings of France and England! That I have labour'd,
      With all my wits, my pains and strong endeavours,
      To bring your most imperial majesties
      Unto this bar and royal interview,
      Your mightiness on both parts best can witness.
      Since then my office hath so far prevail'd
      That, face to face and royal eye to eye,   30
      You have congreeted, let it not disgrace me,
      If I demand, before this royal view,
      What rub or what impediment there is,
      Why that the naked, poor and mangled Peace,
      Dear nurse of arts, plenties and joyful births,
      Should not in this best garden of the world,
      Our fertile France, put up her lovely visage?
      Alas, she hath from France too long been chased,
      And all her husbandry doth lie on heaps,
      Corrupting in its own fertility.   40
      Her vine, the merry cheerer of the heart,

---

16 *in their bent*] in their sight.
17 *basilisks*] meaning both large cannons and the fabulous serpents that killed men by
    their gaze.
27 *bar*] tribunal.
31 *congreeted*] greeted each other, come together.
33 *rub*] obstacle.
39 *husbandry*] farmlands.

Unpruned dies; her hedges even-pleach'd,
Like prisoners wildly overgrown with hair,
Put forth disorder'd twigs; her fallow leas
The darnel, hemlock and rank fumitory
Doth root upon, while that the coulter rusts
That should deracinate such savagery;
The even mead, that erst brought sweetly forth
The freckled cowslip, burnet and green clover,
Wanting the scythe, all uncorrected, rank,   50
Conceives by idleness, and nothing teems
But hateful docks, rough thistles, kecksies, burs,
Losing both beauty and utility.
And as our vineyards, fallows, meads and hedges,
Defective in their natures, grow to wildness,
Even so our houses and ourselves and children
Have lost, or do not learn for want of time,
The sciences that should become our country;
But grow like savages,—as soldiers will
That nothing do but meditate on blood,—   60
To swearing and stern looks, diffused attire
And every thing that seems unnatural.
Which to reduce into our former favour
You are assembled: and my speech entreats
That I may know the let, why gentle Peace
Should not expel these inconveniences
And bless us with her former qualities.

K. HEN.   If, Duke of Burgundy, you would the peace,
Whose want gives growth to the imperfections
Which you have cited, you must buy that peace   70
With full accord to all our just demands;

42 *even-pleach'd*] matted together, thickly interwoven.
44 *fallow leas*] uncultivated fields.
45 *darnel . . . fumitory*] various types of weeds.
46 *coulter*] the blade of the ploughshare.
47 *deracinate*] root out.
49 *burnet*] a sweet-smelling salad plant.
51 *teems*] grows.
52 *docks*] coarse weeds.
    kecksies] hemlock stalks.
55 *Defective in their natures*] Failing in their proper virtues.
61 *diffused attire*] dishevelled dress.
63 *reduce into . . . favour*] return to our former good appearance.
65 *let*] obstacle.
68 *would*] wish.

Whose tenours and particular effects
You have enscheduled briefly in your hands.
BUR. The king hath heard them; to the which as yet
  There is no answer made.
K. HEN.   Well then the peace,
  Which you before so urged, lies in his answer.
FR. KING. I have but with a cursorary eye
  O'erglanced the articles: pleaseth your grace
  To appoint some of your council presently   80
  To sit with us once more, with better heed
  To re-survey them, we will suddenly
  Pass our accept and peremptory answer.
K. HEN. Brother, we shall. Go, uncle Exeter,
  And brother Clarence, and you, brother Gloucester,
  Warwick and Huntingdon, go with the king;
  And take with you free power to ratify,
  Augment, or alter, as your wisdoms best
  Shall see advantageable for our dignity,
  Any thing in or out of our demands;   90
  And we'll consign thereto. Will you, fair sister,
  Go with the princes, or stay here with us?
Q. ISA. Our gracious brother, I will go with them:
  Haply a woman's voice may do some good,
  When articles too nicely urged be stood on.
K. HEN. Yet leave our cousin Katharine here with us:
  She is our capital demand, comprised
  Within the fore-rank of our articles.
Q. ISA. She hath good leave.

   [*Exeunt all except* HENRY, KATHARINE, *and* ALICE.

K. HEN.   Fair Katharine, and most fair, 100
  Will you vouchsafe to teach a soldier terms
  Such as will enter at a lady's ear
  And plead his love-suit to her gentle heart?

---

72 *tenours and particular effects*] essence and details.
73 *enscheduled*] presented in writing.
78 *cursorary*] cursory, hasty.
82–83 *we will suddenly . . . answer*] we will immediately determine our definite and final
  answer.
91 *consign*] agree.
94 *Haply*] Perhaps.
95 *When . . . stood on*] When trivial matters are senselessly insisted on.
97 *capital*] most important.
98 *fore-rank of our articles*] first part of our listed demands.

KATH.   Your majesty shall mock at me; I cannot speak your
    England.

K. HEN.   O fair Katharine, if you will love me soundly with your
    French heart, I will be glad to hear you confess it brokenly
    with your English tongue. Do you like me, Kate?

KATH.   Pardonnez-moi, I cannot tell vat is "like me."

K. HEN.   An angel is like you, Kate, and you are like an angel.   110

KATH.   Que dit-il? que je suis semblable à les anges?

ALICE.   Oui, vraiment, sauf votre grace, ainsi dit-il.

K. HEN.   I said so, dear Katharine; and I must not blush to affirm
    it.

KATH.   O bon Dieu! les langues des hommes sont pleines de
    tromperies.

K. HEN.   What says she, fair one? that the tongues of men are
    full of deceits?

ALICE.   Oui, dat de tongues of de mans is be full of deceits: dat
    is de princess.   120

K. HEN.   The princess is the better Englishwoman. I' faith, Kate,
    my wooing is fit for thy understanding: I am glad thou canst
    speak no better English; for, if thou couldst, thou wouldst
    find me such a plain king that thou wouldst think I had sold
    my farm to buy my crown. I know no ways to mince it in
    love, but directly to say "I love you:" then if you urge me far-
    ther than to say "Do you in faith?" I wear out my suit. Give
    me your answer; i' faith, do: and so clap hands and a bargain:
    how say you, lady?

KATH.   Sauf votre honneur, me understand vell.   130

K. HEN.   Marry, if you would put me to verses or to dance for
    your sake, Kate, why you undid me: for the one, I have nei-
    ther words nor measure, and for the other, I have no strength
    in measure, yet a reasonable measure in strength. If I could
    win a lady at leap-frog, or by vaulting into my saddle with my

111 *Que . . . anges?*] What does he say? that I'm like the angels?

112 *Oui, . . . dit-il.*] Yes, truly, save your grace, that's what he says.

115–116 *O . . . tromperies.*] O good God! Men's tongues are full of lies!

119–120 *dat is de princess*] The meaning may be "that is the princess's opinion." The
    sentence may possibly be interrupted by the king.

121 *the better Englishwoman*] i.e., she has a real Englishwoman's modesty and suspi-
    cion of flattery.

124 *plain*] unaffected, straightforward.

127 *I wear out my suit*] I have nothing more to add.

128 *clap*] clasp.

132 *you undid me*] you would defeat me.

133–134 *measure . . . measure . . . measure*] meter . . . dancing . . . amount.

armour on my back, under the correction of bragging be it spoken, I should quickly leap into a wife. Or if I might buffet for my love, or bound my horse for her favours, I could lay on like a butcher and sit like a jack-an-apes, never off. But, before God, Kate, I cannot look greenly nor gasp out 140 my eloquence, nor I have no cunning in protestation; only downright oaths, which I never use till urged, nor never break for urging. If thou canst love a fellow of this temper, Kate, whose face is not worth sun-burning, that never looks in his glass for love of any thing he sees there, let thine eye be thy cook. I speak to thee plain soldier: if thou canst love me for this, take me; if not, to say to thee that I shall die, is true; but for thy love, by the Lord, no; yet I love thee too. And while thou livest, dear Kate, take a fellow of plain and uncoined constancy; for he perforce must do thee right, be- 150 cause he hath not the gift to woo in other places: for these fellows of infinite tongue, that can rhyme themselves into ladies' favours, they do always reason themselves out again. What! a speaker is but a prater; a rhyme is but a ballad. A good leg will fall; a straight back will stoop; a black beard will turn white; a curled pate will grow bald; a fair face will wither; a full eye will wax hollow: but a good heart, Kate, is the sun and the moon; or, rather, the sun, and not the moon; for it shines bright and never changes, but keeps his course truly. If thou would have such a one, take me; and take me, 160 take a soldier; take a soldier, take a king. And what sayest thou then to my love? speak, my fair, and fairly, I pray thee.

KATH.   Is it possible dat I sould love de enemy of France?

K. HEN.   No; it is not possible you should love the enemy of France, Kate: but, in loving me, you should love the friend of France; for I love France so well that I will not part with a village of it; I will have it all mine: and, Kate, when France is mine and I am yours, then yours is France and you are mine.

---

137 *buffet*] fight, box.

139 *sit like a jack-an-apes*] sit tight like a monkey.

140 *look greenly*] look like a nervous young lover.

144 *not worth sun-burning*] i.e., so ugly that even the sun couldn't make it worse.

145–146 *let thine eye . . . cook*] let thy gaze fashion me to thy fancy.

149–150 *of plain and uncoined constancy*] as of plain sterling metal, which has not yet been stamped or manipulated for circulation as coinage.

150 *perforce must*] is compelled to.

155 *fall*] fall away, shrink.

KATH.   I cannot tell vat is dat.

K. HEN.   No, Kate? I will tell thee in French; which I am sure
will hang upon my tongue like a new-married wife about her
husband's neck, hardly to be shook off. Je quand sur le possession de France, et quand vous avez le possession de
moi,—let me see, what then? Saint Denis be my speed!—
donc votre est France et vous êtes mienne. It is as easy for
me, Kate, to conquer the kingdom as to speak so much more
French: I shall never move thee in French, unless it be to
laugh at me.

KATH.   Sauf votre honneur, le François que vous parlez, il est
meilleur que l'Anglois lequel je parle.

K. HEN.   No, faith, is 't not, Kate: but thy speaking of my tongue,
and I thine, most truly-falsely, must needs be granted to be
much at one. But, Kate, dost thou understand thus much
English, canst thou love me?

KATH.   I cannot tell.

K. HEN.   Can any of your neighbours tell, Kate? I'll ask them.
Come, I know thou lovest me: and at night, when you come
into your closet, you'll question this gentlewoman about me;
and I know, Kate, you will to her dispraise those parts in me
that you love with your heart: but, good Kate, mock me mer-
cifully; the rather, gentle princess, because I love thee cru-
elly. If ever thou beest mine, Kate, as I have a saving faith
within me tells me thou shalt, I get thee with scambling, and
thou must therefore needs prove a good soldier-breeder:
shall not thou and I, between Saint Denis and Saint George,
compound a boy, half French, half English, that shall go to
Constantinople and take the Turk by the beard? shall we
not? what sayest thou, my fair flower-de-luce?

KATH.   I do not know dat.

170

180

190

200

173–176 Je quand . . . mienne.] When I have possession of France, and you have possession of me . . . then France is yours and you are mine.

175 Saint Denis] patron saint of France.

180–181 Sauf . . . parle.] Save your honor, the French that you speak is better than the
English that I speak.

183 truly-falsely] expressed truthfully but incorrectly.

184 much at one] much alike.

189 closet] private chamber.

192–193 cruelly] intensely.

194 scambling] struggling, fighting.

199 flower-de-luce] lily, fleur-de-lys, the emblem of the French monarchy.

K. HEN.   No; 't is hereafter to know, but now to promise: do but
now promise, Kate, you will endeavour for your French part
of such a boy; and for my English moiety take the word of a
king and a bachelor. How answer you, la plus belle
Katharine du monde, mon très cher et devin déesse?

KATH.   Your majestee ave fausse French enough to deceive de
most sage demoiselle dat is en France.

K. HEN.   Now, fie upon my false French! By mine honour, in
true English, I love thee, Kate: by which honour I dare not
swear thou lovest me; yet my blood begins to flatter me that   210
thou dost, notwithstanding the poor and untempering effect
of my visage. Now, beshrew my father's ambition! he was
thinking of civil wars when he got me: therefore was I created with a stubborn outside, with an aspect of iron, that,
when I come to woo ladies, I fright them. But, in faith, Kate,
the elder I wax, the better I shall appear: my comfort is, that
old age, that ill layer up of beauty, can do no more spoil
upon my face: thou hast me, if thou hast me, at the worst;
and thou shalt wear me, if thou wear me, better and better:
and therefore tell me, most fair Katharine, will you have me?   220
Put off your maiden blushes; avouch the thoughts of your
heart with the looks of an empress; take me by the hand, and
say "Harry of England, I am thine": which word thou shalt
no sooner bless mine ear withal, but I will tell thee aloud
"England is thine, Ireland is thine, France is thine, and
Henry Plantagenet is thine"; who, though I speak it before
his face, if he be not fellow with the best king, thou shalt find
the best king of good fellows. Come, your answer in broken
music; for thy voice is music and thy English broken; therefore, queen of all, Katharine, break thy mind to me in bro-   230
ken English, wilt thou have me?

KATH.   Dat is as it sall please de roi mon père.

---

203 *moiety*] half.
204–205 *la plus . . . déesse?*] . . . the most beautiful Katharine in the world, my very dear
     and divine goddess?
206 *fausse*] false, i.e., both "incorrect" and "deceptive."
211 *untempering effect*] unsoftening, unconciliatory quality.
212 *beshrew*] curse.
216 *wax*] grow, age.
221 *avouch*] acknowledge.
232 *Dat . . . père*] i.e., That's up to my father the king.

K. HEN.   Nay, it will please him well, Kate; it shall please him,
   Kate.
KATH.   Den it sall also content me.
K. HEN.   Upon that I kiss your hand, and I call you my queen.
KATH.   Laissez, mon seigneur, laissez, laissez: ma foi, je ne veux
   point que vous abaissiez votre grandeur en baisant la main
   d'une de votre seigneurie indigne serviteur; excusez-moi, je
   vous supplie, mon très-puissant seigneur.   240
K. HEN.   Then I will kiss your lips, Kate.
KATH.   Les dames et demoiselles pour être baisées devant leur
   noces, il n'est pas la coutume de France.
K. HEN.   Madam, my interpreter, what says she?
ALICE.   Dat it is not be de fashion pour les ladies of France,—I
   cannot tell vat is baiser en Anglish.
K. HEN.   To kiss.
ALICE.   Your majesty entendre bettre que moi.
K. HEN.   It is not a fashion for the maids in France to kiss before
   they are married, would she say?   250
ALICE.   Oui, vraiment.
K. HEN.   O Kate, nice customs courtesy to great kings. Dear
   Kate, you and I cannot be confined within the weak list of a
   country's fashion: we are the makers of manners, Kate; and
   the liberty that follows our places stops the mouth of all find-
   faults; as I will do yours, for upholding the nice fashion of
   your country in denying me a kiss: therefore, patiently and
   yielding. [Kissing her.] You have witchcraft in your lips,
   Kate: there is more eloquence in a sugar touch of them than
   in the tongues of the French council; and they should   260
   sooner persuade Harry of England than a general petition of
   monarchs. Here comes your father.

Re-enter the FRENCH KING and his QUEEN, BURGUNDY, and
   other Lords

BUR.   God save your majesty! my royal cousin, teach you our
   princess English?

237–240 Laissez, . . . seigneur.] Stop, my lord, stop, stop: on my faith, I don't want you
   to lessen your greatness by kissing the hand of one of your unworthy servants; excuse me, I beg you, my most powerful lord.
242–243 Les . . . France.] It isn't the custom in France for ladies or girls to be kissed before they get married.
248 entendre . . . moi] understands better than I.
252 nice . . . courtesy] prudish customs curtsy.
253 weak list] feeble bounds.
255 places] (high) ranks.

K. HEN.   I would have her learn, my fair cousin, how perfectly I
   love her; and that is good English.

BUR.   Is she not apt?

K. HEN.   Our tongue is rough, coz, and my condition is not
   smooth; so that, having neither the voice nor the heart of
   flattery about me, I cannot so conjure up the spirit of love in   270
   her, that he will appear in his true likeness.

BUR.   Pardon the frankness of my mirth, if I answer you for that.
   If you would conjure in her, you must make a circle; if conjure up love in her in his true likeness, he must appear
   naked and blind. Can you blame her then, being a maid yet
   rosed over with the virgin crimson of modesty, if she deny
   the appearance of a naked blind boy in her naked seeing
   self? It were, my lord, a hard condition for a maid to consign
   to.

K. HEN.   Yet they do wink and yield, as love is blind and en-   280
   forces.

BUR.   They are then excused, my lord, when they see not what
   they do.

K. HEN.   Then, good my lord, teach your cousin to consent
   winking.

BUR.   I will wink on her to consent, my lord, if you will teach
   her to know my meaning: for maids, well summered and
   warm kept, are like flies at Bartholomew-tide, blind, though
   they have their eyes; and then they will endure handling,
   which before would not abide looking on.   290

K. HEN.   This moral ties me over to time and a hot summer; and
   so I shall catch the fly, your cousin, in the latter end, and she
   must be blind too.

BUR.   As love is, my lord, before it loves.

K. HEN.   It is so: and you may, some of you, thank love for my
   blindness, who cannot see many a fair French city for one
   fair French maid that stands in my way.

FR. KING.   Yes, my lord, you see them perspectively, the cities
   turned into a maid; for they are all girdled with maiden walls
   that war hath never entered.   300

---

268 *condition*] personality.
273 *conjure . . . make a circle*] Magicians traced a circle within which they summoned
   the spirits they conjured up to appear. Burgundy turns the reference into one of a
   series of bawdy puns.
276 *rosed over*] blushing.
286 *summered*] nurtured.
288 *Bartholomew-tide*] St. Bartholomew's Day, 24 August (when the flies are sluggish).
298 *perspectively*] as in a perspective glass, which was designed to produce optical illusions.

K. HEN.   Shall Kate be my wife?

FR. KING.   So please you.

K. HEN.   I am content; so the maiden cities you talk of may wait
on her: so the maid that stood in the way for my wish shall
show me the way to my will.

FR. KING.   We have consented to all terms of reason.

K. HEN.   Is 't so, my lords of England?

WEST.   The king hath granted every article:
His daughter first, and then in sequel all,
According to their firm proposed natures.   310

EXE.   Only he hath not yet subscribed this:
Where your majesty demands, that the King of France, hav-
ing any occasion to write for matter of grant, shall name your
highness in this form and with this addition, in French,
Notre très-cher fils Henri, Roi d'Angleterre, Héritier de
France; and thus in Latin, Præclarissimus filius noster
Henricus, Rex Angliæ, et Hæres Franciæ.

FR. KING.   Nor this I have not, brother, so denied,
But your request shall make me let it pass.

K. HEN.   I pray you then, in love and dear alliance,   320
Let that one article rank with the rest;
And thereupon give me your daughter.

FR. KING.   Take her, fair son, and from her blood raise up
Issue to me; that the contending kingdoms
Of France and England, whose very shores look pale
With envy of each other's happiness,
May cease their hatred, and this dear conjunction
Plant neighbourhood and Christian-like accord
In their sweet bosoms, that never war advance
His bleeding sword 'twixt England and fair France.   330

ALL.   Amen!

K. HEN.   Now, welcome, Kate: and bear me witness all,
That here I kiss her as my sovereign queen.

                                       [*Flourish.*

Q. ISA.   God, the best maker of all marriages,
Combine your hearts in one, your realms in one!

303–305 *I am content . . . my will*] i.e., Henry will forgo demanding in the negotiations
several French cities in exchange for Katharine.

310 *According . . . natures*] as specified in the proposals.

311 *subscribed*] agreed to.

315–316 *Notre . . . de France*] Our very dear son Henry, king of England, heir of France.

316 *Præclarissimus*] Most renowned. The actual treaty of Troyes calls Henry "præcaris-
simus," but Shakespeare has copied Holinshed's mistake.

As man and wife, being two, are one in love,
So be there 'twixt your kingdoms such a spousal,
That never may ill office, or fell jealousy,
Which troubles oft the bed of blessed marriage,
Thrust in between the paction of these kingdoms, 340
To make divorce of their incorporate league;
That English may as French, French Englishmen,
Receive each other. God speak this Amen!
ALL. Amen!
K. HEN. Prepare we for our marriage: on which day,
My Lord of Burgundy, we'll take your oath,
And all the peers', for surety of our leagues.
Then shall I swear to Kate, and you to me;
And may our oaths well kept and prosperous be!

[*Sennet. Exeunt.*

337 *spousal*] marriage.
338 *ill office*] unfriendly dealings.
    fell] cruel.
340 *paction*] compact, alliance.
349 *Sennet*] Flourish on trumpets.

EPILOGUE

Enter Chorus

CHORUS.   Thus far, with rough and all-unable pen,
    Our bending author hath pursued the story,
    In little room confining mighty men,
    Mangling by starts the full course of their glory.
    Small time, but in that small most greatly lived
    This star of England: Fortune made his sword;
    By which the world's best garden he achieved,
    And of it left his son imperial lord.
    Henry the Sixth, in infant bands crown'd King
    Of France and England, did this king succeed;   10
    Whose state so many had the managing,
    That they lost France and made his England bleed:
    Which oft our stage hath shown; and, for their sake,
    In your fair minds let this acceptance take.   *[Exit.*

2 *bending*] i.e., under the weight of his task.
4 *Mangling by starts*] Distorting by interruptions, by fragmentary treatment.
5 *Small time*] Henry V reigned for only nine years before his death at the age of thirty-
   five.
7 *the world's best garden*] France.
9 *in infant bands*] in swaddling clothes.
13 *Which oft . . . shown*] a reference to the three parts of *Henry VI* and to the dramatic
   pieces on which they were based.
14 *let this acceptance take*] let this play meet with your approval.

APPENDIX

ACT III, SCENE IV Translated into English

KATH. Alice, you've been in England, and you speak the language well.

ALICE. A little, madame.

KATH. I beg you, teach me; I've got to learn to speak. How do you say *la main* in English?

ALICE. *La main*? It's called "de hand."

KATH. De hand. And *les doigts*?

ALICE. *Les doigts*? By my faith, I forget *les doigts*. But it'll come to me. *Les doigts*? I think they're called "de fingers." Yes, de fingers.

KATH. *La main*, de hand; *les doigts*, de fingers. I think I'm a very good student; I've learned two words of English so quickly! How do you say *les ongles*?

ALICE. *Les ongles*? We call them "de nails."

KATH. De nails. Listen, and tell me if I'm speaking correctly: de hand, de fingers, and de nails.

ALICE. That's very good, madame. It's excellent English.

KATH. Tell me the English for *le bras*.

ALICE. "De arm," madame.

KATH. And *le coude*?

ALICE. "De elbow."

KATH. De elbow. Now I'm going to repeat all the words you've taught me.

ALICE. I think that will be very difficult, madame.

KATH. Excuse me, Alice. Listen: de hand, de fingers, de nails, de arma, de bilbow.

ALICE. De elbow, madame.

KATH. O my God, I forgot it! De elbow. How do you say *le col*?

ALICE. "De nick," madame.

KATH. De nick. And *le menton*?

ALICE. "De chin."

KATH. De sin. *Le col*, de nick; *le menton*, de sin.

308

ALICE. Yes. Bless you, you really pronounce the words just as well as if you'd been brought up in England!

KATH. I've got no doubt that, with God's help, I'll learn very quickly.

ALICE. Haven't you already forgotten what I've taught you?

KATH. No. I'll recite for you right now: de hand, de fingers, de mails—

ALICE. De nails, madame.

KATH. De nails, de arm, de ilbow.

ALICE. I beg your pardon, de elbow.

KATH. That's what I said. De elbow, de nick, and de sin. How do you say *le pied* and *la robe*?

ALICE. "De foot," madame; and "de coun." [In Alice's pronunciation, "foot" and "gown" sound like the French words for copulate and for the female pudenda.]

KATH. De foot and de coun! O Lord! Those sound like terrible words, depraved, coarse, and obscene, and not for the use of decent women. I wouldn't say those words in front of the gentlemen of France for all the world. O! le foot and le coun! Nonetheless, I'll recite my entire lesson one more time: de hand, de fingers, de nails, de arm, de elbow, de nick, de sin, de foot, de coun.

ALICE. Excellent, madame!

KATH. That's enough for now; let's go to dinner.

Richard III

Richard III

Richard III was probably written between 1592 and 1593, soon after Shakespeare completed the three Henry VI plays. Shakespeare's primary source for the play's historical events was the 1587 edition of Raphael Holinshed's *Chronicles of England, Scotland and Ireland,* and the basis of his information on Richard was Sir Thomas More's *The Life of Richard III* (1513). More's portrayal of a villainous, deformed Richard is hardly surprising. Henry VIII, whom More served, was the son of Henry Tudor, the Lancastrian claimant to the crown who defeated Richard at the Battle of Bosworth Field and assumed the throne as Henry VII. (Henry's accession effectively ended the long and bloody dynastic civil wars known as the Wars of the Roses [1455–85].)

Despite the character's basis in sixteenth-century propaganda, Shakespeare's fictional Richard is better known than the historical figure. Ruthless and ambitious, the hunchbacked king vies with Iago in his depravity. Richard's political machinations exceed even those of Machiavelli, whom, as he boasts in *3 Henry VI,* he will "set . . . to school" (III. ii. 193). Richard's deformed soul is matched by his deformed physiognomy—he is a "poisonous bunch-backed toad," an "elvish-mark'd, abortive rooting hog," "hell's black intelligencer." But Richard flaunts his physical appearance as readily as his malevolence. Since, as he says in his opening soliloquy, he is not "made to court an amorous looking-glass," he is "determined to prove a villain," a royal deceiver, a plotter extraordinaire. He becomes all this and more—one of Shakespeare's most memorable villains.

Candace Ward

Dramatis Personæ

KING EDWARD the Fourth.
EDWARD, Prince of Wales, afterwards King Edward V, } sons to the King.
RICHARD, Duke of York. }
GEORGE, Duke of Clarence, } brothers to the King.
RICHARD, Duke of Gloucester, afterwards King Richard III. }
A young son of Clarence.
HENRY, Earl of Richmond, afterwards King Henry VII.
CARDINAL BOURCHIER, Archbishop of Canterbury.
THOMAS ROTHERHAM, Archbishop of York.
JOHN MORTON, Bishop of Ely.
DUKE OF BUCKINGHAM.
DUKE OF NORFOLK.
EARL OF SURREY, his son.
EARL RIVERS, brother to Elizabeth.
MARQUIS OF DORSET and LORD GREY, sons to Elizabeth.
EARL OF OXFORD.
LORD HASTINGS.
LORD STANLEY, called also EARL OF DERBY.
LORD LOVEL.
SIR THOMAS VAUGHAN.
SIR RICHARD RATCLIFF.
SIR WILLIAM CATESBY.
SIR JAMES TYRREL.
SIR JAMES BLOUNT.
SIR WALTER HERBERT.
SIR ROBERT BRAKENBURY, Lieutenant of the Tower.
SIR WILLIAM BRANDON.
CHRISTOPHER URSWICK, a priest.
Another Priest.

TRESSEL and BERKELEY, gentlemen attending on the Lady Anne.
Lord Mayor of London.
Sheriff of Wiltshire.

ELIZABETH, queen to King Edward IV.
MARGARET, widow of King Henry VI.
DUCHESS OF YORK, mother to King Edward IV.
LADY ANNE, widow of Edward Prince of Wales, son to King Henry VI;
    afterwards married to Richard.
A young daughter of Clarence (MARGARET PLANTAGENET).

Ghosts of those murdered by Richard III, Lords and other Attendants; a
    Pursuivant, Scrivener, Citizens, Murderers, Messengers, Soldiers, &c.

SCENE: *England*

ACT I.

Scene I. *London. A Street.*

Enter Richard, Duke of Gloucester, *solus*

Glou.   Now is the winter of our discontent
Made glorious summer by this sun of York;[1]
And all the clouds that lour'd upon our house
In the deep bosom of the ocean buried.
Now are our brows bound with victorious wreaths;
Our bruised arms hung up for monuments;
Our stern alarums changed to merry meetings,
Our dreadful marches to delightful measures.
Grim-visaged war hath smooth'd his wrinkled front;
And now, instead of mounting barbed[2] steeds
To fright the souls of fearful adversaries,
He capers nimbly in a lady's chamber
To the lascivious pleasing of a lute.
But I, that am not shaped for sportive tricks,
Nor made to court an amorous looking-glass;
I, that am rudely stamp'd, and want love's majesty
To strut before a wanton ambling nymph;
I, that am curtail'd of this fair proportion,[3]
Cheated of feature by dissembling nature,[4]
Deform'd, unfinish'd, sent before my time
Into this breathing world, scarce half made up,
And that so lamely and unfashionable
That dogs bark at me as I halt by them;

---

1. *this sun of York*] a punning reference to the badge of the "blazing sun" adopted by
Edward IV.
2. *barbed*] caparisoned with warlike trappings.
3. *this fair proportion*] the fair shape (which "serves love's majesty," two lines above).
4. *Cheated . . . nature*] robbed of attractive figure by distorting nature.

317

Why, I, in this weak piping time of peace,[5]
Have no delight to pass away the time,
Unless to spy my shadow in the sun,
And descant on mine own deformity:
And therefore, since I cannot prove a lover,
To entertain these fair well-spoken days,[6]
I am determined to prove a villain,
And hate the idle pleasures of these days.
Plots have I laid, inductions[7] dangerous,
By drunken prophecies, libels and dreams,
To set my brother Clarence and the king
In deadly hate the one against the other:
And if King Edward be as true and just
As I am subtle, false and treacherous,
This day should Clarence closely be mew'd up,[8]
About a prophecy, which says that G
Of Edward's heirs the murderer shall be.
Dive, thoughts, down to my soul: here Clarence comes.[9]

Enter CLARENCE, *guarded, and* BRAKENBURY

Brother, good day: what means this armed guard
That waits upon your grace?
CLAR.   His majesty,
Tendering[10] my person's safety, hath appointed
This conduct[11] to convey me to the Tower.
GLOU.   Upon what cause?
CLAR.   Because my name is George.
GLOU.   Alack, my lord, that fault is none of yours;
He should, for that, commit your godfathers:
O, belike his majesty hath some intent
That you shall be new-christen'd in the Tower.
But what's the matter, Clarence? may I know?
CLAR.   Yea, Richard, when I know; for I protest
As yet I do not: but, as I can learn,
He hearkens after prophecies and dreams;

---

5. *piping time of peace*] The pipe and tabor were usual emblems of peace, as the drum
   and fife were of war.
6. *these fair . . . days*] these happy, prosperous days.
7. *inductions*] preparatory steps, groundwork.
8. *mew'd up*] confined.
9. *a prophecy . . . comes*] G is the initial of Clarence's Christian name George (under
   which he is listed in the *Dramatis Personae*). King Edward purportedly was greatly
   disturbed by a prophecy that Edward would be succeeded by someone whose name
   began with "G."
10. *Tendering*] having tender regard for.
11. *conduct*] escort.

And from the cross-row[12] plucks the letter G,
And says a wizard told him that by G
His issue disinherited should be;
And, for my name of George begins with G,
It follows in his thought that I am he.
These, as I learn, and such like toys as these
Have moved his highness to commit me now.
GLOU.   Why, this it is, when men are ruled by women:
'Tis not the king that sends you to the Tower;
My Lady Grey his wife, Clarence, 'tis she
That tempers[13] him to this extremity.
Was it not she and that good man of worship,
Anthony Woodville, her brother there,
That made him send Lord Hastings to the Tower,
From whence this present day he is deliver'd?
We are not safe, Clarence; we are not safe.
CLAR.   By heaven, I think there's no man is secure,
But the queen's kindred and night-walking heralds,
That trudge betwixt the king and Mistress Shore.
Heard ye not what an humble suppliant
Lord Hastings was to her for his delivery?
GLOU.   Humbly complaining to her deity
Got my lord chamberlain his liberty.
I'll tell you what; I think it is our way,
If we will keep in favour with the king,
To be her men and wear her livery:
The jealous o'erworn widow and herself,[14]
Since that our brother dubb'd them gentlewomen,
Are mighty gossips in this monarchy.
BRAK.   I beseech your graces both to pardon me;
His majesty hath straitly given in charge
That no man shall have private conference,
Of what degree soever, with his brother.
GLOU.   Even so; an 't please your worship, Brakenbury,
You may partake of any thing we say:
We speak no treason, man: we say the king
Is wise and virtuous, and his noble queen
Well struck in years, fair, and not jealous;

---

12. *cross-row*] alphabet; more frequently called "criss-cross-row." "Criss-cross" is a corruption of "Christ's cross," the prayer "Christ's cross be my speed" commonly standing at the head of the alphabet as printed in the elementary school books of the day.
13. *tempers*] frames or disposes.
14. *o'erworn widow and herself*] Edward IV's Queen and Jane Shore, his mistress. Though the latter was influential for a time, after Edward's death she was imprisoned for witchcraft and later died in poverty.

We say that Shore's wife hath a pretty foot,
A cherry lip, a bonny eye, a passing pleasing tongue;
And that the queen's kindred are made gentle-folks:
How say you, sir? can you deny all this?

BRAK.   With this, my lord, myself have nought to do.

GLOU.   Naught to do with Mistress Shore! I tell thee, fellow,
He that doth naught[15] with her, excepting one,
Were best he do it secretly alone.

BRAK.   What one, my lord?

GLOU.   Her husband, knave: wouldst thou betray me?

BRAK.   I beseech your grace to pardon me, and withal
Forbear your conference with the noble duke.

CLAR.   We know thy charge, Brakenbury, and will obey.

GLOU.   We are the queen's abjects,[16] and must obey.
Brother, farewell: I will unto the king;
And whatsoever you will employ me in,
Were it to call King Edward's widow sister,
I will perform it to enfranchise you.
Meantime, this deep disgrace in brotherhood
Touches me deeper than you can imagine.

CLAR.   I know it pleaseth neither of us well.

GLOU.   Well, your imprisonment shall not be long;
I will deliver you, or else lie for you:[17]
Meantime, have patience.

CLAR.   I must perforce. Farewell.

[*Exeunt* CLARENCE, BRAKENBURY, *and* Guard.]

GLOU.   Go tread the path that thou shalt ne'er return,
Simple, plain Clarence! I do love thee so,
That I will shortly send thy soul to heaven,
If heaven will take the present at our hands.
But who comes here? the new-deliver'd Hastings?

Enter LORD HASTINGS

HAST.   Good time of day unto my gracious lord!

GLOU.   As much unto my good lord chamberlain!
Well are you welcome to the open air.
How hath your lordship brook'd imprisonment?

HAST.   With patience, noble lord, as prisoners must:
But I shall live, my lord, to give them thanks
That were the cause of my imprisonment.

---

15. *Naught ... naught*] a quibble between "nought," i.e., nothing, and "naught," i.e., naughtily.
16. *abjects*] base slaves, the scum of the people.
17. *lie for you*] lie imprisoned in your stead.

GLOU.   No doubt, no doubt; and so shall Clarence too;
         For they that were your enemies are his,
         And have prevail'd as much on him[18] as you.
HAST.   More pity that the eagle should be mew'd,[19]
         While kites and buzzards prey at liberty.
GLOU.   What news abroad?
HAST.   No news so bad abroad as this at home;
         The king is sickly, weak and melancholy,
         And his physicians fear him[20] mightily.
GLOU.   Now, by Saint Paul, this news is bad indeed.
         O, he hath kept an evil diet long,
         And overmuch consumed his royal person:
         'Tis very grievous to be thought upon.
         What, is he in his bed?
HAST.   He is.
GLOU.   Go you before, and I will follow you.   [*Exit* HASTINGS.]
         He cannot live, I hope; and must not die,
         Till George be pack'd with post-horse up to heaven.
         I'll in, to urge his hatred more to Clarence,
         With lies well steel'd with weighty arguments;
         And, if I fail not in my deep intent,
         Clarence hath not another day to live:
         Which done, God take King Edward to his mercy,
         And leave the world for me to bustle in!
         For then I'll marry Warwick's youngest daughter.[21]
         What though I kill'd her husband and her father?
         The readiest way to make the wench amends
         Is to become her husband and her father:
         The which will I, not all so much for love,
         As for another secret close intent,
         By marrying her which I must reach unto.
         But yet I run before my horse to market:
         Clarence still breathes; Edward still lives and reigns:
         When they are gone, then must I count my gains.   [*Exit.*]

---

18. *on him*] against him.
19. *mew'd*] hawks were "mewed" or kept in confinement while moulting.
20. *fear him*] fear for, are anxious about, him.
21. *Warwick's youngest daughter*] Anne, younger daughter of the Earl of Warwick, had been affianced (rather than actually married) to Queen Margaret and Henry VI's son, Edward, Prince of Wales, who was slain at the battle of Tewkesbury, May 4, 1471.

SCENE II. *The Same. Another Street*

Enter the corpse of KING HENRY THE SIXTH, *Gentlemen with halberds[1] to guard it;* LADY ANNE *being the mourner*

ANNE.   Set down, set down your honourable load —
      If honour may be shrouded in a hearse —
      Whilst I awhile obsequiously lament
      The untimely fall of virtuous Lancaster.
      Poor key-cold[2] figure of a holy king!
      Pale ashes of the house of Lancaster!
      Thou bloodless remnant of that royal blood!
      Be it lawful that I invocate thy ghost,
      To hear the lamentations of poor Anne,
      Wife to thy Edward, to thy slaughtered son,
      Stabb'd by the selfsame hand that made these wounds!
      Lo, in these windows that let forth thy life
      I pour the helpless balm of my poor eyes.
      Cursed be the hand that made these fatal holes!
      Cursed be the heart that had the heart to do it!
      Cursed the blood that let this blood from hence!
      More direful hap[3] betide that hated wretch,
      That makes us wretched by the death of thee,
      Than I can wish to adders, spiders, toads,
      Or any creeping venom'd thing that lives!
      If ever he have child, abortive be it,
      Prodigious,[4] and untimely brought to light,
      Whose ugly and unnatural aspect
      May fright the hopeful mother at the view;
      And that be heir to his unhappiness!
      If ever he have wife, let her be made
      As miserable by the death of him,
      As I am made by my poor lord and thee!
      Come, now towards Chertsey[5] with your holy load,
      Taken from Paul's[6] to be interred there;
      And still, as you are weary of the weight,

---

1. *halberds*] battle-axes fitted to long poles.
2. *key-cold*] cold as a key; in common use as an intensitive of "cold."
3. *hap*] fortune.
4. *Prodigious*] like a prodigy or monster.
5. *Chertsey*] a monastery near London.
6. *Paul's*] St. Paul's Church, the principal cathedral in London.

Rest you, whiles I lament King Henry's corse.[7]

Enter GLOUCESTER

GLOU.   Stay, you that bear the corse, and set it down.
ANNE.   What black magician conjures up this fiend,
   To stop devoted charitable deeds?
GLOU.   Villains, set down the corse; or, by Saint Paul,
   I'll make a corse of him that disobeys.
GENT.   My lord, stand back, and let the coffin pass.
GLOU.   Unmanner'd dog! stand thou, when I command:
   Advance thy halberd higher than my breast,
   Or, by Saint Paul, I'll strike thee to my foot,
   And spurn upon thee, beggar, for thy boldness.
ANNE.   What, do you tremble? are you all afraid?
   Alas, I blame you not; for you are mortal,
   And mortal eyes cannot endure the devil.
   Avaunt, thou dreadful minister of hell!
   Thou hadst but power over his mortal body,
   His soul thou canst not have; therefore, be gone.
GLOU.   Sweet saint, for charity, be not so curst.
ANNE.   Foul devil, for God's sake, hence, and trouble us not;
   For thou hast made the happy earth thy hell,
   Fill'd it with cursing cries and deep exclaims.
   If thou delight to view thy heinous deeds,
   Behold this pattern of thy butcheries.
   O, gentlemen, see, see! dead Henry's wounds
   Open their congeal'd mouths and bleed afresh.
   Blush, blush, thou lump of foul deformity;
   For 'tis thy presence that exhales[8] this blood
   From cold and empty veins, where no blood dwells;
   Thy deed, inhuman and unnatural,
   Provokes this deluge most unnatural.
   O God, which this blood madest, revenge his death!
   O earth, which this blood drink'st, revenge his death!
   Either heaven with lightning strike the murderer dead,
   Or earth, gape open wide and eat him quick,[9]
   As thou dost swallow up this good king's blood,
   Which his hell-govern'd arm hath butchered!
GLOU.   Lady, you know no rules of charity,
   Which renders good for bad, blessings for curses.

---

7. *corse*] corpse.
8. *exhales*] draws forth. It was a popular notion that a murdered corpse bled in presence of
   the murderer.
9. *quick*] alive.

ANNE.   Villain, thou know'st no law of God nor man:
          No beast so fierce but knows some touch of pity.
GLOU.   But I know none, and therefore am no beast.
ANNE.   O wonderful, when devils tell the truth!
GLOU.   More wonderful, when angels are so angry.
          Vouchsafe, divine perfection of a woman,
          Of these supposed evils, to give me leave,
          By circumstance,[10] but to acquit myself.
ANNE.   Vouchsafe, defused[11] infection of a man,
          For these known evils, but to give me leave,
          By circumstance, to curse thy cursed self.
GLOU.   Fairer than tongue can name thee, let me have
          Some patient leisure to excuse myself.
ANNE.   Fouler than heart can think thee, thou canst make
          No excuse current,[12] but to hang thyself.
GLOU.   By such despair, I should accuse myself.
ANNE.   And, by despairing, shouldst thou stand excused
          For doing worthy vengeance on thyself,
          Which didst unworthy slaughter upon others.
GLOU.   Say that I slew them not?
ANNE.   Why, then they are not dead:
          But dead they are, and, devilish slave, by thee.
GLOU.   I did not kill your husband.
ANNE.   Why, then he is alive.
GLOU.   Nay, he is dead; and slain by Edward's hand.
ANNE.   In thy foul throat thou liest: Queen Margaret saw
          Thy murderous falchion[13] smoking in his blood;
          The which thou once didst bend against her breast,
          But that thy brothers beat aside the point.
GLOU.   I was provoked by her slanderous tongue,
          Which laid their guilt upon my guiltless shoulders.
ANNE.   Thou wast provoked by thy bloody mind,
          Which never dreamt on aught but butcheries:
          Didst thou not kill this king?
GLOU.   I grant ye.
ANNE.   Dost grant me, hedgehog? then, God grant me too
          Thou mayst be damned for that wicked deed!
          O, he was gentle, mild, and virtuous!
GLOU.   The fitter for the King of heaven, that hath him.
ANNE.   He is in heaven, where thou shalt never come.

---

10. *circumstance*] circumstantial detail.
11. *defused*] uncouthly spread, shapeless.
12. *current*] having currency, worth.
13. *falchion*] scimitar.

GLOU.   Let him thank me, that holp to send him thither;
    For he was fitter for that place than earth.
ANNE.   And thou unfit for any place but hell.
GLOU.   Yes, one place else, if you will hear me name it.
ANNE.   Some dungeon.
GLOU.   Your bed-chamber.
ANNE.   Ill rest betide the chamber where thou liest!
GLOU.   So will it, madam, till I lie with you.
ANNE.   I hope so.
GLOU.   I know so. But, gentle Lady Anne,
    To leave this keen encounter of our wits,
    And fall somewhat into a slower method,
    Is not the causer of the timeless[14] deaths
    Of these Plantagenets, Henry and Edward,
    As blameful as the executioner?
ANNE.   Thou art the cause, and most accursed effect.[15]
GLOU.   Your beauty was the cause of that effect;
    Your beauty, which did haunt me in my sleep
    To undertake the death of all the world,
    So I might live one hour in your sweet bosom.
ANNE.   If I thought that, I tell thee, homicide,
    These nails should rend that beauty from my cheeks.
GLOU.   These eyes could never endure sweet beauty's wreck;
    You should not blemish it, if I stood by:
    As all the world is cheered by the sun,
    So I by that; it is my day, my life.
ANNE.   Black night o'ershade thy day, and death thy life!
GLOU.   Curse not thyself, fair creature; thou art both.
ANNE.   I would I were, to be revenged on thee.
GLOU.   It is a quarrel most unnatural,
    To be revenged on him that loveth you.
ANNE.   It is a quarrel just and reasonable,
    To be revenged on him that slew my husband.
GLOU.   He that bereft thee, lady, of thy husband,
    Did it to help thee to a better husband.
ANNE.   His better doth not breathe upon the earth.
GLOU.   He lives that loves you better than he could.
ANNE.   Name him.
GLOU.   Plantagenet.
ANNE.   Why, that was he.
GLOU.   The selfsame name, but one of better nature.

---

14. *timeless*] untimely.
15. *effect*] effecter, doer, executioner. The act is put for the agent. In the next line "effect"
    is employed in the ordinary manner, and means "the deaths of these Plantagenets."

ANNE.   Where is he?
GLOU.   Here. [*She spitteth at him.*] Why dost thou spit at me?
ANNE.   Would it were mortal poison, for thy sake!
GLOU.   Never came poison from so sweet a place.
ANNE.   Never hung poison on a fouler toad.
   Out of my sight! thou dost infect my eyes.
GLOU.   Thine eyes, sweet lady, have infected mine.
ANNE.   Would they were basilisks,[16] to strike thee dead!
GLOU.   I would they were, that I might die at once;
  For now they kill me with a living death.
  Those eyes of thine from mine have drawn salt tears,
  Shamed their aspect with store of childish drops:
  These eyes, which never shed remorseful tear,
  No, when my father York and Edward wept,
  To hear the piteous moan that Rutland made
  When black-faced Clifford shook his sword at him;
  Nor when thy warlike father, like a child,
  Told the sad story of my father's death,
  And twenty times made pause to sob and weep,
  That all the standers-by had wet their cheeks,
  Like trees bedash'd with rain: in that sad time
  My manly eyes did scorn an humble tear;
  And what these sorrows could not thence exhale,[17]
  Thy beauty hath, and made them blind with weeping.
  I never sued to friend nor enemy;
  My tongue could never learn sweet smoothing words;
  But, now thy beauty is proposed my fee,
  My proud heart sues, and prompts my tongue to speak.
                  [*She looks scornfully at him.*]
  Teach not thy lips such scorn, for they were made
  For kissing, lady, not for such contempt.
  If thy revengeful heart cannot forgive,
  Lo, here I lend thee this sharp-pointed sword;
  Which if thou please to hide in this true bosom,
  And let the soul forth that adoreth thee,
  I lay it naked to the deadly stroke,
  And humbly beg the death upon my knee.
        [*He lays his breast open: she offers at it with his sword.*]
  Nay, do not pause; for I did kill King Henry,
  But 'twas thy beauty that provoked me.
  Nay, now dispatch; 'twas I that stabb'd young Edward,
  But 'twas thy heavenly face that set me on.

---

16. *basilisks*] fabulous reptiles who could kill with a look.
17. *exhale*] draw forth.

[Here she lets fall the sword.]

    Take up the sword again, or take up me.

ANNE.   Arise, dissembler: though I wish thy death,
    I will not be the executioner.

GLOU.   Then bid me kill myself, and I will do it.

ANNE.   I have already.

GLOU.   Tush, that was in thy rage:
    Speak it again, and, even with the word,
    That hand, which, for thy love, did kill thy love,
    Shall, for thy love, kill a far truer love;
    To both their deaths shalt thou be accessary.

ANNE.   I would I knew thy heart.

GLOU.   'Tis figured in my tongue.

ANNE.   I fear me both are false.

GLOU.   Then never man was true.

ANNE.   Well, well, put up your sword.

GLOU.   Say, then, my peace is made.

ANNE.   That shall you know hereafter.

GLOU.   But shall I live in hope?

ANNE.   All men, I hope, live so.

GLOU.   Vouchsafe to wear this ring.

ANNE.   To take is not to give.

GLOU.   Look, how this ring encompasseth thy finger,
    Even so thy breast encloseth my poor heart;
    Wear both of them, for both of them are thine.
    And if thy poor devoted suppliant may
    But beg one favour at thy gracious hand,
    Thou dost confirm his happiness for ever.

ANNE.   What is it?

GLOU.   That it would please thee leave these sad designs
    To him that hath more cause to be a mourner,
    And presently repair to Crosby Place;[18]
    Where, after I have solemnly interr'd
    At Chertsey monastery this noble king,
    And wet his grave with my repentant tears,
    I will with all expedient[19] duty see you:
    For divers unknown reasons, I beseech you,
    Grant me this boon.

ANNE.   With all my heart; and much it joys me too,

---

18. *Crosby Place*] a fine house of timber and stone in Bishopsgate Street, London, built a few years before by Sir John Crosby, a prominent citizen of London. Richard occupied it while he was Protector. The building, after undergoing successive renovations, was demolished in January, 1908.

19. *expedient*] expeditious.

To see you are become so penitent.
Tressel and Berkeley, go along with me.
GLOU.   Bid me farewell.
ANNE.   'Tis more than you deserve;
But since you teach me how to flatter you,
Imagine I have said farewell already.

          [*Exeunt* LADY ANNE, TRESSEL, *and* BERKELEY.]

GLOU.   Sirs, take up the corse.
GENT.   Towards Chertsey, noble lord?
GLOU.   No, to White-Friars;[20] there attend my coming.

          [*Exeunt all but* GLOUCESTER.]

Was ever woman in this humour woo'd?
Was ever woman in this humour won?
I'll have her; but I will not keep her long.
What! I, that kill'd her husband and his father,
To take[21] her in her heart's extremest hate,
With curses in her mouth, tears in her eyes,
The bleeding witness of her hatred by;
Having God, her conscience, and these bars against me,
And I nothing to back my suit at all,
But the plain devil and dissembling looks,
And yet to win her, all the world to nothing![22]
Ha!
Hath she forgot already that brave prince,
Edward, her lord, whom I, some three months since,
Stabb'd in my angry mood at Tewksbury?
A sweeter and a lovelier gentleman,
Framed in the prodigality of nature,
Young, valiant, wise, and, no doubt, right royal,
The spacious world cannot again afford:
And will she yet debase her eyes on me,
That cropp'd the golden prime of this sweet prince,
And made her widow to a woful bed?
On me, whose all not equals Edward's moiety?[23]
On me, that halt and am unshapen thus?
My dukedom to a beggarly denier,[24]

---

20. *White-Friars*] According to the 1587 edition of Holinshed's *Chronicles*, one of Shakespeare's major sources for his English history plays, the corpse was taken to the religious house of the Dominicans, in the city of London, known as Blackfriars, and not to White-Friars, a neighbouring house of the Carmelites or white friars. Districts in the city of London are still familiarly known as Blackfriars and Whitefriars.
21. *take*] capture, captivate.
22. *all the world to nothing*] the odds against me being all the world to nothing.
23. *moiety*] one of two equal parts, a half.
24. *denier*] a coin of very small value; from the Latin *denarius*.

I do mistake my person all this while:
Upon my life, she finds, although I cannot,
Myself to be a marvellous proper man.
I'll be at charges[25] for a looking-glass,
And entertain[26] some score or two of tailors,
To study fashions to adorn my body:
Since I am crept in favour with myself,
I will maintain it with some little cost.
But first I'll turn yon fellow in his grave;
And then return lamenting to my love.
Shine out, fair sun, till I have bought a glass,
That I may see my shadow as I pass.

                                                                    [*Exit.*]

SCENE III. *The Palace.*

Enter QUEEN ELIZABETH, LORD RIVERS, *and* LORD GREY

RIV.   Have patience, madam: there's no doubt his majesty
         Will soon recover his accustom'd health.
GREY.   In that you brook[1] it ill, it makes him worse:
         Therefore, for God's sake, entertain good comfort,
         And cheer his grace with quick and merry words.
Q. ELIZ.   If he were dead, what would betide of me?
RIV.   No other harm but loss of such a lord.
Q. ELIZ.   The loss of such a lord includes all harm.
GREY.   The heavens have bless'd you with a goodly son,
         To be your comforter when he is gone.
Q. ELIZ.   Oh, he is young, and his minority
         Is put unto the trust of Richard Gloucester,
         A man that loves not me, nor none of you.
RIV.   Is it concluded he shall be protector?
Q. ELIZ.   It is determined, not concluded[2] yet:
         But so it must be, if the king miscarry.[3]

Enter BUCKINGHAM *and* DERBY

---

25. *at charges*] incur costs for (a looking-glass).
26. *entertain*] take into service.

---

1. *brook*] bear, endure. (Here, the sense is, "If you cannot endure the King's illness, it will make him worse.")
2. *determined, not concluded*] settled, but not formally recorded.
3. *miscarry*] perish, die.

GREY.   Here come the lords of Buckingham and Derby.[4]
BUCK.   Good time of day unto your royal grace!
DER.   God make your majesty joyful as you have been!
Q. ELIZ.   The Countess Richmond,[5] good my Lord of Derby,
   To your good prayers will scarcely say amen.
   Yet, Derby, notwithstanding she's your wife,
   And loves not me, be you, good lord, assured
   I hate not you for her proud arrogance.
DER.   I do beseech you, either not believe
   The envious slanders of her false accusers;
   Or, if she be accused in true report,
   Bear with her weakness, which, I think, proceeds
   From wayward sickness, and no grounded malice.[6]
RIV.   Saw you the king to-day, my Lord of Derby?
DER.   But now the Duke of Buckingham and I
   Are come from visiting his majesty.
Q. ELIZ.   What likelihood of his amendment, lords?
BUCK.   Madam, good hope; his grace speaks cheerfully.
Q. ELIZ.   God grant him health! Did you confer with him?
BUCK.   Madam, we did: he desires to make atonement[7]
   Betwixt the Duke of Gloucester and your brothers,
   And betwixt them and my lord chamberlain;
   And sent to warn them to his royal presence.
Q. ELIZ.   Would all were well! but that will never be:
   I fear our happiness is at the highest.

Enter GLOUCESTER, HASTINGS, *and* DORSET

GLOU.   They do me wrong, and I will not endure it:
   Who are they that complain unto the king,
   That I, forsooth, am stern and love them not?
   By holy Paul, they love his grace but lightly
   That fill his ears with such dissentious rumours.
   Because I cannot flatter and speak fair,
   Smile in men's faces, smooth, deceive and cog,[8]

---

4. *Derby*] In Act III, Sc. ii, and frequently in Act IV, he is called more correctly Lord Stanley. He was Thomas, Lord Stanley, who was created first Earl of Derby by Henry VII, after Richard III's death. The premature designation of Derby is due to Shakespeare's carelessness.
5. *The Countess Richmond*] Margaret, only child of John Beaufort, first Duke of Somerset, and descendant of John of Gaunt, had married Lord Stanley as her third husband. She was mother, by her first husband, Edmund Tudor, Earl of Richmond, of King Henry VII.
6. *grounded malice*] inveterate hatred.
7. *atonement*] reconciliation.
8. *smooth . . . and cog*] cajole . . . and cheat.

Duck with French nods and apish courtesy,
I must be held a rancorous enemy.
Cannot a plain man live and think no harm,
But thus his simple truth must be abused
By silken, sly, insinuating Jacks?[9]

RIV.   To whom in all this presence speaks your grace?

GLOU.   To thee, that hast nor[10] honesty nor grace.
When have I injured thee? when done thee wrong?
Or thee? or thee? or any of your faction?
A plague upon you all! His royal person —
Whom God preserve better than you would wish! —
Cannot be quiet scarce a breathing-while,
But you must trouble him with lewd[11] complaints.

Q. ELIZ.   Brother of Gloucester, you mistake the matter.
The king, of his own royal disposition,
And not provoked by any suitor else;
Aiming, belike, at your interior[12] hatred,
Which in your outward actions shows itself
Against my kindred, brothers, and myself,
Makes him to send; that thereby he may gather
The ground of your ill-will, and to remove it.

GLOU.   I cannot tell: the world is grown so bad,
That wrens make prey where eagles dare not perch:
Since every Jack became a gentleman,
There's many a gentle person made a Jack.

Q. ELIZ.   Come, come, we know your meaning, brother Gloucester;
You envy my advancement and my friends':
God grant we never may have need of you!

GLOU.   Meantime, God grants that we have need of you:
Our brother is imprison'd by your means,
Myself disgraced, and the nobility
Held in contempt; whilst many fair promotions
Are daily given to ennoble those
That scarce, some two days since, were worth a noble.[13]

Q. ELIZ.   By Him that raised me to this careful[14] height
From that contented hap which I enjoy'd,
I never did incense his majesty
Against the Duke of Clarence, but have been

---

9. *Jacks*] contemptuous term for saucy, paltry or silly men.
10. *nor*] neither.
11. *lewd*] vulgar, ignorant.
12. *interior*] inwardly cherished.
13. *a noble*] a pun on the word in the sense of a gold coin, worth about six shillings, eight pence.
14. *careful*] full of care, anxiety.

An earnest advocate to plead for him.
My lord, you do me shameful injury,
Falsely to draw me in these vile suspects.[15]

GLOU.   You may deny that you were not the cause
Of my Lord Hastings' late imprisonment.

RIV.   She may, my lord, for —

GLOU.   She may, Lord Rivers! why, who knows not so?
She may do more, sir, than denying that:
She may help you to many fair preferments;
And then deny her aiding hand therein,
And lay those honours on your high deserts.
What may she not? She may, yea, marry, may she, —

RIV.   What, marry, may she?

GLOU.   What, marry, may she! marry with a king,
A bachelor, a handsome stripling too:
I wis[16] your grandam had a worser match.

Q. ELIZ.   My Lord of Gloucester, I have too long borne
Your blunt upbraidings and your bitter scoffs:
By heaven, I will acquaint his majesty
With those gross taunts I often have endured.
I had rather be a country servant-maid
Than a great queen, with this condition,
To be thus taunted, scorn'd, and baited at:

Enter QUEEN MARGARET,[17] *behind*

Small joy have I in being England's queen.

Q. MAR.   And lessen'd be that small, God, I beseech thee!
Thy honour, state and seat is due to me.

GLOU.   What! threat you me with telling of the king?
Tell him, and spare not: look, what I have said
I will avouch in presence of the king:
I dare adventure to be sent to the Tower.
'Tis time to speak; my pains[18] are quite forgot.

Q. MAR.   Out, devil! I remember them too well:
Thou slewest my husband Henry in the Tower,
And Edward, my poor son, at Tewksbury.

GLOU.   Ere you were queen, yea, or your husband king,
I was a pack-horse in his great affairs;

---

15. *suspects*] suspicions.
16. *I wis*] usually spelled I-wis, meaning surely, certainly.
17. *Queen Margaret*] Margaret of Anjou, widow of Henry VI and mother of Edward Plantagenet (1453–1471), who was killed at the Battle of Tewkesbury by Gloucester and his brothers. She was banished in 1475 and died in France without ever returning to England. Her presence in the play is for dramatic effect and is historically inaccurate.
18. *pains*] labors.

A weeder out of his proud adversaries,
A liberal rewarder of his friends:
To royalise[19] his blood I spilt mine own.
Q. MAR.   Yea, and much better blood than his or thine.
GLOU.   In all which time you and your husband Grey
     Were factious for the house of Lancaster;
     And, Rivers, so were you. Was not your husband
     In Margaret's battle at Saint Alban's slain?
     Let me put in your minds, if you forget,
     What you have been ere now, and what you are;
     Withal, what I have been, and what I am.
Q. MAR.   A murderous villain, and so still thou art.
GLOU.   Poor Clarence did forsake his father, Warwick;
     Yea, and forswore himself, — which Jesu pardon! —
Q. MAR.   Which God revenge!
GLOU.   To fight on Edward's party for the crown;
     And for his meed,[20] poor lord, he is mew'd up.
     I would to God my heart were flint, like Edward's;
     Or Edward's soft and pitiful, like mine:
     I am too childish-foolish for this world.
Q. MAR.   Hie thee to hell for shame, and leave the world,
     Thou cacodemon![21] there thy kingdom is.
RIV.   My Lord of Gloucester, in those busy days
     Which here you urge to prove us enemies,
     We follow'd then our lord, our lawful king:
     So should we you, if you should be our king.
GLOU.   If I should be! I had rather be a pedlar:
     Far be it from my heart, the thought of it!
Q. ELIZ.   As little joy, my lord, as you suppose
     You should enjoy, were you this country's king,
     As little joy may you suppose in me,
     That I enjoy, being the queen thereof.
Q. MAR.   A little joy enjoys the queen thereof;
     For I am she, and altogether joyless.
     I can no longer hold me patient.   [*Advancing.*]
     Hear me, you wrangling pirates, that fall out
     In sharing that which you have pill'd[22] from me!
     Which of you trembles not that looks on me?
     If not, that, I being queen, you bow like subjects,
     Yet that, by you deposed, you quake like rebels?
     O gentle villain, do not turn away!

---

19. *royalise*] make royal.
20. *meed*] reward.
21. *cacodemon*] evil spirit.
22. *pill'd*] pillaged, plundered.

GLOU. Foul wrinkled witch, what makest[23] thou in my sight?
Q. MAR. But repetition of what thou hast marr'd;
That will I make before I let thee go.
GLOU. Wert thou not banished on pain of death?
Q. MAR. I was; but I do find more pain in banishment,
Than death can yield me here by my abode.
A husband and a son thou owest to me;
And thou a kingdom; all of you allegiance:
The sorrow that I have, by right is yours,
And all the pleasures you usurp are mine.
GLOU. The curse my noble father laid on thee,
When thou didst crown his warlike brows with paper,
And with thy scorns drew'st rivers from his eyes,
And then, to dry them, gavest the duke a clout,[24]
Steep'd in the faultless blood of pretty Rutland, —
His curses, then from bitterness of soul
Denounced against thee, are all fall'n upon thee;
And God, not we, hath plagued[25] thy bloody deed.[26]
Q. ELIZ. So just is God, to right the innocent.
HAST. O, 'twas the foulest deed to slay that babe,[27]
And the most merciless that e'er was heard of!
RIV. Tyrants themselves wept when it was reported.
DOR. No man but prophesied revenge for it.
BUCK. Northumberland, then present, wept to see it.
Q. MAR. What! were you snarling all before I came,
Ready to catch each other by the throat,
And turn you all your hatred now on me?
Did York's dread curse prevail so much with heaven,
That Henry's death, my lovely Edward's death,
Their kingdom's loss, my woful banishment,
Could all but answer for that peevish brat?
Can curses pierce the clouds and enter heaven?
Why, then, give way, dull clouds, to my quick curses!
If not by war, by surfeit die your king,

---

23. *makest*] doest.
24. *clout*] cloth.
25. *plagued*] punished.
26. *When . . . bloody deed*] In 3 *Hen. VI*, I, iv, York had defeated Henry VI, who named York (rather than his own son Edward) successor to the throne. Queen Margaret, however, continued the fight against the Yorkists and eventually captured York. In the play, after taking him prisoner, Margaret and her followers taunt him and bid him weep, offering him a handkerchief stained with the blood of his youngest son, the Earl of Rutland, who was killed by Lord Clifford in the preceding battle. She then forces him to wear a paper crown and at the end of the scene she and Clifford stab him to death.
27. *babe*] i.e., Rutland. The term was sometimes used to refer to older children.

As ours by murder, to make him a king!
Edward thy son, which now is Prince of Wales,
For Edward my son, which was Prince of Wales,
Die in his youth by like untimely violence!
Thyself a queen, for me that was a queen,
Outlive thy glory, like my wretched self!
Long mayst thou live to wail thy children's loss;
And see another, as I see thee now,
Deck'd in thy rights, as thou art stall'd in mine!
Long die thy happy days before thy death;
And, after many lengthen'd hours of grief,
Die neither mother, wife, nor England's queen!
Rivers and Dorset, you were standers by,
And so wast thou, Lord Hastings, when my son
Was stabb'd with bloody daggers: God, I pray him,
That none of you may live your natural age,
But by some unlook'd accident cut off!
GLOU. Have done thy charm, thou hateful withered hag!
Q. MAR. And leave out thee? stay, dog, for thou shalt hear me.
If heaven have any grievous plague in store
Exceeding those that I can wish upon thee,
O, let them[28] keep it till thy sins be ripe,
And then hurl down their indignation
On thee, the troubler of the poor world's peace!
The worm of conscience still begnaw thy soul!
Thy friends suspect for traitors while thou livest,
And take deep traitors for thy dearest friends!
No sleep close up that deadly eye of thine,
Unless it be whilst some tormenting dream
Affrights thee with a hell of ugly devils!
Thou elvish-mark'd,[29] abortive, rooting hog![30]
Thou that wast seal'd in thy nativity
The slave of nature and the son of hell!
Thou slander of thy mother's heavy womb
Thou loathed issue of thy father's loins!
Thou rag of honour! thou detested—
GLOU. Margaret.
Q. MAR.   Richard!
GLOU.   Ha!
Q. MAR.   I call thee not.

---

28. *them*] heaven; the word has a collective or plural significance.
29. *elvish-mark'd*] the common superstition that persons born with scars or deformities had been marked by wicked fairies or elves.
30. *hog*] Richard's heraldic blazon featured a boar.

GLOU.   I cry thee mercy then, for I had thought
    That thou hadst call'd me all these bitter names.
Q. MAR.   Why, so I did; but look'd for no reply.
    O, let me make the period to my curse!
GLOU.   'Tis done by me, and ends in "Margaret."
Q. ELIZ.   Thus have you breathed your curse against yourself.
Q. MAR.   Poor painted queen, vain flourish of my fortune!
    Why strew'st thou sugar on that bottled spider,[31]
    Whose deadly web ensnareth thee about?
    Fool, fool! thou whet'st a knife to kill thyself.
    The time will come that thou shalt wish for me
    To help thee curse that poisonous bunch-back'd toad.
HAST.   False-boding woman, end thy frantic curse,
    Lest to thy harm thou move our patience.
Q. MAR.   Foul shame upon you! you have all moved mine.
RIV.   Were you well served, you would be taught your duty.
Q. MAR.   To serve me well, you all should do me duty,
    Teach me to be your queen, and you my subjects:
    O, serve me well, and teach yourselves that duty!
DOR.   Dispute not with her; she is lunatic.
Q. MAR.   Peace, master marquess, you are malapert:[32]
    Your fire-new[33] stamp of honour is scarce current.
    O, that your young nobility could judge
    What 't were to lose it, and be miserable!
    They that stand high have many blasts to shake them;
    And if they fall, they dash themselves to pieces.
GLOU.   Good counsel, marry: learn it, learn it, marquess.
DOR.   It toucheth you, my lord, as much as me.
GLOU.   Yea, and much more: but I was born so high,
    Our aery buildeth in the cedar's top,
    And dallies with the wind and scorns the sun.
Q. MAR.   And turns the sun to shade; alas! alas!
    Witness my son, now in the shade of death;
    Whose bright out-shining beams thy cloudy wrath
    Hath in eternal darkness folded up.
    Your aery buildeth in our aery's nest.
    O God, that seest it, do not suffer it;
    As it was won with blood, lost be it so!
BUCK.   Have done! for shame, if not for charity.
Q. MAR.   Urge neither charity nor shame to me:
    Uncharitably with me have you dealt,

---

31. *bottled spider*] an exceptionally large or bottle-shaped spider.
32. *malapert*] pert, forward, saucy.
33. *fire-new*] brand-new.

And shamefully by you my hopes are butcher'd.
My charity is outrage, life my shame;
And in that shame still live my sorrow's rage!
BUCK.   Have done, have done.
Q. MAR.   O princely Buckingham, I'll kiss thy hand,
In sign of league and amity with thee:
Now fair befall thee[34] and thy noble house!
Thy garments are not spotted with our blood,
Nor thou within the compass of my curse.
BUCK.   Nor no one here; for curses never pass
The lips of those that breathe them in the air.
Q. MAR.   I'll not believe but they ascend the sky,
And there awake God's gentle-sleeping peace.
O Buckingham, take heed of yonder dog!
Look, when he fawns, he bites; and when he bites,
His venom tooth will rankle to the death:
Have not to do with him, beware of him;
Sin, death, and hell have set their marks on him,
And all their ministers attend on him.
GLOU.   What doth she say, my Lord of Buckingham?
BUCK.   Nothing that I respect, my gracious lord.
Q. MAR.   What, dost thou scorn me for my gentle counsel?
And soothe the devil that I warn thee from?
O, but remember this another day,
When he shall split thy very heart with sorrow,
And say poor Margaret was a prophetess.
Live each of you the subjects to his hate,
And he to yours, and all of you to God's!   [*Exit.*]
HAST.   My hair doth stand on end to hear her curses.
RIV.   And so doth mine: I muse why she's at liberty.
GLOU.   I cannot blame her: by God's holy mother,
She hath had too much wrong; and I repent
My part thereof that I have done to her.
Q. ELIZ.   I never did her any, to my knowledge.
GLOU.   But you have all the vantage of her wrong.
I was too hot to do somebody good,
That is too cold in thinking of it now.
Marry, as for Clarence, he is well repaid;
He is frank'd up[35] to fatting for his pains:
God pardon them that are the cause of it!

---

34. *fair befall thee*] good fortune attend you!
35. *frank'd up*] cooped up as in a pen or sty, which was commonly called a "frank." The
    verb is used of animals, especially hogs, being fattened for the butcher.

RIV.   A virtuous and a Christian-like conclusion,
     To pray for them that have done scathe[36] to us.
GLOU.   So do I ever: [*Aside*] being well advised:
     For had I cursed now, I had cursed myself.

Enter CATESBY

CATES.   Madam, his majesty doth call for you;
     And for your grace; and you, my noble lords.
Q. ELIZ.   Catesby, we come. Lords, will you go with us?
RIV.   Madam, we will attend your grace.
                     [*Exeunt all but* GLOUCESTER.]
GLOU.   I do the wrong, and first begin to brawl.
     The secret mischiefs that I set abroach[37]
     I lay unto the grievous charge of others.
     Clarence, whom I, indeed, have laid in darkness,
     I do beweep to many simple gulls;[38]
     Namely, to Hastings, Derby, Buckingham;
     And say it is the queen and her allies
     That stir the king against the duke my brother.
     Now, they believe it; and withal whet me
     To be revenged on Rivers, Vaughan, Grey:
     But then I sigh; and, with a piece of Scripture,
     Tell them that God bids us do good for evil:
     And thus I clothe my naked villany
     With old odd ends[39] stolen out of holy writ;
     And seem a saint, when most I play the devil.

Enter two Murderers

     But, soft! here come my executioners.
     How now, my hardy stout resolved mates!
     Are you now going to dispatch this deed?
FIRST MURD.   We are, my lord; and come to have the warrant,
     That we may be admitted where he is.
GLOU.   Well thought upon; I have it here about me.
                     [*Gives the warrant.*]
     When you have done, repair to Crosby Place.
     But, sirs, be sudden in the execution,
     Withal obdurate, do not hear him plead;
     For Clarence is well-spoken, and perhaps
     May move your hearts to pity, if you mark him.

---

36. *scathe*] injury, hurt.
37. *set abroach*] to cause, set into action, agitate.
38. *gulls*] tricks, impositions.
39. *old odd ends*] quoted tags, odds and ends.

FIRST MURD.   Tush!
    Fear not, my lord, we will not stand to prate;
    Talkers are no good doers: be assured
    We come to use our hands and not our tongues.
GLOU.   Your eyes drop millstones,[40] when fools' eyes drop tears.
    I like you, lads: about your business straight.
    Go, go, dispatch.
FIRST MURD.   We will, my noble lord.   [*Exeunt.*]

SCENE IV. *London. The Tower.*

Enter CLARENCE *and* BRAKENBURY

BRAK.   Why looks your grace so heavily to-day?
CLAR.   O, I have pass'd a miserable night,
    So full of ugly sights, of ghastly dreams,
    That, as I am a Christian faithful[1] man,
    I would not spend another such a night,
    Though 't were to buy a world of happy days,
    So full of dismal terror was the time!
BRAK.   What was your dream? I long to hear you tell it.
CLAR.   Methoughts that I had broken from the Tower,
    And was embark'd to cross to Burgundy;
    And, in my company, my brother Gloucester;
    Who from my cabin tempted me to walk
    Upon the hatches: thence we look'd toward England,
    And cited up a thousand fearful times,
    During the wars of York and Lancaster,
    That had befall'n us. As we paced along
    Upon the giddy footing of the hatches,
    Methought that Gloucester stumbled; and, in falling,
    Struck me, that thought to stay him, overboard,
    Into the tumbling billows of the main.
    Lord, Lord! methought, what pain it was to drown!
    What dreadful noise of waters in mine ears!
    What ugly sights of death within mine eyes!
    Methought I saw a thousand fearful wrecks;

---

40. *Your eyes drop millstones*] an expression very commonly applied to hard-natured
    persons who were not in the habit of weeping at all.

---

1. *faithful*] as opposed to "infidel."

Ten thousand men that fishes gnaw'd upon;
Wedges of gold, great anchors, heaps of pearl,
Inestimable stones, unvalued[2] jewels,
All scattered in the bottom of the sea:
Some lay in dead men's skulls; and in those holes
Where eyes did once inhabit, there were crept,
As 't were in scorn of eyes, reflecting gems,
Which woo'd[3] the slimy bottom of the deep,
And mock'd the dead bones that lay scattered by.

BRAK.   Had you such leisure in the time of death
To gaze upon the secrets of the deep?

CLAR.   Methought I had; and often did I strive
To yield the ghost: but still the envious[4] flood
Kept in my soul, and would not let it forth
To seek the empty, vast and wandering air;
But smothered it within my panting bulk,[5]
Which almost burst to belch it in the sea.

BRAK.   Awaked you not with this sore agony?

CLAR.   O no, my dream was lengthened after life;
O, then began the tempest to my soul,
Who pass'd, methought, the melancholy flood,
With that grim ferryman which poets write of,[6]
Unto the kingdom of perpetual night.
The first that there did greet my stranger soul,
Was my great father-in-law, renowned Warwick;
Who cried aloud, "What scourge for perjury
Can this dark monarchy afford false Clarence?"
And so he vanish'd: then came wandering by
A shadow like an angel, with bright hair
Dabbled in blood; and he squeak'd out aloud,
"Clarence is come; false, fleeting,[7] perjured Clarence,
That stabb'd me in the field by Tewksbury:[8]
Seize on him, Furies, take him to your torments!"
With that, methoughts, a legion of foul fiends
Environ'd me about, and howled in mine ears
Such hideous cries, that with the very noise
I trembling waked, and for a season after
Could not believe but that I was in hell,

---

2. *unvalued*] invaluable.
3. *woo'd*] ogled.
4. *envious*] cruel, malicious.
5. *bulk*] body, frame, trunk.
6. *Who pass'd . . . poets write of*] a reference to the myth of Charon, the Stygian ferryman.
7. *fleeting*] wavering, inconstant.
8. *A shadow . . . Tewksbury*] the ghost of Edward Plantagenet, Prince of Wales.

Such terrible impression made the dream.

BRAK.　No marvel, my lord, though it affrighted you;
　　I promise you, I am afraid to hear you tell it.

CLAR.　O Brakenbury, I have done those things,
　　Which now bear evidence against my soul,
　　For Edward's sake; and see how he requites me!
　　O God! if my deep prayers cannot appease thee,
　　But thou wilt be avenged on my misdeeds,
　　Yet execute thy wrath in me alone;
　　O, spare my guiltless wife[9] and my poor children!
　　I pray thee, gentle keeper, stay by me;
　　My soul is heavy, and I fain would sleep.

BRAK.　I will, my lord: God give your grace good rest!

　　　　　　　　　　　　　　　　　　[CLARENCE *sleeps.*]

Sorrow breaks seasons and reposing hours,
Makes the night morning and the noon-tide night.
Princes have but their titles for their glories,
An outward honour for an inward toil;
And, for unfelt imagination,
They often feel a world of restless cares:[10]
So that, betwixt their titles and low names,
There's nothing differs but the outward fame.

Enter the two Murderers

FIRST MURD.　Ho! who's here?

BRAK.　In God's name what are you, and how came you hither?

FIRST MURD.　I would speak with Clarence, and I came hither on my
　　legs.

BRAK.　Yea, are you so brief?

SEC. MURD.　O sir, it is better to be brief than tedious.
　　Show him our commission; talk no more.

　　　　　　　　　　　　　　　　　　[BRAKENBURY *reads it.*]

BRAK.　I am in this commanded to deliver
　　The noble Duke of Clarence to your hands:
　　I will not reason what is meant hereby,
　　Because I will be guiltless of the meaning.
　　Here are the keys, there sits the duke asleep:
　　I'll to the king; and signify to him
　　That thus I have resign'd my charge to you.

---

9. *guiltless wife*] an historical error. Clarence's wife, Isabella Neville, the elder daughter of the Earl of Warwick, died December 21, 1476, long before Clarence's imprisonment.

10. *for unfelt imagination . . . cares*] In return for imaginary gratification, which does not touch their feeling, they often feel any amount of disturbing cares.

FIRST MURD.   Do so, it is a point of wisdom: fare you well.

           [*Exit* BRAKENBURY.]

SEC. MURD.   What, shall we stab him as he sleeps?

FIRST MURD.   No; then he will say 't was done cowardly, when he wakes.

SEC. MURD.   When he wakes! why, fool, he shall never wake till the judgement-day.

FIRST MURD.   Why, then he will say we stabbed him sleeping.

SEC. MURD.   The urging of that word "judgement" hath bred a kind of remorse in me.

FIRST MURD.   What, art thou afraid?

SEC. MURD.   Not to kill him, having a warrant for it; but to be damned for killing him, from which no warrant can defend us.

FIRST MURD.   I thought thou hadst been resolute.

SEC. MURD.   So I am, to let him live.

FIRST MURD.   Back to the Duke of Gloucester, tell him so.

SEC. MURD.   I pray thee, stay a while: I hope my holy humour will change; 't was wont to hold me but while one would tell[11] twenty.

FIRST MURD.   How dost thou feel thyself now?

SEC. MURD.   Faith, some certain dregs of conscience are yet within me.

FIRST MURD.   Remember our reward, when the deed is done.

SEC. MURD.   'Zounds, he dies: I had forgot the reward.

FIRST MURD.   Where is thy conscience now?

SEC. MURD.   In the Duke of Gloucester's purse.

FIRST MURD.   So when he opens his purse to give us our reward, thy conscience flies out.

SEC. MURD.   Let it go; there's few or none will entertain it.

FIRST MURD.   How if it come to thee again?

SEC. MURD.   I'll not meddle with it: it is a dangerous thing: it makes a man a coward: a man cannot steal, but it accuseth him; he cannot swear, but it checks him; he cannot lie with his neighbour's wife, but it detects him: it is a blushing shamefast spirit that mutinies in a man's bosom; it fills one full of obstacles: it made me once restore a purse of gold, that I found; it beggars any man that keeps it: it is turned out of all towns and cities for a dangerous thing; and every man that means to live well endeavours to trust to himself and to live without it.

FIRST MURD.   'Zounds, it is even now at my elbow, persuading me not to kill the duke.

SEC. MURD.   Take the devil in thy mind, and believe him[12] not: he would insinuate with thee[13] but to make thee sigh.

---

11. *tell*] count to.
12. *him*] i.e., thy conscience.
13. *insinuate with thee*] beguile thee.

FIRST MURD. Tut, I am strong-framed, he cannot prevail with me, I
    warrant thee.
SEC. MURD. Spoke like a tall[14] fellow that respects his reputation.
    Come, shall we to this gear?[15]
FIRST MURD. Take him over the costard[16] with the hilts of thy sword,
    and then we will chop[17] him in the malmsey-butt[18] in the next
    room.
SEC. MURD. O excellent device! make a sop of him.
FIRST MURD. Hark! he stirs: shall I strike?
SEC. MURD. No, first let's reason with him.
CLAR. Where art thou, keeper? give me a cup of wine.
SEC. MURD. You shall have wine enough, my lord, anon.
CLAR. In God's name, what art thou?
SEC. MURD. A man, as you are.
CLAR. But not, as I am, royal.
SEC. MURD. Nor you, as we are, loyal.
CLAR. Thy voice is thunder, but thy looks are humble.
SEC. MURD. My voice is now the king's, my looks mine own.
CLAR. How darkly and how deadly dost thou speak!
    Your eyes do menace me: why look you pale?
    Who sent you hither? Wherefore do you come?
BOTH. To, to, to —
CLAR. To murder me?
BOTH. Ay, ay.
CLAR. You scarcely have the hearts to tell me so,
    And therefore cannot have the hearts to do it.
    Wherein, my friends, have I offended you?
FIRST MURD. Offended us you have not, but the king.
CLAR. I shall be reconciled to him again.
SEC. MURD. Never, my lord; therefore prepare to die.
CLAR. Are you call'd forth from out a world of men
    To slay the innocent? What is my offence?
    Where are the evidence that do accuse me?
    What lawful quest[19] have given their verdict up
    Unto the frowning judge? or who pronounced
    The bitter sentence of poor Clarence' death?
    Before I be convict by course of law,
    To threaten me with death is most unlawful.
    I charge you, as you hope to have redemption

14. *tall*] bold, daring; a common usage.
15. *to this gear*] to this business.
16. *Take him over the costard*] hit him over the head.
17. *chop*] to do something with a quick motion.
18. *malmsey-butt*] a large cask of malmsey (a kind of sweet wine).
19. *quest*] inquest or trial by jury; an empanelled jury.

By Christ's dear blood shed for our grievous sins,
That you depart and lay no hands on me:
The deed you undertake is damnable.

FIRST MURD.   What we will do, we do upon command.

SEC. MURD.   And he that hath commanded is the king.

CLAR.   Erroneous vassal! the great King of kings
Hath in the tables of his law commanded
That thou shalt do no murder: and wilt thou then
Spurn at his edict, and fulfil a man's?
Take heed; for he holds vengeance in his hands,
To hurl upon their heads that break his law.

SEC. MURD.   And that same vengeance doth he hurl on thee,
For false forswearing, and for murder too:
Thou didst receive the holy sacrament,
To fight in quarrel of the house of Lancaster.

FIRST MURD.   And, like a traitor to the name of God,
Didst break that vow; and with thy treacherous blade
Unrip'dst the bowels of thy sovereign's son.

SEC. MURD.   Whom thou wert sworn to cherish and defend.

FIRST MURD.   How canst thou urge God's dreadful law to us,
When thou hast broke it in so dear degree?

CLAR.   Alas! for whose sake did I that ill deed?
For Edward, for my brother, for his sake:
Why, sirs,
He sends ye not to murder me for this;
For in this sin he is as deep as I.
If God will be revenged for this deed,
O, know you yet, he doth it publicly:
Take not the quarrel from his powerful arm;
He needs no indirect nor lawless course
To cut off those that have offended him.

FIRST MURD.   Who made thee then a bloody minister,
When gallant-springing[20] brave Plantagenet,
That princely novice, was struck dead by thee?

CLAR.   My brother's love, the devil, and my rage.

FIRST MURD.   Thy brother's love, our duty, and thy fault,
Provoke us hither now to slaughter thee.

CLAR.   Oh, if you love my brother, hate not me;
I am his brother, and I love him well.
If you be hired for meed, go back again,
And I will send you to my brother Gloucester,
Who shall reward you better for my life,
Than Edward will for tidings of my death.

---

20. *gallant-springing*] like a gallant in the spring of life.

SEC. MURD.   You are deceived, your brother Gloucester hates yo
CLAR.   O, no, he loves me, and he holds me dear:
    Go you to him from me.
BOTH.   Ay, so we will.
CLAR.   Tell him, when that our princely father York
    Bless'd his three sons with his victorious arm,
    And charged us from his soul to love each other,
    He little thought of this divided friendship:
    Bid Gloucester think of this, and he will weep.
FIRST MURD.   Ay, millstones;[21] as he lesson'd us to weep.
CLAR.   O, do not slander him, for he is kind.
FIRST MURD.   Right,
    As snow in harvest. Thou deceivest thyself:
    'Tis he that sent us hither now to slaughter thee.[22]
CLAR.   It cannot be; for when I parted with him,
    He hugg'd me in his arms, and swore, with sobs,
    That he would labour my delivery.
SEC. MURD.   Why, so he doth, now he delivers thee
    From this world's thraldom to the joys of heaven.
FIRST MURD.   Make peace with God, for you must die, my lord.
CLAR.   Hast thou that holy feeling in thy soul,
    To counsel me to make my peace with God,
    And art thou yet to thy own soul so blind,
    That thou wilt war with God by murdering me?
    Ah, sirs, consider, he that set you on
    To do this deed will hate you for the deed.
SEC. MURD.   What shall we do?
CLAR.   Relent, and save your souls.
FIRST MURD.   Relent! 'tis cowardly and womanish.
CLAR.   Not to relent is beastly, savage, devilish.
    Which of you, if you were a prince's son,
    Being pent from liberty, as I am now,
    If two such murderers as yourselves came to you,
    Would not entreat for life?
    My friend, I spy some pity in thy looks;
    O, if thine eye be not a flatterer,
    Come thou on my side, and entreat for me,
    As you would beg, were you in my distress:
    A begging prince what beggar pities not?
SEC. MURD.   Look behind you, my lord.

---

21. *Ay, millstones*] see note 40, Act I, Sc. iii.
22. *'Tis . . . thee*] There is no historical evidence linking Gloucester with the death of
    Clarence. Sixteenth-century chroniclers do report the rumour that he was drowned in
    a butt of malmsey.

FIRST MURD.   Take that, and that: if all this will not do,

                                                     [*Stabs him.*]

    I'll drown you in the malmsey-butt within.

                                       [*Exit, with the body.*]

SEC. MURD.   A bloody deed, and desperately dispatch'd!
    How fain, like Pilate, would I wash my hands
    Of this most grievous guilty murder done!

Re-enter First Murderer

FIRST MURD.   How now! what mean'st thou, that thou help'st me not?
    By heavens, the duke shall know how slack thou art!
SEC. MURD.   I would he knew that I had saved his brother!
    Take thou the fee, and tell him what I say;
    For I repent me that the duke is slain.   [*Exit.*]
FIRST MURD.   So do not I: go, coward as thou art.
    Now must I hide his body in some hole,
    Until the duke take order for his burial:
    And when I have my meed, I must away;
    For this will out, and here I must not stay.   [*Exit.*]

ACT II.

SCENE I. *London. The Palace.*

Flourish. Enter KING EDWARD *sick,* QUEEN ELIZABETH, DORSET, RIVERS, HASTINGS, BUCKINGHAM, GREY, *and others*

K. EDW.   Why, so: now have I done a good day's work:
    You peers, continue this united league:
    I every day expect an embassage
    From my Redeemer to redeem me hence;
    And now in peace my soul shall part[1] to heaven,
    Since I have set my friends at peace on earth.
    Rivers and Hastings, take each other's hand;
    Dissemble not your hatred, swear your love.
RIV.   By heaven, my soul is purged from grudging hate;
    And with my hand I seal my true heart's love.
HAST.   So thrive I, as I truly swear the like!
K. EDW.   Take heed you dally not before your king;

---

1. *part*] depart.

       Lest he that is the supreme King of kings
       Confound[2] your hidden falsehood, and award
       Either of you to be the other's end.
HAST.   So prosper I, as I swear perfect love!
RIV.   And I, as I love Hastings with my heart!
K. EDW.   Madam, yourself are not exempt in this,
       Nor your son Dorset; Buckingham, nor you;
       You have been factious one against the other.
       Wife, love Lord Hastings, let him kiss your hand;
       And what you do, do it unfeignedly.
Q. ELIZ.   Here, Hastings; I will never more remember
       Our former hatred, so thrive I and mine!
K. EDW.   Dorset, embrace him; Hastings, love lord marquess.
DOR.   This interchange of love, I here protest,
       Upon my part shall be unviolable.
HAST.   And so swear I, my lord.   [*They embrace.*]
K. EDW.   Now, princely Buckingham, seal thou this league
       With thy embracements to my wife's allies,
       And make me happy in your unity.
BUCK.   [*To the* QUEEN] Whenever Buckingham doth turn his hate
       On you or yours, but with all duteous love
       Doth[3] cherish you and yours, God punish me
       With hate in those where I expect most love!
       When I have most need to employ a friend,
       And most assured that he is a friend,
       Deep, hollow, treacherous and full of guile,
       Be he unto me! this do I beg of God,
       When I am cold in zeal to you or yours.   [*They embrace.*]
K. EDW.   A pleasing cordial, princely Buckingham,
       Is this thy vow unto my sickly heart.
       There wanteth now our brother Gloucester here,
       To make the perfect period of this peace.
BUCK.   And, in good time, here comes the noble duke.

Enter GLOUCESTER

GLOU.   Good morrow to my sovereign king and queen;
       And, princely peers, a happy time of day!
K. EDW.   Happy indeed, as we have spent the day.
       Brother, we have done deeds of charity;
       Made peace of enmity, fair love of hate,
       Between these swelling wrong-incensed peers.

---

2. *Confound*] ruin, destroy.
3. *but . . . Doth*] and doth not.

GLOU.　A blessed labour, my most sovereign liege:
　　Amongst this princely heap,[4] if any here,
　　By false intelligence, or wrong surmise,
　　Hold me a foe;
　　If I unwittingly, or in my rage,
　　Have aught committed that is hardly borne
　　By any in this presence, I desire
　　To reconcile me to his friendly peace:
　　'Tis death to me to be at enmity;
　　I hate it, and desire all good men's love.
　　First, madam, I entreat true peace of you,
　　Which I will purchase with my duteous service;
　　Of you, my noble cousin Buckingham,
　　If ever any grudge were lodged between us;
　　·Of you, Lord Rivers, and, Lord Grey, of you,
　　That all without desert have frown'd on me;
　　Dukes, earls, lords, gentlemen; indeed, of all.
　　I do not know that Englishman alive
　　With whom my soul is any jot at odds,
　　More than the infant that is born to-night:
　　I thank my God for my humility.
Q. ELIZ.　A holy day shall this be kept hereafter:
　　I would to God all strifes were well compounded.
　　My sovereign liege, I do beseech your majesty
　　To take our brother Clarence to your grace.
GLOU.　Why, madam, have I offer'd love for this
　　To be so flouted in this royal presence?
　　Who knows not that the noble duke is dead?　　[*They all start.*]
　　You do him injury to scorn his corse.
RIV.　Who knows not he is dead! who knows he is?
Q. ELIZ.　All-seeing heaven, what a world is this!
BUCK.　Look I so pale, Lord Dorset, as the rest?
DOR.　Ay, my good lord; and no one in this presence
　　But his red colour hath forsook his cheeks.
K. EDW.　Is Clarence dead? the order was reversed.
GLOU.　But he, poor soul, by your first order died,
　　And that a winged Mercury did bear;
　　Some tardy cripple bore the countermand,
　　That came too lag to see him buried.
　　God grant that some, less noble and less loyal,
　　Nearer in bloody thoughts, but not in blood,

---

4. *heap*] throng, company.

Deserve not worse than wretched Clarence did,
And yet go current[5] from suspicion!

Enter DERBY

DER.   A boon, my sovereign, for my service done!
K. EDW.   I pray thee, peace: my soul is full of sorrow.
DER.   I will not rise, unless your highness grant.
K. EDW.   Then speak at once what is it thou demand'st.
DER.   The forfeit, sovereign, of my servant's life;
    Who slew to-day a riotous gentleman
    Lately attendant on the Duke of Norfolk.
K. EDW.   Have I a tongue to doom my brother's death,
    And shall that tongue give pardon to a slave?
    My brother slew no man; his fault was thought,
    And yet his punishment was cruel death.
    Who sued to me for him? who, in my rage,
    Kneel'd at my feet and bade me be advised?
    Who spake of brotherhood? who spake of love?
    Who told me how the poor soul did forsake
    The mighty Warwick, and did fight for me?
    Who told me, in the field by Tewksbury,
    When Oxford had me down, he rescued me,
    And said "Dear brother, live, and be a king"?
    Who told me, when we both lay in the field
    Frozen almost to death, how he did lap me
    Even in his own garments, and gave himself,
    All thin and naked, to the numb cold night?
    All this from my remembrance brutish wrath
    Sinfully pluck'd, and not a man of you
    Had so much grace to put it in my mind.
    But when your carters or your waiting-vassals
    Have done a drunken slaughter, and defaced
    The precious image of our dear Redeemer,
    You straight are on your knees for pardon, pardon;
    And I, unjustly too, must grant it you:
    But for my brother not a man would speak,
    Nor I, ungracious, speak unto myself
    For him, poor soul. The proudest of you all
    Have been beholding to him in his life;
    Yet none of you would once plead for his life.
    O God, I fear thy justice will take hold

---

5. *go current*] go as though perceived to be honest.

On me, and you, and mine, and yours for this!
Come, Hastings, help me to my closet. Oh, poor Clarence!
                              [*Exeunt some with King and Queen.*]
GLOU.   This is the fruit of rashness. Mark'd you not
     How that the guilty kindred of the queen
     Look'd pale when they did hear of Clarence' death?
     O, they did urge it still unto the king!
     God will revenge it. But come, let us in,
     To comfort Edward with our company.
BUCK.   We wait upon your grace.   [*Exeunt.*]

SCENE II. *The Palace.*

Enter the DUCHESS OF YORK, *with the two children of* CLARENCE

BOY.   Tell me, good grandam,[1] is our father dead?
DUCH.   No, boy.
BOY.   Why do you wring your hands, and beat your breast,
     And cry "O Clarence, my unhappy son"?
GIRL.   Why do you look on us, and shake your head,
     And call us wretches, orphans, castaways,
     If that our noble father be alive?
DUCH.   My pretty cousins,[2] you mistake me much.
     I do lament the sickness of the king,
     As loath to lose him; not your father's death;
     It were lost sorrow to wail one that's lost.
BOY.   Then, grandam, you conclude that he is dead.
     The king my uncle is to blame for this:
     God will revenge it; whom I will importune
     With daily prayers all to that effect.
GIRL.   And so will I.

---

1. *good grandam*] the widow of Richard, Duke of York, who was slain at the battle of
Wakefield, 1460, and the mother of Edward IV, Richard III, and Clarence. She survived
her husband thirty-five years. Her grandchildren, Clarence's son and daughter, with
whom she converses in this scene, were respectively Edward Plantagenet, Earl of
Warwick, who was executed by Henry VII on November 21, 1499, and the famous
Margaret, Countess of Salisbury, mother of Cardinal Pole; the Countess was beheaded
on Tower Hill at Henry VIII's instance on May 27, 1541.
2. *cousins*] This word was used for kinsfolk of any degree.

DUCH. Peace, children, peace! the king doth love you well:
　　Incapable[3] and shallow innocents,
　　You cannot guess who caused your father's death.
BOY. Grandam, we can; for my good uncle Gloucester
　　Told me, the king, provoked by the queen,
　　Devised impeachments to imprison him:
　　And when my uncle told me so, he wept,
　　And hugg'd me in his arm, and kindly kiss'd my cheek;
　　Bade me rely on him as on my father,
　　And he would love me dearly as his child.
DUCH. Oh, that deceit should steal such gentle shapes,
　　And with a virtuous vizard hide foul guile!
　　He is my son; yea, and therein my shame;
　　Yet from my dugs[4] he drew not this deceit.
BOY. Think you my uncle did dissemble, grandam?
DUCH. Ay, boy.
BOY. I cannot think it. Hark! what noise is this?

Enter QUEEN ELIZABETH, *with her hair about her ears;* RIVERS *and*
DORSET *after her*

Q. ELIZ. Oh, who shall hinder me to wail and weep,
　　To chide my fortune and torment myself?
　　I'll join with black despair against my soul,
　　And to myself become an enemy.
DUCH. What means this scene of rude impatience?
Q. ELIZ. To make an act[5] of tragic violence:
　　Edward, my lord, your son, our king, is dead.
　　Why grow the branches now the root is wither'd?
　　Why wither not the leaves the sap being gone?
　　If you will live, lament; if die, be brief,
　　That our swift-winged souls may catch the king's,
　　Or, like obedient subjects, follow him
　　To his new kingdom of perpetual rest.
DUCH. Ah, so much interest have I in thy sorrow
　　As I had title in thy noble husband!
　　I have bewept a worthy husband's death,
　　And lived by looking on his images:[6]
　　But now two mirrors of his princely semblance
　　Are crack'd in pieces by malignant death,

---

3. *Incapable*] i.e., incapable of understanding.
4. *dugs*] teats.
5. *an act*] in a theatrical sense.
6. *his images*] the children who preserve his likeness.

And I for comfort have but one false glass,
Which grieves me when I see my shame in him.
Thou art a widow; yet thou art a mother,
And hast the comfort of thy children left thee:
But death hath snatch'd my husband from mine arms,
And pluck'd two crutches from my feeble limbs,
Edward and Clarence. O, what cause have I,
Thine being but a moiety of my grief,
To overgo thy plaints[7] and drown thy cries!

BOY. Good aunt, you wept not for our father's death,
How can we aid you with our kindred tears?

GIRL. Our fatherless distress was left unmoan'd;
Your widow-dolour likewise be unwept!

Q. ELIZ. Give me no help in lamentation;
I am not barren to bring forth complaints:
All springs reduce[8] their currents to mine eyes,
That I, being govern'd by the watery moon,
May send forth plenteous tears to drown the world!
Oh for my husband, for my dear lord Edward!

CHIL. Oh for our father, for our dear lord Clarence!

DUCH. Alas for both, both mine, Edward and Clarence!

Q. ELIZ. What stay had I but Edward? and he's gone.

CHIL. What stay had we but Clarence? and he's gone.

DUCH. What stays had I but they? and they are gone.

Q. ELIZ. Was never widow had so dear a loss.

CHIL. Were never orphans had so dear a loss.

DUCH. Was never mother had so dear a loss.
Alas, I am the mother of these moans!
Their woes are parcell'd, mine are general.[9]
She for an Edward weeps, and so do I;
I for a Clarence weep, so doth not she:
These babes for Clarence weep, and so do I;
I for an Edward weep, so do not they:
Alas, you three, on me threefold distress'd
Pour all your tears! I am your sorrow's nurse,
And I will pamper it with lamentations.

DOR. Comfort, dear mother: God is much displeased
That you take with unthankfulness his doing:
In common worldly things, 'tis call'd ungrateful,
With dull unwillingness to repay a debt

---

7. *overgo thy plaints*] exceed thy lamentations.
8. *reduce*] bring, lead back.
9. *Their woes ... general*] Their woes are divided up amongst them; each has his own particular woe; my woes cover all theirs.

Which with a bounteous hand was kindly lent;
Much more to be thus opposite with heaven,
For it requires the royal debt it lent you.

RIV.   Madam, bethink you, like a careful mother,
Of the young prince your son: send straight for him;
Let him be crown'd; in him your comfort lives:
Drown desperate sorrow in dead Edward's grave,
And plant your joys in living Edward's throne.

Enter GLOUCESTER, BUCKINGHAM, DERBY, HASTINGS, *and* RATCLIFF

GLOU.   Madam, have comfort: all of us have cause
To wail the dimming of our shining star;
But none can cure their harms by wailing them.
Madam, my mother, I do cry you mercy;
I did not see your grace: humbly on my knee
I crave your blessing.

DUCH.   God bless thee, and put meekness in thy mind,
Love, charity, obedience, and true duty!

GLOU.   [*Aside*] Amen; and make me die a good old man!
That is the butt-end of a mother's blessing:
I marvel why her grace did leave it out.

BUCK.   You cloudy[10] princes and heart-sorrowing peers,
That bear this mutual heavy load of moan,
Now cheer each other in each other's love:
Though we have spent our harvest of this king,
We are to reap the harvest of his son.
The broken rancour[11] of your high-swoln hearts,
But lately splinter'd,[12] knit and join'd together,
Must gently be preserved, cherish'd, and kept:
Me seemeth good, that, with some little train,
Forthwith from Ludlow[13] the young prince[14] be fetch'd
Hither to London, to be crown'd our king.

RIV.   Why with some little train, my Lord of Buckingham?

BUCK.   Marry, my lord, lest, by a multitude,
The new-heal'd wound of malice should break out;
Which would be so much the more dangerous,

---

10. *cloudy*] sullen.
11. *broken rancour*] the rancour that has been broken and destroyed, the cessation of rancour, the reconciliation.
12. *splinter'd*] joined together with splints.
13. *Ludlow*] As Prince of Wales, the young prince, according to established custom, resided at Ludlow Castle on the Welsh border.
14. *the young prince*] the oldest son of Edward IV and Elizabeth Woodville, and soon to be Edward V, king at the age of 13.

By how much the estate[15] is green and yet ungovern'd:
Where every horse bears his commanding rein,
And may direct his course as please himself,
As well the fear of harm as harm apparent,
In my opinion, ought to be prevented.

GLOU.   I hope the king made peace with all of us;
And the compact is firm and true in me.

RIV.   And so in me; and so, I think, in all:
Yet, since it is but green, it should be put
To no apparent likelihood of breach,
Which haply by much company might be urged:
Therefore I say with noble Buckingham,
That it is meet so few should fetch the prince.

HAST.   And so say I.

GLOU.   Then be it so; and go we to determine
Who they shall be that straight shall post to Ludlow.
Madam, and you, my mother, will you go
To give your censures[16] in this weighty business?

Q. ELIZ. ⎤
DUCH. ⎦ With all our hearts.

                [*Exeunt all but* BUCKINGHAM *and* GLOUCESTER.]

BUCK.   My lord, whoever journeys to the prince,
For God's sake, let not us two stay behind;
For, by the way, I'll sort occasion,[17]
As index[18] to the story we late talk'd of,
To part the queen's proud kindred from the king.

GLOU.   My other self, my counsel's consistory,[19]
My oracle, my prophet! — My dear cousin,
I, like a child, will go by thy direction.
Towards Ludlow then, for we'll not stay behind.   [*Exeunt.*]

---

15. *the estate*] the state.
16. *censures*] opinions.
17. *sort occasion*] contrive an opportunity.
18. *index*] prelude, prologue. In early printed books, the index was placed in the preliminary pages.
19. *consistory*] a council or solemn assembly.

SCENE III. *London. A Street.*

Enter two Citizens, *meeting*

FIRST CIT.   Neighbour, well met: whither away so fast?
SEC. CIT.   I promise you, I scarcely know myself:
    Hear you the news abroad?
FIRST CIT.   Ay, that the king is dead.
SEC. CIT.   Bad news, by 'r lady, seldom comes the better:
    I fear, I fear, 'twill prove a troublous world.

Enter another Citizen

THIRD CIT.   Neighbours, God speed!
FIRST CIT.   Give you good morrow, sir.
THIRD CIT.   Doth this news hold of good King Edward's death?
SEC. CIT.   Ay, sir, it is too true; God help the while!
THIRD CIT.   Then, masters, look to see a troublous world.
FIRST CIT.   No, no; by God's good grace his son shall reign.
THIRD CIT.   Woe to that land that's govern'd by a child!
SEC. CIT.   In him there is a hope of government,
    That in his nonage council under him,
    And in his full and ripen'd years himself,
    No doubt, shall then and till then govern well.
FIRST CIT.   So stood the state when Henry the Sixth
    Was crown'd in Paris but at nine months old.
THIRD CIT.   Stood the state so? No, no, good friends, God wot;
    For then this land was famously enrich'd
    With politic grave counsel; then the king
    Had virtuous uncles to protect his grace.
FIRST CIT.   Why, so hath this, both by the father and mother.
THIRD CIT.   Better it were they all came by the father,
    Or by the father there were none at all;
    For emulation now, who shall be nearest,
    Will touch us all too near,[1] if God prevent not.
    O, full of danger is the Duke of Gloucester!
    And the queen's sons and brothers haught[2] and proud:
    And were they to be ruled, and not to rule,
    This sickly land might solace[3] as before.

---

1. *touch . . . near*] injure, hurt, hit.
2. *haught*] a common form of "haughty."
3. *solace*] find comfort, *not* give comfort.

FIRST CIT.   Come, come, we fear the worst; all shall be well.
THIRD CIT.   When clouds appear, wise men put on their cloaks;
     When great leaves fall, the winter is at hand;
     When the sun sets, who doth not look for night?
     Untimely storms make men expect a dearth.
     All may be well; but, if God sort[4] it so,
     'Tis more than we deserve, or I expect.
SEC. CIT.   Truly, the souls of men are full of dread:
     Ye cannot reason almost with a man
     That looks not heavily and full of fear.
THIRD CIT.   Before the times of change, still is it so:
     By a divine instinct men's minds mistrust
     Ensuing dangers; as, by proof, we see
     The waters swell before a boisterous storm.
     But leave it all to God. Whither away?
SEC. CIT.   Marry, we were sent for to the justices.
THIRD CIT.   And so was I: I'll bear you company.   [*Exeunt.*]

SCENE IV. *London. The Palace.*

Enter the ARCHBISHOP OF YORK, *the young* DUKE OF YORK, QUEEN
ELIZABETH, *and the* DUCHESS OF YORK

ARCH.   Last night, I hear, they lay at Northampton;
     At Stony-Stratford will they be to-night:
     To-morrow, or next day, they will be here.
DUCH.   I long with all my heart to see the prince:
     I hope he is much grown since last I saw him.
Q. ELIZ.   But I hear, no; they say my son of York
     Hath almost overta'en him in his growth.
YORK.   Ay, mother; but I would not have it so.
DUCH.   Why, my young cousin, it is good to grow.
YORK.   Grandam, one night, as we did sit at supper,
     My uncle Rivers talk'd how I did grow
     More than my brother: "Ay," quoth my uncle Gloucester,
     "Small herbs have grace, great weeds do grow apace:"
     And since, methinks, I would not grow so fast,

---

4. *sort*] ordain.

Because sweet flowers are slow and weeds make haste.
DUCH.   Good faith, good faith, the saying did not hold
    In him that did object the same to thee:
    He was the wretched'st thing when he was young,
    So long a-growing and so leisurely,
    That, if this rule were true, he should be gracious.
ARCH.   Why, madam, so, no doubt, he is.
DUCH.   I hope so too; but yet let mothers doubt.
YORK.   Now, by my troth, if I had been remember'd,
    I could have given my uncle's grace a flout,
    To touch his growth nearer[1] than he touch'd mine.
DUCH.   How, my pretty York? I pray thee, let me hear it.
YORK.   Marry, they say my uncle grew so fast
    That he could gnaw a crust at two hours old:
    'Twas full two years ere I could get a tooth.
    Grandam, this would have been a biting jest.
DUCH.   I pray thee, pretty York, who told thee this?
YORK.   Grandam, his nurse.
DUCH.   His nurse! why, she was dead ere thou wert born.
YORK.   If 'twere not she, I cannot tell who told me.
Q. ELIZ.   A parlous boy:[2] go to, you are too shrewd.
ARCH.   Good madam, be not angry with the child.
Q. ELIZ.   Pitchers have ears.

Enter a Messenger

ARCH.   Here comes a messenger. What news?
MESS.   Such news, my lord, as grieves me to unfold.
Q. ELIZ.   How fares the prince?
MESS.   Well, madam, and in health.
DUCH.   What is thy news then?
MESS.   Lord Rivers and Lord Grey are sent to Pomfret,
    With them Sir Thomas Vaughan, prisoners.
DUCH.   Who hath committed them?
MESS.   The mighty dukes,
    Gloucester and Buckingham.
Q. ELIZ.   For what offence?
MESS.   The sum of all I can, I have disclosed;
    Why or for what these nobles were committed
    Is all unknown to me, my gracious lady.
Q. ELIZ.   Ay me, I see the downfall of our house!
    The tiger now hath seized the gentle hind;
    Insulting tyranny begins to jet

---

1. *touch ... nearer*] hit, in the slang sense of "get at."
2. *parlous boy*] an *enfant terrible*.

Upon the innocent and aweless throne:[3]
Welcome, destruction, death, and massacre!
I see, as in a map, the end of all.

DUCH. Accursed and unquiet wrangling days,
How many of you have mine eyes beheld!
My husband lost his life to get the crown;
And often up and down my sons were toss'd,
For me to joy and weep their gain and loss:
And being seated, and domestic broils
Clean over-blown, themselves, the conquerors,
Make war upon themselves; blood against blood,
Self against self: O, preposterous
And frantic outrage, end thy damned spleen;
Or let me die, to look on death no more!

Q. ELIZ. Come, come, my boy; we will to sanctuary.[4]
Madam, farewell.

DUCH.   I'll go along with you.

Q. ELIZ. You have no cause.

ARCH.   My gracious lady, go;
And thither bear your treasure and your goods.
For my part, I'll resign unto your grace
The seal[5] I keep: and so betide to me
As well I tender you and all of yours!
Come, I'll conduct you to the sanctuary.   [*Exeunt.*]

ACT III.

SCENE I. *London. A Street.*

The trumpets sound. Enter the young PRINCE, *the Dukes of* GLOUCES-
TER *and* BUCKINGHAM, CARDINAL BOURCHIER, CATESBY, *and others*

BUCK. Welcome, sweet prince, to London, to your chamber.[1]

---

3. *to jet . . . throne*] to encroach upon a throne filled by an innocent child, and one
inspiring no fear.
4. *sanctuary*] the precincts of Westminster Abbey, where no arrests of suspected persons
were permitted.
5. *The seal*] the Great Seal of England.

---

1. *chamber*] London, the capital city of the kingdom, was formally called "camera regis"
(king's chamber).

GLOU.   Welcome, dear cousin, my thoughts' sovereign:
   The weary way hath made you melancholy.
PRINCE.   No, uncle; but our crosses on the way
   Have made it tedious, wearisome, and heavy:
   I want more uncles here to welcome me.
GLOU.   Sweet prince, the untainted virtue of your years
   Hath not yet dived into the world's deceit:
   Nor more can you distinguish of a man
   Than of his outward show; which, God he knows,
   Seldom or never jumpeth with the heart.
   Those uncles which you want were dangerous;
   Your grace attended to their sugar'd words,
   But look'd not on the poison of their hearts:
   God keep you from them, and from such false friends!
PRINCE.   God keep me from false friends! but they were none.
GLOU.   My lord, the mayor of London comes to greet you.

Enter the Lord Mayor, *and his train*

MAY.   God bless your grace with health and happy days!
PRINCE.   I thank you, good my lord; and thank you all.
   I thought my mother and my brother York
   Would long ere this have met us on the way:
   Fie, what a slug is Hastings, that he comes not
   To tell us whether they will come or no!

Enter LORD HASTINGS

BUCK.   And, in good time here comes the sweating lord.
PRINCE.   Welcome, my lord: what, will our mother come?
HAST.   On what occasion, God he knows, not I,
   The queen your mother and your brother York
   Have taken sanctuary: the tender prince
   Would fain have come with me to meet your grace,
   But by his mother was perforce withheld.
BUCK.   Fie, what an indirect and peevish course
   Is this of hers! Lord cardinal, will your grace
   Persuade the queen to send the Duke of York
   Unto his princely brother presently?
   If she deny, Lord Hastings, go with him,
   And from her jealous arms pluck him perforce.
CARD.   My Lord of Buckingham, if my weak oratory
   Can from his mother win the Duke of York,
   Anon expect him here; but if she be obdurate
   To mild entreaties, God in heaven forbid

    We should infringe the holy privilege
    Of blessed sanctuary! not for all this land
    Would I be guilty of so deep a sin.
BUCK.   You are too senseless-obstinate,[2] my lord,
    Too ceremonious and traditional:
    Weigh it but with the grossness of this age,[3]
    You break not sanctuary in seizing him.
    The benefit thereof is always granted
    To those whose dealings have deserved the place,
    And those who have the wit to claim the place:
    This prince hath neither claim'd it nor deserved it;
    And therefore, in mine opinion, cannot have it:
    Then, taking him from thence that is not there,
    You break no privilege nor charter there.
    Oft have I heard of sanctuary men;
    But sanctuary children ne'er till now.
CARD.   My lord, you shall o'er-rule my mind for once.
    Come on, Lord Hastings, will you go with me?
HAST.   I go, my lord.
PRINCE.   Good lords, make all the speedy haste you may.
                         [*Exeunt* CARDINAL *and* HASTINGS.]
    Say, uncle Gloucester, if our brother come,
    Where shall we sojourn till our coronation?
GLOU.   Where it seems best unto your royal self.
    If I may counsel you, some day or two
    Your highness shall repose you at the Tower:
    Then where you please, and shall be thought most fit
    For your best health and recreation.
PRINCE.   I do not like the Tower, of any place.
    Did Julius Cæsar build that place, my lord?
BUCK.   He did, my gracious lord, begin that place;
    Which, since, succeeding ages have re-edified.
PRINCE.   Is it upon record, or else reported
    Successively from age to age, he built it?
BUCK.   Upon record, my gracious lord.
PRINCE.   But say, my lord, it were not register'd,
    Methinks the truth should live from age to age,
    As 'twere retail'd[4] to all posterity,
    Even to the general all-ending day.
GLOU.   [*Aside*] So wise so young, they say, do never live long.

---

   2. *senseless-obstinate*] unreasonable in obstinacy.
   3. *Weigh . . . age*] Consider it in the light of the unlicensed temper of the times (which
      calls for high-handed action).
   4. *retail'd*] recounted, rehearsed.

PRINCE.   What say you, uncle?
GLOU.   I say, without characters,[5] fame lives long.
    [*Aside*] Thus, like the formal vice, Iniquity,[6]
    I moralize two meanings in one word.
PRINCE.   That Julius Cæsar was a famous man;
    With what his valour did enrich his wit,
    His wit set down to make his valour live:
    Death makes no conquest of this conqueror;
    For now he lives in fame, though not in life.
    I'll tell you what, my cousin Buckingham, —
BUCK.   What, my gracious lord?
PRINCE.   An if I live until I be a man,
    I'll win our ancient right in France again,
    Or die a soldier, as I lived a king.
GLOU.   [*Aside*] Short summers lightly[7] have a forward spring.

Enter young YORK, HASTINGS, *and the* CARDINAL

BUCK.   Now, in good time, here comes the Duke of York.
PRINCE.   Richard of York! how fares our loving brother?
YORK.   Well, my dread lord; so must I call you now.
PRINCE.   Ay, brother, to our grief, as it is yours:
    Too late[8] he died that might have kept that title,
    Which by his death hath lost much majesty.
GLOU.   How fares our cousin, noble Lord of York?
YORK.   I thank you, gentle uncle. O, my lord,
    You said that idle weeds are fast in growth:
    The prince my brother hath outgrown me far.
GLOU.   He hath, my lord.
YORK.   And therefore is he idle?
GLOU.   O, my fair cousin, I must not say so.
YORK.   Then he is more beholding to you than I.
GLOU.   He may command me as my sovereign;
    But you have power in me as in a kinsman.
YORK.   I pray you, uncle, give me this dagger.
GLOU.   My dagger, little cousin? with all my heart.
PRINCE.   A beggar, brother?

---

5. *without characters*] without the help of letters or inscriptions.
6. *Thus . . . Iniquity*] In the old Morality plays the leading character in attendance on the
    Devil bore the conventional ("formal") designation of "The Vice," and indulged in
    persistent word-play. The character was occasionally known by the more specific name
    of "Iniquity" or "Hypocrisy" or some other sin.
7. *lightly*] commonly; a rare usage deduced from the meaning of "easily" or "readily"
    which often attaches to the word.
8. *late*] lately, recently.

YORK.   Of my kind uncle, that I know will give;
 And being but a toy, which is no grief to give.
GLOU.   A greater gift than that I'll give my cousin.
YORK.   A greater gift! O, that's the sword to it.[9]
GLOU.   Ay, gentle cousin, were it light enough.
YORK.   O, then, I see, you will part but with light gifts;
 In weightier things you'll say a beggar nay.
GLOU.   It is too heavy for your grace to wear.
YORK.   I weigh it lightly,[10] were it heavier.
GLOU.   What, would you have my weapon, little lord?
YORK.   I would, that I might thank you as you call me.
GLOU.   How?
YORK.   Little.
PRINCE.   My Lord of York will still be cross[11] in talk:
 Uncle, your grace knows how to bear with him.
YORK.   You mean, to bear me, not to bear with me:
 Uncle, my brother mocks both you and me;
 Because that I am little, like an ape,
 He thinks that you should bear me on your shoulders.
BUCK.   With what a sharp-provided wit he reasons!
 To mitigate the scorn he gives his uncle,
 He prettily and aptly taunts himself:
 So cunning and so young is wonderful.
GLOU.   My lord, will 't please you pass along?
 Myself and my good cousin Buckingham
 Will to your mother, to entreat of her
 To meet you at the Tower and welcome you.
YORK.   What, will you go unto the Tower, my lord?
PRINCE.   My lord protector needs will have it so.
YORK.   I shall not sleep in quiet at the Tower.
GLOU.   Why, what should you fear?
YORK.   Marry, my uncle Clarence' angry ghost:
 My grandam told me he was murder'd there.
PRINCE.   I fear no uncles dead.
GLOU.   Nor none that live, I hope.
PRINCE.   An if they live, I hope I need not fear.
 But come, my lord; and with a heavy heart,
 Thinking on them, go I unto the Tower.
 [A *Sennet.*[12] *Exeunt all but* GLOUCESTER, BUCKINGHAM *and*
                                                          CATESBY.

---

9. *the sword to it*] The belt, which carried the dagger, bore a sword in addition.
10. *I . . . lightly*] I should mind very little.
11. *cross*] at cross purposes, malapert.
12. *A Sennet*] a flourish on a trumpet, marking the entrance or exit of a procession.

BUCK.   Think you, my lord, this little prating York
    Was not incensed by his subtle mother
    To taunt and scorn you thus opprobriously?
GLOU.   No doubt, no doubt: O, 'tis a parlous boy;
    Bold, quick, ingenious, forward, capable:
    He is all the mother's, from the top to toe.
BUCK.   Well, let them rest. Come hither, Catesby.
    Thou art sworn as deeply to effect what we intend,
    As closely to conceal what we impart:
    Thou know'st our reasons urged upon the way;
    What think'st thou? is it not an easy matter
    To make William Lord Hastings of our mind,
    For the instalment of this noble duke
    In the seat royal of this famous isle?
CATE.   He for his father's sake so loves the prince,
    That he will not be won to aught against him.
BUCK.   What think'st thou then of Stanley? what will he?
CATE.   He will do all in all as Hastings doth.
BUCK.   Well, then, no more but this: go, gentle Catesby,
    And, as it were far off, sound thou Lord Hastings,
    How he doth stand affected[13] to our purpose;
    And summon him to-morrow to the Tower,
    To sit about the coronation.
    If thou dost find him tractable to us,
    Encourage him, and show him all our reasons:
    If he be leaden, icy-cold, unwilling,
    Be thou so too; and so break off your talk,
    And give us notice of his inclination:
    For we to-morrow hold divided councils,[14]
    Wherein thyself shalt highly be employ'd.
GLOU.   Commend me to Lord William: tell him, Catesby,
    His ancient knot of dangerous adversaries
    To-morrow are let blood[15] at Pomfret-castle;
    And bid my friend, for joy of this good news,
    Give Mistress Shore[16] one gentle kiss the more.
BUCK.   Good Catesby, go, effect this business soundly.
CATE.   My good lords both, with all the heed I may.
GLOU.   Shall we hear from you, Catesby, ere we sleep?
CATE.   You shall, my lord.

---

13. *stand affected*] feel disposed.
14. *divided councils*] two separate councils, one of Gloucester's supporters and the other of the young prince's.
15. *let blood*] killed, executed.
16. *Mistress Shore*] On Edward IV's death, according to Holinshed's *Chronicles*, Hastings made Jane Shore his mistress.

GLOU. At Crosby Place, there shall you find us both.
                                                    [*Exit* CATESBY.]
BUCK. Now, my lord, what shall we do, if we perceive
       Lord Hastings will not yield to our complots?[17]
GLOU. Chop off his head, man; somewhat we will do:
       And, look, when I am king, claim thou of me
       The earldom of Hereford, and the moveables[18]
       Whereof the king my brother stood possess'd.
BUCK. I'll claim that promise at your grace's hands.
GLOU. And look to have it yielded with all willingness.
       Come, let us sup betimes, that afterwards
       We may digest our complots in some form.   [*Exeunt.*]

SCENE II. *Before Lord Hastings' House.*

Enter a Messenger

MESS. What, ho! my lord
HAST. [*Within*] Who knocks at the door?
MESS. A messenger from the Lord Stanley.

Enter LORD HASTINGS

HAST. What is 't o'clock?
MESS. Upon the stroke of four.
HAST. Cannot thy master sleep these tedious nights?
MESS. So it should seem by that I have to say.
       First, he commends him to your noble lordship.
HAST. And then?
MESS. And then he sends you word
       He dreamt to-night the boar had razed his helm:[1]
       Besides, he says there are two councils held;
       And that may be determined at the one
       Which may make you and him to rue at the other.
       Therefore he sends to know your lordship's pleasure,
       If presently you will take horse with him,
       And with all speed post with him toward the north,
       To shun the danger that his soul divines.

---

17. *complots*] conspiracies.
18. *moveables*] any property, such as furniture, not fixed in place.

1. *razed his helm*] tore off his head. The boar refers to Gloucester.

HAST.   Go, fellow, go, return unto thy lord;
   Bid him not fear the separated councils:
   His honour and myself are at the one,
   And at the other is my servant Catesby;
   Where nothing can proceed that toucheth[2] us,
   Whereof I shall not have intelligence.
   Tell him his fears are shallow, wanting instance:[3]
   And for his dreams, I wonder he is so fond
   To trust the mockery of unquiet slumbers:
   To fly the boar before the boar pursues,
   Were to incense the boar to follow us,
   And make pursuit where he did mean no chase.
   Go, bid thy master rise and come to me;
   And we will both together to the Tower,
   Where, he shall see, the boar will use us kindly.
MESS.   My gracious lord, I'll tell him what you say.   [*Exit.*]

Enter CATESBY

CATE.   Many good morrows to my noble lord!
HAST.   Good morrow, Catesby; you are early stirring:
   What news, what news, in this our tottering state?
CATE.   It is a reeling world indeed, my lord;
   And I believe 'twill never stand upright
   Till Richard wear the garland of the realm.
HAST.   How! wear the garland! dost thou mean the crown?
CATE.   Ay, my good lord.
HAST.   I'll have this crown of mine cut from my shoulders,
   Ere I will see the crown so foul misplaced.
   But canst thou guess that he doth aim at it?
CATE.   Ay, on my life, and hopes to find you forward
   Upon his party for the gain thereof:
   And thereupon he sends you this good news,
   That this same very day your enemies,
   The kindred of the queen, must die at Pomfret.
HAST.   Indeed, I am no mourner for that news,
   Because they have been still[4] mine enemies:
   But, that I'll give my voice on Richard's side,
   To bar my master's heirs in true descent,
   God knows I will not do it, to the death.
CATE.   God keep your lordship in that gracious mind!

---

2. *toucheth*] injureth.
3. *wanting instance*] without example or proof.
4. *still*] always.

HAST. But I shall laugh at this a twelve-month hence,
That they who brought me in my master's hate,
I live to look upon their tragedy.
I tell thee, Catesby, —
CATE. What, my lord?
HAST. Ere a fortnight make me elder,
I'll send some packing that yet think not on it.
CATE. 'Tis a vile thing to die, my gracious lord,
When men are unprepared and look not for it.
HAST. O monstrous, monstrous! and so falls it out
With Rivers, Vaughan, Grey: and so 'twill do
With some men else, who think themselves as safe
As thou and I; who, as thou know'st, are dear
To princely Richard and to Buckingham.
CATE. The princes both make high account of you;
[*Aside*] For they account his head upon the bridge.[5]
HAST. I know they do; and I have well deserved it.

Enter LORD STANLEY

Come on, come on; where is your boar-spear, man?
Fear you the boar, and go so unprovided?
STAN. My lord, good morrow; good morrow, Catesby:
You may jest on, but, by the holy rood,[6]
I do not like these several councils, I.
HAST. My lord,
I hold my life as dear as you do yours;
And never in my life, I do protest,
Was it more precious to me than 'tis now:
Think you, but that I know our state secure,
I would be so triumphant as I am?
STAN. The lords at Pomfret, when they rode from London,
Were jocund and supposed their state was sure,
And they indeed had no cause to mistrust;
But yet, you see, how soon the day o'ercast.
This sudden stab of rancour I misdoubt:
Pray God, I say, I prove a needless coward!
What, shall we toward the Tower? the day is spent.
HAST. Come, come, have with you.[7] Wot[8] you what, my lord?
To-day the lords you talk of are beheaded.

---

5. *they account . . . bridge*] It was customary to put the heads of those who were executed
for high treason on a pole fixed to the roof of a tower on London Bridge.
6. *rood*] the cross (on which Christ died).
7. *have with you*] I will go along with you.
8. *Wot*] know.

STAN.   They, for their truth, might better wear their heads,
    Than some that have accused them wear their hats.
    But come, my lord, let us away.

Enter a Pursuivant[9]

HAST.   Go on before; I'll talk with this good fellow.

                            [Exeunt STANLEY *and* CATESBY.]
    How now, sirrah! how goes the world with thee?
PURS.   The better that your lordship please to ask.
HAST.   I tell thee, man, 'tis better with me now,
    Than when I met thee last where now we meet:
    Then was I going prisoner to the Tower,
    By the suggestion of the queen's allies;
    But now, I tell thee — keep it to thyself —
    This day those enemies are put to death,
    And I in better state than e'er I was.
PURS.   God hold it,[10] to your honour's good content!
HAST.   Gramercy,[11] fellow: there, drink that for me.

                               [Throws him his purse.]
PURS.   God save your lordship.
                                    [Exit.]

Enter a Priest

PRIEST.   Well met, my lord; I am glad to see your honour.
HAST.   I thank thee, good Sir John,[12] with all my heart.
    I am in your debt for your last exercise:[13]
    Come the next Sabbath, and I will content you.

                              [He whispers in his ear.]

Enter BUCKINGHAM

BUCK.   What, talking with a priest, lord chamberlain?
    Your friends at Pomfret, they do need the priest;
    Your honour hath no shriving work[14] in hand.
HAST.   Good faith, and when I met this holy man,
    Those men you talk of came into my mind.
    What, go you toward the Tower?
BUCK.   I do, my lord; but long I shall not stay:
    I shall return before your lordship thence.

---

  9. *Pursuivant*] Properly, an attendant on a herald, an officer of the college of arms, but the word was more often used, as here, for any messenger of a court of justice. It is also found in the general sense of messenger.

10. *God hold it*] God continue your good fortune.

11. *Gramercy*] great thanks.

12. *good Sir John*] "Sir" was a courtesy title given to all clergymen.

13. *exercise*] religious exhortation, sermon.

14. *shriving work*] confession.

HAST.   'Tis like enough, for I stay dinner there.
BUCK.   [*Aside*] And supper too, although thou know'st it not.
    Come, will you go?
HAST.   I'll wait upon your lordship.   [*Exeunt.*] ·

SCENE III. *Pomfret Castle.*

Enter SIR RICHARD RATCLIFF, *with halberds, carrying* RIVERS, GREY,
and VAUGHAN *to death*

RAT.   Come, bring forth the prisoners.
RIV.   Sir Richard Ratcliff, let me tell thee this:
    To-day shalt thou behold a subject die
    For truth, for duty, and for loyalty.
GREY.   God keep the prince from all the pack of you!
    A knot you are of damned blood-suckers.
VAUG.   You live that shall cry woe for this hereafter.
RAT.   Dispatch; the limit of your lives is out.
RIV.   O Pomfret, Pomfret! O thou bloody prison;
    Fatal and ominous to noble peers!
    Within the guilty closure[1] of thy walls
    Richard the second here was hack'd to death;
    And, for more slander to thy dismal seat,
    We give thee up our guiltless blood to drink.
GREY.   Now Margaret's curse is fall'n upon our heads,
    For standing by when Richard stabb'd her son.
RIV.   Then cursed she Hastings, then cursed she Buckingham,
    Then cursed she Richard. O, remember, God,
    To hear her prayers for them, as now for us!
    And for my sister and her princely sons,
    Be satisfied, dear God, with our true blood,
    Which, as thou know'st, unjustly must be spilt.
RAT.   Make haste; the hour of death is expiate.[2]
RIV.   Come, Grey, come, Vaughan, let us all embrace:
    And take our leave, until we meet in heaven.   [*Exeunt.*]

---

1. *closure*] enclosure, compass.
2. *expiate*] brought to a close, finished.

SCENE IV. *The Tower of London.*

Enter BUCKINGHAM, DERBY, HASTINGS, *the* BISHOP OF ELY, RATCLIFF, LOVEL, *with others, and take their seats at a table*

HAST.   My lords, at once: the cause why we are met
     Is, to determine of the coronation.
     In God's name, speak: when is the royal day?
BUCK.   Are all things fitting for that royal time?
DER.   It is, and wants but nomination.[1]
ELY.   To-morrow then I judge a happy day.
BUCK.   Who knows the lord protector's mind herein?
     Who is most inward[2] with the noble duke?
ELY.   Your grace, we think, should soonest know his mind.
BUCK.   Who, I, my lord! We know each other's faces,
     But for our hearts, he knows no more of mine
     Than I of yours;
     Nor I no more of his, than you of mine.
     Lord Hastings, you and he are near in love.
HAST.   I thank his grace, I know he loves me well;
     But, for his purpose in the coronation,
     I have not sounded him, nor he deliver'd
     His gracious pleasure any way therein:
     But you, my noble lords, may name the time;
     And in the duke's behalf I'll give my voice,
     Which, I presume, he'll take in gentle part.

Enter GLOUCESTER

ELY.   Now in good time, here comes the duke himself.
GLOU.   My noble lords and cousins all, good morrow.
     I have been long a sleeper; but, I hope,
     My absence doth neglect no great designs,
     Which by my presence might have been concluded.
BUCK.   Had not you come upon your cue, my lord,
     William Lord Hastings had pronounced your part, —
     I mean, your voice, — for crowning of the king.
GLOU.   Than my Lord Hastings no man might be bolder;
     His lordship knows me well, and loves me well.
HAST.   I thank your grace.

---

1. *nomination*] the naming of the day.
2. *inward*] intimate.

GLOU.   My Lord of Ely!
ELY.   My lord?
GLOU.   When I was last in Holborn,
    I saw good strawberries in your garden there:
    I do beseech you send for some of them.
ELY.   Marry, and will, my lord, with all my heart.   [*Exit.*]
GLOU.   Cousin of Buckingham, a word with you.
                                    [*Drawing him aside.*]
    Catesby hath sounded Hastings in our business,
    And finds the testy gentleman so hot,
    As he will lose his head ere give consent
    His master's son, as worshipful he terms it,
    Shall lose the royalty of England's throne.
BUCK.   Withdraw you hence, my lord, I'll follow you.
                    [*Exit* GLOUCESTER, BUCKINGHAM *following.*]
DER.   We have not yet set down this day of triumph.
    To-morrow, in mine opinion, is too sudden;
    For I myself am not so well provided
    As else I would be, were the day prolong'd.

Re-enter BISHOP OF ELY

ELY.   Where is my lord protector? I have sent for these strawberries.
HAST.   His grace looks cheerfully and smooth to-day;
    There's some conceit or other likes him[3] well,
    When he doth bid good morrow with such a spirit.
    I think there's never a man in Christendom
    That can less hide his love or hate than he;
    For by his face straight shall you know his heart.
DER.   What of his heart perceive you in his face
    By any likelihood he show'd to-day?
HAST.   Marry, that with no man here he is offended;
    For, were he, he had shown it in his looks.
DER.   I pray God he be not, I say.

Re-enter GLOUCESTER *and* BUCKINGHAM

GLOU.   I pray you all, tell me what they deserve
    That do conspire my death with devilish plots
    Of damned witchcraft, and that have prevail'd
    Upon my body with their hellish charms?
HAST.   The tender love I bear your grace, my lord,
    Makes me most forward in this noble presence

---

3. *some conceit . . . likes him*] Some thought or other pleases him.

       To doom the offenders, whatsoever they be:
       I say, my lord, they have deserved death.
GLOU.   Then be your eyes the witness of this ill:
       See how I am bewitch'd; behold, mine arm
       Is like a blasted sapling, withered up:
       And this is Edward's wife, that monstrous witch,
       Consorted with that harlot strumpet Shore,
       That by their witchcraft thus have marked me.
HAST.   If they have done this thing, my gracious lord, —
GLOU.   If! thou protector of this damned strumpet,
       Tellest thou me of "ifs"? Thou art a traitor:
       Off with his head! Now, by Saint Paul I swear,
       I will not dine until I see the same.
       Lovel and Ratcliff, look that it be done:
       The rest that love me, rise and follow me.
               [*Exeunt all but* HASTINGS, RATCLIFF *and* LOVEL.]
HAST.   Woe, woe for England! not a whit for me;
       For I, too fond, might have prevented this.
       Stanley did dream the boar did raze his helm;
       But I disdain'd it, and did scorn to fly:
       Three times to-day my foot-cloth horse did stumble,[4]
       And startled, when he look'd upon the Tower,
       As loath to bear me to the slaughter-house.
       O, now I want the priest that spake to me:
       I now repent I told the pursuivant,
       As 'twere triumphing at mine enemies,
       How they at Pomfret bloodily were butcher'd,
       And I myself secure in grace and favour.
       O Margaret, Margaret, now thy heavy curse
       Is lighted on poor Hastings' wretched head!
RAT.   Dispatch, my lord; the duke would be at dinner:
       Make a short shrift;[5] he longs to see your head.
HAST.   O momentary grace of mortal men,
       Which we more hunt for than the grace of God!
       Who builds his hopes in air of your fair looks,
       Lives like a drunken sailor on a mast,
       Ready, with every nod, to tumble down
       Into the fatal bowels of the deep.
LOV.   Come, come, dispatch; 'tis bootless to exclaim.
HAST. O bloody Richard! miserable England!
       I prophesy the fearfull'st time to thee

---

4. *foot-cloth . . . stumble*] horse adorned with a rich cloth reaching nearly to the ground on
   each side. It was considered an ill omen if one's horse stumbled.
5. *shrift*] confession.

That ever wretched age hath look'd upon.
Come, lead me to the block; bear him my head:
They smile at me that shortly shall be dead.   [*Exeunt.*]

SCENE V. *The Tower-Walls.*

Enter GLOUCESTER *and* BUCKINGHAM, *in rotten*[1] *armour, marvellous ill-favoured*

GLOU.   Come, cousin, canst thou quake, and change thy colour,
      Murder thy breath in middle of a word,
      And then begin again, and stop again,
      As if thou wert distraught and mad with terror?
BUCK.   Tut, I can counterfeit the deep tragedian,
      Speak and look back, and pry on every side,
      Tremble and start at wagging of a straw,
      Intending[2] deep suspicion: ghastly looks
      Are at my service, like enforced smiles;
      And both are ready in their offices,
      At any time, to grace my stratagems.
      But what, is Catesby gone?
GLOU.   He is; and, see, he brings the mayor along.

Enter the Mayor *and* CATESBY

BUCK.   Lord mayor,—
GLOU.   Look to the drawbridge there!
BUCK.   Hark! a drum.
GLOU.   Catesby, o'erlook the walls.
BUCK.   Lord mayor, the reason we have sent—
GLOU.   Look back, defend thee, here are enemies.
BUCK.   God and our innocency defend and guard us!
GLOU.   Be patient, they are friends, Ratcliff and Lovel.

Enter LOVEL *and* RATCLIFF, *with* HASTINGS' *head*

LOV.   Here is the head of that ignoble traitor,
      The dangerous and unsuspected Hastings.
GLOU.   So dear I loved the man, that I must weep.
      I took him for the plainest harmless creature

---

1. *rotten*] rusty.
2. *Intending*] pretending.

That breathed upon this earth a Christian;
Made him my book, wherein my soul recorded
The history of all her secret thoughts:
So smooth he daub'd his vice with show of virtue
That, his apparent open guilt omitted,[3]
I mean, his conversation[4] with Shore's wife,
He lived from all attainder of suspect.[5]

BUCK.   Well, well, he was the covert'st shelter'd traitor
That ever lived.
Would you imagine, or almost believe,
Were 't not that, by great preservation,
We live to tell it you, the subtle traitor
This day had plotted, in the council-house
To murder me and my good Lord of Gloucester?

MAY.   What, had he so?

GLOU.   What, think you we are Turks or infidels?
Or that we would, against the form of law,
Proceed thus rashly to the villain's death,
But that the extreme peril of the case,
The peace of England and our persons' safety,
Enforced us to this execution?

MAY.   Now, fair befall you![6] he deserved his death;
And you, my good lords both, have well proceeded,
To warn false traitors from the like attempts.
I never look'd for better at his hands,
After he once fell in with Mistress Shore.

GLOU.   Yet had not we determined he should die,
Until your lordship came to see his death;
Which now the loving haste of these our friends,
Somewhat against our meaning, have prevented:
Because, my lord, we would have had you heard
The traitor speak and timorously confess
The manner and the purpose of his treason;
That you might well have signified the same
Unto the citizens, who haply may
Misconstrue us in him and wail his death.

MAY.   But, my good lord, your grace's word shall serve,
As well as I had seen and heard him speak:
And doubt you not, right noble princes both,
But I'll acquaint our duteous citizens

---

3. *apparent . . . omitted*] manifest . . . excepted.
4. *conversation*] criminal conversation.
5. *from all attainder of suspect*] free from all taint of suspicion.
6. *fair befall you!*] Good fortune attend you!

With all your just proceedings in this cause.
GLOU.   And to that end we wish'd your lordship here,
To avoid the carping censures of the world.
BUCK.   But since you come too late of our intents,[7]
Yet witness what you hear we did intend:
And so, my good lord mayor, we bid farewell.   [*Exit* Mayor.]
GLOU.   Go, after, after, cousin Buckingham.
The mayor towards Guildhall hies him in all post:
There, at your meet'st advantage[8] of the time,
Infer[9] the bastardy of Edward's children:
Tell them how Edward put to death a citizen,
Only for saying he would make his son
Heir to the crown, meaning indeed his house,
Which, by the sign thereof, was termed so.[10]
Moreover, urge his hateful luxury
And bestial appetite in change of lust;[11]
Which stretched to their servants, daughters, wives,
Even where his lustful eye or savage heart,
Without control, listed to make his prey.
Nay, for a need, thus far come near my person:
Tell them, when that my mother went with child
Of that unsatiate Edward, noble York,
My princely father, then had wars in France;
And, by just computation of the time,
Found that the issue was not his begot;
Which well appeared in his lineaments,
Being nothing like the noble duke my father:
But touch this sparingly, as 'twere far off;
Because you know, my lord, my mother lives.
BUCK.   Fear not, my lord, I'll play the orator,
As if the golden fee for which I plead
Were for myself: and so, my lord, adieu.
GLOU.   If you thrive well, bring them to Baynard's Castle;[12]

---

7. *too late of our intents*] too late for our plans or purposes.
8. *meet'st advantage*] fittest opportunity.
9. *Infer*] allege, suggest.
10. *a citizen . . . termed so*] The historian Edward Hall (c. 1498–1547) describes the execution by Edward IV's order, on the grounds given in these lines, of a citizen named Burdet, "who dwelt in Cheap Side, *at the signe of the Croune*, . . . over against Soper Lane."
11. *in change of lust*] driven by a constant desire for new mistresses.
12. *Baynard's Castle*] a palatial residence in the city of London, on the north bank of the Thames, not far from the south side of St. Paul's Cathedral. It had been recently occupied by Gloucester's father, Richard, Duke of York.

Where you shall find me well accompanied
With reverend fathers and well-learned bishops.
BUCK.   I go; and towards three or four o'clock
Look for the news that the Guildhall affords.   [*Exit.*]
GLOU.   Go, Lovel, with all speed to Doctor Shaw;
   [*To Cate.*] Go thou to Friar Penker;[13] bid them both
Meet me within this hour at Baynard's Castle.
                              [*Exeunt all but* GLOUCESTER.]
Now will I in, to take some privy order,
To draw the brats of Clarence out of sight;
And to give notice, that no manner of person
At any time have recourse unto the princes.   [*Exit.*]

SCENE VI. *The Same. A Street.*

Enter a Scrivener, *with a paper in his hand*

SCRIV.   This is the indictment of the good Lord Hastings;
Which in a set hand fairly is engross'd,
That it may be this day read o'er in Paul's.
And mark how well the sequel hangs together:
Eleven hours I spent to write it over,
For yesternight by Catesby was it brought me;
The precedent[1] was full as long a-doing:
And yet within these five hours lived Lord Hastings,
Untainted, unexamined, free, at liberty.
Here's a good world the while! Why, who's so gross,
That seeth not this palpable device?
Yet who's so blind, but says he sees it not?
Bad is the world; and all will come to nought,
When such bad dealing must be seen in thought.[2]   [*Exit.*]

---

13. *Doctor Shaw ... Friar Penker*] well-known preachers of the day. Doctor Shaw was
   brother of the Lord Mayor.

---

1. *precedent*] first draft.
2. *in thought*] in silence, unvoiced.

SCENE VII. *Baynard's Castle.*

Enter GLOUCESTER *and* BUCKINGHAM, *at several doors*

GLOU.   How now, my lord, what say the citizens?
BUCK.   Now, by the holy mother of our Lord,
    The citizens are mum, and speak not a word.
GLOU.   Touch'd you the bastardy of Edward's children?
BUCK.   I did; with his contract with Lady Lucy,
    And his contract by deputy in France;[1]
    The insatiate greediness of his desires,
    And his enforcement of the city wives;
    His tyranny for trifles; his own bastardy,
    As being got, your father then in France,
    And his resemblance, being not like the duke:
    Withal I did infer your lineaments,
    Being the right idea of your father,
    Both in your form and nobleness of mind;
    Laid open all your victories in Scotland,
    Your discipline in war, wisdom in peace,
    Your bounty, virtue, fair humility;
    Indeed left nothing fitting for the purpose
    Untouch'd or slightly handled in discourse:
    And when mine oratory grew to an end,
    I bid them that did love their country's good
    Cry "God save Richard, England's royal king!"
GLOU.   Ah! and did they so?
BUCK.   No, so God help me, they spake not a word;
    But, like dumb statuës[2] or breathing stones,
    Gazed each on other, and look'd deadly pale.
    Which when I saw, I reprehended them;
    And ask'd the mayor what meant this wilful silence:
    His answer was, the people were not wont
    To be spoke to but by the recorder.
    Then he was urged to tell my tale again:
    "Thus saith the duke, thus hath the duke inferr'd;"

---

1. *contract . . . France*] It was said that Edward was contracted to marry a woman named Elizabeth Lucy before his marriage to Lady Elizabeth Grey; a proposal that Edward IV should marry Lady Bona, the sister of King Louis XI of France, was made by the Earl of Warwick, acting as the king's deputy, but did not get beyond the stage of discussion.
2. *statuës*] This word is always a trisyllable in Shakespeare, and is often written "statuas."

But nothing spake in warrant from himself.
When he had done, some followers of mine own
At the lower end of the hall hurl'd up their caps,
And some ten voices cried "God save King Richard!"
And thus I took the vantage of those few,
"Thanks, gentle citizens and friends!" quoth I,
"This general applause and loving shout
Argues your wisdoms and your love to Richard;"
And even here brake off, and came away.
GLOU.   What tongueless blocks were they! would they not speak?
BUCK.   No, by my troth, my lord.
GLOU.   Will not the mayor then and his brethren come?
BUCK.   The mayor is here at hand: intend[3] some fear;
Be not you spoke with, but by mighty suit:
And look you get a prayer-book in your hand,
And stand betwixt two churchmen, good my lord;
For on that ground I'll build a holy descant:[4]
And be not easily won to our request;
Play the maid's part, still answer nay, and take it.
GLOU.   I go; and if you plead as well for them
As I can say nay to thee for myself,
No doubt we'll bring it to a happy issue.
BUCK.   Go, go up to the leads;[5] the lord mayor knocks.

                                        [*Exit* GLOUCESTER.]

Enter the Mayor *and* Citizens

Welcome, my lord: I dance attendance here;
I think the duke will not be spoke withal.

Enter CATESBY

Here comes his servant: how now, Catesby,
   What says he?
CATE.   My lord, he doth entreat your grace
To visit him to-morrow or next day:
He is within, with two right reverend fathers,
Divinely bent to meditation;
And in no worldly suit would he be moved,
To draw him from his holy exercise.
BUCK.   Return, good Catesby, to thy lord again;

---

3. *intend*] pretend.
4. *ground . . . descant*] "Ground" is the core melody to which "descant" is added as an accompaniment, usually in a higher voice.
5. *the leads*] the roof, the topmost part of the building, which was covered with sheets of lead.

Tell him, myself, the mayor and citizens,
In deep designs and matters of great moment,
No less importing than our general good,
Are come to have some conference with his grace.

CATE. I'll tell him what you say, my lord. [*Exit.*]

BUCK. Ah, ha, my lord, this prince is not an Edward!
He is not lolling on a lewd day-bed,
But on his knees at meditation;
Not dallying with a brace of courtezans,
But meditating with two deep divines;
Not sleeping, to engross[6] his idle body,
But praying, to enrich his watchful soul:
Happy were England, would this gracious prince
Take on himself the sovereignty thereof:
But, sure, I fear, we shall ne'er win him to it.

MAY. Marry, God forbid his grace should say us nay!

BUCK. I fear he will.

Re-enter CATESBY

How now, Catesby, what says your lord?

CATE. My lord,
He wonders to what end you have assembled
Such troops of citizens to speak with him,
His grace not being warn'd thereof before:
My lord, he fears you mean no good to him.

BUCK. Sorry I am my noble cousin should
Suspect me, that I mean no good to him:
By heaven, I come in perfect love to him;
And so once more return and tell his grace. [*Exit* CATESBY.]
When holy and devout religious men
Are at their beads, 'tis hard to draw them thence,
So sweet is zealous contemplation.

Enter GLOUCESTER *aloft, between two* Bishops. CATESBY *returns*

MAY. See, where he stands between two clergymen!

BUCK. Two props of virtue for a Christian prince,
To stay him from the fall of vanity:
And, see, a book of prayer in his hand,
True ornaments to know a holy man.
Famous Plantagenet, most gracious prince,
Lend favourable ears to our request;
And pardon us the interruption
Of thy devotion and right Christian zeal.

---

6. *engross*] make gross, fatten.

GLOU.   My lord, there needs no such apology:
    I rather do beseech you pardon me,
    Who, earnest in the service of my God,
    Neglect the visitation of my friends.
    But, leaving this, what is your grace's pleasure?
BUCK.   Even that, I hope, which pleaseth God above,
    And all good men of this ungovern'd isle.
GLOU.   I do suspect I have done some offence
    That seems disgracious in the city's eyes,
    And that you come to reprehend my ignorance.
BUCK.   You have, my lord: would it might please your grace,
    At our entreaties, to amend that fault!
GLOU.   Else wherefore breathe I in a Christian land?
BUCK.   Then know, it is your fault that you resign
    The supreme seat, the throne majestical,
    The scepter'd office of your ancestors,
    Your state of fortune and your due of birth,
    The lineal glory of your royal house,
    To the corruption of a blemish'd stock:
    Whilst, in the mildness of your sleepy thoughts,
    Which here we waken to our country's good,
    This noble isle doth want her proper limbs;
    Her face defaced with scars of infamy,
    Her royal stock graft with ignoble plants,
    And almost shoulder'd in[7] the swallowing gulf
    Of blind forgetfulness and dark oblivion.
    Which to recure,[8] we heartily solicit
    Your gracious self to take on you the charge
    And kingly government of this your land;
    Not as protector, steward, substitute,
    Or lowly factor for another's gain;
    But as successively,[9] from blood to blood,
    Your right of birth, your empery,[10] your own.
    For this, consorted with the citizens,
    Your very worshipful and loving friends,
    And by their vehement instigation,
    In this just suit come I to move your grace.
GLOU.   I know not whether to depart in silence,
    Or bitterly to speak in your reproof,
    Best fitteth my degree or your condition:

---

7. *shoulder'd in*] jostled into.
8. *recure*] cure.
9. *successively*] in due succession.
10. *empery*] dominion.

If not to answer, you might haply think
Tongue-tied ambition, not replying, yielded
To bear the golden yoke of sovereignty,
Which fondly you would here impose on me;
If to reprove you for this suit of yours
So season'd with your faithful love to me,
Then, on the other side, I check'd my friends.
Therefore, to speak, and to avoid the first,
And then, in speaking, not to incur the last,
Definitively thus I answer you.
Your love deserves my thanks, but my desert
Unmeritable shuns your high request.
First, if all obstacles were cut away
And that my path were even to the crown,
As my right revenue and due by birth;
Yet so much is my poverty of spirit,
So mighty and so many my defects,
As I had rather hide me from my greatness,
Being a bark[11] to brook no mighty sea,
Than in my greatness covet to be hid,
And in the vapour of my glory smother'd.
But, God be thanked, there's no need of me,
And much I need to help you,[12] if need were;
The royal tree hath left us royal fruit,
Which, mellow'd by the stealing hours of time,
Will well become the seat of majesty,
And make, no doubt, us happy by his reign.
On him I lay what you would lay on me,
The right and fortune of his happy stars;
Which God defend that I should wring from him!
BUCK.   My lord, this argues conscience in your grace;
But the respects thereof are nice[13] and trivial,
All circumstances well considered.
You say that Edward is your brother's son:
So say we too, but not by Edward's wife;
For first he was contract[14] to Lady Lucy —
Your mother lives a witness to that vow —
And afterward by substitute betroth'd
To Bona, sister to the King of France.
These both put by, a poor petitioner,

---

11. *bark*] a boat propelled by oars or sails.
12. *need*] lack (the capacity to help you).
13. *nice*] punctilious, fanciful.
14. *contract*] betrothed.

A care-crazed mother of a many children,
A beauty-waning and distressed widow,
Even in the afternoon of her best days,
Made prize and purchase of his lustful eye,
Seduced the pitch[15] and height of all his thoughts
To base declension and loathed bigamy:[16]
By her, in his unlawful bed, he got[17]
This Edward, whom our manners term the prince.
More bitterly could I expostulate,
Save that, for reverence to some alive,
I give a sparing limit to my tongue.
Then, good my lord, take to your royal self
This proffer'd benefit of dignity;
If not to bless us and the land withal,
Yet to draw forth your noble ancestry
From the corruption of abusing times,
Unto a lineal true-derived course.

MAY.   Do, good my lord, your citizens entreat you.
BUCK. Refuse not, mighty lord, this proffer'd love.
CATE. O, make them joyful, grant their lawful suit!
GLOU. Alas, why would you heap these cares on me?
I am unfit for state and majesty:
I do beseech you, take it not amiss;
I cannot nor I will not yield to you.
BUCK. If you refuse it, — as, in love and zeal,
Loath to depose the child, your brother's son;
As well we know your tenderness of heart
And gentle, kind, effeminate remorse,[18]
Which we have noted in you to your kin,
And egally[19] indeed to all estates, —
Yet whether you accept our suit or no,
Your brother's son shall never reign our king;
But we will plant some other in the throne,
To the disgrace and downfall of your house:
And in this resolution here we leave you.
Come, citizens: 'zounds![20] I'll entreat no more.

---

15. *pitch*] a common term in falconry for the hawk's highest flight.
16. *bigamy*] According to canon law in Edward IV's time, marriage with a widow consti-
    tuted bigamy.
17. *got*] begot, sired.
18. *remorse*] sense of pity.
19. *egally*] equally.
20. *'zounds!*] an oath contracted from "God's wounds!", a reference to the wounds Christ
    received at his trial and on the Cross.

GLOU.   O, do not swear, my lord of Buckingham.

                   [*Exit* BUCKINGHAM *with the* Citizens.]

CATE.   Call them again, my lord, and accept their suit:

ANOTHER.   Do, good my lord, lest all the land do rue it.

GLOU.   Would you enforce me to a world of care?

     Well, call them again. I am not made of stones,

     But penetrable to your kind entreats,

     Albeit against my conscience and my soul.

Re-enter BUCKINGHAM *and the rest*

     Cousin of Buckingham, and you sage, grave men,

     Since you will buckle fortune on my back,

     To bear her burthen, whether I will or no,

     I must have patience to endure the load:

     But if black scandal or foul-faced reproach

     Attend the sequel of your imposition,

     Your mere enforcement shall acquittance[21] me

     From all the impure blots and stains thereof;

     For God he knows, and you may partly see,

     How far I am from the desire thereof.

MAY.   God bless your grace! we see it, and will say it.

GLOU.   In saying so, you shall but say the truth.

BUCK.   Then I salute you with this kingly title:

     Long live Richard, England's royal king!

MAY. AND CIT.   Amen.

BUCK.   To-morrow will it please you to be crown'd?

GLOU.   Even when you please, since you will have it so.

BUCK.   To-morrow then we will attend your grace:

     And so most joyfully we take our leave.

GLOU.   Come, let us to our holy task again.

     Farewell, good cousin; farewell, gentle friends.   [*Exeunt.*]

---

21. *acquittance*] acquit.

ACT IV.

SCENE I. *Before the Tower.*

Enter, on one side, QUEEN ELIZABETH, DUCHESS OF YORK, *and* MAR-
QUESS OF DORSET; *on the other,* ANNE, DUCHESS OF GLOUCESTER,
leading LADY MARGARET PLANTAGENET, CLARENCE'S *young daughter*

DUCH.   Who meets us here? my niece[1] Plantagenet
     Led in the hand of her kind aunt Gloucester?[2]
     Now, for my life, she's wandering to the Tower,
     On pure heart's love to greet the tender princes.
     Daughter, well met.
ANNE.   God give your graces both
     A happy and a joyful time of day!
Q. ELIZ.   As much to you, good sister! Whither away?
ANNE.   No farther than the Tower, and, as I guess,
     Upon the like devotion as yourselves,
     To gratulate the gentle princes there.
Q. ELIZ.   Kind sister, thanks: we'll enter all together.

Enter BRAKENBURY

     And, in good time, here the lieutenant comes.
     Master lieutenant, pray you, by your leave,
     How doth the prince, and my young son of York?
BRAK.   Right well, dear madam. By your patience,
     I may not suffer you to visit them;
     The king hath straitly charged the contrary.
Q. ELIZ.   The king! why, who's that?
BRAK.   I cry you mercy: I mean the lord protector.
Q. ELIZ.   The Lord protect him from that kingly title!
     Hath he set bounds betwixt their love and me?
     I am their mother; who should keep me from them?
DUCH.   I am their father's mother; I will see them.
ANNE.   Their aunt I am in law,[3] in love their mother:

---

1. *niece*] granddaughter.
2. *aunt Gloucester*] Anne, widow, or rather affianced bride, of Prince Edward, Henry VI's
son and heir, was solicited in marriage by Gloucester while acting as chief mourner at
Henry VI's funeral and is now married to him. Lady Margaret Plantagenet, whom she
holds by the hand, was daughter of her sister, the late Duchess of Clarence.
3. *in law*] by marriage.

Then bring me to their sights; I'll bear thy blame,
And take thy office from thee, on my peril.

BRAK.   No, madam, no; I may not leave it[4] so:
I am bound by oath, and therefore pardon me.   [*Exit.*]

Enter LORD STANLEY

STAN.   Let me but meet you, ladies, one hour hence,
And I'll salute your grace of York as mother,
And reverend looker on, of two fair queens.
[*To Anne.*] Come, madam, you must straight to Westminster,
There to be crowned Richard's royal queen.

Q. ELIZ.   O, cut my lace in sunder, that my pent heart
May have some scope to beat, or else I swoon
With this dead-killing news!

ANNE.   Despiteful tidings! O unpleasing news!

DOR.   Be of good cheer: mother, how fares your grace?

Q. ELIZ.   O Dorset, speak not to me, get thee hence!
Death and destruction dog thee at the heels;
Thy mother's name is ominous to children.
If thou wilt outstrip death, go cross the seas,
And live with Richmond,[5] from the reach of hell:
Go, hie thee, hie thee from this slaughter-house,
Lest thou increase the number of the dead;
And make me die the thrall of Margaret's curse,
Nor mother, wife, nor England's counted queen.

STAN.   Full of wise care is this your counsel, madam.
Take all the swift advantage of the hours;
You shall have letters from me to my son
To meet you on the way, and welcome you.
Be not ta'en tardy by unwise delay.

DUCH.   O ill-dispersing wind of misery!
O my accursed womb, the bed of death!
A cockatrice[6] hast thou hatch'd to the world,
Whose unavoided eye is murderous.

STAN.   Come, madam, come; I in all haste was sent.

ANNE.   And I in all unwillingness will go.
I would to God that the inclusive verge
Of golden metal that must round my brow

---

4. *leave it*] part from my office, infringe my duty.
5. *cross . . . Richmond*] Henry Tudor, Earl of Richmond (later Henry VII) and head of the
House of Lancaster after Henry VI's death, was in Brittany at the time.
6. *cockatrice*] a fabulous serpent, also known as the basilisk, whose glance was deadly.

Were red-hot steel,[7] to sear me to the brain!
Anointed let me be with deadly venom,
And die, ere men can say, God save the queen!

Q. ELIZ. Go, go, poor soul, I envy not thy glory;
To feed my humour, wish thyself no harm.

ANNE. No! why? When he that is my husband now
Came to me, as I follow'd Henry's corse,
When scarce the blood was well wash'd from his hands
Which issued from my other angel husband,
And that dead saint which then I weeping follow'd;
O, when, I say, I look'd on Richard's face,
This was my wish: "Be thou," quoth I, "accursed,
For making me, so young, so old a widow!
And, when thou wed'st, let sorrow haunt thy bed;
And be thy wife — if any be so mad —
As miserable by the death of thee
As thou hast made me by my dear lord's death!"
Lo, ere I can repeat this curse again,
Even in so short a space, my woman's heart
Grossly grew captive to his honey words,
And proved the subject of my own soul's curse,
Which ever since hath kept my eyes from rest;
For never yet one hour in his bed
Have I enjoy'd the golden dew of sleep,
But have been waked by his timorous dreams.
Besides, he hates me for my father Warwick;
And will, no doubt, shortly be rid of me.

Q. ELIZ. Poor heart, adieu! I pity thy complaining.

ANNE. No more than from my soul I mourn for yours.

DOR. Farewell, thou woful welcomer of glory!

ANNE. Adieu, poor soul, that takest thy leave of it!

DUCH. [To DORSET] Go thou to Richmond, and good fortune guide
thee!
[To ANNE] Go thou to Richard, and good angels guard thee!
[To QUEEN ELIZ.] Go thou to sanctuary, and good thoughts possess
thee!
I to my grave, where peace and rest lie with me!
Eighty odd years of sorrow have I seen,
And each hour's joy wreck'd with a week of teen.[8]

Q. ELIZ. Stay, yet look back with me unto the Tower.

---

7. *red-hot steel*] Regicides or conspirators against the lives of kings were often punished in
the middle ages by setting on their brows a crown of iron heated red-hot.

8. *teen*] grief.

Pity, you ancient stones, those tender babes
Whom envy hath immured within your walls!
Rough cradle for such little pretty ones!
Rude ragged nurse, old sullen playfellow
For tender princes, use my babies well!
So foolish sorrow bids your stones farewell.   [*Exeunt.*]

SCENE II. *London. The Palace.*

Sennet. Enter RICHARD, *in pomp, crowned;* BUCKINGHAM, CATESBY, *a* Page, *and others*

K. RICH.   Stand all apart. Cousin of Buckingham!
BUCK.   My gracious sovereign?
K. RICH.   Give me thy hand. [*Here he ascendeth the throne.*] Thus
     high, by thy advice
     And thy assistance, is king Richard seated:
     But shall we wear these honours for a day?
     Or shall they last, and we rejoice in them?
BUCK.   Still live they, and for ever may they last!
K. RICH.   O Buckingham, now do I play the touch,[1]
     To try if thou be current gold indeed:
     Young Edward lives: think now what I would say.
BUCK.   Say on, my loving lord.
K. RICH.   Why, Buckingham, I say, I would be king.
BUCK.   Why, so you are, my thrice renowned liege.
K. RICH.   Ha! am I king? 'tis so: but Edward lives.
BUCK.   True, noble prince.
K. RICH.   O bitter consequence,
     That Edward still should live true noble prince!
     Cousin, thou wert not wont to be so dull:
     Shall I be plain? I wish the bastards dead;
     And I would have it suddenly perform'd.
     What sayest thou? speak suddenly; be brief.
BUCK.   Your grace may do your pleasure.
K. RICH.   Tut, tut, thou art all ice, thy kindness freezeth:
     Say, have I thy consent that they shall die?
BUCK.   Give me some breath, some little pause, my lord,
     Before I positively speak herein:

---

1. *play the touch*] make play with the touchstone, or true test (of metals).

I will resolve[2] your grace immediately.   . .   [*Exit.*]
CATE.   [*Aside to a stander by*] The king is angry: see, he bites the lip.
K. RICH.   I will converse with iron-witted[3] fools
    And unrespective[4] boys: none are for me
    That look into me with considerate eyes:
    High-reaching Buckingham grows circumspect.
    Boy!
PAGE.   My lord?
K. RICH.   Know'st thou not any whom corrupting gold
    Would tempt unto a close exploit of death?
PAGE.   My lord, I know a discontented gentleman,
    Whose humble means match not his haughty mind:
    Gold were as good as twenty orators,
    And will, no doubt, tempt him to any thing.
K. RICH.   What is his name?
PAGE.   His name, my lord, is Tyrrel.
K. RICH.   I partly know the man: go, call him hither.   [*Exit* Page.]
    The deep-revolving witty[5] Buckingham
    No more shall be the neighbour to my counsel:
    Hath he so long held out with me untired,
    And stops he now for breath?

Enter STANLEY

    How now! what news with you?
STAN.   My lord, I hear the Marquis Dorset's fled
    To Richmond, in those parts beyond the seas
    Where he abides.   [*Stands apart.*]
K. RICH.   Catesby!
CATE.   My lord?
K. RICH.   Rumour it abroad
    That Anne, my wife, is sick and like to die:
    I will take order[6] for her keeping close.
    Inquire me out some mean-born gentleman,
    Whom I will marry straight to Clarence' daughter:
    The boy is foolish, and I fear not him.
    Look, how thou dream'st! I say again, give out
    That Anne my wife is sick, and like to die:
    About it; for it stands me much upon,[7]

---

2. *resolve*] definitely answer, satisfy.
3. *iron-witted*] dull-witted, wooden-headed.
4. *unrespective*] careless, thoughtless.
5. *witty*] knowing, clever.
6. *take order*] take measures, arrange.
7. *it stands me much upon*] It is a matter of importance for me.

To stop all hopes whose growth may damage me.

[Exit CATESBY.*]*

I must be married to my brother's daughter,[8]
Or else my kingdom stands on brittle glass.
Murder her brothers, and then marry her!
Uncertain way of gain! But I am in
So far in blood that sin will pluck on[9] sin:
Tear-falling pity dwells not in this eye.

Re-enter Page, *with* TYRREL

    Is thy name Tyrrel?
TYR.   James Tyrrel, and your most obedient subject.
K. RICH.   Art thou, indeed?
TYR.   Prove me, my gracious sovereign.
K. RICH.   Darest thou resolve to kill a friend of mine?
TYR.   Ay, my lord;
    But I had rather kill two enemies.
K. RICH.   Why, there thou hast it: two deep enemies,
    Foes to my rest and my sweet sleep's disturbers
    Are they that I would have thee deal upon:[10]
    Tyrrel, I mean those bastards in the Tower.
TYR.   Let me have open means to come to them,
    And soon I'll rid you from the fear of them.
K. RICH.   Thou sing'st sweet music. Hark, come hither, Tyrrel:
    Go, by this token: rise, and lend thine ear: *[Whispers.]*
    There is no more but so: say it is done,
    And I will love thee, and prefer thee too.
TYR.   'Tis done, my gracious lord.
K. RICH.   Shall we hear from thee, Tyrrel, ere we sleep?
TYR.   Ye shall, my lord.   *[Exit.]*

Re-enter BUCKINGHAM

BUCK.   My lord, I have consider'd in my mind
    The late demand that you did sound me in.
K. RICH.   Well, let that pass. Dorset is fled to Richmond.
BUCK.   I hear that news, my lord.
K. RICH.   Stanley, he is your wife's son:[11] well, look to it.
BUCK.   My lord, I claim your gift, my due by promise,
    For which your honour and your faith is pawn'd;

---

    8. *my brother's daughter*] Edward IV's eldest daughter Elizabeth, who happily escaped
       marriage with her uncle and became the wife of his successor Henry VII.
    9. *pluck on*] excite, cause.
   10. *deal upon*] deal with.
   11. *Stanley . . . son*] Stanley was married to Margaret Beaufort, the widow of Edmund
       Tudor, Richmond's father.

The earldom of Hereford and the moveables
The which you promised I should possess.

K. RICH.   Stanley, look to your wife: if she convey
Letters to Richmond, you shall answer it.

BUCK.   What says your highness to my just demand?

K. RICH.   As I remember, Henry the Sixth
Did prophesy that Richmond should be king,
When Richmond was a little peevish boy.
A king, perhaps, perhaps, —

BUCK.   My lord!

K. RICH.   How chance the prophet could not at that time
Have told me, I being by, that I should kill him?

BUCK.   My lord, your promise for the earldom, —

K. RICH.   Richmond! When last I was at Exeter,
The mayor in courtesy show'd me the castle,
And call'd it Rougemont: at which name I started,
Because a bard of Ireland told me once,
I should not live long after I saw Richmond.

BUCK.   My lord!

K. RICH.   Ay, what's o'clock?

BUCK.   I am thus bold to put your grace in mind
Of what you promised me.

K. RICH.   Well, but what's o'clock?

BUCK.   Upon the stroke of ten.

K. RICH.   Well, let it strike.

BUCK.   Why let it strike?

K. RICH.   Because that, like a Jack,[12] thou keep'st the stroke
Betwixt thy begging and my meditation.
I am not in the giving vein to-day.

BUCK.   Why, then resolve me whether you will or no.

K. RICH.   Tut, tut,
Thou troublest me; I am not in the vein.

                                                            [*Exeunt all but* BUCKINGHAM.]

BUCK.   Is it even so? rewards he my true service
With such deep contempt? made I him king for this?
O, let me think on Hastings, and be gone
To Brecknock,[13] while my fearful[14] head is on!   [*Exit.*]

---

12. *a Jack*] a small mechanical figure that struck the hour on the bell of a clock.
13. *Brecknock*] Brecknock Castle, in South Wales, was one of the Duke of Buckingham's residences.
14. *fearful*] full of fear.

SCENE III. *The Same.*

Enter TYRREL

TYR.   The tyrannous and bloody deed is done,
    The most arch[1] act of piteous massacre
    That ever yet this land was guilty of.
    Dighton and Forrest, whom I did suborn
    To do this ruthless piece of butchery,
    Although they were flesh'd[2] villains, bloody dogs,
    Melting with tenderness and kind compassion
    Wept like two children in their deaths' sad stories.
    "Lo, thus," quoth Dighton, "lay those tender babes:"
    "Thus, thus," quoth Forrest, "girdling one another
    Within their innocent alabaster arms:
    Their lips were four red roses on a stalk,
    Which in their summer beauty kiss'd each other.
    A book of prayers on their pillow lay;
    Which once," quoth Forrest, "almost changed my mind;
    But O! the devil" — there the villain stopp'd;
    Whilst Dighton thus told on: "We smothered
    The most replenished[3] sweet work of nature
    That from the prime creation e'er she framed."
    Thus both are gone with conscience and remorse;
    They could not speak; and so I left them both,
    To bring this tidings to the bloody king.
    And here he comes.

Enter KING RICHARD

                All hail, my sovereign liege!
K. RICH.   Kind Tyrrel, am I happy in thy news?
TYR.   If to have done the thing you gave in charge
    Beget your happiness, be happy then,
    For it is done, my lord.
K. RICH.   But didst thou see them dead?
TYR.   I did, my lord.
K. RICH.   And buried, gentle Tyrrel?

---

1. *arch*] consummate, notable.
2. *flesh'd*] inured to bloodshed.
3. *replenished*] complete, perfect.

TYR.   The chaplain of the Tower hath buried them;
    But how or in what place I do not know.
K. RICH.   Come to me, Tyrrel, soon at after supper,[4]
    And thou shalt tell the process of their death.
    Meantime, but think how I may do thee good,
    And be inheritor of thy desire.
    Farewell till soon.   [*Exit* TYRREL.]
    The son of Clarence have I pent up close;
    His daughter meanly have I match'd in marriage;[5]
    The sons of Edward sleep in Abraham's bosom,
    And Anne my wife hath bid the world good night.
    Now, for I know the Breton Richmond aims
    At young Elizabeth, my brother's daughter,
    And, by that knot, looks proudly o'er the crown,
    To her I go, a jolly thriving wooer.

Enter CATESBY

CATE.   My lord!
K. RICH.   Good news or bad, that thou comest in so bluntly?
CATE.   Bad news, my lord: Ely[6] is fled to Richmond;
    And Buckingham, back'd with the hardy Welshmen,
    Is in the field, and still his power increaseth.
K. RICH.   Ely with Richmond troubles me more near
    Than Buckingham and his rash-levied army.
    Come, I have heard that fearful commenting
    Is leaden servitor to dull delay;
    Delay leads impotent and snail-paced beggary:[7]
    Then fiery expedition[8] be my wing,
    Jove's Mercury,[9] and herald for a king!
    Come, muster men: my counsel is my shield;
    We must be brief when traitors brave the field.[10]   [*Exeunt.*]

---

4. *soon at after supper*] about the time when supper is over.
5. *His . . . marriage*] Clarence's daughter Margaret was married to Sir Richard Pole, who
   was of somewhat better birth than the text indicates. Contrary to the statement of the
   text, the union took place about 1491, some years after Richard's death, by direction of
   Henry VII.
6. *Ely*] John Morton, Bishop of Ely, afterwards Archbishop of Canterbury, by the appointment of Henry VII.
7. *fearful . . . beggary*] timorous reflection serves the slow purpose of sluggish procrastination; procrastination superinduces feeble and creeping beggary.
8. *fiery expedition*] rapidity of fire or lightning.
9. *Mercury*] the swift messenger of Jove.
10. *brave the field*] vauntingly challenge (us) to the battlefield.

SCENE IV. *Before the Palace.*

Enter QUEEN MARGARET

Q. MAR.   So, now prosperity begins to mellow
    And drop into the rotten mouth of death.
    Here in these confines slily have I lurk'd,
    To watch the waning of mine adversaries.
    A dire induction[1] am I witness to,
    And will to France, hoping the consequence
    Will prove as bitter, black, and tragical.
    Withdraw thee, wretched Margaret: who comes here?

Enter QUEEN ELIZABETH *and the* DUCHESS OF YORK

Q. ELIZ.   Ah, my young princes! ah, my tender babes!
    My unblown flowers, new-appearing sweets!
    If yet your gentle souls fly in the air,
    And be not fix'd in doom perpetual,
    Hover about me with your airy wings,
    And hear your mother's lamentation!
Q. MAR.   Hover about her; say, that right for right
    Hath dimm'd your infant morn to aged night.[2]
DUCH.   So many miseries have crazed my voice,
    That my woe-wearied tongue is mute and dumb.
    Edward Plantagenet, why art thou dead?
Q. MAR.   Plantagenet doth quit[3] Plantagenet,
    Edward for Edward pays a dying debt.
Q. ELIZ.   Wilt thou, O God, fly from such gentle lambs,
    And throw them in the entrails of the wolf?
    When didst thou sleep when such a deed was done?
Q. MAR.   When holy Harry died, and my sweet son.
DUCH.   Blind sight, dead life, poor mortal living ghost,
    Woe's scene, world's shame, grave's due by life usurp'd,
    Brief abstract and record of tedious days,

---

1. *induction*] preparation, prelude.
2. *right for right . . . night*] Supreme right, justice answering the claims of justice, has dimmed or blotted out the bright dawn of your infant's life and put in its place the darkness of death, which commonly awaits old age. The losses which Queen Margaret has suffered cause her to regard Queen Elizabeth's bereavement as just retribution for the removal of her own kindred.
3. *quit*] requite.

Rest thy unrest on England's lawful earth,   [*Sitting down.*]
Unlawfully made drunk with innocents' blood!
Q. ELIZ.   O, that thou wouldst as well afford a grave
As thou canst yield a melancholy seat!
Then would I hide my bones, not rest them here.
O, who hath any cause to mourn but I?   [*Sitting down by her.*]
Q. MAR.   If ancient sorrow[4] be most reverend,
Give mine the benefit of seniory,[5]
And let my woes frown on the upper hand.
If sorrow can admit society,   [*Sitting down with them.*]
Tell o'er your woes again by viewing mine:
I had an Edward, till a Richard kill'd him;
I had a Harry, till a Richard kill'd him:
Thou hadst an Edward, till a Richard kill'd him;
Thou hadst a Richard, till a Richard kill'd him.
DUCH.   I had a Richard too, and thou didst kill him;
I had a Rutland too, thou holp'st to kill him.
Q. MAR.   Thou hadst a Clarence too, and Richard kill'd him.
From forth the kennel of thy womb hath crept
A hell-hound that doth hunt us all to death:
That dog, that had his teeth[6] before his eyes,
To worry lambs and lap their gentle blood,
That foul defacer of God's handiwork,
That excellent grand tyrant of the earth,
That reigns in galled eyes of weeping souls,
Thy womb let loose, to chase us to our graves.
O upright, just, and true-disposing God,
How do I thank thee, that this carnal[7] cur
Preys on the issue of his mother's body,
And makes her pew-fellow[8] with others' moan!
DUCH.   O Harry's wife, triumph not in my woes!
God witness with me, I have wept for thine.
Q. MAR.   Bear with me; I am hungry for revenge,
And now I cloy me with beholding it.
Thy Edward he is dead, that stabb'd my Edward;
Thy other Edward dead, to quit my Edward;
Young York he is but boot,[9] because both they

---

4. *ancient sorrow*] sorrow of age.
5. *seniory*] seniority.
6. *dog . . . teeth*] Richard was reported to have been born with teeth.
7. *carnal*] flesh-consuming, cannibal.
8. *pew-fellow*] companion, comrade, partner.
9. *boot*] a mere trifle (an extra bit of merchandise thrown in by a vendor to entice potential buyers).

      Match not the high perfection of my loss:
      Thy Clarence he is dead that kill'd my Edward;
      And the beholders of this tragic play,
      The adulterate[10] Hastings, Rivers, Vaughan, Grey,
      Untimely smother'd in their dusky graves.
      Richard yet lives, hell's black intelligencer,[11]
      Only reserved their[12] factor,[13] to buy souls
      And send them thither: but at hand, at hand,
      Ensues his piteous and unpitied end:
      Earth gapes, hell burns, fiends roar, saints pray,
      To have him suddenly convey'd away.
      Cancel his bond of life, dear God, I pray,
      That I may live to say, The dog is dead!
Q. ELIZ.   O, thou didst prophesy the time would come
      That I should wish for thee to help me curse
      That bottled spider, that foul bunch-back'd toad!
Q. MAR.   I call'd thee then vain flourish of my fortune;
      I call'd thee then poor shadow, painted queen;
      The presentation of but what I was;
      The flattering index[14] of a direful pageant;
      One heaved a-high, to be hurl'd down below;
      A mother only mock'd with two sweet babes;
      A dream of what thou wert, a breath, a bubble,
      A sign of dignity, a garish flag
      To be the aim of every dangerous shot;
      A queen in jest, only to fill the scene.
      Where is thy husband now? where be thy brothers?
      Where are thy children? wherein dost thou joy?
      Who sues to thee, and cries "God save the queen"?
      Where be the bending peers that flattered thee?
      Where be the thronging troops that followed thee?
      Decline all this,[15] and see what now thou art:
      For happy wife, a most distressed widow;
      For joyful mother, one that wails the name;
      For queen, a very caitiff[16] crown'd with care;
      For one being sued to, one that humbly sues;
      For one that scorn'd at me, now scorn'd of me;

---

10. *adulterate*] adulterous.
11. *intelligencer*] agent, emissary, informer.
12. *their*] i.e., hell's (treated as a plural because it signifies a community of evil spirits).
13. *factor*] agent (of hell).
14. *index*] prelude.
15. *Decline all this*] Go through all this (as through the declension of a verb or noun in a grammar book).
16. *caitiff*] wretch, slave.

For one being fear'd of all, now fearing one;
For one commanding all, obey'd of none.
Thus hath the course of justice wheel'd about,
And left thee but a very prey to time;
Having no more but thought of what thou wert,
To torture thee the more, being what thou art.
Thou didst usurp my place, and dost thou not
Usurp the just proportion of my sorrow?
Now thy proud neck bears half my burthen'd yoke;
From which even here I slip my weary neck,
And leave the burthen of it all on thee.
Farewell, York's wife, and queen of sad mischance:
These English woes will make me smile in France.
Q. ELIZ.   O thou well skill'd in curses, stay awhile,
And teach me how to curse mine enemies!
Q. MAR.   Forbear to sleep the nights, and fast the days;
Compare dead happiness with living woe;
Think that thy babes were fairer than they were,
And he that slew them fouler than he is:
Bettering thy loss[17] makes the bad causer worse:
Revolving this will teach thee how to curse.
Q. ELIZ.   My words are dull; O, quicken them with thine!
Q. MAR.   Thy woes will make them sharp and pierce like mine. [*Exit.*]
DUCH.   Why should calamity be full of words?
Q. ELIZ.   Windy attorneys to their client woes,
Airy succeeders of intestate joys,[18]
Poor breathing orators of miseries!
Let them have scope: though what they do impart
Help not at all, yet do they ease the heart.
DUCH.   If so, then be not tongue-tied: go with me,
And in the breath of bitter words let's smother
My damned son, which thy two sweet sons smother'd.
I hear his drum: be copious in exclaims.

Enter KING RICHARD, *marching, with drums and trumpets*

K. RICH.   Who intercepts my expedition?
DUCH.   O, she that might have intercepted thee,
By strangling thee in her accursed womb,
From all the slaughters, wretch, that thou hast done!
Q. ELIZ.   Hidest thou that forehead with a golden crown,

---

17. *Bettering thy loss*] exaggeration of thy loss.
18. *Airy succeeders of intestate joys*] breath-born heirs or inheritors of poor joys, which
(with nothing to bequeath) have made no will.

Where should be graven, if that right were right,
The slaughter of the prince that owed[19] that crown,
And the dire death of my two sons and brothers?
Tell me, thou villain slave, where are my children?

DUCH.　Thou toad, thou toad, where is thy brother Clarence?
And little Ned Plantagenet, his son?

Q. ELIZ.　Where is kind Hastings, Rivers, Vaughan, Grey?

K. RICH.　A flourish, trumpets! strike alarum, drums!
Let not the heavens hear these tell-tale women
Rail on the Lord's anointed: strike, I say!　　[*Flourish. Alarums.*]
Either be patient, and entreat[20] me fair,
Or with the clamorous report of war
Thus will I drown your exclamations.

DUCH.　Art thou my son?

K. RICH.　Ay, I thank God, my father, and yourself.

DUCH.　Then patiently hear my impatience.

K. RICH.　Madam, I have a touch of your condition,[21]
Which cannot brook the accent of reproof.

DUCH.　O, let me speak!

K. RICH.　　　　　　　　Do then; but I'll not hear.

DUCH.　I will be mild and gentle in my speech.

K. RICH.　And brief, good mother; for I am in haste.

DUCH.　Art thou so hasty? I have stay'd for thee,
God knows, in anguish, pain and agony.

K. RICH.　And came I not at last to comfort you?

DUCH.　No, by the holy rood, thou know'st it well,
Thou camest on earth to make the earth my hell.
A grievous burthen was thy birth to me;
Tetchy[22] and wayward was thy infancy;
Thy school-days frightful,[23] desperate, wild, and furious,
Thy prime of manhood daring, bold, and venturous,
Thy age confirm'd,[24] proud, subtle, bloody, treacherous;
More mild, but yet more harmful, kind in hatred:
What comfortable hour canst thou name,
That ever graced me in thy company?

K. RICH.　Faith, none, but Humphrey Hour, that call'd your grace

---

19. *owed*] owned.
20. *entreat*] treat, use.
21. *a touch of your condition*] a dash of your temperament.
22. *Tetchy*] fretful, peevish.
23. *frightful*] causing fright.
24. *Thy age confirm'd*] thy ripened age.

To breakfast once forth of[25] my company.[26]
If I be so disgracious in your sight,
Let me march on, and not offend your grace.
Strike up the drum.

DUCH.   I prithee, hear me speak.

K. RICH.   You speak too bitterly.

DUCH.   Hear me a word;
For I shall never speak to thee again.

K. RICH.   So.

DUCH.   Either thou wilt die, by God's just ordinance,
Ere from this war thou turn a conqueror,
Or I with grief and extreme age shall perish
And never look upon thy face again.
Therefore take with thee my most heavy curse;
Which, in the day of battle, tire thee more
Than all the complete armour that thou wear'st!
My prayers on the adverse party fight;
And there the little souls of Edward's children
Whisper the spirits of thine enemies,
And promise them success and victory.
Bloody thou art, bloody will be thy end;
Shame serves thy life and doth thy death attend.   [Exit.]

Q. ELIZ.   Though far more cause, yet much less spirit to curse
Abides in me; I say amen to all.

K. RICH.   Stay, madam; I must speak a word with you.

Q. ELIZ.   I have no moe sons of the royal blood
For thee to murder: for my daughters, Richard,
They shall be praying nuns, not weeping queens;
And therefore level not to hit their lives.

K. RICH.   You have a daughter call'd Elizabeth,
Virtuous and fair, royal and gracious.

Q. ELIZ.   And must she die for this? O, let her live,
And I'll corrupt her manners, stain her beauty;
Slander myself as false to Edward's bed;
Throw over her the veil of infamy:
So she may live unscarr'd of bleeding slaughter,
I will confess she was not Edward's daughter.

---

25. *forth of*] away from.

26. *Humphrey Hour ... company*] The reference is probably to the hour when the
Duchess gave birth to Richard, and to the first meal which she took after her delivery.
According to homely wit, after delivery the mother traditionally breakfasted apart from
the child whom she had hitherto fed in her womb along with herself. "To dine with the
Duke of Humphrey," meant to go hungry, to go without one's dinner.

K. RICH.   Wrong not her birth, she is of royal blood.
Q. ELIZ.   To save her life, I'll say she is not so.
K. RICH.   Her life is only safest in her birth.
Q. ELIZ.   And only in that safety died her brothers.
K. RICH.   Lo, at their births good stars were opposite.[27]
Q. ELIZ.   No, to their lives bad friends were contrary.
K. RICH.   All unavoided[28] is the doom of destiny.
Q. ELIZ.   True, when avoided grace makes destiny:
      My babes were destined to a fairer death,
      If grace had bless'd thee with a fairer life.
K. RICH.   You speak as if that I had slain my cousins.
Q. ELIZ.   Cousins, indeed; and by their uncle cozen'd
      Of comfort, kingdom, kindred, freedom, life.
      Whose hand soever lanced their tender hearts,
      Thy head, all indirectly,[29] gave direction:
      No doubt the murderous knife was dull and blunt,
      Till it was whetted on thy stone-hard heart,
      To revel in the entrails of my lambs.
      But that still use[30] of grief makes wild grief tame,
      My tongue should to thy ears not name my boys,
      Till that my nails were anchor'd in thine eyes;
      And I, in such a desperate bay of death,
      Like a poor bark, of sails and tackling reft,
      Rush all to pieces on thy rocky bosom.
K. RICH.   Madam, so thrive I in my enterprise,
      And dangerous success of bloody wars,
      As I intend more good to you and yours,
      Than ever you or yours were by me wrong'd!
Q. ELIZ.   What good is cover'd with the face of heaven,
      To be discover'd, that can do me good?
K. RICH.   The advancement of your children, gentle lady.
Q. ELIZ.   Up to some scaffold, there to lose their heads?
K. RICH.   No, to the dignity and height of honour,
      The high imperial type[31] of this earth's glory.
Q. ELIZ.   Flatter my sorrows with report of it;
      Tell me what state, what dignity, what honour,
      Canst thou demise to any child of mine?
K. RICH.   Even all I have; yea, and myself and all,

---

27. *opposite*† hostile, in opposition; an astrological term.
28. *unavoided*] unavoidable.
29. *indirectly*] wickedly, disingenuously.
30. *still use*] continual habit.
31. *type*] symbol, emblem, crown.

        Will I withal endow a child of thine;
        So in the Lethe[32] of thy angry soul
        Thou drown the sad remembrance of those wrongs,
        Which thou supposest I have done to thee.

Q. ELIZ.   Be brief, lest that the process of thy kindness
        Last longer telling than thy kindness' date.

K. RICH.   Then know, that from my soul I love thy daughter.

Q. ELIZ.   My daughter's mother thinks it with her soul.

K. RICH.   What do you think?

Q. ELIZ.   That thou dost love my daughter from[33] thy soul:
        So from thy soul's love didst thou love her brothers;
        And from my heart's love I do thank thee for it.

K. RICH.   Be not so hasty to confound my meaning:
        I mean, that with my soul I love thy daughter,
        And mean to make her queen of England.

Q. ELIZ.   Say then, who dost thou mean shall be her king?

K. RICH.   Even he that makes her queen: who should be else?

Q. ELIZ.   What, thou?

K. RICH.   I, even I: what think you of it, madam?

Q. ELIZ.   How canst thou woo her?

K. RICH.   That would I learn of you,
        As one that are best acquainted with her humour.

Q. ELIZ.   And wilt thou learn of me?

K. RICH.   ·   Madam, with all my heart.

Q. ELIZ.   Send to her, by the man that slew her brothers,
        A pair of bleeding hearts; thereon engrave
        Edward and York; then haply she will weep:
        Therefore present to her, — as sometime Margaret
        Did to thy father, steep'd in Rutland's blood, —
        A handkerchief; which, say to her, did drain
        The purple sap from her sweet brother's body,
        And bid her dry her weeping eyes therewith.
        If this inducement force her not to love,
        Send her a story of thy noble acts;
        Tell her thou madest away her uncle Clarence,
        Her uncle Rivers; yea, and, for her sake,
        Madest quick conveyance with her good aunt Anne.

K. RICH.   Come, come, you mock me; this is not the way
        To win your daughter.

Q. ELIZ.   There is no other way;

---

32. *Lethe*] in classical mythology, the river of forgetfulness.
33. *from*] here meaning "away from," as opposed to "from the depths of," which is Richard's use of the preposition.

Unless thou couldst put on some other shape,
And not be Richard that hath done all this.

K. RICH.　Say that I did all this for love of her.

Q. ELIZ.　Nay, then indeed she cannot choose but hate thee,
Having bought love with such a bloody spoil.

K. RICH.　Look, what is done cannot be now amended:
Men shall deal unadvisedly sometimes,
Which after-hours give leisure to repent.
If I did take the kingdom from your sons,
To make amends, I'll give it to your daughter.
If I have kill'd the issue of your womb,
To quicken your increase, I will beget
Mine issue of your blood upon your daughter:
A grandam's name is little less in love
Than is the doting title of a mother;
They are as children but one step below,
Even of your mettle, of your very blood;
Of all one pain, save for a night of groans
Endured of her, for whom you bid like sorrow.[34]
Your children were vexation to your youth,
But mine shall be a comfort to your age.
The loss you have is but a son being king,
And by that loss your daughter is made queen.
I cannot make you what amends I would,
Therefore accept such kindness as I can.
Dorset your son, that with a fearful soul
Leads discontented steps in foreign soil,
This fair alliance quickly shall call home
To high promotions and great dignity:
The king, that calls your beauteous daughter wife,
Familiarly shall call thy Dorset brother;
Again shall you be mother to a king,
And all the ruins of distressful times
Repair'd with double riches of content.
What! we have many goodly days to see:
The liquid drops of tears that you have shed
Shall come again, transform'd to orient pearl,
Advantaging[35] their loan with interest
Of ten times double gain of happiness.
Go then, my mother, to thy daughter go;
Make bold her bashful years with your experience;
Prepare her ears to hear a wooer's tale;

---

34. *Endured . . . sorrow*] endured by her for whom you suffered like grief.
35. *Advantaging*] increasing.

  Put in her tender heart the aspiring flame
  Of golden sovereignty; acquaint the princess
  With the sweet silent hours of marriage joys:
  And when this arm of mine hath chastised
  The petty rebel, dull-brain'd Buckingham,
  Bound with triumphant garlands will I come,
  And lead thy daughter to a conqueror's bed;
  To whom I will retail my conquest won,
  And she shall be sole victress, Cæsar's Cæsar.
Q. ELIZ. What were I best to say? her father's brother
  Would be her lord? or shall I say, her uncle?
  Or, he that slew her brothers and her uncles?
  Under what title shall I woo for thee,
  That God, the law, my honour and her love,
  Can make seem pleasing to her tender years?
K. RICH. Infer fair England's peace by this alliance.
Q. ELIZ. Which she shall purchase with still lasting war.
K. RICH. Say that the king, which may command, entreats.
Q. ELIZ. That at her hands which the king's King forbids.
K. RICH. Say, she shall be a high and mighty queen.
Q. ELIZ. To wail the title, as her mother doth.
K. RICH. Say, I will love her everlastingly.
Q. ELIZ. But how long shall that title "ever" last?
K. RICH. Sweetly in force unto her fair life's end.
Q. ELIZ. But how long fairly shall her sweet life last?
K. RICH. So long as heaven and nature lengthens it.
Q. ELIZ. So long as hell and Richard likes of it.
K. RICH. Say, I, her sovereign, am her subject love.
Q. ELIZ. But she, your subject, loathes such sovereignty.
K. RICH. Be eloquent in my behalf to her.
Q. ELIZ. An honest tale speeds best being plainly told.
K. RICH. Then in plain terms tell her my loving tale.
Q. ELIZ. Plain and not honest is too harsh a style.
K. RICH. Your reasons are too shallow and too quick.
Q. ELIZ. O no, my reasons are too deep and dead;[36]
  Too deep and dead, poor infants, in their grave.
K. RICH. Harp not on that string, madam; that is past.
Q. ELIZ. Harp on it still shall I till heart-strings break.
K. RICH. Now, by my George,[37] my garter, and my crown, —
Q. ELIZ. Profaned, dishonour'd, and the third usurp'd.

---

36. *quick . . . dead*] Richard uses "quick" in its ordinary sense of "rapid," "nimble." Queen Elizabeth quibblingly takes it in the sense of "alive," of which "dead" is the negative.

37. *George*] a jewel in the shape of a figure of England's patron saint, which formed part of the insignia of the Order of the Garter.

K. RICH.   I swear —
Q. ELIZ.   By nothing; for this is no oath:
    The George, profaned, hath lost his holy honour;
    The garter, blemish'd, pawn'd his knightly virtue;
    The crown, usurp'd, disgraced his kingly glory.
    If something thou wilt swear to be believed,
    Swear then by something that thou hast not wrong'd.
K. RICH.   Now, by the world —
Q. ELIZ.   'Tis full of thy foul wrongs.
K. RICH.   My father's death —
Q. ELIZ.   Thy life hath that dishonour'd.
K. RICH.   Then, by myself —
Q. ELIZ.   Thyself thyself misusest.
K. RICH.   Why then, by God —
Q. ELIZ.   God's wrong is most of all.
    If thou hadst fear'd to break an oath by Him,
    The unity the king thy brother made
    Had not been broken, nor my brother slain:
    If thou hadst fear'd to break an oath by Him,
    The imperial metal, circling now thy brow,
    Had graced the tender temples of my child,
    And both the princes had been breathing here,
    Which now, two tender playfellows for dust,
    Thy broken faith hath made a prey for worms.
    What canst thou swear by now?
K. RICH.   The time to come.
Q. ELIZ.   That thou hast wronged in the time o'erpast;
    For I myself have many tears to wash
    Hereafter time, for time past wrong'd by thee.
    The children live, whose parents thou hast slaughter'd,
    Ungovern'd youth, to wail it in their age;
    The parents live, whose children thou hast butcher'd,
    Old withered plants, to wail it with their age.
    Swear not by time to come; for that thou hast
    Misused ere used, by time misused o'erpast.[38]
K. RICH.   As I intend to prosper and repent,
    So thrive I in my dangerous attempt
    Of hostile arms! myself myself confound!
    Heaven and fortune bar me happy hours!
    Day, yield me not thy light; nor, night, thy rest!
    Be opposite all planets of good luck
    To my proceedings, if, with pure heart's love,

---

38. *for that . . . o'erpast*] for thou hast misused the future before it was at your disposal, by
    virtue of the misuse to which you have put the time that is over and past.

Immaculate devotion, holy thoughts,
I tender not thy beauteous princely daughter!
In her consists my happiness and thine;
Without her, follows to this land and me,
To thee, herself, and many a Christian soul,
Death, desolation, ruin and decay:
It cannot be avoided but by this;
It will not be avoided but by this.
Therefore, good mother, — I must call you so —
Be the attorney of my love to her:
Plead what I will be, not what I have been;
Not my deserts, but what I will deserve:
Urge the necessity and state of times,
And be not peevish-fond[39] in great designs.

Q. ELIZ. Shall I be tempted of the devil thus?
K. RICH. Ay, if the devil tempt thee to do good.
Q. ELIZ. Shall I forget myself to be myself?
K. RICH. Ay, if yourself's remembrance wrong yourself.
Q. ELIZ. But thou didst kill my children.
K. RICH. But in your daughter's womb I bury them:
  Where in that nest of spicery[40] they shall breed
  Selves of themselves, to your recomforture.[41]
Q. ELIZ. Shall I go win my daughter to thy will?
K. RICH. And be a happy mother by the deed.
Q. ELIZ. I go. Write to me very shortly,
  And you shall understand from me her mind.
K. RICH. Bear her my true love's kiss; and so, farewell.

          [*Exit* QUEEN ELIZABETH.]

Relenting fool, and shallow, changing woman!

Enter RATCLIFF; CATESBY *following*

How now! what news?
RAT. My gracious sovereign, on the western coast
  Rideth a puissant[42] navy; to the shore
  Throng many doubtful hollow-hearted friends,
  Unarm'd, and unresolved to beat them back:
  'Tis thought that Richmond is their admiral;

---

39. *peevish-fond*] perversely stupid.
40. *nest of spicery*] an allusion to the fable of the phœnix, which was consumed every thousand years on a funeral pyre of spices on which the bird was at the same time reincarnated.
41. *recomforture*] comfort, consolation.
42. *puissant*] mighty, powerful.

And there they hull,[43] expecting but the aid
Of Buckingham to welcome them ashore.
K. RICH.　Some light-foot friend post to the Duke of Norfolk:
　　Ratcliff, thyself, or Catesby; where is he?
CATE.　Here, my lord.
K. RICH.　Fly to the duke. [*To* RATCLIFF] Post thou to Salisbury:
　　When thou comest thither, — [*To* CATESBY] Dull unmindful villain,
　　Why stand'st thou still, and go'st not to the duke?
CATE.　First, mighty sovereign, let me know your mind,
　　What from your grace I shall deliver to him.
K. RICH.　O, true, good Catesby: bid him levy[44] straight
　　The greatest strength and power he can make,
　　And meet me presently[45] at Salisbury.
CATE.　I go.　　　　　　　　　　　　　　　　　　　　[*Exit.*]
RAT.　What is't your highness' pleasure I shall do
　　At Salisbury?
K. RICH.　Why, what wouldst thou do there before I go?
RAT.　Your highness told me I should post before.
K. RICH.　My mind is changed, sir, my mind is changed.

Enter LORD STANLEY

　　How now, what news with you?
STAN.　None good, my lord, to please you with the hearing;
　　Nor none so bad, but it may well be told.
K. RICH.　Hoyday,[46] a riddle! neither good nor bad!
　　Why dost thou run so many mile about,
　　When thou mayst tell thy tale a nearer way?
　　Once more, what news?
STAN.　　　　　　　　　　　　Richmond is on the seas.
K. RICH.　There let him sink, and be the seas on him!
　　White-liver'd runagate,[47] what doth he there?
STAN.　I know not, mighty sovereign, but by guess.
K. RICH.　Well, sir, as you guess, as you guess?
STAN.　Stirr'd up by Dorset, Buckingham, and Ely,
　　He makes for England, there to claim the crown.
K. RICH.　Is the chair empty? is the sword unsway'd?
　　Is the king dead? the empire unpossess'd?
　　What heir of York is there alive but we?
　　And who is England's king but great York's heir?

---

43. *hull*] to float, drift with sails furled.
44. *levy*] raise (an army).
45. *presently*] immediately.
46. *Hoyday*] an exclamation of contemptuous surprise.
47. *White-liver'd runagate*] cowardly runaway.

      Then, tell me, what doth he upon the sea?
STAN.   Unless for that, my liege, I cannot guess.
K. RICH.   Unless for that he comes to be your liege,
    You cannot guess wherefore the Welshman[48] comes.
    Thou wilt revolt and fly to him, I fear.
STAN.   No, mighty liege; therefore mistrust me not.
K. RICH.   Where is thy power then to beat him back?
    Where are thy tenants and thy followers?
    Are they not now upon the western shore,
    Safe-conducting the rebels from their ships?
STAN.   No, my good lord, my friends are in the north.
K. RICH.   Cold friends to Richard: what do they in the north,
    When they should serve their sovereign in the west?
STAN.   They have not been commanded, mighty sovereign:
    Please it your majesty to give me leave,
    I'll muster up my friends, and meet your grace
    Where and what time your majesty shall please.
K. RICH.   Ay, ay, thou wouldst be gone to join with Richmond:
    I will not trust you, sir.
STAN.   Most mighty sovereign,
    You have no cause to hold my friendship doubtful:
    I never was nor never will be false.
K. RICH.   Well,
    Go muster men; but, hear you, leave behind
    Your son, George Stanley: look your faith be firm,
    Or else his head's assurance is but frail.
STAN.   So deal with him as I prove true to you.   [*Exit.*]

Enter a Messenger

MESS.   My gracious sovereign, now in Devonshire,
    As I by friends am well advertised,[49]
    Sir Edward Courtney, and the haughty prelate
    Bishop of Exeter, his brother there,[50]
    With many moe confederates, are in arms.

Enter another Messenger

SEC. MESS.   My liege, in Kent, the Guildfords are in arms;

---

48. *the Welshman*] i.e., Richmond. Richmond's grandfather was Owen Tudor, who married the widow of Henry V, Catharine of France. Richmond was descended on the maternal side through the Beauforts to John of Gaunt (son of Edward III) and Catherine Swynford, from which connection he derived his claim to the throne.
49. *advertised*] informed, notified. The accents fall on the second and fourth syllables.
50. *brother there*] Peter Courtney, the Bishop of Exeter, was cousin, *not* brother, of Sir Edward Courtney.

And every hour more competitors[51]
Flock to their aid, and still their power increaseth.

Enter another Messenger

THIRD MESS.   My lord, the army of the Duke of Buckingham —
K. RICH.   Out on you, owls! nothing but songs of death?
                                                        [*He striketh him.*]
   Take that, until thou bring me better news.
THIRD MESS.   The news I have to tell your majesty
   Is, that by sudden floods and fall of waters,
   Buckingham's army is dispersed and scatter'd;
   And he himself wander'd away alone,
   No man knows whither.
K. RICH.   I cry thee mercy:
   There is my purse to cure that blow of thine.
   Hath any well-advised friend proclaim'd
   Reward to him that brings the traitor in?
THIRD MESS.   Such proclamation hath been made, my liege.

Enter another Messenger

FOURTH MESS.   Sir Thomas Lovel and Lord Marquess Dorset,
   'Tis said, my liege, in Yorkshire are in arms.
   Yet this good comfort bring I to your grace,
   The Breton navy is dispersed by tempest:
   Richmond, in Dorsetshire, sent out a boat
   Unto the shore, to ask those on the banks
   If they were his assistants, yea or no;
   Who answer'd him, they came from Buckingham
   Upon his party:[52] he, mistrusting them,
   Hoised sail and made away for Brittany.
K. RICH.   March on, march on, since we are up in arms;
   If not to fight with foreign enemies,
   Yet to beat down these rebels here at home.

Re-enter CATESBY

CATE.   My liege, the Duke of Buckingham is taken;
   That is the best news: that the Earl of Richmond
   Is with a mighty power landed at Milford,
   Is colder tidings, yet they must be told.
K. RICH.   Away towards Salisbury! while we reason here,

---

51. *competitors*] confederates, associates.
52. *Upon his party*] to join his party, to take his side.

A royal battle might be won and lost:
Some one take order[53] Buckingham be brought
To Salisbury; the rest march on with me.   [*Flourish. Exeunt.*]

SCENE V. *Lord Derby's House.*

Enter DERBY *and* SIR CHRISTOPHER URSWICK[1]

DER.   Sir Christopher, tell Richmond this from me:
        That in the sty of this most bloody boar
        My son George Stanley is frank'd up[2] in hold:
        If I revolt, off goes young George's head;
        The fear of that withholds my present aid.
        But, tell me, where is princely Richmond now?
CHRIS.   At Pembroke, or at Ha'rford-west,[3] in Wales.
DER.   What men of name resort to him?
CHRIS.   Sir Walter Herbert, a renowned soldier;
        Sir Gilbert Talbot, Sir William Stanley;
        Oxford, redoubted Pembroke, Sir James Blunt,
        And Rice ap Thomas, with a valiant crew,
        And many moe of noble fame and worth:
        And towards London they do bend their course,
        If by the way they be not fought withal.
DER.   Return unto thy lord; commend me to him:
        Tell him the queen hath heartily consented
        He shall espouse Elizabeth her daughter.
        These letters will resolve[4] him of my mind.
        Farewell.
                                                        [*Exeunt.*]

---

53. *take order*] take measures, arrange.

 1. *Sir Christopher Urswick*] a priest in the service of the Countess of Richmond, and
    employed by her in confidential communication with her son.
 2. *frank'd up*] cooped up, confined.
 3. *Ha'rford-west*] Haverfordwest, on the coast of Pembrokeshire.
 4. *resolve*] inform, satisfy.

ACT V.

Scene I. *Salisbury. An open place.*

Enter the Sheriff, *and* Buckingham, *with halberds, led to execution*

Buck. Will not King Richard let me speak with him?
Sher. No, my good lord; therefore be patient.
Buck. Hastings, and Edward's children, Rivers, Grey,
  Holy King Henry, and thy fair son Edward,
  Vaughan, and all that have miscarried
  By underhand corrupted foul injustice,
  If that your moody discontented souls
  Do through the clouds behold this present hour,
  Even for revenge mock my destruction!
  This is All-Souls' day,[1] fellows, is it not?
Sher. It is, my lord.
Buck. Why, then All-Souls' day is my body's doomsday.
  This is the day that, in King Edward's time,
  I wish'd might fall on me when I was found
  False to his children or his wife's allies;
  This is the day wherein I wish'd to fall
  By the false faith of him I trusted most;
  This, this All-Souls' day to my fearful soul
  Is the determined respite of my wrongs:[2]
  That high All-seer that I dallied with
  Hath turn'd my feigned prayer on my head,
  And given in earnest what I begg'd in jest.
  Thus doth he force the swords of wicked men
  To turn their own points on their masters' bosoms:
  Now Margaret's curse is fallen upon my head;
  "When he," quoth she, "shall split thy heart with sorrow,
  Remember Margaret was a prophetess."
  Come, sirs, convey me to the block of shame;
  Wrong hath but wrong, and blame the due of blame. [*Exeunt.*]

---

1. *All-Souls' day*] November 2 was the festival day appointed by the Roman Catholic
 Church in honor of the souls of all the dead, and was believed to be a time when spirits
 communicated with the living.
2. *determined . . . wrongs*] the term or close of the period to which the punishment of my
 offences was postponed.

SCENE II. *The Camp near Tamworth.*

Enter RICHMOND, OXFORD, BLUNT, HERBERT, *and others, with drum and colours*

RICHM.   Fellows in arms, and my most loving friends,
    Bruised underneath the yoke of tyranny,
    Thus far into the bowels of the land
    Have we march'd on without impediment;
    And here receive we from our father Stanley
    Lines of fair comfort and encouragement.
    The wretched, bloody, and usurping boar,
    That spoil'd your summer fields and fruitful vines,
    Swills your warm blood like wash,[1] and makes his trough
    In your embowell'd[2] bosoms, this foul swine
    Lies[3] now even in the centre of this isle,
    Near to the town of Leicester, as we learn:
    From Tamworth thither is but one day's march.
    In God's name, cheerly on, courageous friends,
    To reap the harvest of perpetual peace
    By this one bloody trial of sharp war.
OXF.   Every man's conscience is a thousand swords,
    To fight against that bloody homicide.
HERB.   I doubt not but his friends will fly to us.
BLUNT.   He hath no friends but who are friends for fear,
    Which in his greatest need will shrink from him.
RICHM.   All for our vantage. Then, in God's name, march:
    True hope is swift, and flies with swallow's wings;
    Kings it makes gods, and meaner creatures kings.   [*Exeunt.*]

---

1. *Swills . . . like wash*] drinks . . . as a boar sucks up hogwash.
2. *embowell'd*] ripped up, disembowelled.
3. *Lies*] sojourns.

SCENE III. *Bosworth Field.*

Enter KING RICHARD *in arms with* NORFOLK, *the* EARL OF SURREY, *and others*

K. RICH.   Here pitch our tents, even here in Bosworth field.
　　My Lord of Surrey, why look you so sad?
SUR.   My heart is ten times lighter than my looks.
K. RICH.   My Lord of Norfolk, —
NOR.   　　　　　　　　Here, most gracious liege.
K. RICH.   Norfolk, we must have knocks; ha! must we not?
NOR.   We must both give and take, my gracious lord.
K. RICH.   Up with my tent there! here will I lie to-night:
　　But where to-morrow? Well, all's one for that.
　　Who hath descried the number of the foe?
NOR.   Six or seven thousand is their utmost power.
K. RICH.   Why, our battalion trebles that account:
　　Besides, the king's name is a tower of strength,
　　Which they upon the adverse party want.[1]
　　Up with my tent there! Valiant gentlemen,
　　Let us survey the vantage of the field;
　　Call for some men of sound direction:[2]
　　Let's want no discipline, make no delay;
　　For, lords, to-morrow is a busy day.   [*Exeunt.*]

Enter, on the other side of the field, RICHMOND, SIR WILLIAM BRAN-DON, OXFORD, *and others. Some of the* Soldiers *pitch Richmond's tent*

RICHM.   The weary sun hath made a golden set,
　　And by the bright track of his fiery car
　　Gives signal of a goodly day to-morrow.
　　Sir William Brandon, you shall bear my standard.
　　Give me some ink and paper in my tent:
　　I'll draw the form and model of our battle,
　　Limit each leader to his several charge,
　　And part in just proportion our small strength.
　　My Lord of Oxford, you, Sir William Brandon,
　　And you, Sir Walter Herbert, stay with me.
　　The Earl of Pembroke keeps[3] his regiment:

---

1. *want*] lack.
2. *sound direction*] sound judgment, tried skill in leadership.
3. *keeps*] stays with.

> Good Captain Blunt, bear my good-night to him,
> And by the second hour in the morning
> Desire the earl to see me in my tent:
> Yet one thing more, good Blunt, before thou go'st,
> Where is Lord Stanley quarter'd, dost thou know?

BLUNT.   Unless I have mista'en his colours much,
> Which well I am assured I have not done,
> His regiment lies half a mile at least
> South from the mighty power of the king.

RICHM.   If without peril it be possible,
> Good Captain Blunt, bear my good-night to him,
> And give him from me this most needful scroll.

BLUNT.   Upon my life, my lord, I'll undertake it;
> And so, God give you quiet rest to-night!

RICHM.   Good night, good Captain Blunt. Come, gentlemen,
> Let us consult upon to-morrow's business:
> In to our tent! the air is raw and cold.

> > *[They withdraw into the tent.]*

Enter, to his tent, KING RICHARD, NORFOLK, RATCLIFF, CATESBY, *and others*

K. RICH.   What is't o'clock?

CATE.   It's supper-time, my lord;
> It's nine o'clock.

K. RICH.   I will not sup to-night.
> Give me some ink and paper.
> What, is my beaver⁴ easier⁵ than it was!
> And all my armour laid into my tent?

CATE.   It is, my liege; and all things are in readiness.

K. RICH.   Good Norfolk, hie thee to thy charge;
> Use careful watch, choose trusty sentinels.

NOR.   I go, my lord.

K. RICH.   Stir with the lark to-morrow, gentle Norfolk.   *[Exit.]*

NOR.   I warrant you, my lord.

K. RICH.   Catesby!

CATE.   My lord?

K. RICH.   Send out a pursuivant at arms
> To Stanley's regiment; bid him bring his power
> Before sunrising, lest his son George fall
> Into the blind cave of eternal night.   *[Exit CATESBY.]*
> Fill me a bowl of wine. Give me a watch.⁶

---

4. *beaver*] properly the part of the helmet that could be drawn up and down over the face, but often used for the helmet itself.

5. *easier*] more loosely fitting.

6. *watch*] watchlight, candle.

Saddle white Surrey[7] for the field to-morrow.
Look that my staves[8] be sound, and not too heavy.
Ratcliff!

RAT.   My lord?

K. RICH.   Saw'st thou the melancholy Lord Northumberland?

RAT.   Thomas the Earl of Surrey, and himself,
Much about cock-shut time,[9] from troop to troop
Went through the army, cheering up the soldiers.

K. RICH.   So, I am satisfied. Give me a bowl of wine:
I have not that alacrity of spirit,
Nor cheer of mind, that I was wont to have.
Set it down. Is ink and paper ready?

RAT.   It is, my lord.

K. RICH.   Bid my guard watch. Leave me. Ratcliff,
About the mid of night come to my tent,
And help to arm me. Leave me, I say.

             [*Exeunt* RATCLIFF *and the other attendants.*]

Enter DERBY *to* RICHMOND *in his tent, Lords and others attending*

DER.   Fortune and victory sit on thy helm!

RICHM.   All comfort that the dark night can afford
Be to thy person, noble father-in-law!
Tell me, how fares our loving mother?

DER.   I, by attorney,[10] bless thee from thy mother,
Who prays continually for Richmond's good:
So much for that. The silent hours steal on,
And flaky darkness[11] breaks within the east.
In brief, for so the season bids us be,
Prepare thy battle early in the morning,
And put thy fortune to the arbitrement[12]
Of bloody strokes and mortal-staring[13] war.
I, as I may — that which I would I cannot, —
With best advantage will deceive the time,
And aid thee in this doubtful shock of arms:
But on thy side I may not be too forward,
Lest, being seen, thy brother, tender George,
Be executed in his father's sight.

---

7. *white Surrey*] According to historical sources, Richard was "mounted on a great white courser." The horse's name was presumably Shakespeare's invention.
8. *staves*] the wooden shafts of the lances.
9. *cock-shut time*] twilight.
10. *by attorney*] by deputy, messenger.
11. *flaky darkness*] darkness streaked with light.
12. *arbitrement*] decision.
13. *mortal-staring*] looking with deadly glance.

Farewell: the leisure[14] and the fearful time
Cuts off the ceremonious vows of love,
And ample interchange of sweet discourse,
Which so long sunder'd friends should dwell upon:
God give us leisure for these rites of love!
Once more, adieu: be valiant, and speed well!
RICHM.   Good lords, conduct him to his regiment:
I'll strive, with troubled thoughts, to take a nap,
Lest leaden slumber peise[15] me down to-morrow,
When I should mount with wings of victory:
Once more, good night, kind lords and gentlemen.

                              [*Exeunt all but* RICHMOND.]

O Thou, whose captain I account myself,
Look on my forces with a gracious eye;
Put in their hands thy bruising irons of wrath,
That they may crush down with a heavy fall
The usurping helmets of our adversaries!
Make us thy ministers of chastisement,
That we may praise thee in the victory!
To thee I do commend my watchful soul,
Ere I let fall the windows of mine eyes:
Sleeping and waking, O, defend me still!   [*Sleeps.*]

Enter the Ghost of PRINCE EDWARD, *son to* HENRY THE SIXTH

GHOST.   [*To* RICHARD] Let me sit heavy on thy soul to-morrow!
Think, how thou stab'dst me in my prime of youth
At Tewksbury: despair, therefore, and die!
[*To* RICHMOND] Be cheerful, Richmond; for the wronged souls ·
Of butcher'd princes fight in thy behalf:
King Henry's issue, Richmond, comforts thee.

Enter the Ghost of HENRY THE SIXTH

GHOST.   [*To* RICHARD] When I was mortal, my anointed body
By thee was punched full of deadly holes:
Think on the Tower and me: despair, and die!
Harry the Sixth bids thee despair and die!
[*To* RICHMOND] Virtuous and holy, be thou conqueror!
Harry, that prophesied thou shouldst be king,
Doth comfort thee in thy sleep: live, and flourish!

Enter the Ghost of CLARENCE

GHOST.   [*To* RICHARD] Let me sit heavy on thy soul to-morrow!

---

14. *leisure*] time at our free disposal.
15. *peise*] weigh.

I, that was wash'd to death with fulsome wine,[16]
Poor Clarence, by thy guile betray'd to death.
To-morrow in the battle think on me,
And fall thy edgeless sword: despair, and die!
[*To* RICHMOND] Thou offspring of the house of Lancaster,
The wronged heirs of York do pray for thee:
Good angels guard thy battle! live, and flourish!

Enter the Ghosts of RIVERS, GREY, *and* VAUGHAN

GHOST OF R.   [*To* RICHARD] Let me sit heavy on thy soul to-morrow,
     Rivers, that died at Pomfret! despair, and die!
GHOST OF G.   [*To* RICHARD] Think upon Grey, and let thy soul despair!
GHOST OF V.   [*To* RICHARD] Think upon Vaughan, and, with guilty
     fear,
     Let fall thy lance: despair, and die!
ALL.   [*To* RICHMOND] Awake, and think our wrongs in Richard's bosom
     Will conquer him! awake, and win the day!

Enter the Ghost of HASTINGS

GHOST.   [*To* RICHARD] Bloody and guilty, guiltily awake,
     And in a bloody battle end thy days!
     Think on Lord Hastings: despair, and die!
     [*To* RICHMOND] Quiet untroubled soul, awake, awake!
     Arm, fight, and conquer, for fair England's sake!

Enter the Ghosts of the two young Princes

GHOSTS.   [*To* RICHARD] Dream on thy cousins smothered in the Tower:
     Let us be lead within thy bosom, Richard,
     And weigh thee down to ruin, shame, and death!
     Thy nephews' souls bid thee despair and die!
     [*To* RICHMOND] Sleep, Richmond, sleep in peace, and wake in joy;
     Good angels guard thee from the boar's annoy![17]
     Live, and beget a happy race of kings!
     Edward's unhappy sons do bid thee flourish.

Enter the Ghost of LADY ANNE *his wife*

GHOST.   [*To* RICHARD] Richard, thy wife, that wretched Anne thy wife,
     That never slept a quiet hour with thee,
     Now fills thy sleep with perturbations:
     To-morrow in the battle think on me,
     And fall thy edgeless sword: despair, and die!
     [*To* RICHMOND] Thou quiet soul, sleep thou a quiet sleep:

---

16. *fulsome wine*] abundance or surfeit of wine.
17. *boar's annoy*] injury from the boar, i.e. Richard.

Dream of success and happy victory!
Thy adversary's wife doth pray for thee.

Enter the Ghost of BUCKINGHAM

GHOST.   [*To* RICHARD] The first was I that help'd thee to the crown;
The last was I that felt thy tyranny:
O, in the battle think on Buckingham,
And die in terror of thy guiltiness!
Dream on, dream on, of bloody deeds and death:
Fainting, despair; despairing, yield thy breath!
[*To* RICHMOND] I died for hope[18] ere I could lend thee aid:
But cheer thy heart, and be thou not dismay'd:
God and good angels fight on Richmond's side;
And Richard falls in height of all his pride.
            [*The Ghosts vanish.* KING RICHARD *starts out of his dream.*]
K. RICH.   Give me another horse: bind up my wounds.
Have mercy, Jesu! — Soft! I did but dream.
O coward conscience, how dost thou afflict me!
The lights burn blue.[19] It is now dead midnight.
Cold fearful drops stand on my trembling flesh.
What do I fear? myself? there's none else by:
Richard loves Richard; that is, I am I.
Is there a murderer here? No. Yes, I am:
Then fly. What, from myself? Great reason why:
Lest I revenge. What, myself upon myself?
Alack, I love myself. Wherefore? for any good
That I myself have done unto myself?
O, no! alas, I rather hate myself
For hateful deeds committed by myself!
I am a villain: yet I lie, I am not.
Fool, of thyself speak well: fool, do not flatter.
My conscience hath a thousand several tongues,
And every tongue brings in a several tale,
And every tale condemns me for a villain.
Perjury, perjury, in the high'st degree;
Murder, stern murder, in the direst degree;
All several sins, all used in each degree,
Throng to the bar,[20] crying all "Guilty! guilty!"
I shall despair. There is no creature loves me;
And if I die, no soul will pity me:
Nay, wherefore should they, since that I myself

---

18. *for hope*] for lack of hope, in despair.
19. *lights burn blue*] thought to be the usual effect of ghostly apparitions.
20. *bar*] the railing at which prisoners stand when on trial.

Find in myself no pity to myself?
Methought the souls of all that I had murder'd
Came to my tent, and every one did threat
To-morrow's vengeance on the head of Richard.

Enter RATCLIFF

RAT. My lord!
K. RICH. 'Zounds! who is there?
RAT. Ratcliff, my lord; 'tis I. The early village-cock
Hath twice done salutation to the morn;
Your friends are up, and buckle on their armour.
K. RICH. O Ratcliff, I have dream'd a fearful dream!
What thinkest thou, will our friends prove all true?
RAT. No doubt, my lord.
K. RICH.   O Ratcliff, I fear, I fear, —
RAT. Nay, good my lord, be not afraid of shadows.
K. RICH. By the apostle Paul, shadows to-night
Have struck more terror to the soul of Richard,
Than can the substance of ten thousand soldiers
Armed in proof,[21] and led by shallow Richmond.
It is not yet near day. Come, go with me;
Under our tents I'll play the eaves-dropper,
To see if any mean to shrink from me.   [*Exeunt.*]

Enter the Lords *to* RICHMOND, *sitting in his tent*

LORDS. Good morrow, Richmond!
RICHM. Cry mercy, lords and watchful gentlemen,
That you have ta'en a tardy sluggard here.
LORDS. How have you slept, my lord?
RICHM. The sweetest sleep, and fairest-boding dreams
That ever enter'd in a drowsy head,
Have I since your departure had, my lords.
Methought their souls, whose bodies Richard murder'd,
Came to my tent, and cried on[22] victory:
I promise you, my soul is very jocund
In the remembrance of so fair a dream.
How far into the morning is it, lords?
LORDS. Upon the stroke of four.
RICHM. Why, then 'tis time to arm and give direction.

---

21. *Armed in proof*] equipped in proved, tested armour.
22. *cried on*] called out.

His oration to his soldiers.

More than I have said, loving countrymen,
The leisure and enforcement of the time
Forbids to dwell upon: yet remember this,
God and our good cause fight upon our side;
The prayers of holy saints and wronged souls,
Like high-rear'd bulwarks, stand before our faces.
Richard except, those whom we fight against
Had rather have us win than him they follow:
For what is he they follow? truly, gentlemen,
A bloody tyrant and a homicide;
One raised in blood, and one in blood establish'd;
One that made means to come by what he hath,
And slaughter'd those that were the means to help him;
A base foul stone, made precious by the foil
Of England's chair, where he is falsely set;[23]
One that hath ever been God's enemy:
Then, if you fight against God's enemy,
God will in justice ward you as his soldiers;
If you do sweat to put a tyrant down,
You sleep in peace, the tyrant being slain;
If you do fight against your country's foes,
Your country's fat[24] shall pay your pains the hire;
If you do fight in safeguard of your wives,
Your wives shall welcome home the conquerors;
If you do free your children from the sword,
Your children's children quit[25] it in your age.
Then, in the name of God and all these rights,
Advance your standards, draw your willing swords.
For me, the ransom of my bold attempt[26]
Shall be this cold corpse on the earth's cold face;
But if I thrive, the gain of my attempt
The least of you shall share his part thereof.
Sound drums and trumpets boldly and cheerfully;
God and Saint George! Richmond and victory!   [*Exeunt.*]

Re-enter KING RICHARD, RATCLIFF, *Attendants and Forces*

K. RICH.   What said Northumberland as touching Richmond?.

---

23. *chair . . . set*] throne . . . set, as in a jewel.
24. *fat*] wealth.
25. *quit*] requite.
26. *the ransom . . . attempt*] the fine due from me in requital of my boldness.

RAT.   That he was never trained up in arms.
K. RICH.   He said the truth: and what said Surrey, then?
RAT.   He smiled and said "The better for our purpose."
K. RICH.   He was in the right; and so indeed it is.

[The clock striketh.]

Tell the clock there. Give me a calendar.
Who saw the sun to-day?
RAT.   Not I, my lord.
K. RICH.   Then he disdains to shine; for by the book[27]
He should have braved[28] the east an hour ago:
A black day will it be to somebody.
Ratcliff!
RAT.   My lord?
K. RICH.   The sun will not be seen to-day;
The sky doth frown and lour upon our army.
I would these dewy tears were from the ground.
Not shine to-day! Why, what is that to me
More than to Richmond? for the selfsame heaven
That frowns on me looks sadly upon him.

Re-enter NORFOLK

NOR.   Arm, arm, my lord; the foe vaunts in the field.
K. RICH.   Come, bustle, bustle. Caparison my horse.
Call up Lord Stanley, bid him bring his power:
I will lead forth my soldiers to the plain,
And thus my battle shall be ordered:
My foreward[29] shall be drawn out all in length,
Consisting equally of horse and foot;
Our archers shall be placed in the midst:
John Duke of Norfolk, Thomas Earl of Surrey,
Shall have the leading of this foot and horse.
They thus directed, we will follow
In the main battle, whose puissance[30] on either side
Shall be well winged with our chiefest horse.
This, and Saint George to boot![31] What think'st thou, Norfolk?
NOR.   A good direction, warlike sovereign.
This found I on my tent this morning.

---

27. *book*] almanac.
28. *braved*] made splendid, glorified.
29. *foreward*] vanguard.
30. *puissance*] armed force.
31. *This, and Saint George to boot!*] this order of battle and the favour of our patron saint in addition!

[*He sheweth him a paper.*]

K. RICH.   [*Reads*] "Jockey of Norfolk, be not so bold,
For Dickon³² thy master is bought and sold."
A thing devised by the enemy.
Go, gentlemen, every man unto his charge:
Let not our babbling dreams affright our souls:
Conscience is but a word that cowards use,
Devised at first to keep the strong in awe:
Our strong arms be our conscience, swords our law.
March on, join bravely, let us to't pell-mell;
If not to heaven, then hand in hand to hell.

His oration to his Army

What shall I say more than I have inferr'd?³³
Remember whom you are to cope withal;
A sort³⁴ of vagabonds, rascals, and runaways,
A scum of Bretons, and base lackey peasants,
Whom their o'er-cloyed country vomits forth
To desperate ventures and assured destruction.
You sleeping safe, they bring to you unrest;
You having lands and blest with beauteous wives,
They would restrain³⁵ the one, distain the other.
And who doth lead them but a paltry fellow,
Long kept in Bretagne at our mother's cost?³⁶
A milk-sop, one that never in his life
Felt so much cold as over shoes in snow?
Let's whip these stragglers o'er the seas again,
Lash hence these overweening rags of France,
These famish'd beggars, weary of their lives,
Who, but for dreaming on this fond exploit,
For want of means, poor rats, had hang'd themselves:
If we be conquer'd, let men conquer us,
And not these bastard Bretons, whom our fathers

---

32. *Dickon*] a colloquial form of Richard. "Bought and sold" means "betrayed."
33. *inferr'd*] alleged.
34. *sort*] set, company.
35. *restrain*] put restraint on, withhold from lawful owners.
36. *our mother's*] Shakespeare is following Richard's speech as it appears in the *second* edition of Holinshed's *Chronicle*, where Richmond is said to have been "brought up by *my moothers* meanes . . . in the court of Francis, Duke of Britaine." Hall's *Chronicle* and the *first* edition of Holinshed read *brother's* for *mother's*. There is little doubt that *brother's* is the right reading. Richard's brother, King Edward IV, had arranged with the Duke of Brittany for Richmond to reside at his court.

Have in their own land beaten, bobb'd,[37] and thump'd,
And in record left them the heirs of shame.
Shall these enjoy our lands? lie with our wives?
Ravish our daughters? [*Drum afar off.*] Hark! I hear their drum.
Fight, gentlemen of England! fight, bold yeomen!
Draw, archers, draw your arrows to the head!
Spur your proud horses hard, and ride in blood;
Amaze the welkin[38] with your broken staves!

Enter a Messenger

What says Lord Stanley? will he bring his power?[39]
MESS.   My lord, he doth deny to come.
K. RICH.   Off with his son George's head!
NOR.   My lord, the enemy is past the marsh:
   After the battle let George Stanley die.
K. RICH.   A thousand hearts are great within my bosom:
   Advance our standards, set upon our foes;
   Our ancient word of courage, fair Saint George,
   Inspire us with the spleen of fiery dragons!
   Upon them! Victory sits on our helms.   [*Exeunt.*]

SCENE IV. *Another Part of the Field.*

Alarum: excursions. Enter NORFOLK *and forces fighting; to him* CATESBY

CATE.   Rescue, my Lord of Norfolk, rescue, rescue!
   The king enacts more wonders than a man,
   Daring an opposite[1] to every danger:
   His horse is slain, and all on foot he fights,
   Seeking for Richmond in the throat of death.
   Rescue, fair lord, or else the day is lost!

Alarums. Enter KING RICHARD

K. RICH.   A horse! a horse! my kingdom for a horse!
CATE.   Withdraw, my lord; I'll help you to a horse.
K. RICH.   Slave, I have set my life upon a cast,

---

37. *bobb'd*] buffeted.
38. *the welkin*] the skies.
39. *power*] force, army.

---

1. *Daring an opposite*] venturing to oppose himself.

And I will stand the hazard of the die.
I think there be six Richmonds in the field;
Five have I slain to-day instead of him.
A horse! a horse! my kingdom for a horse!   [*Exeunt.*]

SCENE V. *Another Part of the Field.*

Alarum. Enter RICHARD *and* RICHMOND; *they fight.* RICHARD *is slain.*
Retreat and flourish. Re-enter RICHMOND, DERBY *bearing the crown,*
with divers other Lords

RICHM.   God and your arms be praised, victorious friends!
          The day is ours; the bloody dog is dead.
DER.   Courageous Richmond, well hast thou acquit thee.
          Lo, here, this long usurped royalty
          From the dead temples of this bloody wretch
          Have I pluck'd off, to grace thy brows withal:
          Wear it, enjoy it, and make much of it.
RICHM.   Great God of heaven, say amen to all!
          But, tell me, is young George Stanley living?
DER.   He is, my lord, and safe in Leicester town;
          Whither, if it please you, we may now withdraw us.
RICHM.   What men of name are slain on either side?
DER.   John Duke of Norfolk, Walter Lord Ferrers, Sir Robert Braken-
          bury, and Sir William Brandon.
RICH.   Inter their bodies as becomes their births:
          Proclaim a pardon to the soldiers fled,
          That in submission will return to us:
          And then, as we have ta'en the sacrament,
          We will unite the white rose and the red.
          Smile heaven upon this fair conjunction,
          That long have frown'd upon their enmity!
          What traitor hears me, and says not amen?
          England hath long been mad, and scarr'd herself;
          The brother blindly shed the brother's blood,
          The father rashly slaughter'd his own son,
          The son, compell'd, been butcher to the sire:
          All this divided York and Lancaster,
          Divided in their dire division,
          O, now let Richmond and Elizabeth,

The true succeeders of each royal house,
By God's fair ordinance conjoin together!
And let their heirs, God, if thy will be so,
Enrich the time to come with smooth-faced peace,
With smiling plenty and fair prosperous days!
Abate the edge[1] of traitors, gracious Lord,
That would reduce[2] these bloody days again,
And make poor England weep in streams of blood!
Let them not live to taste this land's increase,
That would with treason wound this fair land's peace!
Now civil wounds are stopp'd, peace lives again:
That she may long live here, God say amen!   [*Exeun*

1. *Abate the edge*] dull the force or spirit.
2. *reduce*] bring back.